THE
BOATING BOOK

By John Roberts

Fiber Glass Boats: Construction,
Repair, and Maintenance

Choosing Your Boat *(with Maria Mann)*

The Boating Book

THE
BOATING BOOK

A Practical Guide to
Safe Pleasure Boating
Power and Sail

By

John Roberts

W·W·NORTON & COMPANY
NEW YORK   LONDON

The text of this book is composed in Baskerville,
with the display set in Palatino.
Composition by Vail-Ballou Press.
Manufacturing by Maple-Vail Book Group.

First Edition.

ISBN 0-393-03342-2

W.W. Norton & Company, Inc., 500 Fifth Avenue, New York, N.Y. 10110
W.W. Norton & Company, Ltd., 10 Coptic Street, London WC1A 1PU

1 2 3 4 5 6 7 8 9 0

Dedication

This book is dedicated to the memory of Timmy Weller, who drowned November 24, 1989, in Maryland's Choptank River. Timmy, twenty-four, was duck hunting with two companions when their overloaded boat began taking on water and sank. He was not wearing a life jacket.

Contents

List of Figures

Acknowledgments

Two individuals and one news organization have contributed importantly to this book and deserve special recognition for those contributions. They are my wife and boating partner, Susan; our friend and fellow member of the North East River (Maryland) Power Squadron, Past Commander Kenneth G. Smith; and *Soundings,* the monthly boating newspaper.

While the scope of Susan's role varies from book to book, there is one core function that I have come to rely on heavily and value highly—that is, her function as a reviewer. As each chapter is written, she reads it critically, raising questions and offering suggestions. As the chapters are revised, she reads them a second time to ensure that the revisions hit the mark. When the manuscript is completed, she reads the entire book from start to finish—again critically, but this time considering it as a whole unit. Throughout the process, Susan's questions, her critiques, and her suggestions greatly influence the shape and quality of the final manuscript. And this book has been no exception.

Ken Smith, a U.S. Coast Guard licensed captain and a delivery skipper, has been around boats of one type or another for most of his life. He also has been active for many years in boating education with the United States Power Squadrons. Among his many activities today, he teaches the Maryland Boating Safety Course and is an instructor for a sailing school in Annapolis, Maryland. Because of his background and interest in boating safety education, we could think of no one better qualified than Ken to review this book from a technical perspective to ensure that the opinions, the advice, and the facts contained in these pages stand on solid ground. Like Susan, Ken was not bashful about offering suggestions, and both this book and all who read it are beneficiaries of his work.

Soundings proved to be an invaluable resource for the many news reports I wanted to include in this book as a means of bringing home the importance of safety. The organization could not have been more generous, inviting me to use their computer index to identify articles that might be relevant and then helping me find and copy the articles themselves from their back issues. The importance of their assistance will be apparent to all who read this book.

To Susan, Ken, and the staff at *Soundings,* a hearty "Thank you."

John Roberts
Galena, Maryland
September 1990

Introduction

This book is about enjoying your boat. It's based on one underlying premise: If you know how to operate the boat safely and competently, you'll feel better about yourself and your boat. Moreover, your confidence and competence will be contagious. Your family and other passengers or crew will respect your leadership as captain, and all of you—skipper, crew, and passengers—will be more relaxed and better able to enjoy boating as a result. So, the pages that follow focus on safety and small-boat handling for both powerboaters and sailors. While the text does not teach "how to sail," it does cover critical sailing skills which may be needed in case of engine failure.

In preparing to write, I came across a comment in John Russell's *The Book of Seamanship* that expressed my own feelings about the broad subject of boating safety better than any words I would have chosen. Russell wrote:

> Almost any discussion on safety . . . turns out to be not about forethought and priorities but about equipment, and moreover equipment whose purpose is not to ensure safety but to retrieve the situation when safety has been lost. It was deplorable sloppy thinking that stuck the label "safety equipment" onto such things as liferafts, fire extinguishers, and distress flares. These things are emergency, or if you prefer it, danger or survival equipment. Examples of true safety equipment are the humble electric fuse, the lifeline and harness, the white flare, and, *foremost of all, the pound or two of slush that every one of us carries around for life in his skull.*[1] [The added emphasis is my own.]

During my research, I was also repeatedly struck by how remote or impersonal most of the guidance on safety seemed. So, I decided to try something different by including in this book stories from magazines and newspapers as well as anecdotes from our own experiences in an effort to relate safety to people and, therefore, give it more meaning.

This book is aimed at forethought, priorities, and the most potentially effective piece of safety equipment that will be on your boat—the "pound or two of slush" that fills the space between your ears (i.e., your brain). The chapters that follow take you down to your boat, out onto the water, and back to land—even out onto the highway with a boat trailer. In the process, they cover such subjects as understanding your boat, preparing to get underway, maneuvering in close quarters, docking, anchoring, picking up a mooring, using a boat ramp, rules of the road, basic piloting, and avoiding and handling problems. Moreover, with Russell's admonition clearly in mind, the emphasis throughout is on planning and prevention.

But these pages are also aimed at your heart, with the hope that the sometimes humorous but more often tragic or near-tragic experiences of others will make safety a little more personal to you. I, for one, will never forget this plaint of a grieving father: "It's so crazy that we didn't have them put the [life] jackets on. I don't let my kids get in a car without putting their seat belts on. But the life jackets are so uncomfortable."[2]

1. *The Book of Seamanship*, by John Russell. Ziff Davis Publishing Company, New York, 1979; pp. 12–13.
2. "Sunday Fishing Outing Turns to Horror for Family," *News-Journal*, Wilmington, Delaware, April 24, 1986.

THE
BOATING BOOK

I

A Perspective on Safety

The overriding difference between boating and almost any other recreational activity is that boating involves traveling on water. That one fact introduces hazards we don't normally have to deal with. It requires a different set of skills, knowledge, and judgments than are normally required by our other activities. And, it creates extraordinary opportunity for personal and family enjoyment, which is why boating is so popular.

In this section, I'll use comparisons with familiar circumstances and activities ashore as well as examples from my own and other people's experience to explore the special hazards presented by the water, explain why and how the skills required for safe boating are special, address the problems of drinking and operating a boat, and demonstrate the fundamental connection between boating pleasure and boating safety.

1

The Keys to Boating Pleasure

Nothing will ruin a happy day on your boat faster than an accident. And it doesn't make any difference whether it involves a motorboat or a sailboat. I know that from personal experience. I was twelve years old when my father bought a 16-foot sailboat for my brother and me. I had studied a book entitled *How to Sail* for several weeks—literally memorizing its lessons—before picking up the bag of sails and heading down to our new boat to take it out for the first time.

From the moment I started putting on the sails, everything went just as it was described in the book—until I attempted to sail back to our mooring. I followed the instructions I had memorized so carefully, but when the boat stopped short of the buoy, I didn't know what to do. The book hadn't covered that detail; it assumed that everything went right, and I didn't know enough to have anticipated the problem. As a result, when the wind caught the sails again, my boat plowed straight into a molded-plywood speedboat moored nearby.

Fortunately, I wasn't hurt, but I sure was scared. I had put a hole in the speedboat's bow a few inches above the waterline, and I didn't know what to expect from either the boat's owner or my father.

I never did learn what the other boat's owner had to say; my father talked to him. I do know, however, that it was an expensive repair. I also know that my father learned a lesson. The day after the accident, he found someone who could take me out in our boat to teach me some of the more practical aspects of sailing—for example, what to do if you miss your mooring buoy.

Too often, as in my case forty years ago, a day on the water for a new, first-time boat owner and his crew is an accident waiting to happen. Why? Because a boat floating in water is a very different vehicle than any of us has ever driven. It requires a different set of skills and reactions than most of us have ever needed before. Moreover, there are different laws, rules, and courtesies required than we are accustomed to. Ironically, however, in the same society that requires people who want to drive an automobile on public roadways to pass tests demanding a minimum level of driving skills and knowledge of safe-driving laws, we have allowed almost anyone—even a twelve-year-old, as I was—to get behind the wheel of a boat and "drive" that boat on the nation's waterways.

There is a reason for this circumstance, of course. It is one element of the traditional freedom that is the hallmark of our society. That freedom, however, carries with it a responsibility for everyone to operate his or her boat safely. Moreover, that isn't just a moral responsibility; it is a legal responsibility as well. The skipper of a boat involved in an accident is legally responsible for the accident and its consequences if it results from his failure to maintain or operate his boat according to generally accepted standards of good seamanship.

BOATER PLEADS GUILTY—A Marathon, Florida, man has pleaded guilty to vehicular homicide in the operation of a boat that resulted in the death of a college woman near Marathon last Easter Sunday.

An assistant state attorney said Bruce Schofield, 23, of Marathon, has entered a negotiated plea of guilty to charges of vehicular homicide. In turn, the state dropped manslaughter charges. The officer said Schofield was to be sentenced to a year and a day in state prison.

Schofield was accused of operating a 17-foot speedboat through Vaca Cut at dusk, running over an anchored aluminum boat on which four persons were fishing. Killed was Nancy Rodriguez, a 20-year-old University of Florida freshman from Hialeah who was visiting her parents over the holiday. Others in the boat were not injured seriously, reports showed.

Investigating officers said tests showed Schofield had been drinking, but there was insufficient evidence to determine whether he was legally drunk.

Officials said if the case had gone to trial, Schofield could have drawn a more severe sentence.[1]

With waterways becoming more crowded and high-speed motorboats commonplace, concern about public safety is gradually leading state and local officials to the conclusion that it is not sufficient simply to hold people responsible for operating their boats safely. Instead, they are reaching the conclusion that the state itself has a responsibility for boating safety that goes beyond mere law enforcement. At this writing, only one state—Connecticut—has enacted a requirement for a boat operator's license. However, efforts to amend the law make the final requirements and the effective date still uncertain.

Three other states—Maryland, New Jersey and Vermont—have enacted boating safety education requirements. The Maryland law, as an example, requires anyone born after July 1, 1972, who operates a numbered vessel (i.e., all motorboats except those documented by the U.S. Coast Guard) on Maryland waters without supervision to possess a "certificate of boating safety education." The required certificate can be obtained by passing a boating safety course approved by the Maryland Department of Natural Resources or by passing an approved equivalency exam.

It's not difficult to find a boating safety course. Each year, for example, hundreds of thousands of people take boating courses sponsored by the United States Power Squadrons (USPS), the U.S. Coast Guard Auxiliary, and by the offices of boating safety in many of our states. These courses range from one class period to twelve or more, at the end of which the students are tested to be certain they have mastered the lessons. Some other people—albeit a much smaller number—take boating courses offered by profit-making organizations.

For people who, for whatever reason, cannot take a boating

1. *Soundings*, Essex, Connecticut, January 1986.

safety course, there are books intended to help people learn how to operate their boats in a safe manner. This is one such book. While it is designed to complement and reinforce the lessons of boating safety courses offered by local USPS units and Coast Guard Auxiliary units, and many state agencies, it is also written for people who cannot yet take one of those courses. It is intended to help you and all members of your boating family enjoy boating to the fullest extent possible by learning to understand, take care of, and operate your boat safely.

One additional comment must be made, however. Neither taking a course, studying this book, nor any combination of the two can make you a safe boater. One other element is necessary: You have to work consciously to apply what you learn in the classroom or from the book every time you go out on either your own or someone else's boat. It's much like having seat belts in your automobile. Seat belts won't protect you unless you wear them properly—and consistently. They also won't protect your passengers unless they're worn. Similarly, knowing how to maintain and operate your boat safely won't protect you, your family, and friends unless you put that knowledge to work every time you go out on your boat.

Testing What You've Learned
(Answers can be found in Appendix C)

1. When can the skipper of a boat be held legally responsible for damage or injury caused by his boat?

2. What restrictions are imposed by most states on eligibility for operating a motorboat?

3. In states having unusual requirements for operating a motorboat, what are those requirements?

4. What was the fundamental error the author and his father made many years ago that resulted in the author running his sailboat into a motorboat while trying to pick up his mooring?

5. Name three organizations which regularly offer boating safety courses to the public.

2

The Water: A Different Environment

Boating is a special activity. For example, I can be tense from a tough day at work or a problem at home, and the tension dissolves as I drive into our marina. Get me onto a boat, and I don't want to get off. Introduce me to a fellow boater anywhere in the world, and we've got lots to talk about. Boating can be that relaxing, that much fun, and that entertaining. But you don't have to take my word for it. If you don't yet have the experience to confirm my feelings about boating, your common sense will do the job.

Consider this: More than sixty-eight million people in the United States—that's more than one out of every four of us—participate in boating in one form or another. About half of that number own powerboats or sailboats; add in people who own canoes or kayaks, and the fraction jumps to more than 60 percent of the sixty-eight million American boat owners.

As you know yourself, most of us are not wealthy. We're spending hard-earned dollars on our boating activities, and it's a safe bet that we're doing it for some positive reason. It may be that we enjoy the feeling of power as we speed across the water at 50 miles per hour or even faster. Possibly we are captivated by the thrill of running rapids in a kayak or canoe. Or perhaps it's the challenge of using the wind to get from one place to another, or the competitive spirit of racing, whether by sail or motor. Maybe it's satisfaction of a different sort—the excitement of landing a fish or netting a crab, or simply the tranquility of a peaceful afternoon or evening on the water away from the hustle and bustle of everyday life ashore.

Whatever the reasons for enjoying our boats, we should never lose sight of the fact that boats are used on the water. It is an obvious, but important distinction—important because the water provides a very different playground than the dry land we're accustomed to. While these differences help create the lure of boating, they also present a new set of risks and hazards that we are simply not accustomed to dealing with. For example:

• If we fall on land, we might scrape a knee or get a few bruises. If we fall on the water, we might drown. We might drown either because we can't swim well enough to stay afloat until we're rescued, or because we're incapacitated by hypothermia (low body temperature) resulting from our body's reaction to the chilly water. And it can happen even to experienced boaters.

WORLD RACER ROB JAMES DROWNED OFF THE ENGLISH COAST—Rob James, veteran of two Whitbread Round the World races, two-time winner of the Round Britain Race, and winner of the Doublehanded Transatlantic Race, was drowned off the south coast of England on March 20. . . . James, who was working on deck, lost his footing and fell into the safety net between the hulls [of the trimaran]. The net failed, throwing him into the water. He was not wearing a safety harness or life jacket.

The crew threw a buoy; then one of them went overboard with a line tied around himself. He reached James, but in the swell James could not be brought aboard. The crew member was finally hauled out, exhausted, suffering from hypothermia. . . . James was finally recovered by helicopter about two hours after he fell overboard. He was pronounced dead at a hospital in Plymouth, England.[1]

• If we spill some gasoline while filling up the tank in our car, our biggest concern usually is to wipe it from the fender so that it won't trap dirt and look bad. If, on the other hand, we spill some gas while filling the tank in our boat, or develop a leak in our boat's fuel system, we can blow the boat and ourselves to smithereens if we're not careful.

1. *Sail*, Charlestown, Massachusetts, May 1983; p. 149.

BOAT BLAST INJURES FOUR AT DOCK—One person was seriously injured and three others suffered burns July 25 when a 25-foot cabin cruiser exploded moments after being filled with gasoline at the dock at Hoffman's Anchorage, Brielle, New Jersey.

The blast came as the ignition was [switched on] after the tank of the *Sea Hawk* was filled, according to Brielle Fire Inspector Kenneth Miller.

Todd Sokoli, 15, and his 20-year-old brother, Scott, apparently were thrown or jumped out of the boat at the time of the explosion. Their mother, Marilyn, and grandmother, Clara Moro, were trapped inside and were rescued by occupants of nearby boats.

"As far as we can determine, they filled the tank with gas and were returning the gas nozzle to the dockmaster," Miller said. "He hung it back up, and after that one of the boys turned the ignition on. Approximately 20 seconds later, the explosion occurred."

The cause of the fire is under investigation, but fire officials suspect a leak in a gasoline line.[2]

• If we're driving along the road in a car and need to stop quickly, we can put on the brakes. Boats don't have brakes, as too many new boaters learn the first few times they come in to a dock. Moreover, if some outboard motorboats are slowed down too quickly under the wrong conditions, the boat can end up filled with water from waves piling up on the stern and surging over the transom. For example, this item appeared recently in one of the boating magazines.

RUNABOUT SWAMPED; PASSENGER RESCUED—Answering a Coast Guard request to move back [from a tall ship], a small runabout containing four people spurted ahead, which seemed to depress her stern so much that when she slowed she was pooped [flooded] by her own stern wave. She promptly started to sink. . . . [When the last person was rescued], just 2 feet of the runabout's bow remained above water.[3]

• If we don't get home before dark while driving a car, we can simply maintain our speed and turn on the headlights to light the way. Boats, however, don't have headlights. At night, we

2. *Soundings*, October 1986.
3. *Yachting*, Times-Mirror Magazines, Cos Cob, Connecticut, September 1986; p. 32.

rely on red, green, and white flashing lights on channel markers to find our way and on the small red, green, and white running lights on other boats to avoid collision. The result is that we can't see very well at night out on the water, so it's always a good idea to go much slower than in daylight. Moreover, as with automobiles, drinking and driving do not mix.

> DYING FOR A DRINK—In one of the worst boating accidents in recent years, five people died on Fox Lake in Illinois when two high-speed ski boats collided at about 2:00 A.M. on Labor Day. Toxicology tests showed that both operators had been drinking, one with a blood alcohol content (BAC) of .24, twice the amount set as legally drunk.
>
> The fatal collision occurred when a 21-foot powerboat traveling at about 45 mph was hit nearly head on, then run over by a 19-foot boat. The bow was torn off the 21-footer, and all three of its occupants died. Two people aboard the smaller vessel were killed. . . . The operator of the 19-foot boat had a BAC of .088 percent, slightly less than legally drunk but considered "under the influence."[4]

Even the weather assumes a different level of importance on the water. A sudden storm on land may mean we have to close our windows and rescue the lawn furniture. The same storm on the water can put us in real danger, depending upon the kind of boat we have and our boat-handling skills. For that reason, marine police generally have the authority to order a boat into the harbor if bad weather is approaching and the boat isn't suited to the approaching weather conditions. In fact, many of our boats—particularly outboards used for fishing, water-skiing, or just plain running about—simply are not designed for use in the kind of short, steep waves that can be piled up very quickly in larger rivers, lakes, and bays by the strong winds of a thunderstorm or severe rain squall. As a point of reference, nearly 10 percent of boating accidents—and 15 percent of boating fatalities—are caused by rough water or strong currents, according to Coast Guard statistics.

What these differences between being on land and on the

---

4. *BOAT / US Reports,* BOAT / US, Alexandria, Virginia, November / December 1986; p. 2.

water mean, of course, is that anyone who wants to enjoy boating must acquire a whole new set of skills and the knowledge base required to make good judgments while on the water. Some of this knowledge involves understanding the differences between various boat types and designs. It involves learning how to perform basic maneuvers with your own boat, and practicing them until they become second nature. It also requires learning about rules and regulations affecting boats, fundamental safety procedures, and how to read the marine version of traffic signs and road maps—in this case, the system of aids to navigation used to mark our waterways and navigation charts.

BOATING ACCIDENTS—FACTS AND FIGURES

How important is learning about your boat and how to operate it safely? There are an estimated fifty thousand boating accidents every year that kill well over a thousand people and injure another twenty-five thousand. Added to that human toll is millions of dollars in property damage.

Nearly half of the boats involved in these accidents are cruising—just traveling from one place to another. Another 10 percent are drifting, perhaps while fishing. And another nearly 10 percent are tied up at a dock. While all boat types are involved, most are motorboats and well over half are less than 26 feet long. Horsepower is definitely a factor, with nearly half of the accidents involving boats with engines of more than 75 horsepower. Add those in the 26- to 75-horsepower range, and you've accounted for another 15 percent.

Who's driving these boats? Their ages range from under twelve years old to over fifty. And, the accidents happen virtually everywhere. In any given year, for example, every state may have at least one fatal boating accident. About 45 percent of the accidents happen in lakes, ponds, reservoirs, and gravel pits; 20 percent are on rivers, lakes, and streams; and another 20 percent occur in bays, inlets, sounds, harbors, and the Intracoastal Waterway.

What causes these accidents? It's not generally any failure of equipment. In fact, equipment failure accounts for less than one accident in ten. Nor is it bad weather, most of the time. Although I noted earlier that about 10 percent of accidents do happen in rough or very rough water, the other side of that statistic is that 90 percent of boating accidents do not happen in rough or very rough water. In fact, about half of these accidents occur in calm water. The point is this: *The single largest cause of boating accidents is operator error.* "People" mistakes— ignorance, carelessness, not paying attention, not keeping a good enough lookout—are what cause about half of our boating accidents. And these mistakes, when they happen, turn pleasant days on the water into nightmares.

WATER AND ALCOHOL

There is one additional area of safety that needs to be discussed right up front. I touched on it with the news report about the Fox Lake accident in which five people died. The subject is booze—alcoholic beverages—and boats.

Consider these facts: Nine of every ten people who die in boating accidents drown. As many as 69 percent of all drowning victims may have been drinking. An estimated 38 percent of all fatal boating accidents involve people who are legally drunk. In one study, 75 percent of people who drowned after falling off a boat or dock had a blood alcohol content of 0.15; in other words, they were drunk.[5] In another study, the California Department of Waterways showed that alcohol was a factor in 59 percent of that state's boating fatalities.

Faced by facts like these, more and more state legislatures are enacting tough drunk-boating laws. And, for those states that don't enact their own laws, the U.S. Coast Guard has issued a national drunk-boating regulation that accomplishes the same purpose. In effect, these measures extend drunk-driving laws from the highways to our waterways. This includes authorizing the use of breathalyzers to test blood alcohol levels.

5. *Family Safety & Health,* National Safety Council, Chicago, Illinois, Vol. 45, No. 3 (Fall 1986), "Alcohol & the Other Accidents"; p. 18.

The problem, however, won't be solved by law enforcement alone. It can only be solved by convincing individual boaters that alcohol—including beer—is one of the single greatest threats to their boating safety and enjoyment. In fact, as great as the risks are from drinking and driving on land, they are much greater drinking and boating. Why? On land, you can always park your car or have someone else drive you home. On water, even if you "park" your boat, you are still "on the water." Moreover, as long as you're on your boat, you are "on call" and may need to react with responsible, coordinated action if a problem arises—for example, a change in weather, a guest falling overboard, or a mechanical failure. That's tough to do when you've had too much to drink. As for your passengers, I said it earlier: If they should stumble and fall on land, they might scrape a knee. If they stumble and fall on your boat—particularly if they've been drinking—they may well fall overboard and drown. *And you are responsible.*

My family and I learned this lesson very innocently but also very powerfully a few years ago—fortunately without tragedy. I normally do not drink much. However, one June weekend Susan, our two youngest daughters, and I were cruising with several other boats. At the end of a hot, humid summer day, we tied up alongside our friends at anchor to form a raft and enjoy a cocktail party in a quiet cove in one of the many rivers that run into the Chesapeake Bay. By policy, we—John and Susan—will not keep our boat as part of a raft overnight. Instead, we break off before dark to anchor away from the raft by ourselves because we believe it is safer. We've seen strong winds wreak havoc with rafts of boats in the middle of the night, resulting in injured people and damaged boats.

In any case, while we were rafted I failed to keep track of how much I was drinking, and, in the camaraderie of the moment, I simply drank too much. As dark approached, we separated from the raft and went out to anchor. I know we did, because we were anchored off by ourselves when I awoke the next morning. But I don't remember doing it. I also learned the next morning that my wife and daughters had spent two tense hours the night before trying to keep me seated in the cockpit until I finally could be persuaded to go to sleep in the cabin below. I kept wanting to go forward to check the anchor, but was so drunk that Susan was fearful that I would lose my balance and fall overboard. We both know that people who fall into the water when they are drunk frequently just go right to the bottom and drown. Even if I had surfaced, however, Susan was concerned that she would not have been able to get me back onto the boat. Her fear was not without merit. While less than 5 percent of all boating accidents involve people falling overboard, that relatively small number of accidents accounts for nearly 20 percent of the fatalities. Moreover, that night the nearest help was several hundred feet away, all still enjoying the cocktail party. As we talked about it over the next several days, I developed still another concern—that I would have been worthless, and possibly even dangerous, had a problem arisen during the night.

In thinking about that episode, I was frightened enough that I later talked to my friends about it, and we've stopped having organized cocktail parties when we're at anchor. As for ourselves, Susan and I now consciously limit our drinking while sailing or motoring to an occasional can of beer or small glass of wine. At all other times, our limit is one or, possibly, two drinks. Then we turn to water, iced tea, or soft drinks. In any case, I am no longer a casual drinker; I now pay close attention to how much I am drinking, whether we're on land or on the water. The potential cost for being casual about drinking—or about any other area of boating safety, for that matter—is just too high. It would take the fun out of our boating.

Testing What You've Learned
(Answers can be found in Appendix C)

1. Name five factors that may create safety risks on boats which we don't normally encounter when driving cars.

2. What type and size of boat is most often involved in accidents?

3. TRUE or FALSE: Motorboats with engines larger than 75 horsepower are involved in relatively few accidents.

4. Which of the following is the cause of most boating accidents?
   a. Bad weather
   b. Operator error
   c. Failure of equipment

5. TRUE or FALSE: Alcohol plays a major role in boating accidents.

6. Are there any laws where you live that make it illegal to operate a boat under the influence of alcohol?

II

Understanding Your Boat

One of the keys to becoming a skilled boater is understanding how your boat relates to the water. In that one sense alone, learning to operate your boat is similar to learning to drive a car or truck. Boats—like cars and trucks—come in an almost endless variety of sizes, shapes, and descriptions. They are designed for a wide range of uses. There are major differences in the way various boats handle as well as in their stability and maneuverability. And, there are differences in the level of skill required to operate them safely.

This section will look at the performance characteristics, advantages, and limitations of powerboats and sailboats, considering basic hull and / or engine configurations in boats ranging from small johnboats and daysailers to large sportfishermen and sailboats for ocean racing or cruising.

3

Planing, Displacement, and Stability

In an ideal world, safe boating begins with choosing a craft that is suitable for what you want to do. For many of us, however, safe boating begins with understanding the boat we already have—the kind of use it's suited for and the advantages and limitations of its particular design.

This notion shouldn't be revolutionary. Leaving boats aside, for a moment, that's how we deal with cars or trucks every day. If we're interested in "driving" a car, we'll probably be looking for a sports car. For efficient transportation to and from work or just around town, perhaps we'll choose a high-mileage sub-compact. For a lot of long-distance highway driving, we'll more than likely need a larger, heavier sedan. Off-the-road exploring calls for a four-wheel-drive truck or Jeep, possibly with oversized tires. If it's luxury we want, there's a wide selection of expensive cars from which to choose.

Often, of course, the realities of family, pocketbook, or other circumstances force us to make compromises. As a result, we may end up with a "sporty" car in place of a real sports car, an intermediate-sized car instead of either a compact or large sedan, or possibly a four-wheel-drive sedan rather than a four-wheel-drive Jeep or truck. Moreover, we can often serve our desire for luxury with the options we choose in a less expensive car, rather than starting with a $25,000 base sticker price.

On the surface, it might look as if all of these choices among automobiles is simply a marketing ploy. A closer look, however, suggests that these different types of cars have been developed to meet people's needs.

The same can be said of the boating industry. A wide range of boats has been developed to meet consumer needs. Some of these boats are produced for specialized uses ranging from fishing in lakes or rivers to fishing far offshore for large game fish; from dockside living or entertaining to weekend or even long-distance cruising; or from racing in local regattas to participation in major offshore events, power or sail. Others are compromises among these and other purposes, including a wide variety of utility motorboats and small sailboats.

As in the world of automobiles, differences from one boat to another may be substantial. They may also have significant impact on safety as well as on practicality. For example, a boat intended for fishing in the relatively calm waters of an inland lake or small river probably would not be safe for use on a large coastal bay, the Great Lakes, or on the ocean, where the water can get quite rough in a short time. In the same way, a boat intended for weekend sailing on Long Island Sound probably isn't really safe for sailing out to Bermuda.

There's another consideration as well: Most people can move from one car to another and drive either one without compromising safety; if not, car rental agencies would be in big trouble. It's not quite the same when moving from one boat to another. Differences in boat size and type, hull shape, steering system, and engine(s) may require different—sometimes substantially different—skills of the skipper.

Leaving aside for the moment the obvious distinction between motorboats and sailboats, variations among boats begin with the two fundamentally different types of boat hulls—planing hulls and displacement hulls. A second major difference involves stability. From the perspective of safety, an understanding of each is key to recognizing the capabilities and limitations of your boat.

DISPLACEMENT

When any object is put into water, it pushes aside, or *displaces,* an amount of water equal to its weight. We've all proved this to ourselves many times over—every time we've filled a glass too full and then put in a couple of ice cubes. What happened? The glass overflowed. Why? Because the ice cubes displaced an amount of the drink equal to their own weight, forcing the liquid over the top of the glass.

The same thing happens when a boat is launched. It displaces a volume of water equal to its weight—one gallon of water for about every 8.3 pounds of boat. Moreover, every time something else is put into the boat (making it heavier), the boat sinks a little lower and displaces a bit more water.

In dealing with boats, the concept of displacement as volume—or space—is as important as the relationship of displacement to weight. If you'd like to do a little experiment, this can be illustrated easily with three Styrofoam or paper cups, a pan of water, and some sand or small stones. The cups will be your "boats." The sand or pebbles will serve as ballast to make the cups heavy enough to settle down to their waterlines when you put them in the pan of water.

Draw a line around the first cup about an inch above the bottom, and then fill it with just enough sand or stones to make it float with the water right at its waterline (WL) as shown in (a) of Figure 1. That done? Congratulations, you've just made a light-displacement "boat"!

On the second cup, draw the waterline about an inch and a half above the bottom. After adding ballast to sink this cup to its waterline, you will have made a moderate-displacement "boat."

Following the same procedure, give your third "boat" a waterline that is two inches above the bottom and add the sand or stones as ballast, to make a heavy-displacement boat.

Finally, put the three cups next to each other in the water, as shown in (b) of Figure 1, and make a mark on the sides of the two "taller" cups that is even with the top of the "shortest" cup. The idea is to cut the tops from the two cups that are floating highest in the water so that the tops of all three cups will be

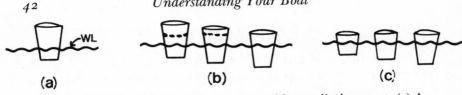

(a)   **(b)**   **(c)**

FIG. 1.   Illustration of light, moderate, and heavy displacement: (a) A
small amount of sand or gravel will make the first cup relatively stable
in the water (light displacement). (b) Progressively larger amounts of
sand or gravel will make the second (moderate displacement) and third
(heavy displacement) cups sit lower in the water. (c) After cutting off
the tops so that all three cups float with the same height above the water,
you have created light-, moderate-, and heavy-displacement "boats."

about the same height above the water's surface, as illustrated
in (c) of Figure 1.

Now you can compare your three "boats." One similarity is
that all three have about the same amount of volume above the
waterline. One difference, on the other hand, is that there is
a lot more cup (volume) beneath the water in the heavy-
displacement "boat" than in either of the other two. Another
key difference is that the heavy-displacement boat weighs more
than the others because you had to add more sand or pebbles
to weigh it down to its waterline.

This illustrates how heavier-displacement boats have more
interior volume below the waterline. It also illustrates how heavier
boats make bigger holes in the water. If you push your "boats"
through the water gently, you may be able to see that heavier-
displacement boats make bigger waves because they have to push
more water out of the way. Moreover, though you probably
can't feel it because your fingers aren't sensitive enough, you'll
need to push a little harder to get the heavier-displacement
"boats" moving. Their bottoms are bigger, there's more water
to be pushed aside, and there's more friction between the "boat"
bottom and the water than in the lighter-displacement "boats."

From a practical viewpoint, of course, essentially all boats are
displacement boats in that they displace a certain amount of
water. Moreover, when they're moving at a slow speed, they
simply push their way *through* the water, and the "hole" they
make in the water stays the same size—just like your cup "boats."

At these low speeds, all boats are said to be operating in a "displacement" mode.

Planing Hulls

Some boats, because of the shape of their hulls, can climb partly or almost completely up on top of the water when they get moving fast enough. When this happens, they are said to be "planing." In general, these boats have long, flat sections in the bottom of their hulls and relatively powerful engines. They also tend to have lighter displacements. As they gain speed, the force of the water moving under the flat hull sections lifts the boat up over its bow wave and out of its "hole" to skim along the top of the water. Depending upon the type and size of boat, a planing hull may be capable of speeds that range from less than 10 knots (nautical miles per hour) to well over 100 knots.

Displacement Hulls

The so-called "displacement hull" is at the opposite end of the spectrum from the planing designs. Boats designed with displacement hulls are not intended for speed. More likely, they are designed for comfort, interior space, and economy of operation. Frequently, their hulls are round, with few (if any) flat surfaces. Moreover, they generally have a heavier displacement for their length than semi-displacement or planing hulls. As a result, they make bigger holes in the water.

As do all boats, displacement hulls create a system of waves that extend out from the side of the boat near the bow (front) and stern (back) as they begin to move through the water. As the boat moves faster, these waves tend to get larger and larger, gradually moving closer to the bow and stern until the boat is literally riding between the two wave systems (Figure 2). Within limits, the heavier a boat's displacement, the larger these waves tend to be.

In theory, the boat at this point is going as fast as it is capable of going, because its combination of power and hull design will not let it climb out of its hole. For that reason, this speed is

FIG. 2. Wave formation at hull speed: As a boat approaches its theoretical maximum hull speed, waves forming at the bow and stern create
a "hole." A large increase in power is required to make the boat move
faster.

called the "maximum theoretical hull speed," or most often,
simply the boat's "hull speed."

An individual boat's hull speed can be determined by finding
the square root of the waterline length and multiplying that by
1.34. For example, hull speed for a displacement design with a
waterline length of 16 feet is about 5.4 knots. (For reference
purposes, one knot is equal to 1.15 miles per hour as measured
by your car's speedometer.) Hull speed for a boat with a 25-
foot waterline is about 6.7 knots. On a 36-foot waterline, it is
about 8.0 knots.

In practice, it is relatively easy to get displacement designs to
go about 80 percent of hull speed; beyond that, a substantial
increase in power from engine or sails is needed to make the
boat go faster (Figure 3).

Semi-Displacement Hulls

Frequently, boat designers try to blend the best features of
displacement and planing hulls into a single boat. The result is
the so-called "semi-displacement" or "semi-planing" hull. Compared to a planing hull, a semi-displacement boat has less flat
area on its bottom. As a result, it can only get partway up onto
a "plane." When you see a semi-displacement vessel going down-
channel, its bow is high, its stern low, and it may look like it
is trying to climb out of a hole. In fact, that's just what it's
doing—trying to climb over its bow wave to get up on top of the
water—but not quite, or just barely, making it. For that reason,
the speeds of semi-displacement boats tend to be in the lower
end of the range for planing boats. Some, however, are equipped

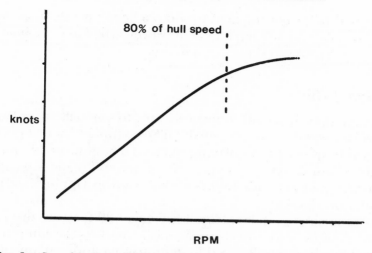

80% of hull speed

knots

RPM

FIG. 3. Speed curve—displacement hull: The speed curve for a typical displacement boat shows the dramatic increase in engine RPM required for small boosts in boat speed as you approach the boat's theoretical maximum hull speed.

with devices called "trim tabs." These are metal plates hinged to the bottom of a boat's transom so that they can be adjusted up and down hydraulically from the helm (Figure 4). When the trim tabs are pushed down, the water flowing under them creates

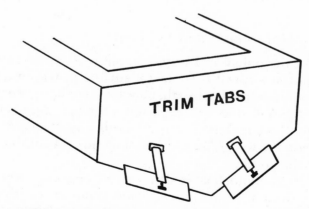

TRIM TABS

FIG. 4. Trim tabs: Adjustable trim tabs mounted on a motorboat's stern help get the boat onto a plane, improving engine efficiency.

a lift that helps get the boat up onto a better plane, increasing boat speed. Too much trim tab, however, will make the boat go down in the bow and reduce stability.

Sailboat Hulls

These same broad descriptions apply to sailboats as well as to powerboats. For example, small sailboats (under 20 feet overall length) frequently have planing hulls, which, in favorable winds, enable them to get up on top of the water and plane—an exhilarating experience for sailors accustomed to ripping along at all of 4 or 5 knots.

For the most part, larger sailboats (over 20 feet) are displacement designs whose performance is subject to the same theoretical maximum hull speed limitations that apply to any other displacement boat. The most obvious exceptions to this are catamarans and trimarans, which are discussed separately later in this chapter. Less obvious exceptions, however, are found among some of the light- or ultralight-displacement sailboats designed specifically for racing. These are analogous to the semi-displacement hulls used for powerboats. Although the design compromises required for seaworthiness and the practical limitations on the size of sails usually won't allow these larger sailboats to get up on a sustained plane, the hulls are designed to surf easily under the right wind and wave conditions.

Surfing—Motorboats and Sailboats

Usually, the only way a displacement hull can be made to go faster than hull speed is to start it surfing in large waves. The skipper positions the boat so that a wave coming up from behind will give a boost to its speed, pushing the boat up over its bow wave onto the larger wave crest. In this way, the crew uses the boat to ride the waves, much like someone on a surfboard rides waves at the beach.

Surfing in a motorboat is always extremely dangerous.

Surfing in a sailboat under racing conditions with a highly experienced crew is exhilarating, but it too is clearly risky.

Surfing in a sailboat *unintentionally,* however, is more than risky; it can be every bit as treacherous as surfing in a motorboat. When the force of moving water in storm waves on the open ocean or breaking waves in an inlet takes over control of either a motorboat or sailboat, pushing it too fast down the front of the wave, the boat may either plunge bow-first into the water and be flipped over lengthwise by the wave—called "pitchpoling"—or slue (turn) sideways and be rolled over, called "broaching." Although a sailboat's ballast keel should make it come back to its feet, the boat may be severely damaged and the crew injured or thrown overboard. If a motorboat rolls over, usually it stays that way—upside down. In other words, either form of capsize—pitchpoling or broaching—is dangerous.

SUNDAY FISHING OUTING TURNS TO HORROR FOR FAMILY—Sunday looked like a fine day for fishing, with no hint of the tragedy that would meet the Mangini family at Indian River Inlet [Delaware].

The family has "100 years of experience on that water," Albert P. Mangini, Jr., of Newark said Wednesday. "We've been out there so many times, with never so much as a close call."

But Sunday morning, as Mangini, 32, and his 57-year-old father were turning their boats from the ocean into the inlet after a disappointing couple of hours looking for fish, the older man's boat capsized.

One child, Mangini's five-year-old niece, drowned. Another child, his five-year-old son, is missing. Neither was wearing a life jacket, although both boats carried them.

"It's so crazy that we didn't have them put the jackets on. I don't let my kids get in a car without putting their seat belts on. But the life jackets are so uncomfortable," he said.

The cause of the capsizing remains a mystery. The elder Mangini's boat had a deep-vee hull, which the younger man said could normally ride out the 4- to 5-foot waves they encountered at the inlet.

James B. Ramsey, supervisor of the Delaware Marine Police, said . . . "it appears from our investigation that the boat had a following sea and it was surfing. It apparently went down under a wave."[1]

1. *News-Journal,* Wilmington, Delaware, April 24, 1986.

STABILITY

Have you ever been in a canoe? If so, you've probably learned firsthand what is meant by stability. Canoes are very unstable if you get your weight too high. That's one reason why people shouldn't stand up in a canoe—or in any other small boat, for that matter. On the other hand, if you keep your weight low and know how to handle them, canoes and other small boats can safely take you through quite rough waters.

There are different kinds of stability, but right now we're interested in transverse stability: Will it tip or roll over?

In general, stability is a function of two major factors: hull shape, and where the weight is located. As a result, there are basically two ways to increase or decrease a boat's transverse stability. One is obvious in our experience with canoes: Put weight up high, and they will turn over easily, because you have reduced their stability; put the weight low, and they're remarkably steady, because you have increased stability. You will get somewhat the same effect when you put a tall flying bridge or tuna tower on a sportfisherman, or a heavy lead keel on the bottom of a sailboat. The flying bridge tends to reduce stability; the heavy keel tends to increase it.

The second way to affect stability involves hull shape, the so-called "form stability"—that is, stability gained or lost by the width and shape of the hull below the waterline. In general, you can increase form stability by making a boat wider and / or by flattening the bottom. By the same token, you can reduce form stability by making the hull narrower and / or designing a round or distinctly vee bottom.

In practice, a designer will try to strike a balance between weight distribution and hull shape to give optimum performance for a boat. Among sailboats, for example, a boat designed for use in shallow water probably will be a bit beamier (wider) than a boat with a deep keel intended for deeper waters. Among motorboats, bassboats and family runabouts tend to be a bit beamier than high-speed runabouts. Similarly, sportfishing boats tend to be quite beamy to support their high flying bridges and tuna towers. What all of this means, of course, is that you need to be careful about adding a center console and tall seat or tall fishing seats to your utility outboard, or a flying bridge to your cabin cruiser. If the boat has not been designed to accommodate the added weight above the deck—and that includes the weight of the people who will sit in those chairs or ride up on the flying bridge—the addition could make your boat unstable in some conditions and, therefore, make it unsafe.

Testing What You've Learned
(Answers can be found in Appendix C)

1. TRUE or FALSE: If you can handle your own boat well, you should be able to step into any other boat and handle it easily and safely.

2. The amount of water a boat pushes aside when it is put in the water is a measure of its _____ .

3. The heavier a boat's displacement is, the more _____ it will have below the waterline.

4. A boat designed so that it can get up and run on top of the water is said to have what type of hull?
   a. Displacement hull
   b. Semi-displacement hull
   c. Planing hull
   d. (a) and (b) above
   e. (b) and (c) above

5. A boat that can get only partway up onto a plane is said to have either a _____ or a _____ hull.

6. TRUE or FALSE: A boat with a displacement hull is designed primarily for speed.

7. TRUE or FALSE: It is relatively easy to get a displacement hull moving at hull speed.

8. What is the hull speed of a 30-foot sailboat whose waterline length is 25 feet?

9. What is the hull speed of a 38-foot trawler whose waterline length is 36 feet?

10. What two dangerous situations can arise when a motorboat or sailboat begins surfing down a wave? Describe what can happen in each situation.

11. What are three factors affecting boat stability?

12. Why is it not safe to stand up in a small boat?

4

The Shape of Your Boat's Bottom

After displacement and stability, the third major difference from one boat hull to another is the shape below the waterline—the part of the hull that is underwater when the boat is standing still. These shapes range from flat to round, with many variations between the two extremes. From a practical viewpoint, we're interested in six basic shapes: flat bottom, vee bottom, cathedral, deep vee, modified vee, and round, as shown in Figure 5, (a) through (f).

POWERBOAT BOTTOM CONFIGURATIONS

Flat Bottoms

In the purest sense, a flat-bottomed boat is just that: it has a flat bottom. Where the bottom meets the sides, it forms about a 90-degree angle, and the boat is said to have a "hard chine." The boat may also have a square, blunt bow instead of the traditional pointy bow.

In the days before fiberglass, flat bottoms made wooden boat building easier and less expensive; today, they still make building with steel or aluminum easier. Flat bottoms, however, have other attractions as well. A flat-bottomed boat, for example, can be beached easily. In shallow bays, a flat-bottomed boat with its propeller in a tunnel can skim through water just a few inches

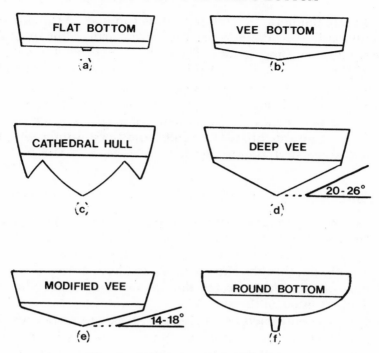

FIG. 5.   Basic motorboat hull shapes.

deep. All other things being equal, flat-bottomed boats will plane easily, which allows for good boat speed. And they are relatively stable *if they are not too narrow.* The flat bottom means that the support of the water on the boat's bottom is spread evenly across the whole boat, offering relatively good initial stability; in other words, the boat is not "tippy."

There are disadvantages to flat bottoms as well, of course. On the stability front, while the flat bottom can provide good initial stability, once a flat-bottomed boat begins to tip over, that stability is quickly lost and the boat will go all the way over with relative ease. This is particularly true in heavy waves that may catch the boat sideways. Also, while flat-bottomed boats generally are not initially "tippy," they tend to have a relatively abrupt rocking motion in waves—called a "quick" motion.

On the speed front, the flat bottom will pound terribly on a plane, even in small waves, because the waves just bang against that broad, flat bottom. That pounding can make a ride uncomfortable and even dangerous. We were startled, for example, one summer evening, in a 6-mile-per-hour controlled speed area of the Maryland's Sassafras River, to see two youngsters thrown from a lightweight boat. It had begun to buck because of the way the bow was being thrown up in the air as the boat pounded across the low wakes of the slow-moving larger boats. Fortunately, no one was hurt. Hopefully, the person operating the small boat learned something.

Vee Bottoms

The vee bottom represents an effort to provide a gentler ride without sacrificing the positive features of a flat bottom. Beginning at the bow, the bottom quickly flows into a vee shape intended to cut through the waves. As the lines move aft (toward the rear of the boat), the vee flattens out until it may be only barely discernible at the stern.

Often, vee-bottomed boats also have hard chines because the angle formed by the joint of the bottom and side for much of the boat's length still is not much more than 90 degrees. In any case, the sides of the vee provide the long, flat surfaces needed for a planing hull.

Depending upon how quickly the vee flattens out, the boat may retain much of the initial stability advantage of the flat bottom. And, in wood, aluminum, or steel boat construction, the vee shape is still relatively easy to build.

What about the comfort factor? How quickly the vee is flattened out as it moves from bow to stern is a trade-off between the pounding characteristics of the boat and its initial stability. In small waves, the sharp vee bottom near the bow cuts through the waves to soften the ride. Depending upon the weight of the boat and how far back from the bow the steeper sides of the vee are carried before they flatten out, the ride begins to deteriorate as waves get larger or boat speed increases. In any case, pounding can be reduced by running at lower speeds so that the waves are taken farther forward, where the steeper vee softens the impact. Of course, slowing down will lessen the impact from pounding in any boat.

Cathedral Bottoms

The cathedral hull was developed in an effort to maximize stability—make the boat less tippy—while providing some of the advantages of a vee bottom from a comfort viewpoint. In effect, the cathedral hull uses the vee shape down the center of the hull and adds extra flotation down each side so that a fisherman (or child) moving to the side of the boat will not make it tip or lean as much as it would otherwise. The idea is that the vee-shaped bow section will cut through small waves more effectively than would a flat-bottomed boat. Carrying the vee on aft is supposed to reduce the flat surfaces involved in pounding. In addition, air is said to be trapped between the side and center portions of the hull, providing a softer ride. It all works to some extent, but cathedral-hull boats, like the flat- and vee-bottomed types, must be run at reduced speeds in choppy water to keep pounding to an acceptable level; otherwise, their ride begins to deteriorate as waves get larger.

Deep-Vee Bottoms

The deep vee was developed for running at high speeds in heavy seas. Typically, the sharp vee-shape is flattened only a small amount so that the deep-vee form is carried all the way to the stern. The effect is to create a hull form that can plunge from one wave to the next without pounding. As the hull comes down onto the wave, it knifes into the water until the outward slope of the bottom provides enough buoyancy to stop downward motion and the boat lifts to the next wave.

Handled skillfully, a deep-vee hull can be operated at substantially higher speeds in rough water than can cathedral-, vee-, or flat-bottomed designs. That advantage, however, is not a license to drive through rough water at any speed. The boat can still buck like a bronco—and just as dangerously.

There are also some trade-offs: The ease with which a boat will get up on the water and plane relates directly to the amount of relatively horizontal, flat surface area on its bottom. As a result, the deep-vee shape provides an inefficient planing surface, and these boats require considerably more horsepower to get up and go. They also frequently are given trim tabs to help them plane more efficiently.

In addition, the less-abrupt joints between the sides and bottom of a deep-vee hull (called "soft" chines) result in a less stable boat *at slow speeds* and at anchor because the shape provides relatively little buoyancy out along the sides of the boat. In other words, these boats are "tippier."

To help compensate for these trade-offs, deep-vee boats typically have flat sections along the outer edges of the bottom for a better planing surface. Many also have a series of flat "lift strakes" (narrow planks or ridges) running the length of the bottom—again, to help give a more efficient planing surface, as shown in Figure 6(a). On some deep-vee boats, particularly the larger sportfishing boats, designers also carry the sides of the hull along the after two-thirds of the boat well below the waterline to create hard chines, as shown in Figure 6(b); these provide an extra measure of buoyancy along the sides of the boat to support high flying bridges and tuna towers. Deep-vee cabin cruisers and sportfishermen with flying bridges usually are also quite beamy to compensate for their top-heaviness.

Modified Vee

In an effort to combine the ability of the deep-vee hull to run through heavy seas at high speed with the initial stability of a vee-bottomed hull at low speeds, designers have developed the so-called "modified vee." Depending upon boat size, the term "modified vee" tends to have one of two meanings. In smaller boats, the builder usually means his boat has a somewhat shallower vee shape than that of a typical deep-vee hull. In larger boats (from about 40 feet up), "modified vee" can also mean that the deep-vee shape is carried from the bow back for about 65 percent of the boat's bottom, after which the bottom flattens out abruptly to provide both increased stability and a strong planing surface for more efficient cruising speeds.

Round Bottoms

Round-bottomed boats have been valued by coastal sport and commercial fishermen for many years. In some parts of the

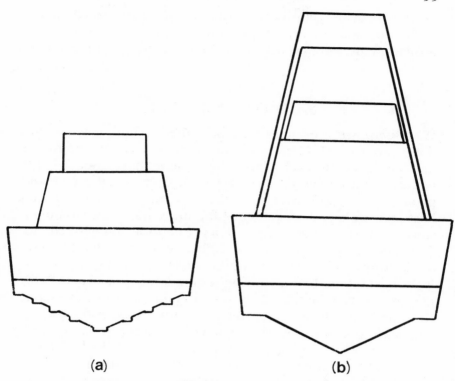

(a) **(b)**

FIG. 6. (a) Lift strakes running along the boat's bottom provide stronger planing surfaces on many deep-vee hulls. (b) The sides of deep-vee sportfishing boats often extend well below the waterline to provide extra buoyancy along the sides, and increased stability.

country, they still are because round bottoms give boats a softer motion. In plain English, this means that round-bottomed boats tend to roll more, but they do it more slowly and more gently. The reason for the softer motion is at least twofold: (1) Usually, more of a round-bottomed boat's mass is lower in the water; and, (2) the smooth curve of the bottom into the side means there isn't any sudden change in the amount of buoyancy along the outer edges of the hull as the boat rolls.

The trade-off in a round-bottomed boat is speed. A round bottom is generally a displacement design, with boat speed limited to the theoretical maximum hull speed. One compromise intended to achieve both planing speeds and an easy motion involves providing a fuller, rounder bottom forward and a flatter bottom aft. Usually, this kind of compromise yields a semi-displacement hull that will plane, but not with great efficiency.

SAILBOAT BOTTOMS

With the possible exception of the cathedral hull, you can find these same five bottom configurations in sailboat design. As mentioned, many smaller boats—daysailers—have essentially flat bottoms that enable them to get up on top of the water and plane under good wind conditions. A number of other sailboats, particularly those designed for amateur construction using wood or steel, have some kind of a vee bottom with hard chines. These boats, like their motor-driven counterparts, tend to have a relatively quick motion, but high initial stability.

Sailboats described as having a "moderate" or "heavy" displacement are generally deep-vee or round-bottomed designs. In some heavy-displacement sailboats, the shape of the bottom amidships (halfway between the bow and stern) is almost semicircular, as shown in Figure 7(c). Others have a wineglass shape, as in (b). In still others, the shape is definitely a deep vee, with just a stubby keel. These designs generally provide maximum interior space and—as does a round bottom in motorboats—an easy motion at sea.

As we saw in our cup "boats," the lighter the displacement, the less boat there is below the surface of the water. As a result, while most light- and ultralight-displacement sailboats still have curved bottoms, the curves are quite flat, as in (a), to provide both the most streamlined shape possible to move through the water, high initial stability, and the lift needed for surfing when wind and wave conditions permit.

KEELS AND SKEGS, CENTERBOARDS AND RUDDERS

In traditional wood, steel, and aluminum construction of rowboats, motorboats, and sailboats, a structural frame runs right

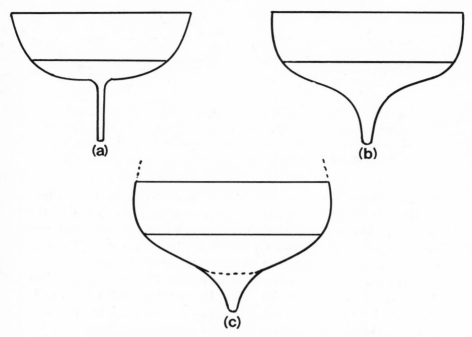

FIG. 7.   Basic sailboat hull shapes: (a) Light displacement; (b) moderate displacement; and (c) heavy displacement.

down the middle of the boat's bottom. This internal frame, called the keel, may or may not be present in fiberglass construction. Whether or not a boat has a structural internal keel, there may be a fin hanging from the bottom of the hull which is also called a "keel." Sometimes the fin, or external keel, runs along the centerline for much of the boat's underwater length, as in Figure 8(a). If there is no external keel, or it runs only part of the boat's length, there may be a small fin called a skeg near the stern (b). In any case, both the skeg and the external keel of a motorboat have three principal functions: (1) They help the boat travel in a straight line; (2) they help keep the boat from skidding sideways in a turn; and (3) frequently they extend deep enough to protect the propeller, rudder, and even the bottom of the hull from damage if the boat runs aground (hits the bottom).

(a)   **(b)**

FIG. 8.   Motorboat keel and skeg: (a) The external keel of a motorboat
hull extends over most of the boat's length. (b) A shorter skeg provides
an alternative means for providing directional stability, but with generally less protection for the propeller.

On sailboats, the keel and skeg have added functions. They
do, in fact, help the boat travel in a straight line. But the keel
also (1) provides resistance to the wind's tendency to push the
boat sideways; (2) provides a lift (much like a wing) as it moves
through the water, helping the boat travel closer to the wind;
and (3) provides the balancing force to counter the tipping force
of the wind blowing on the sails. In fact, the ballast in a sailboat's keel should be enough to stand the boat up again if it is
knocked over by the wind; it should even be enough to turn the
boat right-side up again if the boat were turned completely upside
down in severe conditions.

The shapes of sailboat keels vary greatly (Figure 9). Traditionally, the keel has run essentially the full underwater length
of the boat. Modern racing designs now have keels that are relatively short fore-and-aft, but quite deep. Some keels on racing
boats are shorter at the top than the bottom, making them look
almost as if they had been put on upside down. Moreover, the
keel may have small wings at the bottom. All of these differences in keel shape have implications for the boat's sailing
performance.

Sailboats may also combine a relatively shallow keel with a
"centerboard"—a fin that can be lowered to extend below the
keel to help the boat sail more efficiently. In shallower waters,
the centerboard is simply raised to keep the boat from running
aground. Some sailboats—mostly those under 20 feet in length—
have no external keel, relying instead solely on the centerboard
to provide the wing-like lift needed for the boat to move across
or against the wind.

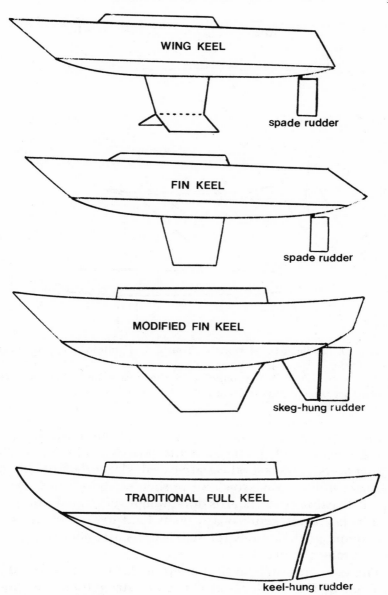

FIG. 9. Basic sailboat keel and rudder arrangements: Wing-keel and fin-keel boats typically have "spade" rudders. Other boats have their rudders supported by some kind of skeg or by the keel.

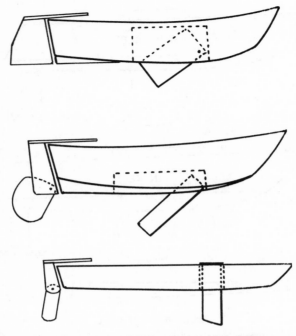

Fig. 10. Sailboat centerboards: From top to bottom, a conventional centerboard, a swing keel, and a daggerboard. The rudder on the top boat is protected from grounding by the small skeg. The other two boats are shown with different styles of "kick-up" rudders.

Centerboards also come in a variety of configurations (Figure 10). Some are called simply "centerboards"; others are called "swing keels"; and still others are called "daggerboards" because they are long and narrow and pushed straight down into the water. Because centerboards don't weigh very much (compared to a ballast keel), centerboard boats tend to rely on the width and shape of their hulls for stability. As a result, they usually are beamier than keel boats.

The skeg on a sailboat (if there is one) is normally found just in front of the rudder and is used to strengthen the rudder assembly. Depending upon its size and shape, a skeg may also improve the flow of water past the rudder, enhancing particularly the downwind steering effectiveness. Many sailboats, however, don't have skegs. Instead, the rudder is hinged either directly to the stern or keel or it stands alone, supported by the rudder shaft.

Rudders

The shape and size of your boat's rudder is a function of the boat's propulsion system. Although you probably do not have any choice as to what type of rudder your boat has, its size and design have important impact on the maneuverability of your boat and the vulnerability of the boat's rudder(s).

Motorboat rudders are most often one of two types: relatively small fins supported only by the rudder shaft; or much larger rudders supported at the top by the rudder shaft and at the bottom by a strut from the keel.

In general, small rudders are used on runabouts and on twin-engine boats. In the case of runabouts, only a small rudder is needed to steer the boat when it is moving fast. However, these boats may be somewhat difficult to maneuver at the slow speeds required around a dock. In the case of twin-engine boats, a small rudder is positioned behind each propeller. These rudders are well able to steer the boat when it is moving at all but the slowest speeds. At speeds so slow that the rudders are not efficient, the boat is more effectively turned by using the engines (see Chapters 10, 13, and 14). The principal disadvantage of these rudders is their vulnerability to damage because they are not supported at the bottom.

Single-engine inboards that operate at displacement or semi-displacement speeds require relatively large rudders to provide effective steering at the slower speeds. Because of their large size, these rudders must be supported at the bottom, which is why they are usually tied into the boat's keel in some way. The large size of these rudders is particularly useful when coming up to a dock or getting into a slip; by turning the rudder to one side or the other and using your propeller to thrust a surge of water against that large rudder, it's possible to push the stern to one side or the other—a technique discussed in more detail in Chapter 10.

Sailboat rudders come in a wide variety of sizes, shapes, and descriptions. On keel boats, there are three fundamental rudder types—spade rudders, skeg-hung rudders, and keel-hung rudders. All are illustrated in Figure 9. A spade rudder often looks almost as if someone took a shovel or "spade," pushed the handle up through the boat's bottom, and used the blade that was left protruding below the bottom as a rudder. Spade rudders are found principally on fin-keel boats.

A skeg-hung rudder represents a compromise between the speed and efficiency of the fin keel and spade rudder combination on the one hand and a desire for security and ease of steering on the other. The skeg strengthens the rudder assembly and makes steering easier, but it also makes the boat somewhat "slower" in light winds—a negative for racing. Keel-hung rudders are found on full-keel boats and tend to be considerably larger than spade or skeg-hung rudders to compensate for their relative inefficiency. In fact, the rudders on some "traditional" designs are affectionately called "barn door rudders" because of their size and shape.

Small sailboats—daysailers—usually have either a "fixed" or a "kick-up" rudder mounted on the transom, as illustrated in Figure 10. Fixed rudders are less common today because they are unforgiving if you run hard aground. "Kick-up" rudders, which come in a variety of shapes and configurations, all are hinged so that the below-water part of the rudder will "kick up" if the rudder hits either the bottom or some other obstruction.

Testing What You've Learned
(Answers can be found in Appendix C)

1. Name two advantages and two disadvantages of flat-bottomed boats.

2. What advantage does the vee bottom have over the flat bottom?

3. What advantage is the cathedral hull intended to offer, compared to other designs?

4. Name the principal advantage and two disadvantages of deep-vee designs.

5. TRUE or FALSE: A round-bottomed boat is capable of the same speeds as a deep-vee design.

6. Which has a softer motion, a vee bottom or round bottom?

7. Which would tend to have a flatter bottom, a light-displacement sailboat or a heavy-displacement sailboat?

8. Where is the internal keel found on a boat? What is its principal function?

9. What are three functions of an external keel on a motorboat? On a sailboat?

10. What three functions can a skeg serve on a motorboat?

11. What are two functions of a skeg on a sailboat?

5

An Engine System for Every Need

In motorboats, the choice in engine systems is basically a choice between outboard, inboard/outboard, and inboard. Once that decision is made, you can choose between having just one engine or more than one. Finally, if you've chosen inboard power, you can make still another decision—gasoline or diesel. In sailboats, the choices are more limited, but even so, there are alternatives ranging from not having any engine at all to having more power than your boat can use.

From a practical perspective, the reasons for choosing one engine system or another may not be profound. If you have a 16-foot open aluminum boat, for example, it obviously will be used with an outboard motor. On the other hand, if you want a 50-foot luxury motor yacht, you will probably turn to diesel inboard power, although not necessarily; Huckins Yacht Corporation in Jacksonville, Florida, has provided one owner with a specially designed 50-foot yacht powered by four 205-horsepower outboards.

The point is this: Boats, like cars, can be powered by a variety of engine configurations. For many uses, it doesn't make much difference what engine is used, so long as it's compatible with the design and construction of the boat. But there are differences—pros and cons—to each engine system. Moreover, safe boating means knowing both the advantages and disadvantages of the system in your boat.

OUTBOARD MOTORS

Historically, outboards were developed to provide low-horsepower engines that could be taken on and off a boat for easy transportation and storage. That need still exists today. However, although modern outboard motors provide relatively lightweight, flexible, and highly reliable power systems, many are so large and powerful that they must be bolted onto the boat's stern and can't be removed for repair, replacement, or storage without using a chain hoist.

Outboard engines are almost ideally suited for boats that will be kept on a trailer and / or used in relatively shallow water. Outboards can be tilted so that many times you can push your boat right up to the beach. Quite frankly, however, once you get into mid-sized boats, there's another attraction: Outboard motorboats don't cost as much as equivalent inboards or inboard / outboards do.

There are several reasons for the cost difference. The outboard boat itself may cost less to build. Use of an inboard motor imposes a special set of Coast Guard safety requirements, because the engine is enclosed instead of hanging out on the stern. The outboard also may use portable gas tanks rather than built-in fuel tanks—again, simplifying construction from a safety perspective and lowering the cost of the boat.

There are other differences between an outboard and an inboard. For example, the outboard boat doesn't need a rudder since the engine itself is turned to steer the boat. Moreover, the builder's job is simplified. Instead of installing different-sized engines on the assembly line to meet various consumer needs, the boat manufacturer simply builds one boat and lets the dealer hang the customer's engine of choice on the stern.

As you might expect, there are disadvantages to using outboards in some boats. The engines themselves are highly sophisticated, and most of us aren't familiar with their systems. It's also just plain hard to work on an engine when you have to hang out over the water to do it, even for normal maintenance. For the same reasons, troubleshooting when the engine fails out in the middle of the river, lake, or bay is also more difficult with outboard engines. (Engine maintenance and troubleshooting are discussed in Chapter 19.)

Another disadvantage to outboards is that the engine weight is all the way aft. This makes the boat bounce more in waves than if the engine were farther forward, demanding careful attention from the skipper when he's running at high speed.

The transom (stern) of the outboard motorboat is yet another consideration. Many outboards require a large cut-out in the top of the transom so that the engine can be mounted low enough to put the propeller down into the water. While the cut-out or "low transom" is required for mounting the engine, it may present a flooding hazard to you in operating the boat.

Any boat running at planing speeds across the water pulls along a relatively large stern wave. The wave doesn't look big, because you're moving so fast that it stretches out as a "wake" behind you. However, when the boat is slowed down abruptly and settles down into its hole in the water, the stern wave keeps rolling on forward and piles up against the transom. If a boat has a large cut-out in the transom, the stern wave can surge right over the cut-out and into the boat.

A boat is particularly vulnerable to this kind of swamping when running in the same direction as the natural waves. What happens in this situation is that the boat's stern wave is piled on top of a natural wave so that both of them come over the transom at the same time—if the boat is slowed down too quickly.

To help prevent the swamping problem, many boats have a secondary "transom" forward of the outboard (Figure 11). On some boats, this secondary "transom" is fixed in place; on others, it is hinged to provide easier access to the engine. It is very important to keep this secondary "transom" locked in place (closed) when using your boat; otherwise, you might as well not have it if the stern wave surges over and through the cut-out and into your boat.

While today's outboard boats up to 20 feet long should not sink when flooded because of Coast Guard flotation requirements, any boat's stability will be reduced if it's swamped, and it may turn over.

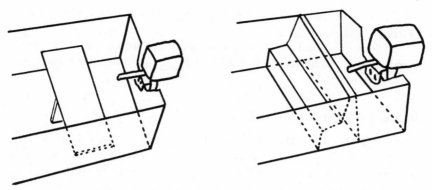

FIG. 11. "Low-transom" outboard motorboats: If a wave surges through the cut-out in the transom of the boat on the left, it can swamp the entire boat. In the same situation, the secondary transom behind the seat on the boat on the right will prevent swamping.

THIRD FEARED DROWNED—A five-year-old boy and his grandfather drowned and the child's stepfather was presumed dead after their fishing boat capsized in Saginaw Bay [Michigan], authorities said Sunday.

Five people were on the 15-foot boat when it began taking on water and capsized.[1]

Believe it or not, there is still one other disadvantage to outboard engines: They can fall off the boat if they are not bolted on. This means that you must check frequently to be certain your motor clamps are screwed down tight. It also means that you should have a safety chain attaching the motor to your boat. Otherwise, the result can be, at best, expensive and, at worst, tragic.

SEARCH IS ON FOR BOATER—Volunteer firefighters for Delaware County, Pennsylvania, were assisting Coast Guard crews today looking for a missing boater on the Delaware River north of the Delaware state line.

Two people were boating on the river south of Tinicum Island when the outboard motor of their 15-foot runabout fell off as the

1. *News-Journal,* Wilmington, Delaware, April 29, 1985.

craft hit a wave—and the boat overturned—according to a Coast
Guard spokesman.

One of the boaters, whose names were not immediately released,
managed to swim to shore and call for help. The other man was
unaccounted for.[2]

Bracket Mounts for Outboards

Some boats are offered with an outboard option that avoids
the shortcomings of low transoms. This option involves hanging the motors on specially designed brackets bolted or built
onto the transom by the boatbuilder. One such system is OMC's
Sea Drive unit, but many boatbuilders have developed their own
bracket systems that can be used with a variety of motors.

Bracket mounting for outboards is rapidly gaining popularity. Not only does bracket mounting overcome the low-transom
problem, it gives more efficient operation. By putting the motor
out beyond the transom, the engine can be mounted about 6
inches higher and the propeller will run in clearer, less dis-
turbed water. As a result, drag is reduced because there is less
engine hanging in the water and the propeller is more efficient.
Increases of 5 knots in boat speed and of 4 to 8 percent in fuel
efficiency have been reported.

Aside from the added cost, the major disadvantage of the
bracket-mount system is to make the already difficult jobs of
maintenance and troubleshooting even more difficult because
the engine is hanging even farther off the stern. Also, because
the bracket mount puts the engine weight even farther aft than
normal, *the boat must be designed and balanced for it.*

INBOARD / OUTBOARDS (STERNDRIVES)

This system consists basically of an inboard engine connected
to a propeller unit that hangs on the stern and can be turned
like an outboard motor to steer the boat. The drive unit also
can be lifted so that it does not project down below the bottom
of the boat. As a result, inboard / outboards—also called "I / Os"

2. *News-Journal,* Wilmington, Delaware, July 11, 1986.

and "sterndrives"—offer the shallow-water advantage of the outboard, the same beaching capability, and the same ease of trailering.

In addition, however, I / O systems offer what many believe are the advantages of an inboard engine. Properly maintained, the engine will last longer than an outboard because it operates at lower engine speeds. Moreover, because the I / O uses a car engine adapted to boats and the engine usually is readily accessible, the engine is easy to service, and many boat owners save money by doing their own engine maintenance. In smaller boats, an I / O system may also make it possible to use a larger engine. Even though the inboard weighs more, the engine weight is farther forward.

The principal disadvantages of the I / O when compared to outboards are higher cost, lack of flexibility in being able to change engines, corrosion on the sterndrive unit, and frequent replacement of the "rubber boot."

The corrosion problem, of course, is a salt-water problem. It occurs because you can't get the sterndrive unit completely out of the water when it's not in use, even though you can tilt the sterndrive up from its normal down position. As a result, the aluminum casing is susceptible to corrosion as long as the boat is in salt water, and repairs can be very expensive.

The I / O system is also more complex than that for an outboard. As a result, such things as added seals, more complicated cooling systems, and the hydraulic system used to raise and lower the sterndrive unit lead to higher maintenance costs.

From a cost perspective, an I / O boat is usually more costly than a comparable outboard boat. As mentioned earlier, the inboard engine requires engineroom safety features not needed in an outboard to reduce the potential for a gasoline fire or explosion. In addition, the engine installation is more complex and, therefore, more expensive.

From a flexibility perspective, outboards win hands down. Changing to a larger engine—or, possibly, even to a different make of engine—with an I / O system represents major surgery. By contrast, while a chain hoist may be needed to make the change, it's relatively easy to install a larger outboard unit if the boat is designed for the added weight and horsepower.

You simply take one engine off the transom or mounting bracket, and hang and hook up the new one.

That leaves the "rubber boot." Although the sterndrive unit is bolted to the transom, the drive-shaft connection between the sterndrive and the engine goes through a hole in the transom. Since the sterndrive has to tilt up and down and swing sideways for steering, a "rubber boot"—a flexible rubber cover surrounding the joints in the drive unit—is used to allow that freedom of movement while sealing off the hole in the transom.

In time, the drive unit's rubber boot will begin to deteriorate and must be replaced. This can happen after as little as a single season or as long as several seasons. In any case, *the importance of replacing the boot at the first sign of wear or aging cannot be overstated. More than one boat has been sunk by a leak in the rubber boot on its I / O drive unit.*

INBOARD ENGINES

On small and mid-sized boats, the choice of inboard or I / O may simply be a matter of personal preference, the builder's choice, or whatever fits the particular design. As boats get much beyond 30 feet in length, however, larger engines are often required, and the standard inboard installation is generally more practical.

Standard inboard engine systems, however, introduce two important dimensions to boats not considered so far: First, boats equipped with inboard engines are steered by a rudder—not by the propeller, as are outboards and I / O boats. Second, the propeller shaft and (usually) the rudder shaft are run through the bottom of the boat. As a result, the propeller unit and rudder of an inboard may be more vulnerable to damage than the sterndrive units of outboards or I / Os.

The difference in steering systems is especially important from a safety perspective, particularly when maneuvering in close quarters. For example, frequently you can put your engine in neutral and coast up to a dock in an inboard boat, steering in to a perfect landing. Not so with an I / O or outboard. Insofar as these boats are steered by turning the drive unit to change the direction of the propeller thrust, you have to drive the I/O or outboard right up to the dock—keeping the propeller turning until the moment you make your landing—and shift into reverse to stop.

Inboards, on the other hand, are steered with their rudders. As long as the boat is moving through the water—whether or not the propeller is turning—the force of the water going past the rudder will turn the boat. However, just because the boat is moving does not mean you can steer it. A boat drifting in a current is moving, but as long as it is moving at the same speed and in the same direction as the current, you have no steering control because there is no water flowing past the rudder.

This distinction between steering with a rudder or a drive unit may sound academic, but it has some very practical implications. For example, our first experience going through a drawbridge, where a narrow waterway created a strong current under the bridge, was downright scary. As we and several other boats approached the drawbridge from both directions and it opened as scheduled, I slowed to what I thought was a safe speed . . . only to discover that I couldn't steer. The tidal current was rushing us toward the bridge at about 4 knots, but my idling speed didn't give us enough steerage to have any effect. Moreover, it took me a moment to figure out what was happening and to speed up my engine to regain steerage.

At 8 knots over the ground—4 knots of current plus 4 knots of boat speed—I had good steering, but we were going so much faster than usual that getting through the bridge in the midst of the heavy traffic was nerve-wracking. Everything was happening too fast for comfort. Even now, those conditions make my adrenalin flow because I know the limitations of my boat; moving at those speeds in that kind of circumstance doesn't give me the margin of safety I like to have.

ONE ENGINE OR TWO?

Single-screw or twin-screw—this is a question that relates principally to motorboats. Sailboats generally have only one engine, and usually it is relatively small. Displacement-hull motorboats frequently have only one engine as well, though it may be fairly large. For most other motorboats, two engines may be an option, beginning with boats in the 16- to 20-foot range, whether you're dealing with outboard, I / O, or inboard power.

Until you get to fairly large boats, however, there are only two reasons for having two engines: safety, and maneuverability at slow speeds. In a planing hull, two engines may be necessary to provide the power needed to attain planing speeds once boat length gets much above 30 to 35 feet. In smaller boats, however, two engines are not generally required to achieve top boat speeds. To the contrary, if a particular boat is designed for a maximum of 250 horsepower, it will usually have a higher top speed with one 250-horsepower engine than with two of 125 horsepower. The reason is twofold: Two engines are heavier than one; and, having two drive and steering assemblies below the water increases drag.

For the small sacrifice in speed, however, twin engines will give you a major boost in safety, simply because you have a spare engine. If one engine fails, you can keep the boat moving on the second. I learned that lesson dramatically at about the age of fifteen when my father and I were entering Barnegat (New Jersey) Inlet in his twin-screw, 30-foot Jersey sea skiff.

To enter from seaward, you headed in toward the beach north of the inlet until you were close in, then turned 90 degrees to port (left) and ran parallel to the shore (broadside to the waves) for one or two hundred yards, before making a 90-degree turn to starboard (right) to enter the inlet itself.

As we entered, the weather was deteriorating and waves were breaking across the approach to the inlet. After we made the first turn to port, we had cresting waves coming at us broadside, threatening to break. And, of course, that was when we lost our starboard engine.

Had that been our only engine, we—and our boat—would have been in real danger. As it was, we were able to keep on going with our port engine, maintaining boat control and steerage adequate to let us snake over the waves until we could make our starboard turn to come on into the inlet safely. Since that time, I have been an advocate of twin engines for any motorboat that will be used in coastal waters.

The maneuverability question can also relate to safety because it involves the issue of how much control you have over your boat. In smaller boats, maneuvering a single-engine outboard or I/O boat at slow speeds is pretty straightforward once you've gained some experience. Insofar as you steer by turning the drive unit, the propeller simply pushes or pulls the boat in the direction you want to go, whether you're trying to go forward or backward.

Maneuvering a single-engine inboard boat in tight quarters is a bit more difficult when you're moving forward and a great deal more difficult when going in reverse. You have to rely mostly on the water pushing against the rudder to steer the boat. As a result, moving a single-engine inboard around in tight quarters at slow speed—as when trying to get into a tight docking area—demands a fair amount of skill, particularly when the wind is blowing.

With twin engines, on the other hand, you can use the propellers to help steer the boat (see Chapter 10) and, with experience, you can dock a twin-screw, inboard-powered 45-foot yacht just about as easily as you'd park a large car.

What's the trade-off? Assuming that a given boat is designed to enable you to choose between one engine or two, the trade-off is simply one of cost. Two engines generally cost more than a single engine of equivalent power. The installation costs are about double. All of the controls and instrumentation costs are doubled. Fuel consumption may be higher. And maintenance costs certainly will be higher.

However, if you will be boating in coastal waters or in any large bay, sound, or lake where you can be several miles from help if a storm comes up and an engine fails, that extra cost may be well worthwhile—even if it means getting a slightly smaller boat to be able to afford the added cost of the second engine.

GASOLINE OR DIESEL?

It would be nice if all boats could have diesel engines. The reason is simple: Diesel fuel is many times safer in use than gasoline. (The safe operation of gasoline engines is covered in detail in Chapter 8.) If you develop a leak in your fuel lines or tank with diesel fuel, the worst-case situation is probably only a tankful of diesel fuel in the boat's bottom—smelly and a lot of trouble to clean up, but not really dangerous. The same leak with gasoline would put you in very real risk of blowing up your boat.

CRUISER EXPLODES AT DOCK—Bernard Towey has been boating since 1949, and he may get a new boat someday. But if he does, it will be different from the one that blew up July 20.

"It will be a diesel or a sailboat," he said. "I won't play games with gasoline anymore."

His 37-foot gasoline-powered cabin cruiser was destroyed when it exploded as he finished refueling at Cassidy's Breton Woods Marina, Brick Township, New Jersey.

Officer Ronald Bahr of the New Jersey marine police, the investigating officer, said the explosion looked like it was an accident.

He said the blast could have been caused by fumes in the cabin and bilge, or by a leaky fuel line.

Towey had just finished fueling the vessel, and said he had been running the bilge blower for about five minutes when he went up to the bridge and turned on the ignition. Suddenly, he felt his body rising straight up into the air.

He was thrown to the dock and saw the boat catch fire, but there were no subsequent blasts.[3]

But safety is not the only advantage offered by diesel engines. Lower maintenance and better fuel economy are two other advantages. The lower maintenance comes about because diesel engines don't have electrical ignition systems. The fuel economy is perhaps even more significant, resulting in lower operating costs and longer range. For example, our 23-horsepower, two-cylinder diesel engine will push our 18,000-pound-displacement sailboat along at about 6 knots under moderate sea and wind conditions, burning only one-half of a gallon per hour. As a result, our 85-gallon fuel tank gives us a range of about 1,000 miles under power.

3. *Soundings*, October 1986.

With that difference in safety and economy of operation, why would boaters want gasoline engines? There are two major reasons: (1) They cost less than diesels; and, (2) they give you more horsepower per pound than diesels do.

In small to mid-sized motorboats, for example, where engine weight and cost can become significant factors, builders can use gasoline engines to pack in the horsepower without overloading either the boats or their customers' pocketbooks.

Where horsepower, weight, and cost are not issues, however, diesels have taken over the market. Auxiliary-powered sailboats, which generally require only small engines, are one such market segment. The incremental cost and weight of the diesel compared to a gasoline engine in most sailboats are relatively small and easily offset by the diesel's advantages of safety, reliability, and fuel economy. As a result, most if not all auxiliary sailboats sold today in the United States are delivered with diesel engines. Similarly, in larger motorboats where the engines represent a smaller fraction of total boat weight, the development of lightweight, higher-horsepower, turbo-charged engines has made the use of diesels more common. However, the premium paid for diesel power in these boats is significant. In a 38- to 40-foot motorboat, for example, the use of diesels at this writing adds from $50,000 to $60,000 to the cost of the boat. For that reason, diesels are still considered optional equipment, even in many larger boats.

Testing What You've Learned
(Answers can be found in Appendix C)

1. What are three advantages of outboard motors?

2. What are three disadvantages of outboard motors?

3. If you are operating an outboard motorboat with a cut-out in the transom, what precaution should you take to avoid swamping the boat when slowing down?

4. List two reasons that bracket-mount outboard systems are becoming more popular.

5. TRUE or FALSE: Any conventional outboard motorboat can be converted easily to a bracket-mount outboard system.

6. What advantages are offered by inboard/outboard systems, compared to outboards?

7. What are the principal disadvantages of the I/O systems?

8. Why is the rubber boot on the I/O drive unit a potential safety hazard?

9. TRUE or FALSE: Inboard engines are more likely to be found on boats larger than about 30 feet in length than are outboards or I/Os. Why?

10. What is the major difference, from a safety perspective, between an inboard engine and an I/O system?

11. Why does tidal or river current affect steering with an inboard engine more than it does with an I/O system?

12. What safety advantage, if any, is offered by having two engines instead of one?

13. Insofar as diesel engines generally cost more than comparable gasoline engines, why would anyone prefer diesel power?

14. What are the two major advantages of gasoline engines compared to diesels?

15. Why have diesel engines effectively taken over the auxiliary-powered-sailboat market?

6

Basic Motorboats

There are six basic types of motorboats for pleasure use: john-boats, runabouts, utility / fishing boats, high-speed runabouts, sportfishing boats, and large and small cabin cruisers (Figures 12 and 13). In practice, it is sometimes difficult to decide where a particular boat fits within these categories, mostly because the boat companies are trying to meet more than one marketing need with a single boat style. But, regardless, it is here that the basic hull configurations—planing, semi-displacement, and dis-placement—are brought together with hull shape to create a boat suited for a particular use.

JOHNBOATS

The johnboat is a basic, flat-bottomed boat that is either rowed or used with a small outboard motor for fishing or simple trans-portation in the protected waters of our smaller rivers, lakes, and bays. Often, it has a square bow and is made of wood or aluminum. Where I did my boating as a youngster, we'd prob-ably have called this a rowboat with an outboard on it. In any case, johnboats are not intended for any but calm waters where shore is close at hand.

RUNABOUTS

Runabouts are general-purpose outboard, I / O, or inboard boats, usually with a vee or modified-vee bottom, that are capable of

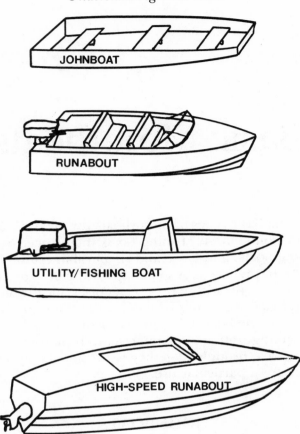

Fig. 12. Basic motorboats.

speeds from 20 or 25 miles per hour on up. It's useful to sub-divide these boats into two groups—general-purpose run-abouts, and high-speed runabouts.

General-purpose runabouts range from about 12 feet to 20 feet in length and are used for water-skiing, fishing, riding around, or simply for going from one place to another. While they are principally open boats, they may have small cuddy cabins with minimal accommodations, including a vee-berth, space for a stereo tape deck, a porta-potti, and, possibly, a small sink. However, they are seldom intended for use out of sight of land.

High-speed runabouts, on the other hand, may be 40 feet or

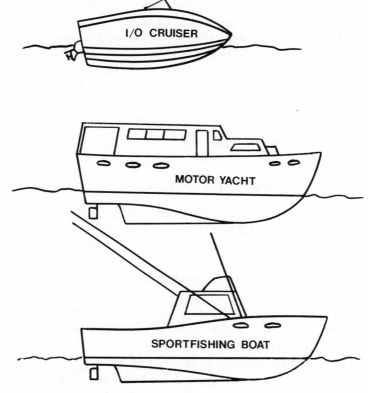

FIG. 13. Basic motorboats (cont.).

more in length with hull designs ranging from vee to deep-vee, depending upon whether they're intended for use in calm waters or for high-speed operation offshore. The best of these boats are heavily constructed (read that "strong," not "heavy") using the most advanced boatbuilding materials and techniques. The largest runabouts may have interior accommodations which, on a smaller scale, are comparable to a luxurious apartment.

UTILITY / FISHING BOATS

These are generally open boats with vee, modified-vee, or cathedral bottoms for good speed and a generous beam for the stability needed for fishing, swimming from the boat, or for diving. They are usually powered by outboard engines, either transom mounted or, increasingly, bracket mounted. Included in this group are boats ranging from about 13 feet long and suited only for use in protected waters, to 20- to 25-footers suitable for fishing in nearby offshore waters in good weather, provided they have proper safety equipment. Some of these, popularly called "bassboats," are equipped with one or more high swivel seats for fishing in calm waters.

SPORTFISHING BOATS

Serious sportfishing boats begin in the 26- to 28-foot range and go up to well over 50 feet in length. They often have modified vee or deep-vee bottoms so that they can make fast runs offshore, even in moderately rough sea conditions, to the canyons where the big fish are found and then get back to port when the fishing day is over. It's not unusual for these boats to run from 50 to 100 miles offshore to fishing grounds. In general, sportfishing boats are characterized by large aft cockpits with a minimum of obstructions in order to provide the open space needed to play and eventually land large fish.

Depending upon boat length, these boats may have anything from quite functional living quarters—one or two sleeping cabins, a head, galley and eating area—to accommodations that are luxurious by any standard. Almost invariably, sportfishing boats are equipped with a flying bridge from which the skipper has an unobstructed view of the water around the boat. Some of these boats also have a tuna tower extending some 10 feet or more above the flying bridge as an aid to spotting fish. As noted earlier, boats with flying bridges and tuna towers require a hefty beam and good buoyancy along the sides to support their weight as the boat rolls in a seaway.

CABIN CRUISERS

There are "cabin cruisers" designed to fit almost every pocketbook and cruising need. They come as trawlers, high-speed cruisers, and large motor yachts. The smallest generally range from 20 to 25 feet long. They usually have a modified vee or deep-vee hull, are I/O powered to provide speeds in the range of 25 to 30 miles per hour, and may be trailerable. Frequently, the effort to provide a minimum 6 feet of headroom results in the smaller cruisers being somewhat stubby in appearance and having a relatively high center of gravity. That stubbiness is also often a comment on their seaworthiness. These boats generally are intended for use only in protected or semi-protected waters. They are not meant for use in the ocean, except on a calm day when you are never more than a few miles from an easy inlet (i.e., no breaking waves).

As boat length increases, the job of providing adequate accommodations becomes less difficult, boat appearance can become more graceful, and the capabilities of the boat frequently (but not necessarily) are increased. Power options are also expanded. Beyond about 25 or 26 feet, I/O power often gives way to inboard gasoline engines because the boats are too big for trailering. As boat length increases beyond 34 or 35 feet, buyers may consider diesel engines as an alternative to gasoline.

One sub-group of cruisers that bears mentioning is the modern version of a houseboat, usually built on a beamy cathedral hull and with engine(s) large enough to get the boat to plane. While modern houseboats are often very comfortable for cruising in sheltered waters, they should not be taken where they can be caught out in heavy seas. Because of their wide, relatively shallow hulls, they must be run at slow speeds in rough water. This, by itself, might not be so bad; but, unfortunately, their high cabin structure makes them difficult to control in strong winds at slow speeds. In large waves, the combination of poor maneuverability and high cabin structure makes houseboats vulnerable to being rolled dangerously.

Testing What You've Learned
(Answers can be found in Appendix C)

1. What is a johnboat, and how is it used?
2. What is a primary difference between runabouts and utility/fishing boats?

3. What are four features that often distinguish sportfishing boats from other cabin cruisers?

4. Why are many small cabin cruisers not suitable for use in the ocean or other large bodies of open water?

5. TRUE or FALSE: The design of modern houseboats has been improved so that they are now suitable for use in coastal waters as well as in inland bays, lakes, and rivers.

7

Basic Sailboats

There are at least three ways of classifying sailboats: by use, by the number of hulls, and by their rigs. You'd think the most practical place to start is with how the boats are used, and that is certainly true if you are shopping for a boat. But "understanding" moves through the list backwards, starting with the rig, moving on to the number of hulls, and only then looking at how the boat is to be used.

SAILBOAT RIGS

The term "rig" essentially describes the number, size, and placement of the masts and sails on a particular boat. Basic rigs used with modern sailboats include the catboat, sloop, cutter, ketch, yawl, schooner, and cat ketch (Figures 14, 15, and 16). These different rigs exist because the variations offer advantages. Understanding these variations can help you know the strengths and limitations of your own boat.

Sailors talk about "rigging." The expression "standing rigging" refers to the system of wire stays and shrouds used to support the boat's masts. The term "running rigging" refers to the ropes or wires used to raise, lower, and adjust the sails.

Catboats

These are among the easiest to distinguish when you see them. Catboats have only one mast and one sail. The mast is placed

FIG. 14. Basic sailboats.

right up at the bow, and the sail typically is quite large. The sail is raised along the after side of the mast and held out along the bottom by a "boom" hinged to the mast a short distance above the deck. The sail is controlled principally by letting the boom out or pulling it in toward the centerline of the boat.

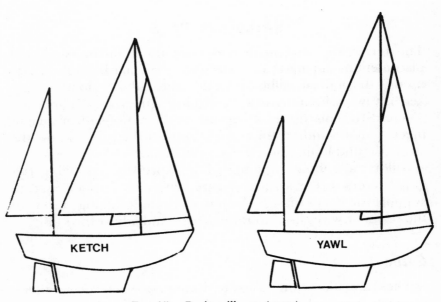

FIG. 15. Basic sailboats (cont.).

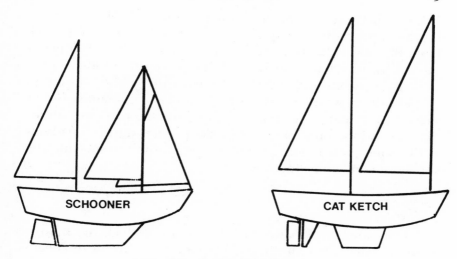

Fig. 16. Basic sailboats (cont.).

Catboats most often are sailed in relatively shallow water and usually have a centerboard and shallow skeg instead of a deep keel. As a result, they usually are quite beamy (wide) in order to provide needed stability. They may also have relatively short masts to keep the heeling (tipping) force of the wind low.

The bow of the catboat generally is also broad and "bluff" (blunt) to keep the boat from "submarining" when sailing downwind in strong winds. The boat I learned to sail on as a youngster (the same boat I had the accident with my first day out) was rigged as a catboat but did not have that characteristic broad, bluff bow. I learned very quickly to avoid sailing directly with the waves when the wind picked up, because the pressure of the wind on the mast tended to push the bow right down under the waves. I could not possibly have kept the boat from diving under the water like a submarine had the bow ever dug in.

Sloops

The most common rig used on modern sailboats is the sloop rig. It is also the most efficient, and most racing sailboats are sloop rigged as a result.

Like a catboat, a sloop has only one mast. Unlike a catboat, however, the mast is stepped about 30 percent of the way back from the bow. The main sail—appropriately called the "mainsail"—fills the triangle formed by the mast and boom, as on a catboat. A second sail called a "headsail" or "jib" is carried in front of the mast, attached to the "forestay." Sometimes, sloops carry two or more headsails of different sizes for use under different wind conditions. Large sloops may rig two headsails at the same time, the larger one raised on the forestay and the smaller on an "inner forestay."

Cutters

The cutter is a variation on the sloop in which the mast is moved farther aft—until it is 40 percent or more of the boat's length from the bow. The practical result is that a cutter has a smaller mainsail than that of a sloop of the same size, and a larger area in front of the mast which permits use of two headsails instead of one (as described above for large sloops). The "method in the madness" is to give a cutter smaller sails than those of a sloop of the same size, allowing greater flexibility in the choice of sails, so that the boat is easier to handle in heavy weather. The cutter rig is particularly suitable for boats between about 30 and 40 feet long that will be sailed by just one person or a couple. There is, of course, a tradeoff: The cutter rig is less efficient when sailing close to the wind than the sloop and, therefore, is less suitable for racing.

Ketches

As boats get larger, sails can quickly begin to get pretty big for one person or a couple to handle. By dividing the sail plan up into more units, it's possible to keep the size of individual sails more manageable. While the cutter rig fills that need well on boats up to about 40 feet in length, larger boats need to break up their sail plans even more. That's the purpose of the ketch rig.

In a typical ketch, the forward 75 to 80 percent of the boat is rigged like a sloop. Then a second mast is placed behind the mainsail. By definition, that second mast—called a "mizzen-mast"—is located in front of the boat's rudderpost. Its sail is a smaller sister of the mainsail and is called a "mizzen sail" or, simply, "the mizzen."

While the ketch offers increased flexibility in sail selection for different wind conditions, the rig generally is less efficient than the sloop or cutter when sailing to "windward" (toward the wind) or directly downwind so that the mizzen blocks the wind from the mainsail. However, when a good breeze is blowing from abeam (the side) or from around toward the stern, the modern ketch rig is a powerhouse, easily driving the boat at or near hull speed.

Yawls

The yawl rig is similar to a ketch. By definition, the distinction between the two lies in the position of the mizzenmast. On a ketch, the mizzenmast is stepped in front of the rudderpost; on a yawl, it is stepped aft of the rudderpost. The practical result is that the yawl's mizzen usually is quite small.

Yawls are relatively uncommon today. They were in their heyday some 20 years ago and earlier when racing rules gave them a rating (handicap) advantage over sloops. Without that rating advantage, the yawl rig makes little sense for most sailors because it is less effective than the ketch rig at breaking up sail area. In practice, the mizzenmast is stepped so far aft that the mainsail is essentially the same size that it would be on a sloop.

From a practical perspective, therefore, many yawls resemble sloops with a small mizzen mounted on the stern almost as an afterthought. On such boats, the mizzen serves mainly as a balancing sail used to fine-tune the boat's performance. It is also useful as a steadying sail when the boat is anchored, helping keep the boat from swinging back and forth in the wind.

On some boats, however, the rudderpost is located far enough forward that the location of the yawl's mizzen mast provides room for a reasonably large mizzen sail. On these boats, there may be little practical difference in sailing and sail-handling characteristics from those provided by a ketch rig on a boat of similar size.

Schooners

To many sailors, a schooner under full sail is one of the most beautiful sights around. What makes a schooner particularly breathtaking is the symmetry of the sail plan. Despite that beauty, however, schooners are even less common today than yawls.

One reason for the scarcity of schooners is that the advantages of the rig don't really become obvious until boat-length goes beyond 50 or 60 feet, at which scale the mainsail even on a ketch or yawl begins to get fairly large. Boats in this size range are beyond the needs of most small-boat sailors.

On those larger boats, however, the schooner rig makes it possible to break up the sail area more effectively because it is not limited to two masts. Depending upon boat size, the schooner may have more than two masts. In all cases, however, the schooner is distinguished by the forward mast—the one closest to the bow—being the same height or shorter than the others.

In addition to breaking up the sail plan into sails of manageable proportions, the schooner rig also facilitates sailing in very light winds. The height and number of the masts give the crew a number of positions from which to hang large, lightweight sails to capture winds that are too light for efficient sailing using normal working sails.

Cat Ketches

The newest rig developed for modern sailboats is the cat ketch. These boats are characterized by two free-standing masts. In other words, the masts are self-supporting; there is no standing rigging.

The foremast of a cat ketch usually is placed right in the bow, like the mast of a catboat; the second mast is placed at about the middle of the boat. Both masts are about the same height and carry nearly identical sails. As in catboats—although to a lesser extent, because the forces are divided between two masts rather than just one—the bow of a cat ketch normally must be somewhat full to provide the extra buoyancy needed to compensate for the downward forces on the mast in the bow.

MULTIHULLS

The second way of categorizing sailboats is by the number of hulls. Traditionally in the western world, sailboats—like motorboats—have had just one hull. These boats are called "monohulls."

More recently, taking a page from the boats of Pacific Ocean islanders, catamarans and trimarans have become increasingly common (Figure 17). A catamaran has two narrow hulls separated by a deck or cabin structure. A trimaran has a rather narrow main hull with two smaller "amas," or streamlined floats, on either side, separated from the main hull by a rigid deck structure. It is not unusual for a trimaran to be wider than it is long.

Both the catamaran and the trimaran—called "multihulls"—are capable of speeds much greater than those attainable by even the fastest monohulls. They are lighter in weight than their single-hulled cousins because they rely on their beam (width) for stability rather than on hull form or ballast keel. Also, they

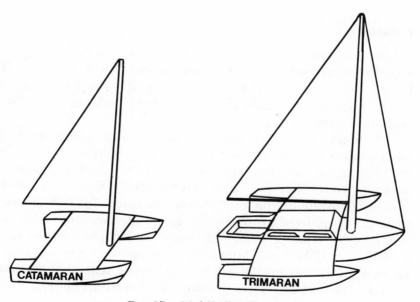

Fig. 17.   Multihull sailboats.

will plane easily, because their hulls are designed for planing.

The Achilles' heel of multihulls is bound up in the matter of stability. While catamarans and trimarans have quite good initial stability, once they begin to go over there is little to stop them. And, once upside down, they are difficult if not impossible to right—particularly if you happen to be 500 miles out in the ocean when the mishap occurs. Despite the stability question—and it is a controversial question for many sailors—multihulls are raced and cruised successfully across most of the world's oceans.

HOW WILL THE BOAT BE USED?

Sailboats fall basically into one of three use categories: daysailing, racing, and cruising. In recent years, however, a fourth category has been added as designers and marketers have tried to combine the strengths of racing and cruising in the same boat, producing what is variously called the "racer / cruiser" or "performance cruiser."

Daysailers

By definition, a daysailer is intended for going out for a sail sometime during the day and coming back in before nightfall. Generally, these boats are not equipped with either lights or an engine, nor do they usually have built-in overnight accommodations.

Daysailers range from simple sailboards and sailing dinghies to catamarans to hi-tech monohulls in the 18- to 20-foot range. In general, they are rigged either as some form of a catboat or as sloops. Some, like the Laser and the Flying Scot, were developed specifically for racing "around the buoys." (Most sailboat races are conducted around a triangular course, often with the points of the triangle marked by buoys put in place by the race committee.) Others are long-time class boats—Lightnings and Comets are two examples—developed many years ago for club racing. The rest are boats developed by entrepreneurial companies to meet a burgeoning market for small sailboats, particularly with the popularization of fiberglass construction in the 1960s and '70s. Moreover, while many of these boats were not developed specifically for racing, there are usually organized races at local yacht clubs and sailing associations wherever a particular boat is popular.

Racers

It is sometimes said that the only real difference between people who buy a racing type of sailboat and those who don't, is that the racers compete openly in organized events. Most cruising sailors—I among them—are closet racers. They're racing every boat on the water, but they're the only ones who know it at the time.

In theory, sailboat races are a test of sailing skill first, and of boats second. This requires finding ways to put competitors on an equal footing. Three approaches have been used most often: (1) The development of "one-design" or "class" boats so that all boats are identical; (2) "handicapping" boats by assigning time penalties or bonuses to offset inherent advantages of the different boats; and (3) creating a complex formula or "rating rule" that imposes limits on the boat's design. While "one-design" and "handicapped" races have been popular for most local and small-boat racing, races of boats designed to a rating rule have dominated major segments of larger-boat (over 30 feet) racing until recent years—including, of course, the America's Cup events. As a result, the rating rules have had enormous impact on sailboat design, particularly as yacht designers have worked within the rules to make boats go faster. In general, modern racers are characterized by very light displacement and relatively shallow bottoms having a long, flat run from bow to stern. Because these boats push less water out of the way as they move forward, they can reach hull speed much more easily than moderate- to heavy-displacement boats. Given half a chance, they will surf easily. While some of these boats are intended for ocean racing, most are not, and many would not be safe on the ocean except in pleasant weather.

The racer's keel is most often a short, deep fin, though new keel designs—including the "winged" keel made famous by the

America's Cup winner *Australia*—are being introduced almost weekly as yacht designers experiment with new shapes. While keel design is in a state of flux, a spade rudder set well aft remains the racer's rudder system of choice. (Of course, in this type of boat, there is no skeg supporting the rudder.)

The quest for speed, however, has also brought trade-offs. For example, the quest for lighter and lighter displacement has often resulted in rather spartan accommodations. Having large areas to stow sails and saving weight are more important to racers than having cabinets and hanging lockers (closets). In addition, the boats carry only enough fuel and water to accommodate the requirements for each race.

Another trade-off involves "stability"—the ability of a boat to resist capsize and, if capsized, to roll back onto its "feet." Analysis after the Fastnet Race in 1979 suggested that the wide, shallow, and light-displacement designs common among racers today may not only make some boats more susceptible to being rolled over in large, breaking waves, it may also make them more likely to stay upside down for several minutes once they've "turned turtle." In the 1979 Fastnet, an ocean race off the southwest coast of England beset by an unusually severe storm, fifteen sailors died, more than one hundred of the 303 boats in the race were "knocked over at least until their masts were horizontal, and about seventy were rolled further. Approximately eighteen boats performed 360-degree rolls, and five capsized yachts reportedly spent periods from thirty seconds to five minutes in a 'turtled' [upside-down] position."[1]

While, at first glance, questions of stability in such severe circumstances may seem important only for people who sail on the ocean or, perhaps, the Great Lakes, their importance is much broader. The winds of a summer thunderstorm can knock down any sailboat caught with too much sail up. Also, any number of today's one-design racers are highly susceptible to broaching while sailing downwind with maximum sail flying. As a result, your safety in such situations is closely tied to your boat's ability to recover from the knockdown.

1. *Desirable and Undesirable Characteristics of Offshore Yachts*, by The Technical Committee of the Cruising Club of America. W. W. Norton, New York, 1987; p. 58.

Cruisers

Cruising means many things to many people. As a result, cruising-type sailboats range from 15-foot sloops or catboats with small cabins barely large enough for a berth, to very large boats. They may be used mostly for a weekend retreat at the dock, for daysailing or weekending in nearby anchorages, for two- or three-week cruises in local waters, for cruising in coastal and nearby offshore waters, and for crossing oceans. They may even become a home for people who choose a cruising lifestyle for a period of months or even years. Some of these people spend those years cruising coastwise; others cross an ocean to cruise Europe or the South Pacific islands; and some just keep cruising along until they've gone around the world.

It should be obvious that not all boats are suitable for every kind of cruising. As a generality, nearly all boats could be used safely for staying at the dock or for weekend sailing in protected waters. Most could probably also be used safely for two- or three-week cruises in protected or semi-protected waters. A considerably smaller number, however, would be suitable for safe cruising in coastal or nearby offshore waters. And fewer still are suitable for crossing oceans safely.

There is no rule that says boats must be more than 35 or 40 feet in length to be suitable for ocean passages. Some excellent designs in the 24- to 28-foot range are successfully cruising the world's oceans. Similarly, some 45-footers make excellent weekenders, but are not suitable for ocean sailing.

There is also no rule for how cruising boats should be rigged. Most cruising boats are sloops—though the percentage diminishes rapidly as boat length goes over 35 feet, because the sails get too big. Some few cruisers are catboats—mostly under 30 feet in length, because that single sail simply gets too big otherwise. Most of the remainder are cutters or ketches, but there are yawls, schooners, and cat ketches sprinkled through the fleet as well.

Cruising boats generally are of moderate to heavy displacement, a design element which gives them larger interior space and a deeper, generally rounder hull shape. The heavier displacement provides greater stability, more interior volume, more complete accommodations, more storage space, and the potential to carry more water and fuel. Frequently, these boats will have a long keel, either a "full keel" running most of the waterline length of the boat, or a "moderate fin keel" extending roughly over the middle 40 percent of the hull length. The rudder of the full-keel boat normally is hinged to the back of the keel. The rudder of the moderate fin-keel boat most often is hinged to a skeg. These cruising designs generally are easier to steer, particularly in adverse conditions, than their racing cousins.

The trade-off for the heavier displacement is a need for larger sails, heavier rigging, and heavier anchors and anchor lines. There is also a trade-off in sailing performance. The heavier-displacement boat simply has to push more water out of the way to move forward, and, since it has a bigger bottom, there's more friction between its bottom and the water. As a result, the cruiser needs more wind-power to get moving than does a light-displacement racing design. Although using larger sails helps compensate for the heavier displacement, the cruising design simply is not as responsive in light air as its lighter cousins. There is a compensating factor, however. Heavier-displacement boats can usually carry their sails longer in stronger winds and require fewer sail changes as winds gain strength.

Racer / Cruisers

In the late 1970s and early 1980s, yacht designers and sailboat marketers created the racer / cruiser. Some have called these boats "performance cruisers." Regardless, their effort was to create a large market for boats that were neither principally race boats nor principally cruisers, but which combined attributes of both. The obvious advantage to these designs is that you will probably get to your destination sooner than in a cruiser because the boat will sail closer to its hull speed a higher percentage of the time.

Today, the technology of fiberglass boat construction has enabled a number of companies to offer light-displacement racer / cruisers with remarkably commodious accommodations and outstanding sailing performance in favorable weather conditions. These boats generally are well suited for cruising and racing in local waters, but they are not suitable for areas where there is risk of being caught out in heavy weather.

There are still trade-offs, however. Because they have relatively lighter displacements, racer/cruisers tend to have less storage area and smaller tanks for water and fuel. They are less comfortable for offshore sailing simply because their lighter weight and flatter bottoms give them a quicker motion in a seaway. Depending upon their keel/rudder configuration, they may be more tiring to steer. And, they may require reducing sail sooner in stronger winds.

Testing What You've Learned
(Answers can be found in Appendix C)

1. Match the rigs listed below with the correct description:

A) Cutter   1) One mast, 30 percent back from the bow; usually has only one headsail and a mainsail

B) Catboat   2) Two masts, with the shorter mast placed near the stern but in front of the rudderpost

C) Schooner   3) Two free-standing masts of approximately equal height

D) Sloop   4) Two or more masts, with the forward mast the same height as or shorter than the others

E) Ketch   5) Two masts, with the shorter mast placed near the stern but aft of the rudderpost

F) Yawl   6) One mast placed right up near the bow; only one sail

G) Cat ketch   7) One mast, 40 percent or more back from the bow; usually has two headsails and a mainsail

2. Which rig is most efficient sailing close to the wind?

3. Why are boats over 40 feet long frequently rigged as ketches, yawls, or schooners?

4. Why would a cutter be preferred over a sloop for ocean cruising?

5. Which are generally faster, monohulls or multihulls?

6. Which are generally more stable, monohulls or multihulls?

7. Why are racing boats or racer/cruisers generally faster than cruising-type sailboats?

8. Why do sailboats designed for cruising generally have heavier displacements than sailboats intended for racing?

III

Getting Underway

The most important part of leaving the launching ramp, your mooring, or a dock is the preparation you make before casting off. This not only involves giving your boat a thorough inspection, but also making a final check on the weather and being sure that your crew and guests know where to find and how to use all safety-related equipment.

This section takes you through the process of checking out your boat and reviews safety equipment required by the U.S. Coast Guard or recommended because it makes good sense. In addition, it suggests ways to combine your system for inspecting your boat with an orientation for your crew and passengers. That orientation includes explaining how you plan to get the boat out onto the water and what your crew and guests should (or should not) do to help as you get underway. Finally, it presents good operating procedures for starting your engine(s), preparing to cast off, and taking your boat away from the beach, raising anchor, dropping your mooring, and leaving from a dock or slip.

8

An Ounce of Prevention . . .

Whether you are leaving the dock or your slip, letting go your mooring, raising anchor, or pushing off from the beach, the most important part of getting underway takes place before the boat starts moving. It's comprised of all of the little things you do before casting off the first line.

You can look at it much as you would preparing for a long car trip. You'd probably check the oil, water, and tire pressure, and then fill up the gas tank. You'd make sure you had packed all the clothes you need. You should check your spare tire to be certain it has sufficient air, and see that the jack and lug wrench are in place. If you had never changed a tire on that particular car, you might even make sure you know how the jack works and where to set it to jack up the car—before you're stuck somewhere away from your home territory after dark in the midst of a rainstorm and have to change a tire. You would also plan your route, using a map and being sure that the map is in the car.

Boating isn't much different, except that virtually every trip on your boat needs the same kind of preparation you'd put into that long car trip—maybe even a bit more. It involves:
• Checking out your boat, its systems (including the engines), equipment, and supplies.
• Plotting your intended course (route) on your nautical chart (map).

• Making a final weather check.

• Taking your crew and passengers through the boat to be sure they know how to use the facilities, which may be strange to them.

• Showing crew and passengers where to find and how to use key safety equipment, and where you'll be going on the chart.

• Starting the engine safely.

• Planning with your crew and passengers how you are going to make your departure so that they know what is expected of them.

Finally, you're ready to go, and the preparation begins to pay off as you make your way competently and safely out onto the waterway to the nodding approval of all the other boat owners who are watching you go—and, believe me, they're watching.

CHECKING OUT YOUR BOAT

Boats, their systems, and equipment live in a hostile environment. If they're not in the water, they may be near it in a "boatel" or some other such convenient storage. Regardless, they're exposed to the marine environment and to the rigors of being taken in and out of the water every time they're used. Or, they're being dragged over the highway at 55 miles per hour, with all of the vibration and jostling that trailering involves, and then being exposed to the marine environment.

Because of these demanding and constantly changing conditions, any system on your boat that worked properly yesterday is a candidate for failure today. If it fails before you leave the dock, you're inconvenienced. If it fails 20 miles from a dock, you may well have a problem. In any case, the way to prevent such problems is by developing a routine for checking out your boat, its systems, and its equipment before you start welcoming passengers and crew aboard, and then correcting any deficiencies you find before you start out. It helps to have a detailed checklist so that you don't forget anything.

The Big Picture

Whether your boat is a small runabout, a daysailer, a large cabin cruiser, or an auxiliary sailboat, the check-out procedure should start with the big picture and then focus increasingly on detail. You can start by stepping back from your boat just to look her over. Walk around her to the extent you can, to see if anything looks different.

Most of the time, everything will look just fine, and you can take the opportunity to admire how nice she looks. But you may find a dock line that has chafed and might otherwise go unnoticed, or possibly you'll see that something has floated down under your stern and could foul your propeller when you put the engine in gear. If your boat is on a trailer, you may find that somehow a roller has become dislodged and your boat's bottom has been damaged. Whatever it is, the one time you find something to correct before it becomes a problem will make all of those other times, when you checked but didn't find anything, worthwhile.

Water in the Bilges

The next place to look is the bilges. For example, if your boat is out of the water, you need to be sure that the drain plug is tightly in place before she is launched. In the autumn, any leaves that may have fallen or been blown into the bilge should be cleaned out before they can clog your bilge pump. It's also worth checking to be sure that all hoses connected to fittings through the hull are in good shape and that the valves to shut off those through-hull fittings are closed. You do not want your boat to fill with water when you launch her.

If your boat is in the water, you need to be sure she hasn't taken on water since you last used her. If you find more water in the bilges than you'd expect, you need to know why—especially if you have a bilge pump that should have pumped that water out automatically. In any case, you'll want to pump it out now.

Electrical System—and the Weather

After checking the bilges, you should make sure that your boat's batteries are properly charged and have adequate water; then turn on your electrical panel and begin inspecting the boat from bow to stern, above deck and below.

If your boat has either a VHF or a weather radio—and you should have at least a weather radio—this is the time to listen to the weather forecast. In that way, you're accomplishing two things at once: you're making sure the radio receiver works, and you're checking the forecast a final time before going out. If the forecast has changed so that deteriorating conditions are expected, you should consider changing your plans in light of the new forecast. You may choose to shorten, or even cancel, your trip.

You should next check your running lights. While you may not plan to be out after dark, it is nice to know that your lights will work if you need them. If you have portable running lights that use their own batteries, you should carry spare batteries and renew them every year.

Anchors, Engines, etc.

With your running lights checked, you can now move on to other systems—for example, testing the engine controls and steering system to be sure they haven't become stiff or frozen. While you're at the controls, it's worth checking your compass. For example, Susan and I know what the compass should read in our slip, and we just look at it to make sure it's reading correctly.

If your boat has a deck locker for anchor and anchor line storage, you'll need to look there to be sure all is in order. That includes being certain that the "bitter end" of the primary anchor line (rode) is tied securely to the boat and that your spare anchor and anchor line are readily accessible. You should check the anchor and anchor line, even if your boat is an open motorboat or daysailer. When your engine fails or your sailboat tips over and you need that anchor, it doesn't help to find that you left it in the garage at home. You should also check to be sure that the shackle used to connect the anchor line to the anchor is securely fastened. Shackle pins have been known to work themselves loose and should be wired so they can't come out (Figure 18). (Anchoring is discussed in Chapter 25.)

If your boat is an outboard and the engines are fastened to the boat with screw clamps, you should make sure that they are

FIG. 18. Securing a shackle pin: By wiring the shackle pin as illustrated, you can be certain it will not come loose.

screwed down tightly and that your safety chain is fastened securely to both the engine and the boat. Never assume that just because everything was in good order last week, it's still in good order this week; a child may have been playing in your boat since the last time you used it.

On any boat with an engine, you'll need to check the oil levels in your engine, transmission, and (if you have one) the vee-drive unit. The condition and adjustment of any drive belts on the engines (e.g., the alternator belt) and the engine coolant level on freshwater-cooled systems also should be checked. (Engine maintenance is covered in more detail in Chapters 19 and 29.)

Some of these checklist items may sound like overkill, but more than one person has discovered after getting out onto the water that he is way off course because someone left a tool lying near the compass, throwing it out of whack because the magnet in the compass needle was attracted by the steel tool. In the same vein, one couple we know had their diesel engine seize when it ran dry of oil; the cost of that repair job was about $2,000. We came close to doing the same thing ourselves before I learned to check the oil every time before starting the engine. Now I chart the oil consumption of our diesel engine so that I can anticipate the need to add oil simply by noting how many hours the engine has run since I last topped it off. These records also let me look for any change in oil consumption.

We haven't had to learn all of these lessons through our own mistakes, however. We've also learned from the mistakes of others. The following is condensed from an unpublished article I wrote for *Yachting* magazine several years ago:

> During the night, the anchorage at Cuttyhunk was hit with heavy winds that caused a number of boats to drag anchor as the night wore on. By morning, several boats were moving to better locations as the storm continued unabated, with winds reported at 30 knots, gusting to 40 knots.
>
> Early in the morning, a 26-foot sailboat came around our stern and headed into the wind to re-anchor. As the skipper let out his anchor line, the wind was blowing the boat back quickly until, suddenly, he felt the end of the anchor line go right through his hands. When he got back into the cockpit, he put his outboard motor in gear and quickly gave it the gas, only to have the outboard jump off the stern and sink out of sight.
>
> But he was lucky. As he was blown past another boat, they threw him a line and let him hang from their stern. Otherwise, he'd have been blown out-of-control into the docks a few hundred feet downwind. He did not have another anchor that he could use to stop his boat, and there was not time to put up his neatly stowed sails, even if he had the skill to sail out of the situation.

So, it can happen to any of us—unless we prevent such incidents by checking out all systems thoroughly each time before leaving the dock.

Below-Deck Items

Of course, the larger your boat and the more equipment you have, the longer your checklist will be. On a boat with a cabin, for example, you'll need to go over several items below decks, starting in the bow with the anchor locker—again, to be sure the anchor lines are not tangled and that the bitter end is secure (unless you've taken care of that from above). Although, as you work your way aft, your checklist will be your own because it needs to fit your boat, it might include making sure that:
• Interior lights are working properly; test them as you work your way aft.
• The water pump in the head sink and the seacock or gate

valve for the sink drain are working properly. (It is a good idea to close all through-hull valves when the boat's not in use. Not only will this prevent leakage from a hose failure while you are away from the boat, but the need to open them every time you use the boat will let you be certain the valves are functioning well and can be closed quickly in an emergency.)

• The marine toilet is in good working order, the holding tank is not filled, and there is an adequate supply of any chemicals needed for the head. (It's also worth checking the supply of toilet paper!)

• The galley sink water supply is working properly, and the sink drain seacock (or gate valve) is open.

• The water tanks have adequate fresh water.

• The stove appears to be in good working order and has an adequate supply of fuel (if it will be needed on the trip).

• All electronic equipment—depthsounder, Loran, etc.—is functioning properly; turn each instrument on and check the readings.

• Your engine's exhaust system is intact. As the following extract from a U.S. Coast Guard report details, exhaust leaks on a boat with a cabin can be deadly:

A GOOD WAY TO DIE—How many times have you dismissed a headache and slight nausea as minor seasickness brought on by the combined effects of the sun and waves or too many beers? Did you ever stop to think that you might have been a victim of carbon monoxide poisoning?

The victims of carbon monoxide poisoning feel no particular pain except, perhaps, a severe headache, which they usually attribute to some other cause. In fact, carbon monoxide will dull the senses to the point where the victims feel no fear or danger and have no will to save themselves. An hour after they drift into unconsciousness, they are dead.

In one accident reported to the Coast Guard, a couple and their two daughters were killed by exhaust fumes that escaped from a cracked generator exhaust manifold.

Inspect the engine and generator exhaust systems for cracks in the hot, unjacketed sections of the exhaust manifolds. Check the tightness of the bolts holding the exhaust manifolds to the engine blocks.

Another accident reported to the Coast Guard involved a large, twin-screw yacht. The owner and three of his guests, who were below during a cruise across a lake, were killed by carbon monoxide gas that seeped into the cabin after escaping from a loose hose coupling on the exhaust pipe for one of the engines.

Are rubber exhaust hose connections held by double hose clamps? Be sure that all rubber hose connections in the exhaust system are fitted with two clamps at each end. Make sure the hoses aren't burned through or beginning to show signs of advanced age. If you replace them, be absolutely certain that [the new hoses] are labeled by the manufacturer for use in a marine exhaust system.[1]

Required and Recommended Equipment

With the boat-systems checklist completed, it is time to check all of the equipment required by the U.S. Coast Guard as well as other equipment often recommended for safety purposes (see Appendix B). If your crew (including passengers) is available by this time, it's a good idea to bring them aboard and have them go through the safety equipment check with you. This lets you be sure they know where everything is and provides opportunity to show them how to use it.

Wearable PFDs (Life Jackets): Required equipment begins with Coast Guard-approved wearable PFDs—life jackets or vests (Figure 19). For many years, PFDs have been made using a fibrous material called kapok sealed in plastic bags to provide flotation. More recently, some companies have begun using a closed-cell plastic foam in place of kapok and, frankly, the foam-filled PFDs are my preference. The reason is very simple: It's too easy to puncture the kapok-filled plastic bag so that the kapok can soak up water and become waterlogged, making the PFD useless, or even dangerous, if someone goes into the water wearing it. That hazard doesn't exist with the foam-filled PFDs.

Regardless of which flotation material is used, however, all PFDs need to be checked frequently. The fabric and straps on PFDs are always subject to degradation by sun, salt, and mildew, so you need to tug on the straps to be sure they won't tear

1. United States Coast Guard Boating Safety Circular #64, July 1986; pp. 30–32.

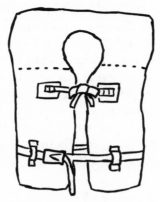

FIG. 19.   Typical Type II PFD (life jacket).

easily. If you have any PFDs made with kapok, you'll need to test them for leaks in the plastic bags by squeezing each part of the flotation very hard between your hands. If any leaks are found (i.e., you can squeeze air out of any of the plastic bags) or the straps are weak, you should tear or cut both the fabric and the plastic bags of kapok so that it is obvious the PFD is no good; then throw it away immediately and replace it with a new one. You don't want the defective PFD on the boat; you also don't want a child finding it in a trash can and using it for swimming, thinking it will help him stay afloat.

Throwable PFDs: In addition to PFDs intended to be worn, you need a Coast Guard-approved throwable device for flotation—for example, a life ring, horseshoe, or cushion. These, too, need to be checked. When putting our horseshoe buoy away for the winter one year, for example, we found to our dismay that its strap had been so weakened by exposure to sunlight that it tore apart when I removed the horseshoe from its rack on the stern rail. We keep the new horseshoe in a locker out of the sunlight when we're not on the boat and check the strap each time we put the buoy into its rack.

PFD cushions, like life jackets, may be made using either closed-cell foam or a kapok-filled plastic bag for flotation. As a result, they require the same kind of test given the wearable PFDs. Moreover, any cushion that might be used in an emergency as a throwable PFD should be checked out, and disposed of and replaced if it doesn't pass muster. You do *not* want a throwable PFD on board that won't do its job.

When testing the condition of your throwable PFDs, you should also review with everyone on the boat—crew and passengers alike—what to do if someone falls overboard. Everyone on the boat should know to yell "Man overboard!", to throw the victim a PFD, and to point toward and keep pointing toward the victim so that he isn't lost from sight. Specific procedures for recovering someone who has fallen overboard are described in Chapter 19.

Boarding Ladders: Unless your boat has a built-in swim platform and ladder, you should carry some kind of boarding ladder—not simply because you may be swimming from the boat, but to help anyone who may fall overboard get back into the boat. Even if you have a small runabout, a two- or three-step boarding ladder that hangs over the side could make a critical difference in getting someone aboard. As you go through your safety checklist and equipment with your crew, be sure to show them and your guests where the boarding ladder is and how to use it.

Fire Extinguishers: Depending upon the size and kind of boat you have, one or more Type B fire extinguishers may be among the required safety equipment. The most common of these are light-in-weight and easily held in one hand. As you inspect your fire extinguishers, show your crew where they are kept and how to get them from their holders. You should also take the time to explain how to use them. *However, never demonstrate or test a fire extinguisher by squirting it, even for a second or two.* Not only would it be messy, it would also reduce the effectiveness of the unit. When you pull the trigger on a fire extinguisher of the size found on most pleasure boats, its entire load is discharged in seconds.

Type B extinguishers are for use on flammable-liquid (kerosene, diesel fuel, alcohol, etc.) and grease fires. The most common ones are dry-chemical extinguishers. Although these extinguishers usually have a pressure gauge you can check to be sure they haven't lost their charge, *checking the pressure gauge isn't good enough.* You also need to make sure the powder hasn't become packed tightly in the bottom of the extinguisher. If the powder is loose, you'll be able to shake it from one end of the extinguisher to the other.

To check the powder, balance the extinguisher on your finger or the edge of your hand to see which end is the heavier. Next, shake the powder to the other end by holding the heavy end up and slapping the side of the extinguisher with the palm of your hand. Finally, balance the extinguisher again on your finger; the other end should be heavier this time. If the powder doesn't move, try slapping the side of the extinguisher a little harder, again holding the heavy end up. If, after two or three efforts, the powder hasn't moved, replace the fire extinguisher.

But don't simply throw the old one away. Take it to the back corner of the boatyard (with the manager's permission, of course) or to your own backyard, and try it out—not on a fire, mind you, but just squirt it onto the ground. The powder is harmless to the environment, and the fire extinguisher may work. If it does, it won't be fully wasted because you'll have had a chance to see what happens when you pull the trigger. When we tried this, we were most impressed with how quickly the fire extinguisher was used up. It obviously was not intended for very large fires.

Signaling Devices / First Aid: After checking the fire extinguishers, it's time to make sure that the horn, bell, and emergency signaling devices are in good order and that everyone on board knows where to find them and how to use them. The first aid kit—not required by law, but advisable—falls in the same category. If any of these items are ever needed, they may be needed in a hurry.

Navigation Charts: Though not required by law, one thing you should have on board whenever you'll be going more than just a few miles from home waters, is a set of charts for the area where you'll be boating. Even if you normally keep the charts on board, they may not always be there. For example, I've taken charts home at times, for one reason or another, and then forgotten to return them to the boat. So, it's worth checking to be sure you have the correct charts on board before you leave the dock. One way to make this check and at the same time increase your crew members' and guests' understanding of where you'll be going is to pull out the charts, show everyone where you're starting from, and then trace the route you plan to follow. Not only does it add interest for them, but you are increasing their ability to be useful should you be injured or become ill. We've also found that most of our guests enjoy keeping track of our progress on the chart throughout the day—again, a real advantage should something happen to you. Of course, if you find that the charts are missing, go get the ones you need before starting out, even if it means buying a second set. (Basic piloting and the use of charts are discussed in Chapter 20.)

VHF Transmitter: Finally, if you have one, it's time to check your VHF transmitter. The radio is not required by any law, but it's an excellent piece of safety equipment—*if* it is working properly and *if* everyone on the boat knows how to use it. Obviously, not everyone needs to know all of the protocol associated with using the radio properly, or how to use all of its features. However, every adult on the boat needs to know where the radio is, how to turn it on, and how to use the microphone to talk and to listen. Moreover, if you take guests out on your boat often, it is probably a good idea to have simplified instructions for using the radio written out, posted, and pointed out to all guests.

In any case, you can check the radio and demonstrate its use simply and quickly. First, explain what you're going to do and how you're going to do it; next, using Channel 16, listen for other boats calling, then call one of those boats, repeating its name three times: "*[Boat name, boat name, boat name],* this is *[your boat name]* calling for a radio check. Please acknowledge and go to Channel 68 [or to 69 or 71] for a radio check." When the skipper of the other boat acknowledges your call and agrees to change channels, switch to the other channel and repeat your call to him for the radio check. He'll tell you how he's receiving you, and you should let him know how you're receiving him. It's also worthwhile to find out where he is so that you can evaluate his response. If the other boat is 15 miles away, you may not expect him to hear you as clearly as if he were within 2 or 3 miles. If he's close by and your signal is weak, then one of you may have a problem with your radio or antenna; you can't tell whether the problem is in your system until you talk with other boats to see if they, too, receive you weakly. When the radio check is over, you should thank the other boat and sign off: "Thank you, *[boat name]*. This is *[your boat name]*, out."

However, a key point: Channel 16 is used only for emergencies or to initiate a call. You should not do your radio check on Channel 16. Instead, as illustrated above, initiate the call on Channel 16, and change to a working channel.

Why, you may ask, is all of that necessary?

I, personally, was a long-term skeptic about the value of a VHF as safety equipment. I figured that as long as we maintained our boat properly, planned our trips thoroughly, stayed in good health, and were sensible about when and where we went out on our boat, we would be able to handle any problems we might encounter. Not only that, but if our engine failed, we could always sail home. We finally put a VHF radio on our boat, but only because Susan insisted.

A few years ago, however, I became "a true believer." We awoke one Sunday morning during a U.S. Power Squadron autumn cruise to find an ambulance at dockside and a man being carried on a stretcher from a sailboat tied across the dock from us. Later, we learned that the man, his wife, and another couple had chartered a boat for a week's cruise in the upper Chesapeake Bay. The skipper, who was the only experienced sailor among the foursome, had suffered an apparent heart attack earlier that morning. When his wife and friends attempted to use the VHF radio to call for help, they couldn't make it work. (They said later that they had never tried to use the radio before that morning.) Fortunately, they were able to attract the attention of people on another boat anchored nearby and have its crew call the Coast Guard to arrange for an ambulance to pick up their skipper at this marina, which was only a few miles from where they were anchored.

By the time the victim's wife and friends got their chartered boat to the marina and tied up, the ambulance was on the scene and paramedics were able to begin ministering to the patient immediately. However, had another boat not been nearby to make that vital radio link, valuable time would have been lost in getting medical attention because the ambulance had to come some 15 to 20 miles to meet the boat. That kind of time loss can be the difference between life and death. So it pays to have a radio, to make sure it is working properly *before* leaving the dock, and to make certain that everyone on the boat knows how to use it.

Fenders: Fenders are used to protect your boat from bumping into a dock or another boat. They come in a variety of styles. Some are thick rectangles of tough, closed-cell foam. The most common are inflated cylinders or balls of tough plastic. Whatever their construction, size, or shape, they are designed to be hung along the side of your hull when you come up to a dock or tie alongside another boat. Their effective use has spared many hands and feet from being caught between boats or between a boat and a dock or piling. They are useful even on small rowboats and dinghies. A minimum of two fenders of a size appropriate to your boat is recommended. If in doubt about what size you should have, err on the side of having fenders that are too big.

Equipment for Smaller Boats

Many of the items discussed so far apply only to mid-sized and larger boats. Smaller boats also have equipment needs that go beyond Coast Guard requirements. For example, a paddle or a pair of oars can be a big help if the wind dies or your engine quits. A spare container—approved for gasoline—of fuel (with the oil already mixed in, if that's required) can also spare you the embarrassment I felt in running out of gas on my second boating date with Susan. In fact, in these days of commercial boat towing, it can save you more than embarrassment. Assistance from a commercial boat-rescue service can be very expensive!

A bailer is a must—something that will scoop out a half gallon of water at a throw. You can make a dandy bailer from an empty plastic bleach or milk bottle. It is also worth having a half dozen 25-foot lengths of 5/16-inch or 3/8-inch nylon stored in a cloth or net bag—not for specific use, but just because they come in very handy.

Other items that may be very important include a whistle or horn, a compass, a chart, a flashlight, a first-aid kit, and some emergency food, water, and warm clothes. You may not plan on being out overnight or when it is cold, but it can easily happen. Of course, you must also have an approved PFD for each person on the boat.

Finally, you should have a small tool-and-spare-parts kit. On a sailboat, you may need only a knife, a screwdriver, pliers, and a roll of rigging tape. On an outboard motorboat, you should also have spare sparkplugs, a sparkplug wrench, and some spare shear pins for the propellers. For both sailboats and outboard motorboats, spare stainless-steel cotter pins of the size used anywhere on the boat are also a good idea. (Maintenance of safety equipment is discussed in Chapter 29. U.S. Coast Guard requirements are detailed in Appendix B.)

Galley and Head Orientation

With the safety check completed, you can well spend a few minutes to show your guests how to use any of the boat's facilities they may need during the outing. For example: How to get water from the sinks. How to get things out of the ice box with minimum loss of coldness. Where food, dishes, glasses, flatware, and any other key galley equipment is kept. And, perhaps most important, how to use the head. Many skippers we know, in fact, have specific instructions for using the head typed and posted. On our boat, we have a needlepoint sign (compliments of Susan's mom) with the instruction: "Gentlemen, please be seated." Operating instructions are given verbally as part of your preparation for leaving the dock, and later as needed.

PFDs for Guests and Crew

Depending upon the type of boat you have, where you'll be going, and the weather conditions, you may also want to find out whether any of your guests or crew are either non-swimmers or weak swimmers. If any of them do not swim reasonably well, you may want to ask them to wear PFDs during the boat ride. The larger and more enclosed your boat is, the less need there is to ask these people (except small children) to wear PFDs; alternatively, the smaller and more open your boat is, the greater the need for them to wear PFDs. It may seem an imposition to ask people who can't swim or who are weak swimmers to wear PFDs, but their lives are your responsibility as long as they're on your boat. Moreover, the risk of a non-swimmer or a weak swimmer drowning from falling or being thrown overboard by an unexpected lurch of the boat is very real.

LACK OF PFDs CITED IN DEATHS—Failure to have life preservers on board may have contributed to the deaths of two men when their boat capsized in Long Island Sound.

The body of Fred Huntley, Jr., 54, of Jersey City, New Jersey, was found by Southold, New York, police divers near Rocky Point, a section of East Marion, New York, on Long Island. His unidentified companion was still missing a month after the accident.

An observer called the Southold police after he saw Huntley clinging to the transom of his 14-foot aluminum rowboat that had flipped over shortly before noon on June 7.

Petty Officer Jim Rockefeller of the Coast Guard station in New Haven, Connecticut, said the seas were relatively calm and the winds were from the southeast at 8 knots when the men moored the boat about 50 yards offshore to fish. Rockefeller could not say why the boat capsized.

"If they had been wearing life jackets, they would have survived," Rockefeller said. "They couldn't have been in the water long enough to die of exposure."[2]

And then, there are the happy outcomes—the times when PFDs are worn. In a nearly tragic accident in Wisconsin, for example, three little girls owe their lives at least in part to the fact that their life jackets kept them afloat until they could be rescued. Had they slipped beneath the water's surface, the likelihood of rescue would have been remote:

SISTERS SAVED BY FAST RESPONSE—Quick action by shoreside observers averted a tragedy when three young girls, all from the same family, were trapped beneath an overturned motorboat on Lake Waubesa, near Madison, Wisconsin.

According to the authorities, Thomas and Nancy Morris of McFarland, Wisconsin, a small lakeshore community, were riding

2. *Soundings*, September 1986.

in a 15-foot motorboat with their three daughters, eight-year-old Nicole, four-year-old Mandy, and two-year-old Lindsey, along with two adult friends and two dogs.

Under gusty 16-mile-per-hour winds, the boat was steadily taking on water and eventually tipped over about 150 yards from shore. Mandy and Lindsey Morris were caught under the bow of the capsized boat in an air pocket, while Nicole was trapped near the middle of the boat. Authorities said all three girls were wearing life preservers.

Accounts of the rescue varied, but . . . [rescuers] managed to pull two of the girls from beneath the boat, and the third was rescued when the swamped craft was righted.

Authorities blamed the mishap on the number of people in the relatively small boat, and the strong winds.[3]

Please note the cause of the Wisconsin accident: Putting too many people—four adults, three children, and two dogs—in the boat for the conditions in which they would be operating. Overloading a boat will be discussed further in Chapter 19.

STARTING THE ENGINE

With all of the other systems and equipment checked out, it's time to start the engine. This, too, is a good thing to show everyone how to do.

Diesel Engines

Depending upon the size and sophistication of your engine(s), the specific procedures for starting diesels may be more involved then those for starting comparable gasoline engine(s). For example, you may have to preheat the cylinders. In any case, those procedures will be outlined in detail in your owner's manual, and you should follow them scrupulously.

From the perspective of safety, however, starting your boat's diesel engine(s) is a much simpler process than it is on similar boats powered by gasoline engines because diesel fuel itself is

3. *Soundings,* August 1986.

safer. On our boat, for example, we begin by opening the cooling-water-intake seacock. We have already checked oil levels and fan belts, so the only other thing that's needed is to go into the cockpit, put the gear lever in neutral, adjust the throttle, and turn the key. Normally, the engine will start promptly, and we simply check the oil-pressure gauge to be sure we have adequate oil pressure, the voltmeter to make certain the alternator is charging properly, and the exhaust to be sure the engine picks up its cooling water. In cold weather, we also have to push the "cold start" button on the engine—something analogous to using a choke on your car.

But, we have a diesel engine. *If you have a gasoline engine, it is a whole different ball game. Gasoline vapors explode. As a result, other safety checks are needed to make sure you do not start a fire or blow up your boat.*

Gasoline Engines

With outboard motors and portable fuel tanks, you'll have to begin by pressurizing the fuel system. You'll also have to check for fuel leaks. Unless you have an open boat, you must then make doubly sure that no gasoline has gotten into the bilge. All gasoline-powered motorboats—including outboards, I/Os, and inboards—that have enclosed gas tanks and/or engines must meet Coast Guard requirements for ventilation. Meeting those requirements, however, does not guarantee that a hazardous condition won't develop. As a result, you must check your bilges to be certain that no gasoline vapors have settled there, waiting for the smallest-possible spark to detonate them. Just for your information: *The vapors from a half cup of gasoline leaked or spilled into the bilge can have the explosive force of six sticks of dynamite.*

FUEL FIRE CONSUMES SMALL BOAT—A small pleasure boat was destroyed after it caught fire at a fuel dock at Essex Island Marina, Essex, Connecticut.

The two boat operators were not injured. Mary Moran of Essex Island Marina said that the boat was refueled at 9:00 A.M. on August 10, and the owners left it at the fuel dock for a few minutes while they ran some errands.

When the owners returned and tried to start the boat, Moran

said, it caught fire. Coast Guard officials from New London, Connecticut, said that the boat was set adrift in the Connecticut River when the fire started.

When the Coast Guard arrived, Saybrook Towing and Salvage had pulled the boat to the side of the river, and the fire had been extinguished.[4]

Not all people, unfortunately, are so lucky:

FOUR-YEAR-OLD DIES IN BOAT EXPLOSION—A boat explosion and fire in the tiny North Carolina town of Bath killed four-year-old Jeremia Leggett, who was too terrified to jump to rescuers' waiting arms.

"When something like this happens, it kind of has a traumatizing effect on the whole community," said Beaufort County Sheriff Nelson Sheppard after the April 23 explosion.

Sheppard said Joseph Thomas Leggett, 33, was severely burned but is expected to live. His wife, Marian Sawyer Leggett, 31, and their 10-year-old daughter, Sandra, were treated and released from a local hospital that same evening.

Sheppard said that the 32-year-old, 30-foot wooden Chris-Craft had just taken on 50 gallons of gasoline at the Quarterdeck Marina on Back Creek about 9:00 P.M. and was pulling into the channel when the explosion occurred. He said the yacht was either not equipped with bilge blowers or they "were not activated or operating."

Three men, Reuben Braddy, J. C. Morgan, and Skip Horney, had just walked past the boat at the gas dock, spoken to the people aboard, and stepped inside the dock house.

The two-engine boat was probably no more than 15 feet from the dock, Sheppard said. One engine was running and Leggett was trying to start the other when the explosion occurred, he said.

"The little girl [Sandra], from the initial explosion, was blown from the boat. They [Braddy, Morgan, and Horney] were able to jump into the creek and reach up to the mother and father, but the heat was so intense, they couldn't go aboard the boat.

"They were able to see the child [Jeremia], and the child was screaming, and they were screaming to the child to jump . . . in my opinion, the child was just terrified and frozen to the spot," Sheppard said.

4. *Soundings*, October 1986.

Sheppard described Leggett as an accomplished boater and part-time fisherman.[5]

The kind of accidents described in these newspaper accounts can be prevented by ventilating the bilges thoroughly before starting your engine(s).

Many boats come equipped with a bilge sniffer—an electronic device designed to detect explosive vapors. These sniffers really do work—most of the time. A better idea is to open a hatch, poke your head through it, and smell the bilge with your nose. If you smell gasoline, immediately order that any smoking materials (cigarettes, etc.) be put out, and get everyone off the boat and a safe distance away from it. Next, if you have a bilge blower—an exhaust fan for the bilge (they are required equipment on all gasoline-powered motorboats built after July 31, 1980)—turn that fan on. Then turn off all other electrical circuits and disconnect the shore power. If you do not have an exhaust fan in the bilge, open all hatches to the bilge and then turn off the boat's power at the battery switch and disconnect any shore power.

If gasoline has been spilled into the bilge, or there is only a very slow leak somewhere, ventilating the bilge thoroughly should take care of the immediate problem by getting rid of the explosive vapors. Then, you need to check the fuel system, including the tank, to see whether you have a leak somewhere. In any case, before you start the engine, you've got to figure out how that gasoline got into the bilge so that you can make sure it doesn't happen again.

If you have a steady fuel leak, the odor won't go away. As fast as you remove the fumes, more gas will leak into the bilge and evaporate to form more fumes. In this circumstance, consult with your marina manager, the marine police, or the fire department to get expert help, and have the boat pulled to someplace where others won't be endangered if the worst happens. You will probably need to "blanket" your bilge with some form of fire suppressant (foam, CO_2, or halon) and have the gasoline pumped from your fuel tank. When the tank is empty, you will need to fill it with halon or CO_2, ventilate the bilge,

5. *Soundings*, July 1987.

then find the leak and have it repaired. Obviously, this is no job for an amateur.

Let's assume, however, that your bilge is clear. Your nose and the electronic sniffer agree—there are no gasoline fumes. Then, if you have a bilge exhaust fan, you should turn that fan on for four to five minutes to exhaust air from the bilge *even though you don't think there are any gasoline vapors down there.* While the fan is running, you can check to see how much fuel you have.

Why, you might ask, don't you turn on the exhaust fan first, let it run, and then check the bilge for fumes? The answer is this: It is critically important to know whether you have a gasoline leak. If you have a slow leak, the exhaust fan might get rid of the evidence temporarily, but not the hazard. So, you sniff first to be certain that you don't have a leak. Then you run the exhaust fan as a back-up precaution against there being explosive fumes hidden somewhere in the bilge. And only after you've done those two things do you go to the control panel and turn the ignition key to start the engine(s).

With the engine(s) running, you'll need to make the same checks for oil pressure, alternator charging, and cooling-water pickup as those needed for a diesel engine. Assuming everything is just as it should be, you should throttle back and let the engine warm up.

Engine Warm-Up

Cold engines have been known to stall at critical moments, so it's not a good idea to just start your engine(s) and cast off your lines. At the same time, however, your engine does not need a long warm-up; four or five minutes is enough. Most experts advise against letting a diesel engine idle for long periods with the gear in neutral. In any case, while the engine warms up, you should gather your crew and passengers to plan your departure from the dock.

PLANNING YOUR DEPARTURE

The most important element involved in making any critical maneuver—and I consider taking your departure a critical maneuver—is the thought that goes into it. In an emergency situation, that thought may take place in milliseconds. But in a non-emergency situation, it should be deliberate and conscious.

The first two things to think about in planning your departure are the strength and direction of the wind and current. Depending upon how strong they are and where they're coming from, either or both the wind and current may have a major effect on how you leave—what order you cast off lines as well as how you maneuver. If you ignore these two forces, they can get you into trouble.

The next thing to check is your surroundings. Are there any obstacles (e.g., anchored boats, another pier, a channel you must follow, boat traffic, fishermen, water-skiers, etc.) that you'll need to consider in making your way out onto the water? For example, whenever we leave anchor in the Harbor of Refuge near Lewes in Delaware Bay, we check to see whether the Lewes–Cape May ferry is getting ready to leave dock or approaching the harbor. Moreover, on occasion we have delayed raising anchor for five or ten minutes to be certain the ferry would be clear.

Once you've looked at the overall picture, you can plan your moves. And as you plan them, you should explain them to all on board and hand out assignments.

First: In what order will you cast off lines, and who will have responsibility for letting each line go at the captain's command? You should show everyone how to get a line ready to be cast off, and then make sure that each person knows what commands you'll use when you're ready for him (her) to cast the line off.

Second: If it's necessary to fend off a piling or other obstacle, who has that responsibility?—again, only when the captain says to fend off. And, does this person know how to do it? He (she) should know to be careful to keep hands, arms, and feet from getting between the piling and the boat where they can get crushed, and push only as hard as necessary to keep the boat off the piling. The idea is to avoid pushing so hard that you push the boat into something on the other side, or interfere with the captain's ability to steer.

Third: Where should people sit or stand so that they won't be in the way if they don't have a duty assigned to them? It's important to tell each person where he (she) should be and what to do or not do.

Fourth: What path will you follow to get out into clear water? Even though you may plan to be at the helm yourself, a situation could arise that would make you hand over the helm to one of the crew. By discussing your plans with others in your crew, you're helping them get ready to step in if needed.

Testing What You've Learned
(Answers can be found in Appendix C)

1. Thinking about your boat, make a list of the systems and equipment you should check before starting your engine or raising the sails.

2. Why is it important to check the integrity of your exhaust if you have an inboard engine and any kind of a cabin?

3. What should you check about your PFDs? How?

4. TRUE or FALSE: PFDs that use closed-cell foam for flotation do not need to be included in your pre-start safety check because you don't have to worry about air leaks in the flotation.

5. TRUE or FALSE: After they are no longer good as PFDs, cushions originally intended as throwable PFDs can be retired to be used as seat cushions.

6. If your boat has one or more fire extinguishers, do you know how to operate them? Have you checked them recently to be sure they haven't lost their charge and to be certain the dry-powder extinguishing agent hasn't become packed tightly in the bottom?

7. What are the only approved (i.e., legal) uses of Channel 16 on the VHF radio?

8. TRUE or FALSE: PFDs are kept aboard boats only for emergencies.

9. Name three pieces of equipment that should be aboard smaller boats, even though they are not required by Coast Guard regulations.

10. On boats with gasoline-powered I/O or inboard engines, what should always be checked before turning on the ignition?

11. What are the first two things to consider when planning your departure? What is the third factor to consider?

12. Experience shows that diligent use of a checklist in going through your boat each day before starting the engine or raising sail will uncover one or more potential problems, how often?

    a. Almost every time you check your boat

    b. On average, about one out of every three times you check your boat

    c. Only once or twice a season

    d. Rarely

9

Leaving from a Beach, Mooring, or Anchor

With your boat and equipment all checked out, your engine warmed up, your departure planned, and your crew and guests all understanding what they are supposed to do, you are ready to get underway. Depending upon whether you're pulled up to a beach, at anchor, or on a mooring, different procedures are required.

LEAVING A BEACH UNDER POWER

Deep Water

When the bottom drops away from the shoreline fast enough that you have moderately deep water right on up to the beach, leaving that beach can be pretty straightforward. First, either someone on shore pushes you off, or you use your engine(s) to pull yourself off the beach. Next, you back away from the beach slowly until there is room to turn the boat, shift to forward, and make your turn. Finally, you head out slowly until you're well clear of the area and can accelerate to cruising speed safely.

Unfortunately, that scenario ignores the real-world hazards usually found at every beach. These may include small children playing in the water (possibly quite close to your boat); swimmers; such underwater obstructions as rocks or shoals (shallow areas); above-water obstructions, including mooring buoys, pilings, docks, channel markers, and other boats; and the wind, current, and waves. One purpose of planning your departure is to avoid all of these hazards.

Shallow Water

When your boat is beached in shallow water where the bottom falls off gradually, it may be necessary to walk the boat out to deeper water before you can start your engine. This means, of course, that you'll have to warm up your engine while someone stands in the water, holding your bow into the wind or current.

Why? The answer is this: If you have an outboard, you shouldn't run the engine until you can lower the drive into the water, because the cooling water intake is in the drive unit. If the drive unit isn't in the water, your water pump can't suck up any cooling water, and it will be damaged quickly. Obviously, too, your engine will overheat.

The answer is a bit muddier when an I/O or standard inboard system is involved, because the cooling-water intake usually is in the bottom of the boat. However, if the water is too shallow to lower an I/O's drive unit, or it is so shallow that there are just a few inches of water between bottom and an inboard motorboat's propeller, there's probably enough mud or sand suspended in the water to be hard on your engine's cooling system. Even if there weren't too much mud or sand suspended in the water naturally, your propeller would stir up a good mess as soon as you put the engine into reverse, creating the same effect. By not starting the engine until the boat is in water two or three feet deep, you're more assured of clean cooling water.

You'll also need to figure out ahead of time how to get the person who walks the boat out, back on board. The best way is to use a boarding ladder that hangs over the side—safely away from the drive unit. When you are ready to go, the person simply turns the bow of the boat away from the beach so that the correct side of the boat swings toward him, and then climbs the boarding ladder. However, *under no circumstances should the engine be put into gear before that person is safely aboard the boat.* If you put the engine in gear while someone is climbing aboard and he or she falls back into the water as the stern comes around, your propeller—even if it is only turning at 600 or 700 RPM—could seriously or even fatally injure the person in the water.

LEAVING THE BEACH UNDER SAIL

Sailing off the beach is somewhat more complex. First, the skipper can't just back away from the shore. Instead, he must get the bow turned around at least parallel to the beach before he starts sailing. On a small daysailer requiring only a foot or two of water depth, it's easy for someone to pull the boat away from the beach, hold the bow into the wind while the sails are raised, and then climb aboard as he (she) turns the boat away from the wind to begin sailing.

On a larger sailboat, particularly one on which it is more difficult to climb aboard, you might consider a different strategy— walking the boat out to deep water, and putting out an anchor. Then you've got plenty of time to get your crew safely aboard, put up your sails, and make sure that everything is ready to go before raising your anchor and sailing away. Alternatively, if there is lots of room and the wind is not strong, the person in the water can walk the boat out to deep water, climb aboard, and then you can raise the sails while the boat simply drifts. But this is somewhat sloppier.

Why not put the sails up, and then have the person in the water simply push the bow off and climb the ladder to get aboard? You should not do this for the same reason that you don't put a motorboat in gear until the crew is safely aboard. Although you don't have to worry about a propeller, you do have to be concerned about the safety of the person in the water. When you push the bow of the sailboat away from the wind, the boat wants to start sailing, making it difficult for anyone to climb aboard—particularly if the wind is blowing hard enough to make the boat heel (lean over) away from the person trying to climb aboard. While it is possible to let the sails luff (flap in the wind) until he or she has climbed aboard, the flapping sails are snapping the lines (ropes) used to control them to and fro, themselves creating a hazard. So it's better to get your crew aboard before the sails are raised.

LEAVING ANCHOR UNDER POWER

Assuming that you've already planned a safe course to open water, the major challenge to leaving anchor under power is getting your anchor up safely and without strain.

On the surface, this may seem like a small challenge. However, depending upon the size of your boat, the weather conditions, and how deeply you've dug in your anchor, getting the anchor up and into the boat safely may be no small feat. For example, if your boat is a 15-foot outboard, the water is calm, the current is light, and you've been anchored for fishing, you can probably just grab your anchor line (rode) and pull it in. If there are waves of any size running, however, it's not quite as simple. First, under these conditions it's important to run the anchor line through a chock on the bow as you pull it in so that your boat is always headed into the wind and waves. If the line doesn't go through such a chock, your boat may try to turn broadside to the waves. In that situation, you can easily swamp the boat trying to pull up the anchor. If the anchor is dug in and hard to break loose, you may be tempted to stand up so that you can pull harder. However, *under no circumstances should you stand up in a small boat to pull in the anchor.*

DOVER MAN MISSING AFTER BOAT OVERTURNS—A Dover man apparently drowned in the Delaware Bay trying to swim to shore Friday night and his fishing partner was rescued after their boat capsized near the mouth of the St. Jones River, police said.

James E. Dukes, 38, and John Gadsden, 39, were fishing about 100 feet from shore in the Delaware Bay about 10:00 P.M. when they decided to head back to shore, police said.

When Dukes stood up in the 14-foot aluminum boat to pull up the anchor, the boat overturned in rough waters, tossing both men into the bay.

Both men held on to the boat before Dukes decided to swim to shore. In his attempt, the tide carried him into the bay, police said. Meanwhile, Gadsden yelled for help [and was rescued].[1]

That news report, as well as others in these pages, testifies also to the importance of staying with your boat if it is capsized or swamped.

On a larger boat, the requirements for getting your anchor in safely are very different. The first requirement is good communication between the person on the bow who is actually raising the anchor, and the person at the steering wheel or tiller. On mid-sized boats, that communication isn't too difficult; the two people can just talk to each other.

However, once boat length gets much above 30 feet, distance and engine noise can make communication between the bow and helm difficult. Why? Three reasons: (1) Usually the boat is coming up into the wind, so the skipper's words shouted forward are blown away by the wind; (2) usually the crew member is facing forward when he (she) tries to shout back to the skipper, and his (her) words can't be understood; and (3) usually the noise of the engine(s) makes it difficult for the skipper to hear, even under the best of circumstances. As a result, it's not at all unusual for the skipper and the crew member on the bow to wind up shouting at each other with anger and frustration. When the two people happen to be husband and wife, or parent and child, the effect can be devastating.

This communication problem, however, is easily solved with a few simple hand signals that can be used day or night if you have a deck light. The thought isn't original with us. Susan and I learned about hand signals in one of the cruising-school courses we took in the first years of our marriage. Since then, we've used them so much that they are now second nature. We use them when anchoring, picking up a mooring, even sometimes when docking.

We have eight basic signals. All but the last one are used with the person on the bow facing forward, his (her) back to the helmsman (Figure 20):

1. Pointing straight ahead with one or both hands means either

1. *News-Journal,* Wilmington, Delaware, August 17, 1987.

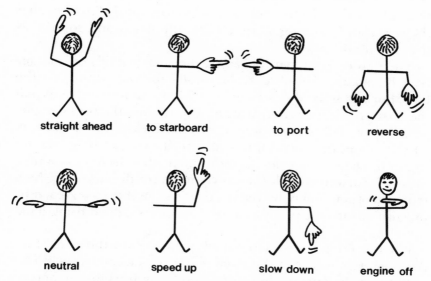

FIG. 20.   Hand signals: A person on the bow can use simple hand signals, like those shown here, to direct the person who is controlling the boat.

"steer straight ahead" or "shift into forward gear," whichever is appropriate.

2. Pointing to starboard means that the helmsman should "steer to starboard" until the pointing stops, then straighten out.

3. Pointing to port means that the helmsman should "steer to port" until the pointing stops, then straighten out.

4. Waving one or both hands down and backward (as if pushing something down and behind you) means "go into reverse."

5. Waving one or both hands sideways with the palms down means "shift into neutral."

6. Holding your arm out to your side and pointing toward the sky with a jabbing motion means "speed up" until the pointing stops.

7. Holding your arm out to your side and pointing down with a jabbing motion means "slow down" until the pointing stops.

8. Turning to face the skipper and drawing a finger across your throat means "turn off the engine."

While these particular signals work well for us, you may find that others work better for you. It makes no difference what the signals are so long as they serve the need, and so long as they are used.

A second essential part of raising the anchor safely on a larger boat is making the job easy physically for the person on the bow. For example, the person on the bow should *not* try to pull the boat up to the anchor. Instead, you can use the boat's engine to move toward the anchor slowly as the anchor line is taken in. In calm conditions with little current, it may not be necessary to put the engine in gear for more than a few seconds at a time to ease it forward. Under more vigorous conditions, more help from the engine may be required. It's something you learn by practicing, with the person on the bow directing you using hand signals.

When the boat is over the anchor, too often the person on the bow tries to break the anchor out of the mud or sand by pulling on the anchor line. It's a good way for him (or her) to hurt his back. Instead, he should simply pull the anchor line tight and snub it around a cleat, being sure it is run properly through the bow chock. If the boat's up-and-down motion in the waves isn't enough to break the anchor out of the mud or sand, you can use the engine to go forward briefly to break it out. If that doesn't do the trick, the anchor may be fouled (caught on something), and you may have to go swimming (with the boat's engine turned off) to get it free.

Once the anchor is loose, it usually comes up easily, and, with the anchor safely on deck, you can begin to make your way slowly to open water. Although you have already planned your path through the anchorage, you'll need to keep alert for any new hazards that you didn't see when you made your earlier check. For example, there may now be a windsurfer nearby that you hadn't seen before, or a couple of small fishing boats drifting with the current. Moreover, there's still one other detail involving the anchor that mustn't be overlooked: The person on the bow has to stow (put away) the anchor securely so that it can't come loose and, possibly, fall overboard.

LEAVING ANCHOR UNDER SAIL

When a boat is lying to its anchor, its bow is generally headed into the wind. This lets you raise your sails safely, even in relatively strong winds. Once the sails are up and you begin pulling the boat up to the anchor (remember, you aren't using your engine this time), you'll find that the bow tends to swing through the wind so that first the wind is on one side, then the other. When the boat is nearly directly over the anchor, you should snub the anchor line so that the boat will break the anchor loose as the bow swings through the wind. And, as soon as the anchor is free, it has to be pulled up quickly so that it can't snag anything as your boat falls off the wind to begin sailing.

From a practical standpoint, you have to plan two paths to open water if you want to sail away from the anchor. Why? Because the path you follow will depend upon which side of the boat the wind is coming from when your anchor breaks loose. You'll have a preferred side, of course, but since things won't always work out the way you prefer, you have to be ready to deal with what you get, not necessarily with what you want.

If it's really important to have the wind on one side or the other when the anchor breaks loose, you can often make that happen by having a second crew member hold the jib out on the "wrong" side of the boat to help the wind push the bow in the desired direction. This procedure is called "backwinding the jib" (Figure 21). With the anchor line snubbed around a cleat, the wind blowing against the jib pushes the bow around the way you want it to go and, hopefully, breaks the anchor

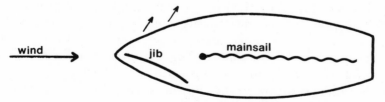

FIG. 21.   Backwinding the jib: By holding the jib out against the wind, you can use the wind to push your bow to the opposite side. Note: In this and subsequent sailboat illustrations, the wavy line is used to illustrate a sail that is "luffing," or flapping loosely in the wind.

loose at the same time. Then it's a matter of getting the jib out of the way by letting it go to the other side and luffing it somewhat to give your crew time to get the anchor up. With it safely on deck, you can bring in your sails and begin sailing along your planned course to open water—again, being alert to any hazards you hadn't noted earlier.

LEAVING YOUR MOORING

Leaving a mooring, whether under power or sail, is not much different strategically than leaving anchor. It is, however, much easier. Instead of pulling up an anchor, you are simply casting off a mooring line. There is, however, an additional obstacle you'll need to avoid, and that is your own mooring line—the one you'll drop into the water. You need to make certain that you don't wrap it around your propeller or snag your rudder as you pull away.

In practice, after you have planned your course to clear water and reviewed it with your crew and guests, the person on the bow simply removes the mooring line from the cleat (or cleats) and drops it overboard at the captain's command, but well away from the boat. Usually, there's a small float attached to the mooring line by a small piece of rope. That float and pendant must be dropped overboard with the mooring line—again, well away from the boat.

If you are under power, you should back one or two boat lengths away from the mooring before turning away and beginning to move forward, so that you don't run over the mooring line you have just cast off. If you're leaving under sail, you should raise the sails before casting off the mooring, and drop the mooring line as the bow passes through the wind toward the direction in which you want to begin sailing. If necessary, you can hold the jib out against the wind (i.e., "backwind" the jib) to help push your bow in the right direction, but usually it's not necessary in this situation.

Testing What You've Learned
(Answers can be found in Appendix C)

1. If you are leaving a beach under power and the bottom falls off gradually, what will you need to do before starting your engine?

2. TRUE or FALSE: If you have an inboard engine, it's OK to warm up your engine even in very shallow water, as long as your boat's not sitting on the bottom.

3. Why should you never put your engine in gear before you've gotten all of your crew into the boat?

4. What would be a safe procedure for leaving the beach under sail with a 25-foot sailboat—assuming its draft is shallow enough to let you get it up close to the beach in the first place?

5. When leaving the beach in a small sailboat, in what direction should you point the bow while raising the sails?

6. Why is it a good idea to run the anchor line through a bow chock when you are raising the anchor on a small boat?

7. What is one solution to the potential communication problem between the person on the bow pulling up the anchor, and the person at the steering position?

8. What's the best way to get a large boat up to its anchor?

9. What's the best way to break your anchor out of the mud or sand?

10. When leaving anchor under sail, why is it important to plan two paths to open water?

11. TRUE or FALSE: Once you've cast off the mooring line and pendant when leaving a mooring under power, you're clear to shift into forward and move on out.

10

Dock-Area Boating Skills

Two basic sets of skills are required for leaving or coming into a dock* or a slip safely: boat-handling skills, and the effective use of dock lines. Although the use of dock lines is essentially the same for all boats, boat-handling skills required for leaving a dock or getting into a slip may be very different, depending upon your boat's engine system. (Although most of the information in this chapter relates to boats with engines, the sections headed *Using the Current* and *Dock Lines* apply to unpowered sailboats as well. Coming up to a dock or slip under sail are covered in Chapters 24 and 25.)

If your boat is an outboard or inboard / outboard, for example, you have an advantage in maneuverability because you use the entire drive unit to steer the boat. Inboard engine systems, on the other hand, require boat-handling skills that involve learning about the so-called "paddle-wheel" effect of the propeller, the difference between "right-hand" and "left-hand" propellers, and the effect of the propeller wash on the rudder. Twin-engine inboards require still additional skills because of the maneuvering capabilities provided by having two engines.

---

* Technically, the word "dock" refers to the area of water in which your boat floats when it is tied up to a pier or a wharf. More commonly, however, "dock" is used to refer to a variety of piers, wharves, and bulkheads at which boats tie up, and that's how the word is used in this book.

THE PADDLE-WHEEL EFFECT

When your boat's propeller begins to turn, it not only pushes the boat forward or pulls it backward, depending upon which gear you're in, it also gives your stern a boost to one side or the other. This tendency of a propeller to push the stern sideways is most easily understood if you imagine the propeller as an old-fashioned paddle wheel like those once used on Mississippi River boats—hence the name, the "paddle-wheel effect." In this case, however, the paddle wheel is mounted sideways. As a result, it wants to push the stern of the boat to one side or the other, depending upon which direction the paddle wheel (propeller) is turning.

This effect can be a major factor when maneuvering a single-engine inboard at very slow speeds or when using only one engine of a twin-screw inboard. Although you do need to compensate for it sometimes by turning your steering wheel slightly when operating an outboard or I/O, the paddle-wheel effect is not usually a major factor in handling outboards or I/O boats, because the propeller unit is turned to steer the boat. Nor is it a factor when running with both engines of a twin-screw inboard, because the two propellers (paddle wheels) turn in opposite directions, canceling each other out.

The paddle-wheel effect is strong when a boat is standing still in the water. As the boat begins to move forward through the water, the paddle-wheel effect becomes negligible because it is quickly overwhelmed by the power of the boat's rudder. On the other hand, the paddle-wheel effect can remain quite strong on single-engine inboards when you are going in reverse, because the boat's rudder is relatively ineffective when moving backward.

"RIGHT-HAND" OR "LEFT-HAND" PROPELLERS?

As you look at a boat from the stern, the propellers on most outboards, I/Os, and single-engine inboards turn clockwise when the boat is going forward. These are called "right-hand" propellers; their blades are oriented to push the boat forward when

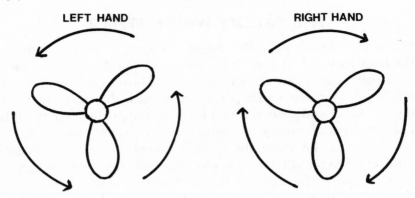

LEFT HAND   RIGHT HAND

FIG. 22. Left-hand and right-hand propellers: Left-hand propellers turn counterclockwise when viewed from the boat's stern. Right-hand propellers turn clockwise.

the propeller is turning to the right (clockwise). As a result of the paddle-wheel effect, right-hand propellers tend to push the stern to the right, or to starboard in forward gear. When operating in reverse, right-hand propellers tend to push the stern to the left, or to port (Figure 22).

On some inboard boats, the engine is mounted using a vee-drive unit, which has the effect of reversing the direction a propeller turns when in forward gear. These boats generally have "left-hand" propellers—propellers whose blades are oriented to push the boat forward when they are rotating to the left, or counterclockwise. As a result, when you shift into forward in a single-engine vee-drive boat, the propeller wants to push the stern to port. When you shift into reverse, the propeller wants to push it to starboard.

TWIN-ENGINE INBOARDS

If a boat has twin engines, both with right-hand propellers, the paddle-wheel effect is quite strong, particularly in reverse. While this has not been a particular problem in twin-engine outboard or I/O installations because the paddle-wheel effect is easily offset by turning the drive units slightly to one side or the other, it would be intolerable with twin-engine inboards. For that rea-

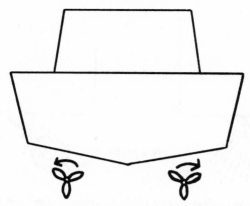

FIG. 23.   Counter-rotating propellers: Twin-engine inboards have a right-hand propeller on the starboard engine, a left-hand propeller on the port engine. Increasingly, I / Os are also using counter-rotating propellers.

son, the engines on twin-screw inboards have been modified so that the starboard engine uses a right-hand propeller and the port engine uses a left-hand propeller (Figure 23). In this way, the paddle-wheel from one engine offsets the paddle-wheel from the other—if both are in the same gear.

Putting one engine in reverse and the other in forward, however, will have both paddle-wheels kicking the stern in the same direction. With one propeller pushing forward and the other pulling backward, they will also tend to twist the boat around on its stern. The practical result is that the paddle-wheel effect of the two propellers works with the twisting effect to make the boat turn in its own length.

Alternatively, it's possible also to use the paddle-wheel effect and thrust of just one engine to move the stern sideways without moving the bow as much. As you will see, the implications of all of these capabilities for maneuvering twin-screw inboards at slow speed are enormous.

PROPELLER WASH

As you shift into forward and the propeller begins to turn, it shoots a stream of water out from the stern of the boat. That

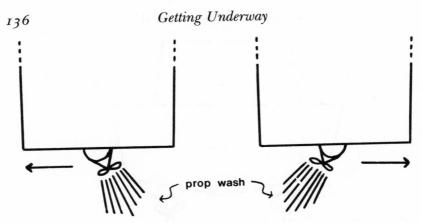

Fig. 24.   Steering outboards and I / Os: Outboards and I / Os are steered by turning the drive unit so that the water thrust from the propeller (the prop wash) pushes the stern to one side or the other.

stream of water is called the "propeller wash," or simply, "prop wash," and is part of what pushes the boat through the water. Moreover, outboards and I / Os are steered by turning the drive unit to direct the prop wash to one side or the other (Figure 24).

Sometimes, the prop wash can also be used to help steer a boat with an inboard engine. For example, when the boat is standing still and you shift into forward, the propeller wash flows past the rudder much faster than the surrounding water does, since the boat hasn't yet started to move. If the rudder is turned to one side or the other, the prop wash will push on the turned rudder and shove the stern sideways (Figure 25).

This effect can be quite useful. For example, if the rudder is turned so that the prop wash and the paddle-wheel effect are working together, you can "kick" the stern a substantial distance to the side. On the other hand, the force of the prop wash on your rudder can be used to offset the paddle-wheel effect when first starting up in a single-engine inboard (Figure 26).

While the propeller wash does not affect steering when the engine is in reverse (because the propeller is shooting the water away from the rudder), you can still use its effect to help you "steer" the boat when moving backward. You simply shift from reverse to forward while the boat continues coasting backward,

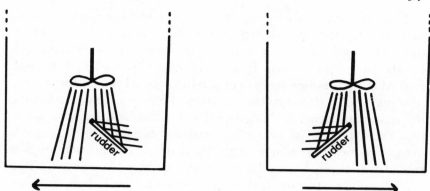

FIG. 25. Steering single-engine inboards: The stern of an inboard can be moved to one side or the other by turning the rudder so that water thrust from the propeller (prop wash) pushes against the rudder, shoving the stern to the side.

give a burst of power (in forward) so that the prop wash pushes against the turned rudder for a few seconds to kick the stern in the desired direction, and then shift back into reverse and continue backing up. The use of the propeller wash to help maneuver your boat will come up repeatedly.

prop wash   paddle wheel

FIG. 26. Using prop wash to offset the paddle-wheel effect: In this illustration the paddle-wheel effect of the right-hand propeller tends to pull the stern to starboard, while the prop wash is pushing against the rudder to move the stern to port.

The effectiveness of prop wash in moving the stern around, however, can vary greatly from one boat to another. For example, some older sailboats have a cut-out in the rudder to make room for the propeller. When those rudders are turned, only a small part of the propeller wash ever pushes against the rudder; most of it just shoots through the aperture. On some newer sailboats, the distance between the propeller and the rudder is so large that the force of the propeller wash pushing on the rudder is greatly reduced. Similarly, high-speed inboards and twin-engine inboards typically have relatively small rudders. As a result, there is less surface area for the prop wash to push against, and the effect on steering at slow speeds is relatively little. For these reasons, you need to experiment with your boat to find out just how useful prop wash can be if your motorboat or auxiliary sailboat has an inboard motor.

(Note: I will repeatedly mention putting your boat in gear and giving a "burst" of power, or a "strong burst" of power, to help maneuver your boat. How strong that burst should be needs to be determined for your boat. On our 18,000-pound-displacement sailboat with a 23-horsepower diesel engine, for example, even a very strong burst of power won't make the boat move dramatically. The same amount of throttle used on a smaller, lighter-weight boat could cause a sudden lurch that would knock someone off his (her) feet or even overboard. So, read the words, understand what is intended, and then experiment with your boat to determine just how much of a "burst of power" you need to give to perform any of these maneuvers.)

USING THE CURRENT

When your boat is standing still at a dock and there is a current running, many times you can move your stern to one side or the other simply by turning your rudder toward or away from the dock.* The water flowing against the rudder will do the

---

* When I speak of turning the rudder "toward" or "away from" the dock, I am referring to the back end of the rudder. Similarly, when I speak of turning the rudder to port or starboard, it is the back end of the rudder that turns to port or starboard.

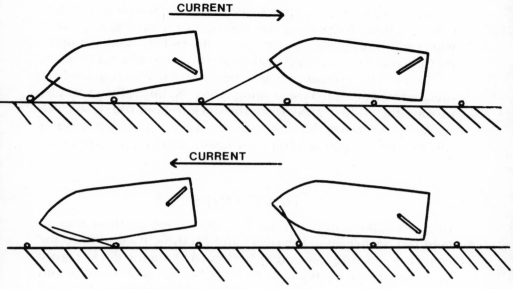

FIG. 27. Using the current to hold your stern close to or away from the dock: When your inboard motorboat is tied to the dock, you can hold your stern toward or off the dock by turning your rudder so that the current pushes the stern in or out.

work for you. For example, if the current is coming from forward, turning the rudder away from the dock will hold the stern close; turning it toward the dock will hold your stern off. If the current comes from astern, it has the opposite effect. You can hold your stern close to the dock by turning your rudder toward the dock. Similarly, your stern will tend to stay off the dock if you turn your rudder away from the dock (Figure 27). Using your rudder in this way to move your stern toward or away from the dock is an important part of coming in to or leaving a dock.

CREATING YOUR OWN "CURRENT"

Sometimes when you're coming in to or getting ready to leave a dock, you need to hold your stern close to or away from the dock while taking care of your dock lines, but there isn't any current to help you. In this situation, you can simply make your own "current" by putting the engine in forward gear so that your prop wash pushes water against the rudder. You can make the "current" stronger or weaker by running the engine faster or slower. Then you simply use the rudder just as you would if there were a real current coming from the bow—for example, turning the rudder away from the dock to hold the stern close in. As noted above, the effectiveness of your propeller wash in this situation depends upon your boat's rudder configuration.

DOCK LINES

In general, boats have two kinds of dock lines: (1) those used to hold the boat close to the dock; and (2) those used to keep the boat from moving forward or backward along the dock (Figure 28). The first group typically includes bow lines, stern lines, and breast lines. The second group includes "spring" lines. Forward spring lines are made fast at the stern or middle of the boat and tied ashore at a point forward so that they keep the boat from drifting backward. Aft spring lines are made fast to the bow or middle of the boat and tied ashore at a point aft so that they keep the boat from drifting forward.

Usually, if you're going to be at a dock for only a short time, bow and stern lines may be all that are needed. If there is a strong current or wind, however, a spring line from the bow or stern may be useful not only for holding the boat in position at

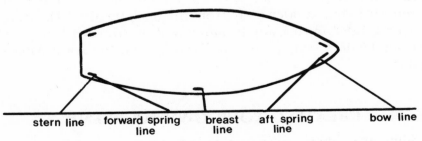

| stern line | forward spring line | breast line | aft spring line | bow line |

FIG. 28. Basic dock lines: The principal function of the bow, stern, and breast lines is to hold the boat close to the dock. The function of spring lines is to keep the boat from moving forward and aft.

the dock, but also when leaving the dock. If you will be tied up for more than a few minutes, forward and aft spring lines should be used, in any case. While breast lines aren't used very often for tying up, they can be very important in leaving a slip when there's a strong wind blowing from one side or the other.

There is still another consideration in placing your dock lines—the tide, if there is one. If there is a rise and fall of the tide of more than a foot or two, you should not run your bow and stern lines perpendicular to the dock. If you do, and the tide drops 5 feet, either your boat will be left hanging by your dock lines, or you'll pull the cleats out of your deck and the boat could be set adrift. The problem is avoided simply by running your stern line to a dock piling or cleat 10 or 12 feet behind your boat and the bow line to a point 10 or 12 feet in front of your boat. In a slip, many boaters cross their stern lines to gain the same advantage. In this way, your boat can go up and down with the tide as if attached to two levers. Of course, you should not use a breast line in this situation; you may, however, still want to use a spring line.

Testing What You've Learned
(Answers can be found in Appendix C)

1. TRUE or FALSE: The paddle-wheel effect is strongest when a boat is moving slowly forward.

2. Why does the paddle-wheel effect in a single-engine inboard have more impact on steering when the boat is moving backward than when the boat is moving forward?

3. TRUE or FALSE: Most boats have right-hand propellers.

4. When in forward, what direction (port or starboard) does a right-hand propeller tend to push the stern?

5. When in reverse, what direction (port or starboard) does a right-hand propeller tend to push the stern?

6. If your single-engine inboard has a right-hand propeller and you have a choice of coming up to a dock from either direction, what side of your boat would you want the dock on to use the paddle-wheel effect to best advantage in docking?

7. What kind of propeller (right-hand or left-hand) is usually found on the port engine of a twin-engine inboard? On the starboard engine?

8. What do you call the stream of water that the propeller shoots out from the stern of the boat?

9. TRUE or FALSE: A boat's prop wash will affect steering more when the engine is in reverse.

10. If you are alongside a dock with a current coming from the bow, what direction should you turn your rudder so that the current will hold your stern close to the dock? Away from the dock?

11. What is the purpose of a forward spring line? Of an aft spring line?

12. What is the purpose of crossing your stern lines if your boat is in a slip?

11

Leaving the Dock

Depending upon the wind, the current, and the crowd, taking your departure from a dock may be as easy as pulling your car away from the curb at six o'clock on a Sunday morning; far more difficult than almost any circumstance you can imagine with your car; or somewhere between the two extremes. In the simplest situation, you may need only let go your lines, push the bow away from the dock, and move out carefully. In the worst situation, you may need to use your dinghy to set an anchor and pull your boat away from the dock by taking in on your anchor line.*

Planning for leaving the dock should begin before you tie up. For example, if you have an outboard, an I/O, or a single-engine inboard boat, you should approach the dock—if you have a choice—so that the paddle-wheel effect will help you when it's time to depart. With a right-hand propeller, that means tying up with the dock to port. With a left-hand propeller, it means putting the dock to starboard. Another example: If you're docking in an area with strong tidal currents, you may want to come up to the dock positioned so that you'll be headed into the current when it's time to take your departure—even though it might make your initial approach a little more difficult. These, at least, are the kinds of things you may want to consider.

When it's time to leave the dock, whether you've been there overnight or for only 30 minutes to take on fuel, your strategy

---

* Although most of this chapter relates to boats with engines, the section headed *"Kedging Off" the Dock* also applies to sailboats without engines.

will be determined by one or more of three factors: first, whether there are other boats in front of you; second, the strength and direction of the wind; third, the strength and direction of the current.

In general, the most common circumstances you'll run into when leaving a dock are contained within the five situations that follow: (1) There are no boats in front of you; (2) you are boxed in by other boats, and the current / wind (whichever will have the greater influence on the boat) is from the bow; (3) you are boxed in by other boats, and the current / wind is from the stern; (4) the wind is blowing off the dock; and (5) the wind is blowing toward the dock. The key to handling all of these situations well is in making good use of your dock lines, the paddle-wheel effect of your propeller, and—depending upon your boat—the effect of the prop wash or current on your rudder. The procedures described in the following pages all assume that you've started and warmed your engine properly before you begin to cast off your dock lines. I assume in all cases that you have fenders in position to keep the boat from bumping against the dock. Where there is a special need to use a fender, it is noted specifically.

Situation No. 1

NO BOATS IN FRONT OF YOU

Most of the time, this is one of the easiest circumstances you can encounter, regardless of where the wind and / or current are coming from. The exception is when there is a strong wind blowing your boat up against the dock. Under that circumstance, it doesn't make any difference whether you're boxed in by other boats or not—getting away from the dock is more difficult, and the procedure is described in Situation No. 5.

Assuming that the wind is not a problem, however, your strategy is straightforward: You should remove your dock lines in a sequence that allows the last line to hold your boat in position at the dock, push the bow away from the dock when the way is clear, cast off the last dock line, and move out. If the current / wind is from astern, you can use a stern line to hold

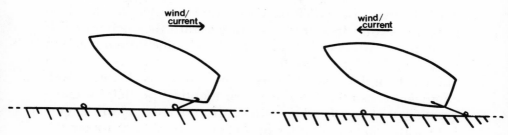

FIG. 29. Leaving a dock—bow-first: When pulling away from a dock bow-first, the last line off should be the stern line.

the boat in position until you're ready to leave. If, however, the current / wind is from the bow, you'd probably use a forward spring line, rigged from your stern cleat, to hold the boat. That spring line will not only hold your boat in position, but it will also let you push the bow away from the dock when you're ready to shove off (Figure 29).

In any case, the specific procedures are as follows:

1. Check to be sure the way is clear for you to leave the dock safely (i.e., there isn't any boat traffic that will create a hazard).

2. Remove all dock lines except either your stern line (if the current / wind is from astern) or the forward spring line (if the current / wind is from the bow).

3. Check the boat traffic once again. When the way is clear, push off at the bow and cast off the last dock line.

4. Put the engine in forward gear, and move on out. If you are moving with the current, remember that you must use enough power to give your boat steerage. While outboards and I / Os have an advantage because the drive unit is what steers the boat, any boat that depends upon a rudder for steering must be moving faster than the water around it for the rudder to be effective; otherwise, you'll just be swept along by the current, unable to steer. Also, you'll need to take the paddle-wheel effect into consideration, as follows:

Outboards and I / Os: Most outboards and I / Os have right-hand propellers. As a result, the paddle-wheel effect will tend to kick your stern safely away from the dock when you shift into forward, if the dock is to port. If, however, the dock is to starboard, the paddle-wheel will try to kick your stern in to the dock. In that case, you'll have to counteract the paddle-wheel by turning your drive unit(s) slightly toward the dock for a few seconds to push your stern away from the dock when you first start moving. The procedure is the same on boats with twin outboards and on most boats with twin I/Os, because both engines are usually equipped with identical propellers, exaggerating the paddle-wheel effect. If you have a twin-engine I/O with counter-rotating propellers, you should follow the procedure described for twin-engine inboards.

Single-Engine Inboards: If you have a right-hand propeller and the dock is to port, the paddle-wheel effect will tend to keep the stern off the dock as you begin to move ahead, particularly if you give an initial one- or two-second burst of power to start the boat moving. That initial surge usually will do more to kick your stern sideways than to push the boat forward.

If the dock is to starboard, you'll need to turn the rudder toward the dock initially so that the prop wash counteracts the paddle-wheel effect (Figure 30). Here, too, an initial one- or two-second burst of power is helpful. Once the boat is moving, just bring the rudder back amidships and steer on out. The same techniques apply if you have a left-hand propeller; the directions are simply reversed.

Twin-Engine Inboards: If your boat is an inboard with two engines or a twin-engine I/O with counter-rotating props, you

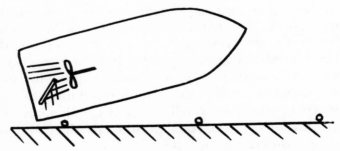

Fig. 30. Keeping your stern clear (single-engine inboard): The paddle-wheel effect may make your stern bump the dock as you begin to pull away. This can be prevented by turning the rudder toward the dock and giving a short surge of power to push the stern out from the dock as you start up. You then simply ease off on the power, straighten out the rudder, and steer on out—carefully.

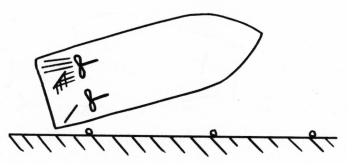

Fig. 31. Keeping your stern clear (twin-engine inboard): You can pull the stern away from the dock by starting out with the "outboard" engine. Both the paddle-wheel and the prop wash on the turned rudder will pull your stern clear of the dock. Then you simply straighten out the rudder, shift the second engine into forward, and steer on out—carefully.

should use the engine that is farther away from the dock for getting underway, because the paddle-wheel effect of that engine will work with the prop wash to pull your stern clear (Figure 31). Turn both rudders toward the dock, give an initial one- or two-second burst of power to maximize the paddle-wheel and prop-wash effects, and, as soon as the stern is clear, put the second engine in gear, straighten out the rudders, and move on out at a safe speed.

Situation No. 2

BOATS FORWARD AND AFT—CURRENT / WIND FROM THE BOW

In the first situation, you'll recall that you had to use a forward spring line rigged from the stern cleat to hold the boat in position when the current / wind was from the bow. Situation No. 2 is not much different, except that there's a boat in front of you. That means you have to get the bow out far enough to clear that boat before you begin to move forward (Figure 32). You may also need to use a fender to cushion your stern against the dock as you push out on the bow. In any case, the procedure is as follows:

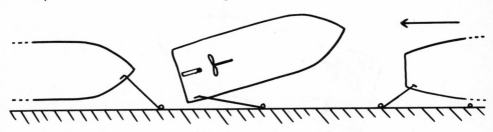

FIG. 32. Leaving a crowded dock—current/wind from the bow (single-engine inboard): When the current/wind is from the bow, you can use a forward spring line to "spring" your bow out from the dock before shifting into forward gear. Then steer as needed to clear the dock.

1. If you do not have a forward spring line running from your stern cleat, rig one. Otherwise, adjust your forward spring as necessary so that it can be cast off easily.

2. Rig a fender at the stern where the boat will push against the dock as the bow swings out.

3. Remove the aft spring line and then the stern line. At this point, only the forward spring and the bow lines should remain.

4. Check boat traffic to be sure the way is clear.

5. Keeping the rudder amidships (in the middle), take off the bow line and push the bow away from the dock.

6. As the bow clears the boat ahead of you, put the engine in forward and cast off your last line. Be careful, however, that the line does not fall into the water where it could get tangled in the propeller.

7. If necessary, steer to offset the paddle-wheel effect so that your stern doesn't bump the dock. Once the stern is clear, just move out slowly into the waterway.

8. Pull all fenders back into the boat.

Situation No. 3

BOATS FORWARD AND AFT—CURRENT/WIND FROM THE STERN

This is one of the more difficult situations. In general, the basic strategy is to go out backward—against the current/wind. The reason for going out stern-first is this: If the current is from astern and at all strong, it may sweep you into the boat in front of you before you can clear the dock, if you try to go out bow-first. A strong wind from astern can have the same effect. So, in this situation, you should back away from the dock to give you better control over your boat (Figure 33). Even when backing out, however, you'll need to keep your stern headed directly enough into the current/wind so that your boat won't be swept forward into another boat. If you get your stern out too far, you'll be nearly sideways to the current/wind and be pushed down along the dock while you are trying to back away from it.

Depending upon whether you have an outboard or I/O, a single-engine inboard, or a twin-engine inboard, there are enough differences in procedure that we'll look at each boat type separately.

Outboards and I/Os: The ease of steering an outboard or I/O in reverse by turning the drive unit to pull the stern where you want it to go, makes getting out in this situation relatively easy. The key point is to get your stern out far enough to clear the boat behind yours. The procedure is as follows:

1. If you do not already have an aft spring line, rig one.

2. Cast off the bow and stern lines, and push the stern far enough away from the dock that you will be able to steer clear of the boat behind you easily.

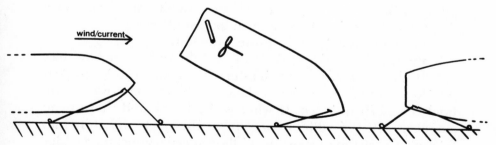

FIG. 33. Leaving a crowded dock—current/wind from astern (single-engine inboard): When the current is from astern, you can use an aft spring line to "spring" your stern away from the dock before reversing out. Note that the rudder in this illustration is turned away from the dock to let the current help swing the stern clear.

3. Turn the drive unit(s) so they are pointed away from the dock, put the engine(s) in slow reverse, and cast off the aft spring line. Either your crew on the bow or someone ashore should fend off the bow to keep it from hitting the dock as you begin to move backward.

4. Back slowly away from the dock at about a 30-degree angle so that the current / wind can't carry you forward into another boat.

5. When you are well clear of the dock and the other boats, shift into forward, turn to your desired heading, and move ahead slowly. Remember, however, that you will be moving with the current; you will need enough boat speed through the water to be able to steer your boat.

Single-Engine Inboards: With an inboard system, you may need to use an aft spring line running from the bow back to a piling or sturdy dock cleat somewhere around the middle of your boat; if there isn't anyone ashore to help you, the spring line should be looped over the dock cleat or piling so that you can cast it off from the boat. You will also need one or more fenders to cushion the bow against the dock as the stern swings out. Finally, because of the time it takes to get lines in and fenders adjusted, you will probably need to use your rudder to help hold the stern to the dock until you're ready to push off.

The procedure for getting clear of the dock with a single-engine inboard in this situation is as follows:

1. If you do not have an aft spring leading from the bow to a piling or dock cleat amidships, rig one. In any case, make sure that the aft spring is snug and can be cast off easily.

2. Put fenders in place to protect the bow.

3. Remove the forward spring line, followed by the bow line.

4. If there is a current from astern, turn your rudder toward the dock so that the force of the current on your rudder will hold the stern in place. If wind is the factor and there is no current, turn the rudder away from the dock and shift into forward to use the prop wash at idling speed against the rudder to hold your stern in place.

5. Remove the stern line. At this point, the aft spring line is doing double duty: it's holding the bow in; and, it's keeping the boat from moving forward. The stern is being held in place by the rudder.

6. Push the stern away from the dock by turning the rudder so that either the current or the propeller wash does the work. If there is a strong wind from astern, it will help push the stern out once you get it away from the dock. In fact, you'll need to be careful lest the wind blow your stern out farther than you had planned—not a problem, just something you may have to deal with.

7. As the stern clears the boat behind you, put the engine in reverse, cast off the spring line, straighten out your rudder, and, with a moderate amount of throttle, begin backing away from the dock at an angle of about 30 degrees. If the wind starts to blow your stern around too far, you may have to turn your rudder toward the dock to help steer your stern against the wind. The person on the bow should get the spring line aboard promptly and pull the fenders up onto the deck.

When backing, you may also need to help steer your boat by using the prop wash on the rudder to kick the stern to one side or the other. As we noted earlier, you do this by: (1) throttling down to idling speed; (2) putting the rudder hard to port (if you want to kick the stern to starboard) or to starboard (if you want to kick it to port); (3) shifting into forward; (4) giving a short burst of power to kick the stern over with the propeller wash; and (5) shifting back into reverse to continue movement backward. While breaking this procedure down into five distinct steps makes it seem complicated, all five steps usually take only ten seconds or so. Done properly, in fact, your boat never fully stops moving backward.

One note of caution: Hold onto the wheel or tiller firmly when turning the rudder while your boat is moving backward. The force of the water on the rudder can jerk the wheel or tiller right out of your hands as the rudder passes through the centerline and over to the other side.

8. When the boat is well clear of the dock, shift into forward and give a good burst of power to stop the backward movement, and turn your rudder to bring the boat around to the desired heading. Then reduce power and move forward carefully.

Twin-Engine Inboards: Having two engines makes life simpler, because you have much more control when backing and turning. However, the basic strategy remains the same: You will need to spring out your stern and back away from the dock. There's also one complicating factor—and that's one of vocabulary. With a twin-engine installation, it is common practice to refer to the engine closest to the dock as the "inboard" engine and the one farther away from the dock as the "outboard" engine. The reference, however, has nothing to do with the type of engine, only its relative position to the dock. With that understood, the detailed procedure is as follows:

1. If you do not have an aft spring leading from the bow to a piling or dock cleat amidships, rig one. In any case, make sure your aft spring is snug and can be cast off easily. Also, rig fenders as needed to protect the bow as you spring your stern out.

2. Remove the forward spring line, followed by the bow line.

3. If there is a current from astern, turn your rudders toward the dock so that the force of the current on them will help hold the stern in place. If there is no current or that doesn't do the job, put the "inboard" engine (the engine closest to the dock) into forward and turn the rudders away from the dock. Usually, the combination of the paddle-wheel effect and the prop wash from the "inboard" engine on the rudder will hold the stern in.

4. Remove the stern line.

5. To move the stern away from the dock, put the "inboard" engine in neutral, turn the rudders toward the dock, and put the "outboard" engine in forward. The combined effects of the paddle-wheel, the propeller wash on the rudder of the "outboard" engine, and the forward thrust against the spring line will normally do the job without your having to use much power.

6. As the stern clears the boat behind you, straighten the rudders, put both engines in reverse, cast off the spring line, and, with a moderate amount of throttle, begin backing away from the dock at an angle of about 30 degrees. The person on the bow should get the spring line aboard promptly and pull the fenders up onto the deck.

When backing away from the dock, you would normally use both engines with the rudders straight—unless the wind is trying to blow your stern around. In that circumstance, you can offset the wind by turning your rudders toward the dock and, if necessary, giving extra power to the "outboard" engine.

7. When the boat is clear of both the dock and the other boats, slow both engines to an idle, shift the "inboard" engine into forward, and give it a short burst of power to turn the boat to the desired heading. When the boat is headed correctly, shift the "outboard" engine into forward and move out with both engines at slow speed.

Situation No. 4
WIND BLOWING OFF THE DOCK

If the wind is blowing your boat away from the dock and there is a strong current, you should just ignore the wind and follow the steps outlined above for either Situation No. 2 or No. 3, depending upon whether the current is from your bow or stern. The wind will simply make it easier for you.

If, however, there is no current to contend with, this is an easy departure and essentially the same for all boats. You simply remove any spring lines, take off the bow line, push the bow out, remove the stern line, and let the wind blow you off the dock. When your bow is clear of the boat in front of you, put the engine(s) in forward and begin to make your way slowly out from the dock.

Situation No. 5
WIND BLOWING TOWARD THE DOCK

The fundamental strategy in this situation is the same for all boats: Spring the stern away from the dock so that it is pointing into the wind. "The stern?" you say. Yes, the stern. The reason is quite simple: Most boats don't have the power to swing their bows away from the dock against much of a wind. By the same token, however, most boats do have the power to spring their sterns out even against a fairly strong wind. And if you think the wind may be too strong to spring your stern out, it's time to think seriously about delaying your departure until the wind eases. The only alternatives are to be towed away from the dock or to take an anchor out in the dinghy and use it to pull the boat out, a procedure described at the end of this chapter.

Assuming the conditions are reasonable, the procedure is essentially the same for all boats—up to the point at which you begin to use your engine. At that point, small but significant differences do emerge, depending on your engine and steering configuration. The procedure begins:

1. If you do not have an aft spring line running from your bow to the dock amidships or a little forward of amidships, rig one. If it's necessary to shift the boat forward or aft to get that line rigged properly, do it.

2. Prepare fenders to cushion the bow against the dock as you spring the stern out. Note: The person at the bow may have to move the fenders as the stern swings away from the dock.

3. Remove the bow line.

4. If the forward spring line is carrying a load (because of a current), remove the stern line and then the forward spring. If the forward spring line is slack (not carrying a load), take off the forward spring and then the stern line.

Outboards and I/Os:

5. When the stern line or forward spring line is removed, turn the drive unit toward the dock and put the engine in forward gear. Gradually increase power as needed to push the stern out and into the wind, all the while keeping a sharp eye for other boat traffic (Figure 34).

6. As the stern comes into the wind, reduce power, shift into reverse, and straighten out the drive unit so that it begins to pull the boat away from the dock. Cast off the last line as soon as the boat begins to move back from the dock. When the line is free, increase power and back away smartly. The person on the bow should get the dock line aboard promptly and then pull all fenders up on deck.

Single-Engine Inboards:

5. When the stern line or forward spring line is removed, turn the rudder toward the dock, put the engine in forward, and give a sharp initial burst of power to kick the stern away from the dock. Reduce power, then increase power slowly as needed to keep the stern moving away from the dock and into the wind.

6. As the stern comes into the wind, reduce power, shift into

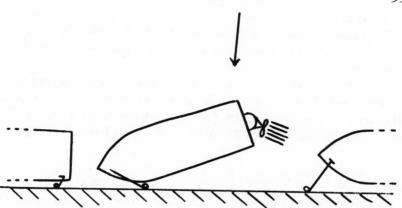

Fig. 34. Springing the stern away from the dock (outboard or I/O): Using an aft spring line, you can push the stern of an outboard or I/O away from the dock, even against a wind blowing perpendicular to the dock. When the stern is directly into the wind, you begin to back away, casting off the last line.

reverse, and increase power just enough to begin pulling the boat away from the dock. Cast off the remaining spring line as soon as the boat begins to move back from the dock. When the line is free, increase power and back away smartly, steering to keep your stern into the wind. The person on the bow should get the line aboard promptly and then pull all fenders up on deck.

Twin-Engine Inboards:

5. When the stern line or forward spring line is removed, turn the rudders toward the dock, put the "outboard" engine in forward, and give a sharp initial burst of power to kick the stern away from the dock. Reduce power, then increase power as needed—still using only the "outboard" engine—to keep the stern moving away from the dock and into the wind.

6. As the stern comes into the wind, reduce power, shift both engines into reverse, straighten out the rudders, and increase power just enough to start the boat moving backward. Cast off the remaining line as soon as the boat begins to move away from the dock. When the line is free, increase power and back away smartly. The person on the bow should get the line aboard promptly and then pull all fenders up on deck.

All Boats:

7. When the boat is well clear of the dock, reduce power, shift into forward, steer toward your desired heading, and move out carefully.

Usually, getting away from the dock in this situation will require help from someone on the dock so that your crew can handle fenders. The person on the dock can help push the stern of your boat away from the dock and cast off your last line.

"Kedging Off" the Dock

In the extreme circumstance that the wind is too strong to try springing your stern out and you cannot wait for the wind to ease, the only way to get your boat away from the dock other than being towed off is to take an anchor out in your dinghy, set it, return to the boat, and pull in on your anchor line to move the boat away from the dock until it is hanging on its anchor. This procedure is called "kedging off." From that point, you simply follow the procedures for leaving anchor under power (Chapter 9). However, there are some points to keep in mind, should you ever need to resort to this method of leaving a dock:

• Taking your anchor out in a dinghy in these conditions is itself very difficult. If you can find someone with a 15-foot outboard motorboat who will take the anchor out for you, have him do so; he'll have a much easier time of it. If you must take the anchor out in your dinghy, wear your life jacket. One technique is to hang the anchor from your dinghy's stern with a piece of light line that you can cut easily, and then coil the anchor line, or "rode," in the dinghy, feeding the line from the top of the coil to the stern of your boat. As you move away from the boat, the line will feed out from the dinghy. When you reach the end of the line, you simply cut the cord holding the anchor, and let the anchor drop. Of course, if your dinghy has an outboard engine, you have to keep the anchor line clear of your propeller. This procedure is best done with two people in the dinghy—one to handle the dinghy, the other to handle the anchor line and anchor.

• Your anchor should be set directly upwind from your stern (Figure 35). The idea is to position the anchor so that your boat

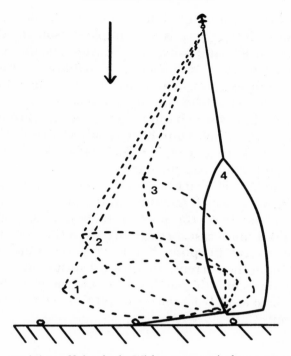

FIG. 35.   Kedging off the dock: With a strong wind or current pinning
your boat against a dock, it may be necessary to kedge (pull) your boat
off by setting an anchor and hauling in on the anchor line to pull the
bow out until it is headed into the wind.

will pivot on its stern rather than drag along the dock as the
bow is pulled out toward the anchor. You need to rig a sturdy
forward spring line from the stern cleat to the dock to hold
your stern in position as you begin to pull your bow away from
the dock.

• Your anchor rode should be twelve times or more the depth
of the water at the point where you drop your anchor, plus the
height of your boat's bow chock off the water. In other words,
if your bow chock is 3 feet above the water and the water is 15
feet deep where you are going to set your anchor, you should
have at least 216 feet of anchor line $[(15+3) \times 12]$. The dock
master should be able to tell you how deep the water is off the
dock.

• Any wind strong enough to pin you against the dock deserves your largest anchor. There is one simple reason for the extra length of anchor line and using your heaviest anchor: You don't have any way to "set" your anchor. You have to count on it digging in firmly as you winch or pull in your line and start to drag the anchor across the bottom. To make sure your anchor is well set, you should winch (pull) a fair amount of tension into your anchor rode while your boat is still secure to the dock. Once you've done that, you can slack off on it until you are ready to begin pulling your boat off.

With the anchor set, you can start the engine, cast off the bow lines, and begin to winch (pull) in on the anchor rode. As the bow is pulled out from the dock, you should ease off on the remaining dock lines, casting them off when they are no longer serving any useful purpose, but leaving the stern line—or, depending upon the current, the forward spring line—until last. As the bow comes into the wind, you should then use the engine to move the boat away from the dock and proceed to raise anchor and move out.

A FINAL NOTE

At times, you may find docks so crowded that the only way you can get in is to tie up alongside another boat. Under those circumstances, it is especially important to be careful when taking your departure. If you ignore the paddle-wheel effect of your propeller, for example, your stern won't simply bump into the dock; it will bump into the boat you've been tied to. Also, if circumstances require that you move your boat backward before you can get clear, think about the paddle-wheel effect. If your propeller in reverse will tend to pull your stern into the line of boats between you and the dock, forget the engine. Instead, move your boat back by hand. It may take a little longer; it might even be a little more work. But at least you and the people on the other boats won't be frantically trying to push your boat off while the paddle-wheel effect of your propeller in reverse keeps trying to scrape your stern along their hulls.

Testing What You've Learned
(Answers can be found in Appendix C)

1. All other things considered, when is the best time to begin planning for leaving a dock?

2. What are the three major factors you need to consider in preparing to leave a dock?

3. TRUE or FALSE: When getting ready to leave a dock, you should cast off all of your lines as nearly at the same time as possible, so that you aren't left hanging by one line while the wind and current try to push you into another boat before you can start using your engine to pull away from the dock.

4. Name three ways to control the stern of your boat at the dock after you have removed most of your dock lines.

5. Given a choice, which side of your boat would you prefer to tie next to the dock if your boat has a right-hand propeller? Which side would you choose if your boat has a left-hand propeller? Why?

6. You are backing your boat and need to kick your boat's stern to starboard using the prop wash to offset the paddle-wheel effect of your propeller. Three questions: Is the propeller in this situation a right-hand or left-hand propeller? Which side should the rudder be turned toward while you're reversing to help offset the paddle-wheel effect? And, which side should the rudder be turned toward when you shift into forward for the prop wash to kick the stern to starboard?

7. In general, if the current or wind, whichever has the strongest effect, is coming from your bow, should you plan to leave the dock moving forward or go out in reverse? Why?

8. In general, if the current or wind, whichever has the strongest effect, is coming from your stern, should you plan to leave the dock moving forward or go out in reverse? Why?

12

Leaving a Slip

The key to leaving a slip is using your dock lines to hold the boat in the best possible position for your departure.* For example, if the wind is coming from the side, you should shorten the lines to windward (the side toward the wind) so that you leave as much room as possible to leeward (the side away from the wind). Shortening your lines in this way lets you offset the tendency of the wind to blow the boat across the slip as you cast off your lines and begin to move out. Being aware of such effects of wind and current lets you compensate for them in planning and making your departure.

It's also important to prepare your lines for taking leave. This means making sure you can remove each line from the cleat or piling rapidly when the order is given to "cast off." In some situations, you may want to take most of the wraps off the cleat, snubbing the line to hold the boat in place so that you can cast the line off quickly when the order is given—*but using care that no line falls into the water where it can become tangled in a propeller.*

In addition, though it may seem self-evident, you should check to be sure it's safe to move out into the traffic before starting out of your slip—much like looking up and down the street before you back your car out of the driveway. This means (1) looking to be sure there aren't any boats coming that will create a hazard, and (2) giving a long blast (four to six seconds) on your horn to warn other boats that you are coming out.

* In general, this chapter relates only to boats with engines. I do not recommend attempting to sail into or out of a slip. Under all but the most favorable circumstances, you do not have adequate control of the boat to be safe in such confined quarters.

The following six situations illustrate the range of circumstances you'll encounter in leaving a slip. As in making any other departure, your engine(s) should be properly warmed up before you cast off your lines, so that they do not fail at a critical point.

Situation No. 1

CURRENT AND/OR WIND FROM THE STERN

In this situation, the idea is to hang from your stern lines until you are ready to go. As a result, your stern lines will be the last ones that you cast off (Figure 36). If, however, you are headed bow-first into the slip, it may be necessary to shorten your stern lines to hold your bow off the dock.

Stern-First in the Slip

Getting out of the slip in this situation is relatively easy. The current or wind will tend to push you out once you've cast off your lines. If the current (wind) is strong, however, you may want to put the engine(s) in reverse with just enough throttle to hold the boat in place before you cast off your stern lines. The procedure is as follows:

1. Adjust the stern lines as necessary to position the boat in the center of the slip.

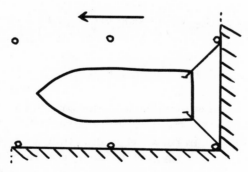

FIG. 36.   Leaving a slip—current/wind astern: When the current/wind is from the stern, the last two lines ashore when leaving a slip should be the stern lines.

2. Remove the spring lines, followed by the bow lines.

3. Put engine(s) in reverse as needed to take the load off the stern lines, and check to be sure the way is clear outside of your slip.

4. Sound a four- to six-second blast, cast off the stern lines, and shift into neutral. The current (wind) should begin pushing the boat forward out of the slip. By going into neutral rather than forward gear, you not only prevent the paddle-wheel effect from kicking your stern to the side, but you also keep your boat speed slow.

Outboards and I / Os:

5. As you clear the slip, shift into forward gear and head out slowly on your desired course, paying particular attention to the effect of the current so that it doesn't sweep you unsuspectingly into a hazardous area.

Single-Engine Inboards:

5. As mentioned earlier, a single-engine inboard boat moving at a slow speed with the current has very little steerage. For that reason, as you clear the slip, you should turn your rudder to steer across the current and shift into forward gear, giving a short burst of power. By using the prop wash to help you head across the current, you can gain steerage quickly without going too fast. If there isn't space to steer across the current, you'll have to gain steerage by shifting into forward and speeding up so that your boat is moving faster than the current. Once you are clear of the dock area, you can adjust your speed and head out on your desired course.

Twin-Engine Inboards:

5. When going with the current, even a twin-engine boat must be moving faster than the current for the rudders to be able to steer the boat. With two engines, however, you have the advantage of being able to use your engines and rudders to turn the boat to the desired course as you clear the slip. For example, if you want to turn to starboard, put the starboard engine in reverse and the port engine in forward gear so that the propellers twist the boat around. For turning to port, you do the opposite— port engine in reverse, starboard engine in forward (Figure 37). When the boat is headed in the correct direction, put both engines in forward and move out at a safe speed.

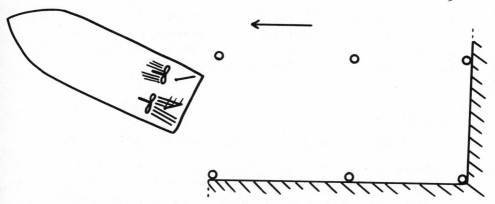

FIG. 37.   Turning across the current (twin-engine inboard): With the current from astern, a twin-engine inboard can use its engines—one in reverse, the other in forward—to turn the boat so that it is heading across the current, for improved steering control.

Bow-First in the Slip

The procedure for backing out of your slip in this situation is as follows:

1. Shorten your stern lines as necessary.

2. Cast off the spring lines, followed by the bow lines.

3. Put the engine(s) in reverse, as needed, to take the load off the stern lines. Check to be certain the way is clear outside your slip.

4. Give a four- to six-second blast with your horn and cast off the stern lines, increasing the throttle or shifting into reverse to back out of the slip when both lines are free.

If your boat is an outboard or I / O, you can simply back out of the slip, steering with the drive unit(s). With a single-engine inboard (no vee drive), you will probably want your rudder over to starboard to help you back up in a straight line. (With a vee drive, the rudder probably will go to port.) With two engines, your rudders should be aligned amidships. As long as both engines are in reverse and running at the same RPM, the boat should back up in a straight line.

5. When you are clear of the slip, turn the wheel or tiller hard over to turn your boat in the desired direction. After shifting

into forward, give a strong burst of power to kick your stern over, and begin your turn. Then ease up on the throttle to motor slowly around to your desired course. With twin engines, you can use your engines to turn the boat.

Situation No. 2
CURRENT AND / OR WIND FROM THE BOW

If the current or wind is coming from the bow, the bow lines are cast off last (Figure 38). Otherwise, you do everything the same as when the current is coming from astern, but in reverse. The procedures are essentially the same for all boats.

Stern-First in the Slip

This is a relatively easy situation. The only trick is in using your steering to counter any paddle-wheel effect when you start moving forward.

1. Shorten the bow lines as necessary to keep your stern from drifting back into the dock when other lines are removed.

2. Remove the spring lines first and then the stern lines.

3. If the current is at all strong, use the engine(s) as needed, in forward gear, to hold the boat against the current, turning

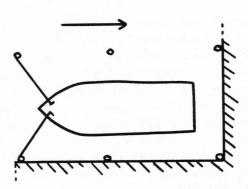

FIG. 38. Leaving a slip—current / wind from the bow: With the current / wind from forward, the last two lines ashore should be the bow lines.

the rudder to offset the paddle-wheel effect. Make sure the way is clear outside your slip.

4. Give a long blast with your horn, cast off your bow lines, and shift into forward, or increase power as needed, to move out of the slip, steering to offset the paddle-wheel.

5. As you clear the slip, turn to your desired heading and continue to move away from the dock area at a safe, slow speed. Steering won't be any problem because you are heading into the current.

Bow-First in the Slip

In this situation, you can simply let the current push you backward out of the slip—if it's strong enough. If not, you can always help with the engine(s). However, while it's sometimes advantageous to use the engine(s) to get the boat started, you can then shift quickly into neutral and coast with the current. In this way, boat speed is kept down and the interference of the paddle-wheel effect is minimized. Moreover, when the boat is drifting back with the current, you don't need to steer.

The procedure is as follows:

1. Adjust the bow lines as necessary to hold the boat in the middle of the slip.

2. Cast off the spring lines, then the stern lines.

3. Shift the engine(s) into forward, as needed, to take the load off the bow lines (using the rudder to help offset the paddle-wheel), but do not use enough throttle to move the boat forward against the current. Check to be sure the way is clear outside your slip.

4. Give a four- to six-second blast on your horn, cast off the bow lines, and shift the engine(s) into neutral to let the current push you out of the slip. If the current is weak, you might need to use your engine(s) in reverse briefly to start your boat moving out the slip, but you should shift into neutral as soon as your boat starts moving backward.

5. When your boat is far enough out of the slip that you can turn safely, put the wheel or tiller hard over to turn in the desired direction, shift into forward, and give a strong burst of power to stop your backward movement and kick your stern around.

Ease up on the throttle, complete your turn, and move out slowly and safely to your desired heading. With twin engines, you can use your engines to turn the boat.

Situation No. 3

WIND FROM THE SIDE

The objective in this situation is to keep your boat from being blown into the pilings or dock as you leave the slip. For that reason, you start out by getting your boat as close to the windward side of the slip (the side closest to the wind) as you can; that gives you the maximum amount of room to leeward (Figure 39). What this means, of course, is that you must be ready to cast off your windward bow and stern lines at the same time so that the wind can't blow one end of your boat sideways while someone struggles to get the line off a cleat at the other end. The procedures are as follows:

Stern-First in the Slip

While it is somewhat more difficult to back into a slip than to head in bow-first, once you've gotten into the slip the hard way, getting out is much easier. In this situation, for example, there's

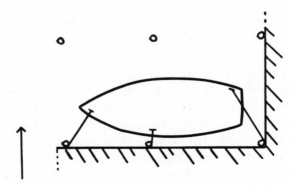

FIG. 39. Leaving a slip—current/wind from abeam: With the current/wind from the side, you should shorten the lines on the up-current or windward side of the boat before casting off.

no need to rig a breast line to help hold your boat against the wind. The bow line will work quite nicely for that function. One of your crew can hold the line and walk aft still holding the line as the boat starts to move out of the slip. The procedure in this situation is as follows:

1. Shorten the windward bow and stern lines to position the boat to the windward side of the slip.

2. Cast off the spring lines, followed by the leeward bow and stern lines.

3. After checking that the way is clear outside your slip, take the windward bow line off the cleat, but do not cast it off. Use it to hold the bow temporarily to windward.

4. Give a long blast with your horn to warn people that you are coming out, cast off your stern line, put the engine(s) in gear, and give enough throttle to start your boat moving out of the slip smartly (quickly).

5. As the boat moves forward, your crew then simply "walks" the windward bow line aft to help hold the boat to windward. When he or she has walked back to about the 'midship mark, the line is cast off. By this time, the boat is moving fast enough that you can control the stern with the rudder.

6. As the boat clears the slip, ease up on the throttle and begin turning to the desired heading. Move out safely into the waterway.

Bow-First in the Slip

1. Begin by shortening up the bow and stern lines to windward.

2. Since you will be backing out of the slip, rig a breast line from the center piling or dock cleat in your slip (if there is one) to a 'midship cleat. When you begin to move out of the slip, one of your crew can walk this line forward to help keep the wind from blowing your bow across the slip into either the far pilings or your neighbor's boat. If there is no center piling or dock cleat, plan to have one of the crew walk the stern line forward for the same purpose.

3. Cast off the spring lines, followed by the leeward bow and stern lines.

4. After checking to be certain the way is clear outside of your slip, prepare the remaining lines so they can be removed easily and, when that is done, give a four- to six-second blast with your horn.

5. With your rudder turned to help you back up in a straight line, remove the stern and breast lines from their cleats, cast off the bow line, and put the engine(s) in reverse, increasing power to get the boat moving smartly. While you don't want to go so fast that you can't stop if a problem develops, the faster you get out of the slip, the less time the wind or the current has to push your boat across the slip into the leeward pilings. As the boat moves backward out of the slip, walk the stern line forward a few steps to help hold the stern against the wind, and then cast the stern line off (unless you are using it in place of a breast line). As the boat continues to move out of the slip, the crew should move forward with the breast or stern line, controlling the bow against the wind.

6. As the bow clears the slip, ease up on the throttle and cast off the last line onto the dock or over the piling carefully.

7. When the boat is well clear of the slip, put the wheel (tiller) hard over, shift into forward, and give a good burst of power to stop the backward momentum and kick the stern around to begin your turn away from the slip. Ease up on the throttle, complete your turn, and move out safely. With twin engines, you can use your engines to turn the boat.

Situation No. 4
CURRENT FROM THE STERN; WIND FROM THE SIDE

The most complicated situation you're likely to encounter occurs when there's a strong wind coming from one side of the slip or the other, along with a good current moving from one end or the other. When you find yourself in this circumstance, you need to combine elements of the three situations described above. For example, you would begin by shortening the windward lines just as if the current were not involved. You would also use your engine(s) to hold the boat against the current, just as if there weren't any wind from the side to contend with. Then you'd put the two together. As in other situations, the challenge is easier if you've gone into your slip stern-first; it's somewhat more complicated if you've gone into it bow-first.

Stern-First in the Slip

In this situation, you can take the time to let the current help you out of the slip, despite the wind, because the most difficult part of your boat to control—the bow—leaves the slip first. Moreover, your crew can simply walk your bow line aft to hold the forward half of the boat against the wind (Figure 40) as it comes out of the slip. An occasional burst of prop wash will keep the stern where it belongs. Remember, however, that your ability to steer may be limited when the boat clears the slip, because you will be moving with the current.

The procedure is as follows:

1. Adjust the bow and stern lines to hold your boat to the windward side of the slip.

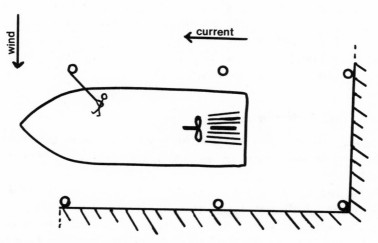

Fig. 40.   Walking your bow line aft: With the current from astern and the wind abeam, you can help hold the boat to windward when headed bow-first out of the slip by walking your bow line aft as the boat moves out.

2. Put the engine(s) in reverse as needed to take the load off the stern lines. Remove the spring lines.

3. Check to be sure the way is clear outside your slip.

4. Give a four- to six-second blast with your horn, cast off the leeward bow and stern lines, followed by the windward stern line.

5. Shift into forward briefly to help get the boat started, then go back into neutral, letting the current push you out of the slip while your crew walks the bow line aft to hold the bow to windward. If necessary, you can shift into forward and use short bursts of prop wash to keep the stern from being blown to leeward and to help your boat out of the slip. When the bow line is amidships, cast it off, being sure that it doesn't fall into the water.

Outboards and I / Os:

6. When the boat clears the slip, shift into forward, increase the throttle enough to provide steerage, and head out into the waterway safely.

Single-Engine Inboards:

6. When the boat clears the slip, shift into forward, put the rudder over to turn the boat in the desired direction, and give a good burst of prop wash to kick the stern around and start the boat moving across the current to give you steerage.

Twin-Engine Inboards:

6. When the boat clears the slip, use your engines to turn the boat toward its desired heading.

Bow-First in the Slip

This is a more difficult situation, mostly because more effort is needed to hold your bow against the wind. The procedure is as follows:

1. Adjust the bow and stern lines as necessary to hold the boat to the windward side of the slip.

2. Rig a breast line that you will be able to walk toward the bow as the boat moves backward from the slip. Alternatively, plan to walk the windward stern line forward.

3. Put the engine(s) in reverse as needed to take the load off

the stern lines, remove the spring lines, and check to be sure the way is clear outside your slip.

4. Cast off the leeward bow and stern lines, continuing to use the engine(s) as necessary to hold the boat against the current. (You may need to turn the rudder so that the force of the current on the rudder offsets the paddle-wheel effect of your propeller in reverse.) Prepare to cast off the windward bow and stern lines.

5. After giving a four- to six-second blast on your horn, shift into reverse or increase power as needed to begin backing out of the slip, casting off the windward bow line as your bow begins to move and steering to offset the paddle-wheel effect. Walk the stern line forward a few steps to help hold the stern against the wind, and then cast it off (unless you are using it in place of a breast line).

6. As the boat continues to move backward out of the slip, walk the breast line (or stern line) forward to keep the bow from being blown off by the wind.

7. As the bow clears the slip, cast the last line onto the dock or over the piling so that it does not hang in the water.

8. When the boat is well clear of the slip, shift into forward, give a burst of power to stop the backward momentum, and steer to start your turn away from the slip. Ease off on the throttle, complete your turn, and move out safely into the waterway. With twin engines, you can use your engines to turn the boat.

Situation No. 5

CURRENT FROM THE BOW; WIND FROM THE SIDE

In this situation, as in the one immediately preceding, the key is controlling your bow against the wind. Depending upon whether your boat is in the slip bow- or stern-first, you may need to rig a breast line to help out. As before, an alternative to a breast line, if that is what's called for, is to walk your stern line forward as the boat moves out of the slip (Figure 41). While

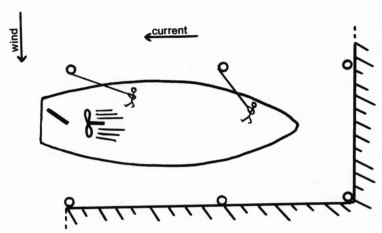

Fig. 41. Walking your breast and stern lines forward: With the current from the bow and the wind abeam, you can help hold the boat to windward when backing out of the slip by walking your breast and stern lines forward.

the stern line is not as effective as a breast line for this purpose because of the time it takes to walk it far enough forward to give you some control over the bow, it is better than nothing.

Stern-First in the Slip

In this situation, you will be motoring forward into the current and can walk your bow line aft to hold your bow to windward as the boat begins to move out of the slip. The procedure is as follows:

1. Adjust your bow and stern lines to hold the boat to the windward side of the slip.

2. Cast off the spring lines, followed by the leeward bow and stern lines.

3. Take the windward bow line from its cleat, holding onto it to keep the bow to windward. (Note: If the wind is strong, it may be desirable to keep the bow line snubbed against the cleat until the stern line is cast off. When the command is given to cast off the stern line, you can unsnub the bow line and prepare to walk it aft as the boat begins to move.)

4. Give a long blast with your horn, cast off the stern line, shift into forward, and increase power to begin moving out of the slip, steering as necessary to offset the paddle-wheel effect and to keep the stern from being blown off to leeward.

5. Walk the bow line aft to help hold the bow to windward, then cast off the bow line when you're amidships.

6. As the boat clears the slip, begin your turn to the desired heading, moving out safely into the waterway.

Bow-First in the Slip

In this situation without a side wind, I suggested you let the current push the boat backward out of the slip, unless you needed a boost from the engine because the current was weak. Not so, this time, if the wind is at all strong. With a good wind from the side and the whole length of the slip for it to push your bow off, you want to get out of the slip promptly and should make full use of your engine to do it. The procedure is as follows:

1. Adjust the bow and stern lines to hold the boat to windward.

2. Rig a breast line, if the slip permits.

3. Put the engine(s) in forward as needed to take the load off the bow lines. Remove the spring lines.

4. After checking to be sure the way is clear outside your slip, cast off the leeward bow and stern lines and continue using the engine(s) as needed to hold the boat's position in the slip. Prepare to cast off or walk your windward lines forward.

5. Give a four- to six-second blast with your horn, reduce power, shift into reverse, and, as the boat begins to move backward, cast off the windward bow line.

6. Increase power, and back out smartly, walking the stern line a few steps forward to help control the stern as the boat begins to move. At that point, unless it will be used in place of a breast line, cast off the stern line.

7. As the boat continues moving out of the slip, walk the breast line (or stern line) forward, using it to hold the bow to windward.

8. As the boat clears the slip, cast off the last line so that it lies securely on the dock or over a piling.

9. When the boat is well clear of the slip, shift into forward, give a burst of power to stop the backward momentum, and steer to begin your turn away from the slip. Ease up on the throttle, complete your turn, and move out safely on the desired heading. With twin engines, you can use your engines to turn the boat.

Situation No. 6
CURRENT FROM THE SIDE; WIND FROM ANY DIRECTION

Although many docks for pleasure boats are built out into the water so that the current runs parallel to the length of the boat slips, you will sometimes find slips in which the current comes from one side or the other. This situation is handled using the basic techniques described for Situations No. 4 and No. 5, where the wind was from the side.

The only real complication might occur if the wind and current are from opposite sides. Then you need to determine which of the two is having the greater effect on your boat. The easy way to do that is to notice which side of the slip your boat lies in. If the wind is dominant, it will push the boat to the leeward or downwind side of the slip; if the current is dominant, it will hold the boat against the windward (upwind) side of the slip. As in earlier situations in which the wind was coming from the side of the slip, the key to getting out of your slip safely is to move out smartly, walking a dock line along the deck to keep your boat from being pushed across the slip against pilings, the dock, or another boat. Once clear of the slip, you can turn toward the channel and be on your way in a seamanlike manner that the people on neighboring boats will admire.

Testing What You've Learned
(Answers can be found in Appendix C)

1. Before planning your departure from a slip, you should observe the strength and direction of both the _____ and the _____.

2. If the wind is coming from the bow and the current from the stern, how can you tell which one will have the most effect on the boat?

3. When the wind is from the side (abeam), what's the purpose of shortening the dock lines on the windward side of your boat before beginning to leave the slip?

4. TRUE or FALSE: It really doesn't matter in what order you remove your dock lines, as long as you don't take too long getting them off.

5. What two things should you always do just before starting out of your slip, no matter what the direction and strength of the wind and current?

6. What effect does moving at a slow speed with the current have on a boat's steering?

7. If your boat is in a slip bow-first and the wind / current is from the bow, what is the advantage of letting the wind or current push the boat out instead of putting it in reverse and backing out under power?

8. When the wind is from one side or the other, what is the only practical way to keep it from blowing your bow off to the side when you are leaving a slip?

IV

Basic Boat-Handling Skills

If one key to becoming a skilled boater is understanding how your boat relates to water, a second key is practicing the basic maneuvers that will be routine every time you go out in your boat. It's much the same as learning to drive a car: After you've been shown the basics, you have to get out on the road and practice them until they become almost second nature.

Within that context, I suggest finding an experienced boater who can go out with you to coach you through your first one or two excursions, to help you in learning the vital maneuvers. This section describes how to handle your boat through such fundamental operations as turning, accelerating, slowing down, maneuvering in close quarters, holding position against a current or wind, and backing up. Throughout these chapters, the importance of encouraging your first mate to learn and practice the same skills is emphasized.

13

Operating Your Boat in Open Water

It's one thing to read a book that tells you how to handle your boat; it's another to get out there and do it. And it's still another matter to get out there and do it well—consistently.

Boating skills, like any others, are first learned and then acquired. They can be learned by trial and error. They are better learned through instruction, either from books or, preferably, from a teacher. But they are *acquired* only through practice.

Remember when you learned to drive a car? I do. I was in eighth grade when a schoolmate took me out into a slightly muddy field on his father's farm with a pickup truck and began by teaching me to use the clutch. I had to start up the truck without stalling or spinning the wheels. It was a tough lesson, and I had to try it over and over again before I finally mastered the technique.

Boating's no different. Operating your boat, whether it's a motorboat or a sailboat, requires a new set of skills, and it takes practice to become good at them. As a twelve-year-old, as mentioned earlier, I indeed put a hole in a speedboat the first time I tried to sail my boat up to its mooring buoy. But after getting a couple of lessons and practicing the maneuver over and over again, I became very good at making that mooring—so good, in fact, that after those first few weeks, I didn't miss my mooring again in four-and-a-half more summers of sailing that boat in all kinds of conditions.

Could I do the same thing today, with our present boat? Possibly, but I doubt it. How about if I practiced it? Absolutely. It's all a matter of learning how far the boat will coast under different conditions. Once you have a feel for that, it's duck soup.

The same comment applies to the whole range of maneuvers you must learn in order to operate your boat safely and comfortably. Once you have in your head how you're supposed to do them, you've got to practice each maneuver again and again in order to drive that knowledge from your head to the seat of your pants. And, quite frankly, I'd suggest that you plan on practicing *with your crew and without guests* until you are confident (1) that you as the skipper can operate your boat safely, and (2) that your first mate (spouse, child, or friend) can do all the things you know how to do. Why the second point? That's in case you become sick or injured and your first mate has to get the boat, and you, safely back to shore.

GETTING STARTED

There are all kinds of ways to begin learning how to operate your boat safely, but they all have one thing in common: You have to admit your ignorance, or inexperience, and be willing to ask for help. If you're into sailboats, there are "sailing schools" in many parts of the country. They are easy to locate by looking in the back advertising pages of sail-oriented magazines, and by using the yellow pages of a telephone book.

Another approach that's suitable for motorboaters and sailors alike is to ask an experienced boater to go out with you the first couple of times you take your boat out. And, I don't mean the salesman. Too often, boat salesmen don't know much more about operating the boats they sell than do first-time buyers. They are salesmen, not necessarily boaters. As a result, you're usually better off asking either someone at your marina or a friend whom you know to be an experienced *and* competent boater. Don't worry about imposing on anyone. Chances are that the person you ask will be delighted. And, I say that from personal experience. I have not only been very flattered to be asked, but have had a delightful time as well. My guess is that almost anyone you'd ask to go out with you would have the same reaction I did.

The first thing you have to learn, of course, is how to get away from the dock. I can assure you that it was much easier for me to write about leaving a dock in the previous section, than it was to perform those procedures the first few times with our new boat in any but favorable conditions. In fact, when we took delivery of our boat, she didn't have rubrails. After I put a 4-inch scratch through the gelcoat one time while getting out of our slip, we decided to give her sturdy rubrails the following spring. Since then, we've made a conscious effort to think through exactly how we're going to get out of our slip, leave the dock, or get out of an anchorage, *before* we get underway.

Not only that, but we practice doing these things. For example, when I decided that I wanted to learn how to maneuver our boat in reverse, I started backing her into the slip every time we returned from a sail. When Susan decided that she wanted to learn how to back our boat into the slip, we did the same thing. But, to speed up the process, it wasn't at all unusual for us to go in and out of the slip four or five times when coming back from a sail—just so that Susan could practice. We confused our neighbors a bit the first couple of times that we rejected their help when they tried to hand us our dock lines, but it wasn't long before they recognized the symptoms and just sat back to watch the progress.

STEERING AND MAKING TURNS

On the face of it, steering a boat seems relatively easy. And it is—most of the time. There are, however, a few tricks of the trade that can help you avoid such inconveniences as running aground or running into a dock or another boat. They can also help you avoid trouble while maneuvering in close quarters.

Steering in a Straight Line

Steering a boat across the water in a straight line, for example, is quite different from steering a car down an arrow-straight,

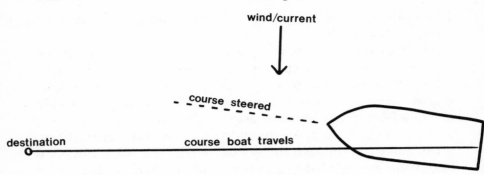

F<small>IG</small>. 42.   Compensating for leeway: By steering a few degrees to wind-ward or up-current, it's possible to compensate for leeway caused by the effect of wind and / or current.

four-lane highway. One reason is that the highway doesn't move. Another is that if the wind affects you at all as you drive down the highway, you know it instantly and can correct for it right on the spot.

Not so with a boat, in either case. The water—your high-way—does move, sometimes rather strongly as tidal or river currents push your boat one way or another. Moreover, when the wind blows, it can push you to one side or the other of your course without you being aware of it, because there aren't any white lines painted along the side of your watery roadway.

What this means, of course, is that you have to take the cur-rent and wind into consideration while you steer. If, for example, you're headed across the wind or current, you'll probably need to steer somewhat to the right or left of your course line to compensate for "leeway," that is, for being pushed sideways by that wind or current (Figure 42). Otherwise, you could run into shallow water unintentionally, or even miss your destination by some miles if it's a long trip across open water, with potentially serious consequences. (Allowing for leeway is covered in more detail in Chapter 20.)

Making Turns

Boats also turn differently than cars do, and you need to learn about those differences. For example, boats turn from the rear

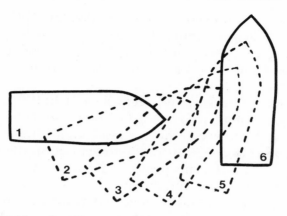

FIG. 43.   Wide swing of the stern in a turn: As a boat turns, the stern swings around until the bow points in the desired direction, pivoting around a point that is about a third of the boat's length back from the bow.

(Figure 43). As a result, your stern makes a wider swing than your bow does—very different from driving a car or truck, where the rear wheels make a shorter turn than the front—and you need to allow for that swing whenever you are turning. If you want to compare the boat to a car, imagine a car in which the front wheels are fixed and the rear wheels do the steering. Or, the next time you visit your local lumberyard, watch someone drive a forklift truck, which is steered by its rear wheels.

Still another factor is that boats slide sideways when they turn, because there aren't any wheels on hard pavement to hold them to a fixed path. At very slow speeds, the slippage is almost unnoticeable. At faster displacement speeds, you can't miss it, and you need to take this slippage into consideration in your planning if there are boats, docks, or other obstacles along the path of your turn.

At planing speeds, sideways slippage is generally even more pronounced. In fact, many planing boats don't really make a discrete turn at high speeds; they sort of skid through the turn. That's why many vee-bottomed boats have hard chines near the stern and a series of vee-shaped strakes running the length of the bottom. As the boat leans into a turn, those strakes and the hard edge of the chine bite into the water to help keep the hull from losing its grip on the water and skidding sideways. On a moderate or deep-vee hull, the vee-form itself helps the hull maintain a grip on the water in the turn. A planing boat with round chines will often have a keel or skeg to help keep it on track in a turn.

Strakes or no strakes, and regardless of hull form or keel, however, you can get into trouble if you try to make a turn too suddenly or if you are going too fast to make the turn in the available space. So, it's worthwhile to get out on the water and practice turns at different speeds until you're comfortable with what you and your boat can do.

Another major difference between making turns in a car and in a boat is that a road doesn't have waves. You do find waves out on the water, however, and, depending upon how big they're running, those waves can make what is ordinarily a perfectly safe turn into an exceedingly dangerous maneuver.

The problem is greatest when you're running on a plane, turning away from the direction of the waves, and your boat gets hit by a wave broadside. Since the boat is already leaning into the turn, the wave's tendency to make the boat roll can provide just enough boost to make the boat go over. The risk is greater in a cabin cruiser than in a low runabout, because of the cruiser's higher center of gravity. It is greater still in a sport-fisherman than in a cruiser, for the same reason. However, even a low runabout can be rolled dangerously in steep, choppy waves or breaking seas, and extra care must be used when turning in these conditions. (See discussion of rough inlets in Chapter 19.)

VIRGINIA WOMAN DROWNS IN CAPSIZE—A 36-year-old Warrenton, Virginia, woman drowned when she was trapped beneath an overturned boat in Hatteras Inlet.

Her four companions were rescued without injury. The dead woman was identified as Jennifer K. Spaulding.

Coast Guard Petty Officer Scott Miller said that on July 10 a passing vessel radioed a report that four people were clinging to the hull of a 20-foot inboard / outboard [boat] near the sea buoy.

Personnel from the nearby station got them out of the water within 30 minutes and, with a second boat, started a search for the missing woman. The woman's body floated out from under the craft as they righted it. She wore a child's life jacket, according to Miller.

Rescuers immediately began cardiopulmonary resuscitation [CPR] as they rushed her to the Coast Guard station, where a local physician pronounced her dead by accidental drowning.

Miller said the inlet was choppy when the accident occurred, with winds of 15 to 17 knots and a rolling sea of 2 to 3 feet.[1]

It's easy, of course, to read that news clipping and say to yourself, "Well, I won't be going out into Hatteras Inlet." The same kind of accident can happen in more benign waters—even in a relatively small river, for example.

MARYLAND BOATER DIES—A small skiff capsized on the Patuxent River in Maryland, killing one of the men aboard and sending the other to the hospital.

Michael Edward Gilbert, 30, of Fort Washington, Maryland, was declared dead at the scene when pulled from the river shortly after the early-evening accident February 1 near the Calvert County line.

With John Max Reese, 29, also of Fort Washington, Gilbert had been fishing the river in a 10-foot skiff. The men were returning to shore when a wave overturned the boat and sent them both into the icy water, according to Department of Natural Resources police.

A passer-by heard screams coming from the river and alerted the police. Reese was flown to Calvert Memorial Hospital, where he was treated for hypothermia and exposure.[2]

The point is this: Waves can make the water more dangerous for your boat, and you'll find them on virtually any body of water. Whenever waves come up, whether they're caused by the wind or other boats, you should use care—particularly when turning your boat at planing speeds.

Another point: *Always look around to both sides and behind you before starting a turn.* You are not on a one-way street. Consider the waterway as an eight- or twelve-lane expressway, with you driving in a middle lane of traffic. While you have to keep a good lookout at all times, it's imperative that you look around (not glance, but look carefully) before starting any turn.

1. *Soundings*, September 1986.
2. *Soundings*, May 1987.

Turning at Slow Speeds

If you need to turn sharply while motoring along at a slow speed, logic suggests that you should turn so that the paddle-wheel effect in forward gear helps to swing your stern through the turn. This is one instance in which the most obvious logic is wrong. You should turn in the direction that lets you use the paddle-wheel effect in reverse and prop wash in forward to kick your stern around by shifting between the two—without coming to a stop. This means turning to starboard in a boat with a right-hand propeller, or to port if your boat has a left-hand propeller. The technique is simple: About 25 to 30 percent of the way through your turn, shift into reverse and give a burst of power to help kick your stern around with the paddle-wheel, then shift back into forward and give a burst of prop wash on your rudder to help you continue your turn. The rudder does not move through any of this; it stays hard over. If you find that your turn is not sharp enough, you can shift into reverse a second time and give a good burst of paddle-wheel to kick your stern further around, and then go back into forward.

A twin-engine inboard or a twin-engine I / O with counter-rotating propellers will turn equally well in either direction with both engines in forward. However, you can shorten the turn by putting the inboard engine into neutral and giving short bursts of power to the outboard engine so that the paddle-wheel effect of the outboard propeller will help pull the stern around.

Turning in One Boat Length

Sometimes it's necessary to turn your boat 90 or even 180 degrees in an extremely short distance—for example, barely more than the length of your boat. Such turns are relatively easy if you have a twin-engine boat. With the boat stopped, you simply put one engine in reverse, the other in forward, turn the rudders in the direction you want to turn, and slowly spin the boat as described in Chapter 12.

With a single-engine outboard or an I / O, it is equally easy, because you can turn the propeller far enough to the side to push the stern around with little or no forward motion. In virtually all instances, however, the turn will be tighter if you stop the boat's forward motion before starting the turn.

With a single-engine inboard, the job is a bit more difficult, but equally possible with most boats. The best technique puts the prop wash to work against the turned rudder with the gear in forward, and uses the paddle-wheel effect with the gear in reverse. Note the strategy here is the same as that used for making a sharp turn while the boat is moving forward at a slow speed.

The first key to the procedure in a single-engine inboard is to have little or no forward motion. The second key is to turn in a direction in which the paddle-wheel effect of your propeller will help you in reverse. (You can ignore the paddle-wheel effect in forward.) If, therefore, you have a right-hand propeller, you should make your turn to starboard (in reverse gear, the propeller will kick your stern to port). Alternatively, if you have a left-hand propeller, make your turn to port.

If your boat is lying still in the water and you have a right-hand propeller, the procedure is as follows (Figure 44):

1. Turn the wheel (or tiller) so that the rudder is hard to starboard. Put the gear in forward and give a two- or three-second burst of power (don't be timid) to use your prop wash against the rudder to kick your stern to port, starting your turn.

2. Throttle back immediately, shift into reverse, and give another burst of power to use the paddle-wheel effect to keep your stern moving to port.

3. Throttle back, shift into forward, and give another burst of power to kick your stern around.

4. Shift into reverse, giving another surge of power.

5. Repeat Steps 3 and 4 over and over as needed to complete the turn.

None of your bursts of power should be long enough to start the boat moving either forward or backward. All you are trying to do is to kick the stern around to port by alternately pushing water suddenly against the turned rudder in forward, and then using the paddle-wheel effect in reverse. Alternating between forward and reverse prevents the boat from moving either forward or backward while you kick the stern around, pivoting your boat around a point about a third of the way back from

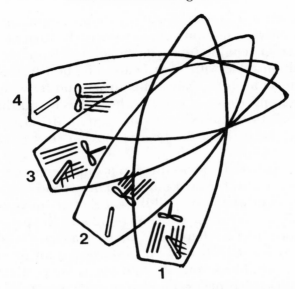

FIG. 44.   Turning a single-engine inboard (right-hand propeller) in one boat length: (1) With the boat stopped, the rudder is turned hard over and the engine put in forward with a brief surge of power. (2) Before the boat starts moving forward, shift into reverse and give a surge of power. (3) Again, before the boat starts moving backward, shift into forward and give another surge, then (4) shift into reverse, and give a surge. By alternately using the prop wash and paddle-wheel effect, the stern is pushed around while the boat stays in essentially the same place.

the bow. The maneuver is easier than it sounds. The only precaution necessary is to throttle down completely before shifting gears.

As long as your rudder is far enough behind the propeller to receive the thrust of water when it is turned, the method works for both motorboats and most auxiliary-powered sailboats. If the rudder is hung on a skeg, it works better because the skeg helps direct the flow of the propeller wash. The method does not work, however, on sailboats whose rudders have a cut-out for the propeller because, as we pointed out earlier, the propeller wash simply shoots back through the cut-out when the rudder is turned. Instead, the paddle-wheel effect in forward will simply offset the paddle-wheel in reverse, and the stern will just wiggle from side to side as you shift back and forth. If you must turn such a boat in that kind of short distance, you will either have to get help from another boat—your own dinghy with an outboard, perhaps—or use a line ashore to help you make the turn.

Learning by Practicing

As noted, the trick to learning how to operate your boat safely is practice. And, hopefully, you'll begin practicing—gingerly, please—the first time you go out in your boat.

It's a good idea to get off by yourself where you won't bother other boats, particularly when you want to practice making turns at planing speeds. And, of course, you should never try to find out how fast you can do something. That's inviting trouble. But simply by doing—making turns—over and over again and at different speeds, you'll begin to develop a feel for what's safe. And once you've got the feel for it on that particular boat, you've got it forever. Your next boat may have a different "feel," but you'll pick that up quickly, too, with a bit of practice.

When practicing any turn, you'll need to locate something in the water that can help you judge distances—how much space you need to turn at each speed. A lot of people use channel markers if there is adequate water all around and boat traffic is light. Practicing maneuvers near a channel is not recommended if you have any choice in the matter, but if you must, it's vitally important to keep a sharp lookout for other boats and to give them lots of room.

A better idea for a marker is to hang a few fishing weights from a balloon or a fender, and put that out as your own "buoy" somewhere away from normal boat traffic. For practicing turns in a single boat length or at slow speeds, you may want two markers so that you can turn between them.

SPEEDING UP AND SLOWING DOWN

Most boats have relatively poor acceleration. You can shift into forward gear, shove open the throttle, and the propeller will just shoot a lot of foam out under the stern before the boat begins picking up speed. The exceptions usually are high-powered runabouts with strong planing surfaces, but even they suffer the same limitations to some extent.

By the same token, boats slow down fairly quickly—up to a point. In both cases, however, it takes practice to learn just how your boat will respond when you push the throttle forward and pull it back.

Accelerating

There are two major obstacles to fast acceleration in a boat. One is the fact that the propeller operates in a fluid. The other is the fact that all boats to some extent are sitting in the water when they're stopped, and you're trying to push the boat through that water—until it gets up on a plane.

In terms of getting the most out of your propeller, the best way to accelerate is to increase the throttle gradually. In actuality, "gradually" may be fairly quickly, but it definitely is not all at once. If you simply shove the throttle forward, you could, of course, stall your engine. But, assuming that doesn't happen, you are essentially trying to shoot all of the water out from under the boat. As a result, the propeller just digs the stern in deeper.

It's almost like trying to start your car quickly in deep sand or snow. Your wheels spin fast because they can't get traction, but the car doesn't start moving very quickly; in fact, you may wind up just digging yourself into a hole. On the other hand, if you accelerate gradually, steadily increasing the throttle as the car—or boat—starts moving, you can get moving quickly and cleanly.

Once a boat starts moving, the next key to fast acceleration is getting up on a plane where there is less resistance from the water. As a result, boats designed to plane quickly (at slow speeds) will generally have the best acceleration. That's why ski boats, for example, frequently have fairly shallow vee bottoms, as opposed to a deep- or even a modified-vee hull design. The strong planing surfaces help them get up on a plane very quickly for the fast acceleration needed to get skiers started.

Obviously, there is great variation from boat to boat, but the point is that you need to practice starting up your boat so that you learn (1) what your boat can and cannot do, and (2) how to bring it up to cruising speed with the least amount of fuss. Again, it's something you get a feel for as you practice.

Slowing Down

A boat speeding across the surface of the water will slow down very quickly if you just cut the power—at first. As it comes down off its plane, it seems to stop almost on the spot. Then the wake catches up with you, surging up against the stern and pushing you forward.

If you have an outboard with a low transom, it's important not to slow abruptly like that in a following sea (with your boat and the waves both headed in the same direction) when the waves are at all high. This is the circumstance mentioned earlier in which your boat's wake, which is catching up to you as you slow down, can combine with a normal wave and surge over your transom, possibly swamping your boat. Under those conditions, you should ease your speed down so that your wake catches you gradually. Once it has caught up with you, you can reduce power further to come the rest of the way off the plane.

When your boat is no longer planing, it will behave just like a displacement boat—it will simply coast through the water until the friction of the water on the hull and the effects of the wind and current bring it to a stop. And, the heavier the boat, the farther it will coast. As a result, the push that you get from your stern wave can send you surging a fair distance through the water. You can always put your engine(s) in reverse to bring your boat to a stop—*maybe*. A careful skipper, however, allows plenty of room so that if something goes wrong—for example, the engine stalls, the folding propeller fails to open in reverse, or something fouls (gets tangled in) the propeller—he's not in a dangerous situation if he can't stop the boat until it simply loses its forward momentum.

Moreover, outboard engines on sailboats, as well as the inboard engines on moderate- and heavy-displacement sailboats, are notoriously ineffective as brakes. The engines are usually relatively small (compared to those on motorboats), and their propellers may be tucked behind a big keel that reduces their efficiency. As a result, it is doubly important for sailors to practice stopping their boats with their engines so that they learn just how much—or how little—help that engine can be.

The practice at slow speeds is particularly important, because that's when you most need to know what to expect. You'd be surprised how many boat owners come up to a dock or into a slip faster than they can stop, and bang their boats up in the process. It not only can be costly from a damage viewpoint, but it's potentially dangerous as well. For example, what happens if you hit a dock and the impact knocks the person on the bow overboard? Moreover, even if they don't cause damage or physical injury, hard landings are very rough on the pride. Everyone who witnesses the incident will tell the story—embroidered as time goes on—many times. Three of our daughters have worked as dock hands at local marinas, and, I can assure you, the stories are not flattering. Nor are newspaper accounts like the one that follows. So, it's worth the practice—even if only to protect your ego.

RUNAWAY SPREADS PEANUT BUTTER TRAIL—A 70-foot Striker sportfisherman plowed through a fuel dock and into the marina store at Tidewater Yacht Marina in Portsmouth, Virginia. It toppled jars of peanut butter, catsup, and coffee from shelves and startled two customers who were looking at boat shoes stacked against the wall.

"The bow went through the window, knocked down shelves, and tore up the store," said marina general manager Becky Zuraw.

Much Too Much, a yacht registered out of Detroit, lived up to its name. When the boat tried to maneuver out of its slip after laying over for the night, it left a gaping hole in the fuel dock and store.

Early on the morning of October 21, Zuraw said, the Florida-bound yacht was leaving the marina, when, the operator claimed, "the gears jammed. He started heading toward the store, and evidently he couldn't get it back into reverse.

"We've had close calls, so many that looked like they were going to crash, but they always seem to get it into reverse in time."

Although larger yachts have safely negotiated the turn from the slip area past the fuel dock and store, Zuraw said that on occasion a few boats have tagged the fuel pier.

She estimated that *Much Too Much* was traveling at about 5 mph when it tagged the pier and drove through it into the store.

No one was injured in the incident.[3]

UNDERSTANDING YOUR BOAT'S WAKE

When discussing the difference between a displacement hull and a planing hull in Chapter 3, I described the waves that boats make as they go through the water. Basically, a system of waves is formed. One begins at the bow. Another comes off the boat initially at about the widest point of the hull, but then moves aft as the boat speeds up. Still other waves come out from the stern, caused by the water rushing around the stern to fill in the hole behind the boat as it moves forward through the water, and by the action of the propeller.

This system of waves forms a boat's wake, which radiates out in a vee shape behind the boat as it moves through the water. When the boat moves very slowly, the waves are small. When it reaches a speed equal to the square root of its waterline length (5 knots for a 25-foot waterline, 6 knots for a 36-foot waterline, etc.), they begin to become more noticeable.

As a boat almost but not quite reaches a plane, the waves that form the wake are at their largest, because the boat is being pushed through the water as fast as it can go without planing; in effect, it is plowing through the water. However, once the boat gets up on top of the water, the waves become smaller. Why? Because the boat isn't pushing as much water out of the way; it's up on top, instead.

This explains why motorboat operators sometimes argue that they will bother other boats less if they go zooming past the fishing or sailing fleet (or marina) at planing speeds rather than moving more slowly at displacement speeds.

It's almost—but not quite—true. If the speed limit is 6 knots and your boat has a 25-foot waterline, you'll probably make bigger waves at 6 knots than when you're moving at three or

3. *Soundings,* January 1986.

four times that speed. The reason is that 6 knots is probably just below your planing speed and you are literally plowing through the water, making your maximum wave.

But, magic! If you'll slow to 4 knots, or to 4½ knots, you'll make almost no wake. And that's really what is needed in many circumstances. It's also certainly what is meant by a buoy or sign that says "No Wake—Limit 6 Knots." That sign means "No Wake," no matter how slowly you have to go to accomplish that. For larger boats whose long waterlines may let them go 7 or 8 knots without making a noticeable wake, it also means that the speed limit is 6 knots. It is not a license to go 6 knots if by doing so you will make waves.

Now, why is this important?

It's important as a part of safe boating. It's important as part of being considerate of other people. And, it's important legally because you, as the skipper of your boat, are responsible for your boat's wake.

For example, if someone sitting in a small fishing boat is thrown overboard and drowns because your wake made his boat rock violently, you could well end up in court if someone noted your boat name and home port, or your boat's state registration number. At this writing, New Jersey authorities are still trying to track down the boat operators involved in this news report:

WAKE CAUSES FATALITY: Two Sport Boats Capsize Anglers— A Fourth of July fishing trip in Egg Harbor Township, New Jersey, ended in tragedy when the wash and wake created by two high-performance sport boats caused a small craft to capsize in the Great Egg Harbor River, killing an 81-year-old Philadelphia man and tossing a companion into the water, State Police at the Marine Bureau in Atlantic City, New Jersey, said.

The body of Christopher Blocker was found on July 6, the day after the accident, about 300 yards from where Blocker's 14-foot Sears Gamefisher overturned in the well-traveled waterway through this Atlantic County community, police said.

Blocker's companion, Columbus Kershaw, also of Philadelphia, managed to swim to shore and didn't require medical treatment, police said.

The two men were fishing in the aluminum boat, which has a 7.5-horsepower engine, July 5 at about 2:00 P.M. when two powerboats came past at a high rate of speed, said Marine Bureau spokesman Ricardo Esteves.

Esteves said the speeding boat operators could face charges of negligent operation of a speedboat, failing to report an accident, and failing to render assistance.

A cash award of up to $2,000 is also being offered by the Atlantic County Crime Stoppers Foundation for information leading to the arrest and indictment of the people wanted in connection with the accident.[4]

Another example: One part of normal sailboat maintenance involves going up your mast to check fittings, change light bulbs, etc. In our case, the masthead is 52 feet above the water. That's about five stories high. We normally perform this maintenance in a slip. The boat is secure and, presumably, the water is calm. Although our marina is not in a "No Wake" area, most boaters are thoughtful enough to slow their boats as they pass by. Unfortunately, however, not all boaters are that thoughtful. Instead, they speed by the marina, pulling water-skiers or simply cruising up the river. I have been moved to blue language many times as I was swept to and fro 52 feet in the air as the effect of those 1- or 1½-foot wakes were greatly magnified by our tall mast as the boat rocked. And mine is not an idle complaint.

WAKE MAY BE FACTOR IN DEATH—An investigation continues in Ocean City, New Jersey, to determine whether a man who fell from the top of his sailboat mast fell as a result of an excessive boat wake.

Patrick Vicars, 45, of Newtown, Pennsylvania, died July 4 after he fell 30 feet from the mast of his sailboat, which was rigged with a boatswain's chair. He was at the top of his mast working on the boat's radar antenna at the time of the accident.

The boat was docked at Nor'easter Residential Marina near Ocean City's Ninth Street Bridge. The area is heavily congested with recreational boat traffic on summer weekends. Police reports indicate there was a possibility of a strong wake from area powerboats, which could have contributed to jarring loose the rope harness.[5]

4. *Soundings*, September 1987.
5. *News-Journal*, Wilmington, Delaware, July 12, 1985.

In short, a safety-conscious boat operator will consider the water in front of any marina a "No Wake" zone, whether or not it is marked as such. And he'll do so for at least three reasons: courtesy, safety, and because he is legally responsible for his boat's wake.

Testing What You've Learned
(Answers can be found in Appendix C)

1. What two factors may push your boat off course when you are traveling on the water with your boat? How can you offset them?

2. When your boat goes through a turn, does it turn from the front or the rear? Why is knowing the answer to this question important?

3. TRUE or FALSE: The faster a boat is traveling through a turn, the more pronounced sideways slippage will be.

4. TRUE or FALSE: When turning your boat, you don't need to worry about being hit broadside by a wave, because the momentum of the turn will keep the boat upright.

5. TRUE or FALSE: When you want to turn in just one boat length, you should stop your boat completely before beginning the turn.

6. To turn a single-engine inboard in its own length, you make use of the _____ against the turned rudder in forward and the _____ of the propeller in reverse.

7. You are in a narrow channel around a marina and have to make a U-turn. Your single-engine boat has a right-hand propeller. In your judgment, there's enough room for you to make it in a single, smooth turn without coming to a stop, but you still want to turn as sharply as possible. In which direction would you make your turn—to port or to starboard? Why?

8. Same situation as above, but the channel is so narrow that you don't think you can make the turn without bringing your boat to a stop and turning essentially in your own boat's length. In which direction would you make your turn—to port or to starboard? Why?

9. What is the best way to accelerate your boat—just go ahead and give it the gas all at once, or increase the throttle gradually?

10. When is it important that you not slow down too quickly?

11. TRUE or FALSE: When coming up to a dock, it isn't really necessary to slow down completely ahead of time, because you can always use reverse gear as a brake.

12. When does a boat make its biggest wake—going forward slowly, almost planing, or when it is planing?

13. TRUE or FALSE: In general, the only time you have to be concerned about the effect of your wake is when operating around a marina or in a "No Wake" zone.

14

Maneuvering in Close Quarters

Just as you can get stuck in heavy traffic in your car, or can have trouble finding parking space during the Christmas shopping season, you can find yourself in heavy traffic out on the water, or without much maneuvering room at a marina. There are four key strategies:

• **Be alert.** Pay attention to the boats around you. If people on your boat want to talk with you at this time, that's OK, as long as you're able to pay attention to surrounding traffic while you talk. If, however, you have any feelings that boat traffic is too heavy for you to be distracted by talking, explain to your guests or crew that things are busy right now and you'd like to concentrate on the traffic around you for the next few minutes.

• **Be predictable.** Operate your boat so that you don't surprise the skippers of any of the boats around you.

• **Go with the flow.** To the extent you can, adjust your speed to that of the other boats. In any case, do not go roaring through a line of heavy boat traffic, throwing a big wake behind you. Your wake can make steering difficult for the boats you're passing.

• **Be courteous.** Be prepared to let the other boat go first, even if you have the right of way. The person running the other boat may not know the rules.

In a confined area where there's heavy traffic, three keys to safe maneuvering are: (1) operating at a slow speed; (2) maintaining a good lookout; and (3) knowing how to handle your boat—i.e., how to make it turn quickly, how to stop forward motion quickly, how to hold your position, and how to maneuver in reverse.

You can turn most quickly by using your prop wash and the paddle-wheel effect, following the procedures outlined in Chapter 13. You can stop forward motion best using your engine, putting it in reverse and giving it a strong burst of power—until the boat is stopped. Holding your position and maneuvering in reverse, however, are more involved.

HOLDING POSITION

Holding position is basically a matter of balancing the forces of your propeller and rudder against the wind and / or current. If there are no wind and current, you don't have much of a challenge. You just stop your boat dead in the water, put the gear in neutral, and the boat will hold its position quite nicely. When the wind is blowing or a current is running, however, the procedures are somewhat more involved.

Current from Ahead, No Wind; or Wind from Ahead, No Current

1. Bring the boat to a stop, headed almost into the current (wind).

2. Put the engine in forward and adjust the throttle so that your slowly turning propeller holds the boat in place against the current (wind). If the wind or current is light, you may have to shift in and out of gear.

3. As necessary, steer slightly to one side or the other to offset the paddle-wheel effect of your propeller in an outboard, I / O, or single-engine inboard, as in Figure 45(a).

Current from Ahead, Wind off the Bow

If the wind is strong, it will be difficult, if not impossible, to hold your bow against it. So, you'd turn the boat around and hold your position stern-to, as in Figure 45(e), by following

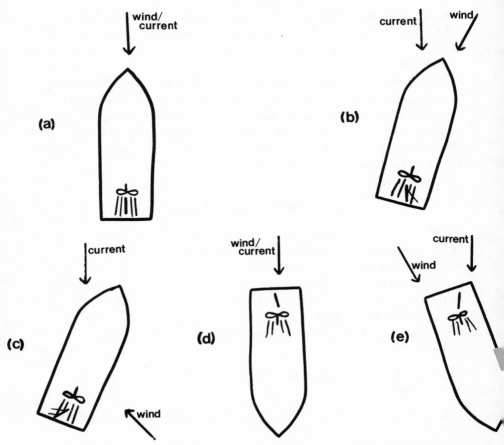

Fig. 45. Holding position against the wind and/or current (single-engine inboard): (a) Wind/current on the bow; (b) wind and current on opposite sides of the bow; (c) wind and current from nearly opposite directions; (d) wind/current from astern; (e) wind and current on opposite sides of the stern.

the procedures outlined below for when the current and wind are from the stern. In milder conditions, however, you can frequently hold your position bow-to by striking a balance between the current and the effect of the wind on your bow, as in Figure 45(b).

1. Bring the boat to a stop, headed so that your bow is pointed about halfway between the current and wind.

2. Turn the rudder or drive unit as if to turn the bow further into the wind.

3. With the gear in forward, adjust the throttle so that the boat does not move forward, but has the propeller turning just fast enough to keep the wind from blowing the bow around and to keep the boat from being pushed backward. Shift in and out of gear as necessary.

Insofar as the strength of the wind has an impact on how your bow is pointed, you'll need to experiment a bit to get the correct balance between the angle of your bow to the wind and the combination of rudder angle and engine speed needed to offset the wind's effect. Once you've practiced a few times, however, it doesn't take long to find the correct balance of forces.

Current from Ahead, Wind off the Stern

The object in this situation is to position your boat so that your prop thrust will offset the effect of the wind on your stern while holding the boat in place against the current, as in Figure 45(c).

1. Bring your boat to a stop so that the current is slightly to one side of the bow and the wind is on your stern from the other side.

2. With your engine in forward, steer to bring your bow more into the current and your stern into the wind.

3. Adjust your engine speed and steering so that the boat stands still.

Current from Astern, No Wind

1. Bring your boat to a stop, with the stern pointed directly into the current.

2. Put the engine in reverse, adjusting the throttle to hold the boat in place, shifting into neutral as needed.

Outboards, I / Os, and Single-Engine Inboards:

3. Turn your rudder or drive unit slightly as needed to offset the paddle-wheel effect, as in Figure 45(d).

Twin-Engine Inboards:

3. Keep your rudders straight so that the current moving past your boat will not push the stern to one side or the other.

Current from Astern, Wind off the Stern

1. Bring your boat to a stop with the stern pointed mostly into the current, but turned slightly toward the wind.

2. Put your engine in reverse, adjusting the throttle to hold the boat in place against the current.

Outboards and I / Os:

3. Turn the drive unit toward the wind as necessary so that the reversing propeller is also holding the stern against the wind. You'll need to play with the throttle and steering to strike the balance needed.

Single and Twin-Engine Inboards:

3. Turn the rudder(s) toward the wind, as in Figure 45(e), so that the current flowing past your boat will tend to push the stern into the wind. You'll need to experiment with boat angle, engine speed, and the angle of the rudder to strike the balance. The paddle-wheel effect may help or hinder in a single-engine boat, depending upon which side of the stern the wind is coming from. If the paddle-wheel is pulling the stern away from the wind, change tactics and point the stern closer to the wind and turn the rudder(s) toward the current. In this way, the flow of the water against your rudder may help balance the paddle-wheel effect.

Current from Astern, Wind off the Bow

Frankly, in this situation, I'd just turn around and put the wind off the stern and the current on the bow, as illustrated in Figure 45(c). If the wind is at all strong, it's difficult, if not impossible, to control your bow against it.

Wind from Astern, No Current

1. Bring your boat to a stop with the stern pointed directly into the wind.

2. Put the engine in reverse and adjust the throttle to hold the boat in place.

Outboards and I / Os:

3. Turn the drive units slightly to offset the paddle-wheel effect so that the stern stays pointed into the wind.

Single-Engine Inboards:

3. When the paddle-wheel effect begins to pull the stern off the wind, shift into forward and use a quick burst of prop wash against a turned rudder to bring the stern back in line.

4. Shift back into reverse and continue holding position, as in Figure 45(d).

Twin-Engine Inboards:

3. If the stern begins to drift off to one side or the other, give a burst of power with the engine on the side falling away from the wind. That should twist the boat back in line.

BACKING UP YOUR BOAT

While different boats require different techniques for backing up, there is one trick that many people find helpful, no matter what kind of boat they have: turning around to face the stern while they back up. This may be difficult in some boats, but if you can do it, I suggest you try it. You'll probably find that everything makes more sense that way. When facing forward, you turn the wheel to the right if you want to steer to your right. When facing the stern, you still turn the wheel to the right if you want to steer to the right.

Backing Up Outboards

In general, outboards make for easy backing up. You have good control over the stern because you are turning the propeller so that it pulls the stern in the direction you want to go. Some precautions are necessary, however.

1. When your boat moves backward, its flat transom is pushing water out of the way. As a result, depending upon how fast you're going, the water can pile up substantially against your stern. If you have a low transom, you need to watch your speed closely so that you don't build up such a wall of water that it will pour in over the transom. Sounds strange, but it happens— particularly if a wave comes along to help—and it can swamp your boat.

2. You also need to watch your bow. If you are backing slowly

and not turning sharply in reverse, the bow will usually follow the stern. If you turn sharply, however, the boat pivots on its stern so that the bow makes a big, wide sweep around. You need to be sure it doesn't hit something or somebody.

3. *Under no circumstances should you back up to a person in the water.* You also need to be particularly careful that you don't accidentally back into something or someone. If you back your outboard into a person in the water, you will cause severe injury. If you back into a log, a rock, or just plain shallow water, you can seriously damage the propeller unit.

Backing Up Inboard / Outboards

In most respects, I / Os are similar to outboards when it comes to maneuvering in reverse. While you usually do not need to worry as much about water building up against the transom, you do need to watch your bow. You have to keep a sharp eye out for swimmers, and watch for obstructions in the water. You also need to be careful that you don't back up too close to a bulkhead or piling. An I / O drive unit is pretty much out of sight, compared to an outboard, and it's easy to forget how far it protrudes beyond the stern. With an I / O, as with an outboard, under no circumstances should you back up to a swimmer in the water. Always come up alongside the person in the water and turn the engine off until he or she is safely aboard the boat. Leaving the engine in gear when you switch it off will immediately stop the propeller from spinning.

Backing Up Twin-Engine Inboards

Two engines offer remarkable maneuverability in reverse. The key, however, is to use the engines, not the rudders. Moreover, most of the time, you can leave the engines at idling speed. The basic procedure is as follows:

1. Put the rudders in the straight-ahead position, and leave them there.

2. To go backward in a straight line, put both engines in reverse. Use the same amount of throttle on each engine.

3. To turn to port slowly, increase the throttle on the star-

board engine while reducing the throttle on the port engine.

4. To turn a bit more quickly, put the port engine in neutral while the starboard engine stays in reverse.

5. To turn more sharply, bring the boat almost to a stop and put the port engine in reverse while the starboard engine stays in forward. The two engines will twist the bow around, pivoting the boat on its stern.

6. To turn to starboard, the procedure is essentially the same. In this case, however, the port engine goes forward while the starboard engine is in reverse.

Again, however, you need to be aware of your bow and of objects or people in the water. When you have one engine in reverse and the other in forward to turn the boat, you are literally pivoting the boat on its stern. As with an outboard or an I/O, this means that the bow sweeps through the turn, and you need to watch carefully to be certain it doesn't hit something.

In really tight quarters, there may not be room for the bow to swing. In that situation, you'll need to make your turn in a series of small steps in which you use both engines in reverse to go back a few feet, use your engines to pivot the bow around a few degrees, back up another few feet, and so on. This technique is particularly useful if you're backing into a tight inside corner slip in a crowded marina.

Backing Up Single-Engine Inboards

If you have only operated an outboard motorboat, an I/O, or a twin-engine inboard, you may not understand why people who have single-engine inboard boats often complain about trying to back up. The reason is quite simple: The boat will effectively turn in only one direction in reverse because of the paddle-wheel effect; it may also go straight back, but then again, it may not. It depends upon the particular boat.

In any case, you'll usually find yourself in one of two situations when you need to back up your boat: either you've got lots of room and are backing for a relatively long distance, or you're just backing up for two or three boat lengths. In the first situation, the boat has time to start moving fast enough in reverse that you may be able to use your rudder to help steer. In the second, you can forget about using your rudder to "steer" the boat in reverse; instead, you use your propeller to move the stern around.

In either circumstance, however, it's not worth trying to back up a single-engine boat if there is too much wind blowing across the bow. How much is too much? You'll learn pretty quickly, but basically the wind is too much if it blows your bow off to the side so that you can't back up in the direction you want to go. In that situation, either plan your maneuver so that having the wind blow the bow around is part of your plan, or forget about going backward, turn your boat around (in its own boat length, if necessary), and head in or out bow-first.

If, however, the wind is from astern, from dead ahead, or from the side but not too strong, a little technique will take you a long way *and* impress the bystanders.

Maneuvers for Longer Distances: For example, let's assume that your boat has a right-hand propeller. In reverse, the paddle-wheel effect will tend to make the stern back around to port. If you want to back around to port, you simply put the rudder to port and begin reversing. The paddle-wheel and the rudder will work together to turn your boat to port, as in Figure 46(a). If, on the other hand, you want to back up in a straight line for a longer distance, the procedure is as follows:

1. Line up the boat so that the path you want to follow as you move backward is slightly to port.

2. Put the engine in reverse, turning your rudder so that it's pointed about 35 degrees to starboard. (If your rudder is turned much farther, it may act more like a brake than a rudder.)

3. As the propeller turns in reverse, the paddle-wheel effect will pull the stern to port so that you are lined up perfectly with your desired pathway. As the boat gains speed moving backward through the water, the force of the water on the turned rudder will tend to push the stern to starboard, offsetting the paddle-wheel effect so that you are now moving backward in a straight line, as in Figure 46(b).

If your rudder is small, it may not be powerful enough to overcome the paddle-wheel effect completely, and, as a result, you may not be able to back up in a straight line. Instead, your stern will make a gradual turn to port. In that case, there are

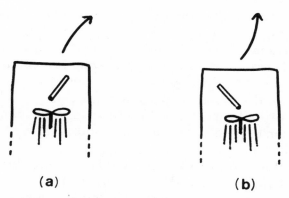

(a)   **(b)**

Fig. 46. Steering a single-engine inboard in reverse: (a) The paddle-wheel and the rudder will work together to make the boat turn, as shown by the curved arrow. (b) Initially, the paddle-wheel effect will make the stern go to port, but as the boat gains speed moving backward, the water pushing against the rudder will overcome the paddle-wheel so that the boat straightens out, as illustrated by the curved arrow.

two maneuvers you can try. If the first one works, go with it. If the first one doesn't do the job, the second one will.

The first maneuver is this—again, assuming your boat has a right-hand propeller: As you're moving backward in reverse and the stern begins to turn to port, slow the engine and shift into neutral. With the propeller stopped, the paddle-wheel effect is also stopped, and your rudder should now begin to push your stern back to starboard. As it comes back in line, go into reverse once again and continue backing. In this way—going into reverse, into neutral, back into reverse, back into neutral, etc.—you can probably back your boat in a more or less straight line.

The second maneuver is the same one described for backing away from a dock: As the stern begins to turn off to port, you simply throttle down, put the rudder over to port carefully, shift into forward, and use a good burst of prop wash to kick your stern back on course. Then, put the rudder back to starboard and shift into reverse to continue backing. As noted earlier, however, it's necessary to hold the wheel or tiller tightly when turning the rudder when your boat is moving backward. The forces on the rudder in reverse are very strong and can snatch the wheel or tiller out of your hands as the rudder crosses the centerline.

Maneuvers for Shorter Distances: When backing shorter distances so that your boat never gets moving fast enough for the rudder to offset the paddle-wheel, you need to use the "two steps backward and half-step sideways" technique. This is similar to the procedure discussed in the paragraph above, except that you don't try to steer with the rudder. The steps, if you have a right-hand propeller, are as follows:

1. With the boat stopped and lined up along the path you want to follow, put the rudder to port, and leave it there. Put the engine in reverse, and give a moderate amount of throttle to begin backing.

2. As the stern is pulled to port by the paddle-wheel, throttle down, shift into forward, and give a short burst of prop wash against the rudder to kick the stern back to starboard where it belongs.

3. Throttle down, shift into reverse, and resume backing.

4. Repeat Steps 2 and 3 as necessary.

Using this procedure, as shown in Figure 47, you can go back 15 or 20 feet, kick the stern to starboard, go back another 20 feet, and kick the stern to starboard again. That's why I call it the "two steps backward and half-step sideways" technique. If

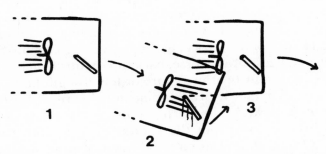

Fig. 47.   Backing a single-engine inboard in a straight line for a short distance: (1) Go into reverse to begin moving backward, with the rudder turned to port. (2) As the stern begins to turn, shift into forward, keeping the rudder turned to port, and give a burst of power to kick the stern back in line. (3) Before the boat stops moving backward, shift into reverse and keep backing. Repeat (2) and (3) as necessary.

you have a left-hand propeller, as we do, the technique is the same, except that you put your rudder to starboard so that the burst of prop wash kicks your stern to port.

There are two keys to using this technique successfully: The first is learning how to kick the stern over, throttle down, shift back into reverse, and start backing up again before the boat has a chance to completely lose its sternway. If you hold the power too long while you are kicking the stern to starboard, the boat will begin to move forward, and that will mess things up. The second key to using this technique is practice. Just go out there and practice it, over and over again. You'll find it works beautifully.

"WALKING" YOUR TWIN-ENGINE INBOARD SIDEWAYS

A particularly useful maneuver when trying to fit your twin-engine inboard boat into a tight dock space, or to position it in tight quarters to back into a slip, is to simply "walk" it sideways. The maneuver works only when the boat is standing still and you aren't trying to go sideways against a wind or current. The procedure is as follows:

To "Walk" to Starboard

1. Turn the rudders all the way to port.
2. With the engines idling, shift the port engine into forward and, at the same time, the starboard engine into reverse.

The prop wash from the port engine pushing against the rudder will push the stern to starboard, as in Figure 48(a). Reversing the starboard engine will twist, or pull, the bow to starboard at the same time. And, the boat will "walk" sideways to starboard. You may have to adjust the throttles slightly, but you'll learn that through practice.

To "Walk" to Port

1. Turn the rudders all the way to starboard.
2. With the engines idling, shift the starboard engine into

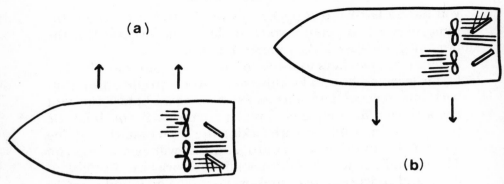

F IG. 48.   "Walking" a twin-engine inboard sideways: (a) To "walk" the
boat to starboard, turn the rudders to port, and put the starboard engine
in reverse and the port engine in forward. (b) To "walk" the boat to
port, turn the rudders to starboard, and put the port engine in reverse
and the starboard engine in forward. You may need to experiment to
find the right throttle settings, but if there's no wind to interfere, the
boat will start moving sideways—just like magic.

forward and, at the same time, the port engine into reverse.

The prop wash from the starboard engine pushing against
the rudder will push the stern to port, as in Figure 48(b).
Reversing the port engine will twist, or pull, the bow to port at
the same time. With the bow and stern both being pulled or
pushed to port, the boat will "walk" sideways to port. Again,
you may have to adjust the throttles slightly, but you'll learn
that through experience.

Testing What You've Learned
(Answers can be found in Appendix C)

1. What are four key strategies for safe boating in heavy traffic?
2. The two major factors you need to consider in attempting to hold
your boat in position are the _____ and _____ of the wind
and current.
3. The fundamental strategy for holding your boat in position is to
orient your boat so that you can strike a balance between the force of
the wind and / or current on your bow or stern and the forces created
by your _____ and _____.

4. Which is generally easier to steer in reverse—an outboard or a single-engine inboard? Why?

5. Why do you need to keep an eye on your bow when turning a boat while moving in reverse?

6. Why should you never back your boat up to a person in the water?

7. When backing a single-engine inboard, why does shifting into neutral help you steer in a more or less straight line?

V

Meeting the Real World

It's one thing to operate your boat under ideal conditions in plenty of open water and with no other boats in sight. It's another to take your boat out into the real world. Among situations that often arise are worsening weather; losing an engine; and waterways crowded by sailboat races, small fishing boats, and large ships, or some combination of the three. Other potential problems run the gamut from losing one of your crew overboard to getting caught out unexpectedly after dark or in a dense fog.

Some of these situations can be handled routinely if you know and follow the Navigation Rules—a formal set of rules promulgated and enforced in the United States by the U.S. Coast Guard. These "rules" serve to regulate traffic on our waterways and describe a series of distress signals for use when emergencies do occur. In addition to prescribing a series of fundamental regulations for operating your boat safely, the Navigation Rules establish "rules of the road" governing who has the right of way when two or more boats are coming together; define the navigation lights to be used on different sizes and types of boats; and prescribe sound signals (made with a horn, whistle, or bell) to be used when operating your boat in traffic or when visibility is reduced, as in fog. The regulations also include one "overriding" rule: If collision is imminent, you should take whatever action is necessary to avoid the collision, even if it means violating the other rules.

While the Navigation Rules are generally agreed upon internationally, there are some differences between the rules for international and U.S. waters. The first three chapters of this section will focus on the rules for U.S. waters. In instances where there are exceptions within the rules to accommodate the special circumstances encountered in the Western Rivers,* the Great Lakes,** and other specified waters, those exceptions are also explained. In the fourth chapter of this section, I'll review distress signals and describe Coast Guard requirements for emergency signaling devices on your boat.

In most other situations that you'll encounter on the water—those that can't be handled simply by adhering to the Navigation Rules—problems can be avoided or minimized with a bit of advance preparation. Accordingly, the last chapter in this section discusses how to prepare for a variety of situations involving the weather, gasoline safety, heavy traffic, mechanical failure, etc., offering suggestions for avoiding them whenever possible and for handling them when it becomes necessary. Finally, we'll talk about water-skiing—an activity, as you'll see from newspaper accounts, that too often is an accident waiting to happen.

---

*The Western Rivers are defined as "the Mississippi River and its tributaries, South Pass and Southwest Pass, to the navigational demarcation lines dividing the high seas from harbors, rivers, and other inland waters of the United States, and the Port Allen–Morgan City Alternate Route, and that part of the Atchafalaya River above its junction with the Port Allen–Morgan City Alternate Route including the Old River and the Red River."

**The Great Lakes are defined as "the Great Lakes and their connecting and tributary waters, including the Calumet River as far as the Thomas J. O'Brien Lock and Controlling Works (between mile 326 and 327), the Chicago River as far as the east side of the Ashland Avenue Bridge (between mile 321 and 322), and the Saint Lawrence River as far east as the lower exit of Saint Lambert Lock."

15

The Rules of the Road

The so-called "rules of the road" basically define who has the right of way when two or more boats are coming together. Officially, these are described in Coast Guard regulations as the "Steering and Sailing Rules," a label which clearly acknowledges that there are differences in the way one determines the right of way for boats operating under power and boats under sail. A boat under power is defined as one whose engine is being used to help push it through the water; a boat under sail is one relying solely on its sails to move through the water. The "steering" rules apply to boats under power; the "sailing" rules apply to boats under sail. As is noted repeatedly in this and other chapters, a boat using both its sails and engine to move through the water is considered "under power" according to the Navigation Rules.

(Readers may obtain the complete text of the Navigation Rules from the U.S. Government Printing Office. At this writing, the cost is six dollars. Send for: *Navigation Rules, International—Inland,* book number COMDTINST M16672.2A. The address is: Superintendent of Documents, U.S. Government Printing Office, Washington, DC 20402.)

FUNDAMENTAL RULES

The Steering and Sailing Rules include a series of fundamental rules that apply to both motorboats and sailboats. They include:
• You must maintain a proper lookout at all times.

• You must operate at a safe speed at all times, so that you can avoid a collision.
• Every boat must use all available means to determine whether the potential for collision exists.
• Action to avoid collision must be taken early and must be recognizable by people on the other boat.
• In narrow channels, you should keep to the right at all times.
• In narrow channels, large boats have the right of way over most pleasure boats.
• In some restricted waters, boats going with the current have the right of way over other boats.
• In a narrow channel, a boat overtaking another boat must use proper signals to communicate intent.
• If collision appears likely despite all other precautions, you may take whatever action is necessary to avoid the collision, even if it means violating the Navigation Rules.

Proper Lookout

The rule is very simple: You are required to keep a proper lookout at all times. In other words, there is no excuse for not seeing another boat. If you are underway in thick fog, for example, you may want to station a crew member at the bow, even if you have only a 16-foot boat. The extra few feet of visibility you gain by putting that lookout forward could make the difference between running into another boat or being able to stop or turn away in time.

FOG CITED IN BOATING ACCIDENT DEATHS ON PAWCA-TUCK—Stonington, Connecticut, police are trying to determine the cause of a boating accident on the Pawcatuck River in which two Connecticut men were killed.

Sergeant Dale Brummund, supervisor of the Stonington marine patrol, said that experts will examine the 18-foot, outboard-powered fiberglass vessel involved in the crash to see whether a mechanical failure may have contributed to the accident.

Police said they believe the boat, a Chris-Craft Corsair powered by a 90-hp Mercury, struck a cement dock on the Connecticut side of the Pawcatuck River sometime during the evening of May 31.

Brummund said police believe the accident occurred when the men were returning from fishing to a marina upriver.

There was fog on the river that evening, Brummund said. "We think that could have played a role in what happened," he said.[1]

Safe Speed

In most waterways, there are no speed limits. Rather, the decision as to what constitutes a safe speed is left to you, the skipper. That means you have to bring good judgment to the operation of your boat because, by definition in this rule, a "safe speed" is determined by the circumstances at hand. Those circumstances include the visibility, the traffic density, the presence of fishing boats, the weather and sea conditions, the draft of your boat relative to the depth of the water, and your boat's maneuverability.

In other words, what is a safe speed in clear daylight may not be considered safe after dark. Similarly, a safe speed after dark may not be safe in fog. Taking it one step further, what is a safe speed along a stretch of water when you're one of just a few boats out there may not be a safe speed when that same stretch of water is more crowded. In any case, if your boat collides with either another boat or some other object (a bridge abutment or dock), almost by definition you either were not traveling at a safe speed, were not maintaining a proper lookout, or both.

TWO PHILADELPHIA MEN HURT IN BOAT ACCIDENT ON C&D CANAL—Two Philadelphia men remained hospitalized Thursday with injuries from a boating accident on the Chesapeake and Delaware Canal, an investigator for the Delaware Marine Police said.

Robert J. Ayars of Audubon, New Jersey, the owner and operator of the 18-foot aluminum Starcraft, was charged with operating at an unsafe speed following the accident late Tuesday just east of Reedy Point Bridge, Officer Bayard Holleger, Jr., said.

According to Holleger, Ayars, 33, was motoring east in the canal when he tried to pass a tanker that was heading in the same direction. Ayars ran his boat into a fishing pier on the canal's south bank.

1. *Soundings*, August 1986.

Holleger said Ayars told investigators he was headed for Salem, New Jersey, after having dinner in Chesapeake City with his friends. Although he had traveled the canal in the daytime, Holleger said, Ayars had not negotiated the passage at night before.[2]

Determining Risk of Collision

This rule includes three key points: First, if you have any doubt whether there is risk of a collision, you should assume the danger does exist and take action to avoid it. Second, if you have radar on your boat, you must use it, along with any other available means, to help determine whether there is, in fact, any risk of collision. Third, by definition, the risk of collision exists when the relative bearing of another boat doesn't change appreciably. For example, if you see a boat about 45 degrees off your starboard bow headed in your general direction and, as it comes closer, its relative bearing (45 degrees off your starboard bow) doesn't change, the two boats are on a collision course. Even if the other boat's relative bearing begins to change as the boats come together, the rule notes that you can't just assume the danger has gone away. If the other boat is very large or a tug with a long tow, or if it is very close, there may still be danger of collision, even though the relative bearing is changing. Once again, it is not enough to know rules; you must also bring good judgment to the situation.

Visible Action Is Required

When you are approaching another boat and there is apparent risk of collision, you have several options. You can maintain your course and speed if you have the right of way. Alternatively, you can change your course, slow down, speed up, go into reverse, or put together some combination of the four. Whatever you do, however, the person steering the other boat must be able to tell what it is that you're doing. If he can't, he may take an action that will make the situation worse. For that reason, making small changes in course and / or speed to ensure

2. *News-Journal*, Wilmington, Delaware, September 4, 1987.

safe passing may not be appropriate. Instead, whatever actions you take should be done deliberately and in a manner that will be obvious to people on the other boats. Sound signals, described in Chapter 17, can be used effectively to help ensure that understanding.

Narrow Channels

Gone are the days when a sailboat automatically had the right of way over all boats under power. Under the "rules of the road," both motorboats shorter than 65.6 feet (12 meters) and sailboats must grant the right of way to *any other boat* that can only navigate safely within the confines of a narrow channel. What this rule means, of course, is that those of us who operate pleasure boats generally must grant the right of way to boats whose size restricts them to running in the channel.

There are, in addition, certain other rules for operating within channels. For example, you are normally required to keep as far to the starboard side of a channel as is practical. Also, if you are overtaking another boat in a narrow channel, you are required either to use the proper sound signals to let that boat know how you plan to pass him or to notify him of your plans by radio. Moreover, the other boat is required to make a reply.

Fishermen take note: No boats are allowed to anchor in a narrow channel unless there is no choice in the matter. Also, contrary to what seems to be popular opinion, fishing boats do not have right of way over other boats operating within a narrow channel. While the rules do not specifically address the kind of fishing you and I might do, they do specifically note that vessels "engaged in fishing shall not impede the passage of any other vessel navigating within a narrow channel or fairway." The rules define boats engaged in fishing as "any vessel fishing with nets, trawls, or other fishing apparatus which restricts maneuverability." Clearly, if commercial fishing boats don't have the right of way in a narrow channel, pleasure fishing boats also do not have any such right of way.

Finally, when operating your boat in the Western Rivers, the Great Lakes, and other specified waters, and around opening bridges (drawbridges, swing bridges, etc.) in areas where there are strong tidal currents, boats moving *with* the current generally have the right of way over boats moving *against* the current. If necessary, the boat headed into the current must hold its position to let the boat coming downstream pass safely. It is the responsibility of the boat headed downstream to propose how he intends to pass, using sound signals or VHF radio communication.

For those of us who do our boating principally on inland lakes or in coastal waters, the highly structured nature of this rule for operating on the Western Rivers, the Great Lakes, etc., may seem excessive. Those who operate their boats in these areas, however, know that the structure is a necessity for survival. This rule also has practical implications if you are waiting in heavy traffic for a drawbridge to go up. If you are headed against the current, don't try to be first through the bridge; you might be run over by the fleet coming the other way, *with* the current! The rationale for this rule, of course, was explained in earlier chapters; boats moving with a current have less steering control and less ability to come to a stop than boats moving against the same current.

The Overriding Rule

This rule, mentioned in the introduction to this section, takes its popular name from the fact that it overrides all of the other rules. The idea behind it is simply this: If there is immediate danger of collision, you may take whatever action is necessary to avoid the collision—even if it means breaking the other rules. I am repeating this rule for the third time in this chapter because it makes an important point: Ultimately, you are the person responsible for avoiding a collision involving your boat. Being able to say that you have followed the Steering and Sailing Rules to the letter while the other boat smashes into your side is not good enough. You must bring your own good judgment to every situation.

STEERING RULES FOR MOTORBOATS

The Steering Rules for motorboats establish the right of way for motorboats when they are within sight of each other and are meeting head-on, are crossing each other's path, and when one boat is overtaking another. These rules define the responsibilities of each boat in these situations. For all except the "overtaking" situation, there are separate rules for sailboats when they are under sail; those Sailing Rules are described later in this chapter. The "overtaking" rule applies to all boats.

Meeting Head-On

When two boats are approaching each other head-on, the skipper of each boat should adjust his course to starboard so that the two boats will pass port-to-port, as in Figure 49(a). This is no different than driving down any road in the U.S.; you keep to the right so that the car coming the other way passes you on the left side.

It should be noted, however, that you can use sound signals or the radio to agree with the skipper of the other boat to pass differently. It should also be noted that if you are not sure whether you are meeting the other boat head-on, you should assume that a head-on situation exists and take the appropriate action.

The only variation from this rule applies to the Western Rivers, the Great Lakes, and other specified waters in which, as noted earlier, the skipper of a boat traveling downstream (with the current) not only has the right of way, but also has the obligation to use sound signals or the VHF radio to tell any approaching boats which side he plans to pass them on.

Crossing Paths

When two boats are in a crossing situation, the boat on the starboard has the right of way, as in Figure 49(b). Expressed differently, if you are crossing paths with another boat and it is on your starboard side, it is your job to keep out of its way. Unless you are clearly going to pass well in front of it, you should change your course and / or speed to let it pass comfortably in front of you.

If the other boat is on your port side, you have the right of way. In this situation, you should maintain your course and speed while the other boat makes necessary adjustments to let you pass.

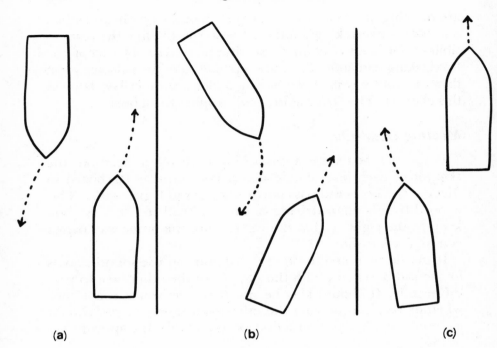

(a) **(b)** **(c)**

FIG. 49. Rules of the road—boats under power: (a) When two boats meet head-on, they should pass port-to-port. (b) When two boats are crossing, the boat to starboard has the right of way. (c) When one boat is overtaking another, the boat being overtaken has the right of way. Conditions permitting, the boat with the right of way should maintain its course and speed.

However, you cannot just assume that the skipper of the other boat knows he's the one who's supposed to slow down or change course. If he simply keeps coming along, you should be prepared to change your course and speed, if necessary, in plenty of time to avoid a collision—despite the fact that you have the right of way. Again, the "overriding" rule.

We should note also that there is an exception to this rule. On the Western Rivers, the Great Lakes, and other specified waters, a boat that is crossing a river must keep clear of boats moving up or down the river. In other words, boats going up or down the river have the right of way over boats wanting to cross the river.

Overtaking Another Boat

This is an easy one: If you are overtaking another boat, it has the right of way. You have to stay clear of it until you're completely past it and clear from any possibility of collision. Even if the boat you're overtaking changes course unexpectedly as you're passing, it is your responsibility to keep clear. That's one good reason for using sound signals or your VHF radio to be sure the other skipper knows what you're doing and agrees to it. It's also a good reason for allowing a safe distance between your boats as you pass.

When are you overtaking another boat? By definition, if you're coming up on another boat from an angle more than 22.5 degrees aft of its beam, as in Figure 49(c), you are overtaking it and must keep clear. Moreover, if you have any doubt as to whether you're overtaking another boat (as opposed to crossing its path), the rule demands that you assume you're overtaking it and keep clear. At night, the only navigation light you will see on the other boat if you're overtaking it is its stern light or, in the case of a tug with a tow, its stern light and yellow towing light (navigation lights are discussed in Chapter 16).

What if your boat is the one being overtaken? Your responsibility is to maintain your course and speed as circumstances will permit. Obviously, if you are following a channel and the channel turns, you will have to turn, too; but you should do it in a safe manner that avoids any risk of collision with the boat that's overtaking you—even though the burden is on the other skipper to keep clear of you.

SAILING RULES

The Sailing Rules are based on wind direction and the relative position of the sailboats to the wind. They apply only to sailboats under sail alone; *if you are motorsailing, you are considered a motorboat.* The rules are:

• When two sailboats are approaching each other and each boat has the wind on a different side, the boat with the wind coming from its starboard side has the right of way, as in Figure 50(a).

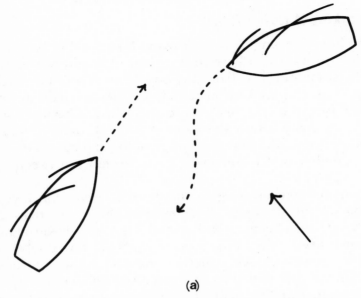

(a)

FIG. 50.   Rules of the road—boats under sail: (a) When two boats are on opposite tacks, the boat on the starboard tack (i.e., the mainsail is to port) has the right of way. (b) When two boats are on the same tack, the leeward (downwind) boat has the right of way. (c) When you are on a port tack (i.e., the mainsail is to starboard) and see another boat to windward but cannot determine what tack the other boat is on, you should assume the other boat has the right of way and steer to keep clear.

The boat with the wind from its port side must change course as necessary to keep clear of the other boat. In sailors' language, the boat on the starboard tack has the right of way; the boat on the port tack has to keep clear.

• When two sailboats have the wind coming from the same side, the downwind boat has the right of way; the upwind boat must keep clear, as in Figure 50(b). In sailors' language, the boat to leeward has the right of way; the boat to windward must keep clear. By definition, the windward side is opposite the side on which the mainsail is set.

• When the skipper of a boat with the wind from the port side sees a boat upwind but can't tell whether the other boat has the wind from its port or starboard, he should assume the other

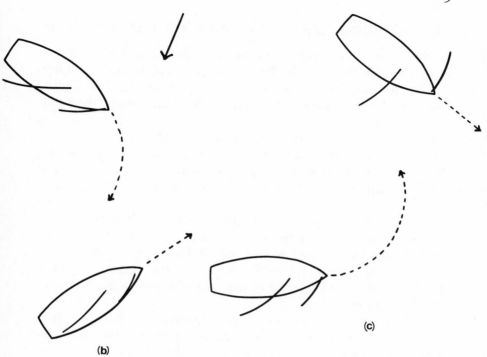

(c)

(b)

boat has the right of way and keep clear of the other boat. This situation is most likely to occur at night, when the upwind boat is running with the wind, as in Figure 50(c). In sailors' language, if you are on a port tack and see another boat upwind but can't tell what tack it's on, assume that it has the right of way, and keep clear.

In addition to these three rules, sailboats under sail are also subject to the "overtaking" rule discussed above. As with boats under power, the boat being overtaken has the right of way. It is the responsibility of the boat that is catching and passing the other one to stay clear. There are refinements to this rule used in sailboat racing, but they do not apply to normal situations and are not discussed here.

RESPONSIBILITIES OF BOATS TO EACH OTHER

In describing the "responsibilities between boats," the Navigation Rules set up a hierarchy of relationships to cover circumstances not specifically addressed by the Steering and Sailing Rules. For that reason, they apply only where one of the other rules does not.

In general, a motorboat that is underway must keep out of the way of (a) a boat that is restricted in its ability to maneuver, (b) a boat engaged in fishing as defined by the rules quoted earlier in this chapter, and (c) a sailboat under sail (without its engine running).

In general, a sailboat under sail must keep out of the way of (a) a boat that is restricted in its ability to maneuver and (b) a boat engaged in fishing, as defined by the rules.

In general, a boat engaged in fishing as defined by the Navigation Rules must keep out of the way of a boat restricted in its ability to maneuver.

And finally, all boats underway must keep clear of any boat which, for some extraordinary reason, is unable to maneuver and cannot, therefore, follow the Navigation Rules. An example might be a barge adrift, or a boat adrift in water too deep for it to anchor.

Testing What You've Learned
(Answers can be found in Appendix C)

1. Is a sailboat using both its sails and engine considered a "sailboat" or a "motorboat" according to the Navigation Rules? Why?

2. TRUE or FALSE: You can usually determine a safe speed at which to travel by following the speed limit set for the body of water on which you are boating.

3. TRUE or FALSE: Sailboats under sail always have the right of way over boats under power.

4. At an opening bridge (drawbridge, swing bridge, etc.), which boats generally have the right of way—boats traveling against the current, or those traveling with the current? Why?

5. What is the so-called "overriding" rule?

6. When two boats under power meet head-on, how should they pass each other?

7. When two boats under power are crossing each other's path, which boat has the right of way?

8. If one boat is overtaking another, which boat has the right of way? What is the responsibility of the boat that does not have the right of way?

9. If one boat under sail is on a port tack and another is on a starboard tack, which one has the right of way?

10. If two sailboats are on the same tack, how do you determine which one has the right of way?

11. If you're sailing on the port tack and see another sailboat, but can't tell what tack it's on, how do you determine who has the right of way?

16

Boat Navigation Lights

As noted in the last chapter, the "rules of the road" apply under all circumstances of visibility—daytime, nighttime, and whatever the weather. From a practical perspective, however, you can't follow the "rules of the road" if you can't see other boats; by the same token, neither can the skippers of other boats you might encounter if they can't see you. That's where boat navigation lights come into play.

Navigation lights fall into three broad categories: running lights, anchor lights, and special-purpose lights. They are to be used in the nighttime hours between sunset and sunrise, or during daylight hours when visibility is severely restricted by dark clouds, fog, rain, or snow. As their name suggests, running lights are to be used whenever your boat is underway, whether under power, under sail, or simply drifting. By definition, the only time a boat is not underway is when it is anchored, aground, or tied to the shore by some means. Similarly, anchor lights must be used when your boat is at anchor—with certain limited exceptions. What we call special-purpose lights are used to help you identify boats engaged in towing, dredging, minesweeping, etc.—special circumstances that restrict the boat's maneuverability.

The navigation lights on your boat serve three fundamental purposes: (1) They enable people on other boats to see you at night or in daytime when visibility is reduced; (2) they enable people on other boats to tell what direction you're headed in, relative to themselves; and (3) they tell people something about your boat—for example, whether you are a boat running under power, a rowboat, a sailboat under sail, or a boat at anchor.

Just as important, the navigation lights on other boats serve those same purposes for you. They make it possible for you to see other boats in the dark of night as well as when visibility is reduced during daylight hours; they let you determine what direction other boats are headed in, relative to you; and they tell you something about any boat that you're seeing—for example, whether it is probably another pleasure boat, a commercial fishing boat dragging nets far behind it, a tug pulling a barge, or a large freighter or tanker.

The importance of these lights to your boating safety makes it critically important for you and your first mate to learn how to read the navigation lights on other boats, particularly if there's even the smallest chance of your being out on a boat at night. It is also equally important for you to be sure that you have the required lights on your own boat, that those lights are working properly, and that you have the spare bulbs and batteries needed to get them working again if a bulb burns out or a battery runs down.

How important is "critically important"? Consider the following two news reports:

CAROLINAS ACCIDENT KILLS TWO NEAR BORDER—Two people were killed and one seriously injured in a midnight boat collision on the North Carolina / South Carolina state line.

Two weeks later, details of the incident, which occurred July 20 on Lake Wylie near Charlotte, North Carolina, remained clouded by confusion. An inquiry was underway.

According to the investigator on the case, Sergeant Alvin Taylor, all that is clear is that an 18-foot Glasstron and a 22-foot Thunderbird collided almost head-on about 12:30 A.M.

Killed were Pamela Kaye Hoffman, 19, and Robert Thomas Heater, 23. Injured were Alan Rutherford, 23, Craig Bell, and Haines Higginbotham, 22, all of Gastonia, North Carolina. Also injured was Terry Gene Drum, Jr., of Wake Forest, North Carolina.

All of the dead and injured had been riding aboard the Glasstron, according to police.[1]

An observation: Had the person steering either one of the two boats involved in that accident seen the navigation lights of the other boat and understood the meaning of those lights, the accident could easily have been avoided.

FOUR KILLED IN SPEEDBOAT CRASH ON ASSAWOMAN BAY—A 23-year-old Baltimore woman was killed and three men were presumed drowned after a fast-moving speedboat rammed an unlighted cabin cruiser late Saturday night in Assawoman Bay, authorities said.

The three were identified as a 38-year-old Baltimore man, a 33-year-old Hagerstown, Maryland, man, and a 26-year-old Hampstead, Maryland, man, said Sergeant Mike Bloxom of the Maryland Natural Resources Police.

All seven people on the moving boat, a 19-foot Beretta, were thrown into the bay when it struck a 25-foot Sea Ray, which authorities say was probably adrift, but possibly at anchor.

The woman, a passenger on the Beretta, was pronounced dead about 30 minutes after the 11:30 P.M. accident, said Sergeant Tim Keane of the Ocean City Police Department. He said authorities are searching for the bodies of three men from the same boat. "They drowned, but they haven't been recovered," Keane said.

The couple aboard the Sea Ray were taken to the shock trauma unit of Johns Hopkins University Hospital in Baltimore.

The Beretta was moving "pretty fast," Keane said. "It took the whole bow off [the Sea Ray], so the boat was really flying at high speed."

Regardless of whether the unlit Sea Ray was anchored or adrift, it would have been violating the law, Bloxom said. He said boats shorter than 20 meters must display a white anchor light while at anchor and red, green, and white running lights while adrift or underway.

An investigation into the collision was launched.[2]

Three weeks later, the operator of the Beretta involved in this accident was charged with four counts of manslaughter by

1. *Soundings,* October 1986.
2. *News-Journal,* Wilmington, Delaware, August 30, 1988.

motorboat. He also faced charges of operating a boat while intoxicated, operating a boat while under the influence of alcohol, negligence, operation so as to endanger a life, reckless operation, speed too great for the conditions, and failure to maintain a proper lookout.

The operator of the cabin cruiser, whose boat was drifting in the bay when the accident occurred, was charged with one count of failure to comply with the Navigation Rules because the stern light on his boat was not operating. He faced a maximum penalty of three months in jail and a $500 fine.

Reviewing the full range of navigation lights required under the Navigation Rules is beyond the scope of this book. Moreover, unless your memory is better than mine, the variety is too great to remember them all, anyway, unless you're out on the water seeing them frequently. So this chapter focuses mainly on lights required by the Inland Rules on most pleasure boats and, in general terms, on larger ships, tugs, and fishing boats.

To fill in the gaps, every skipper should have some kind of reference aboard the boat so that he or she can "look up" any lights whose meanings are not immediately understood. The best reference is the U.S. Coast Guard publication mentioned at the beginning of Chapter 15, *Navigation Rules, International— Inland*. This book contains excellent color drawings to illustrate the lights of many different types of boats. Another less detailed reference is one of the "Quick Reference Navigation Rules" cards found in many marine stores. The reference cards, consisting of abbreviated Navigation Rules, are printed on a sturdy 8½- by-11-inch plastic page. We keep both aboard our boat—one available for immediate reference, the other for more detailed information if needed.

REQUIRED LIGHTS

The Navigation Rules describe seven different types of lights to be used on boats traveling on U.S. waterways. These lights must be used from sunset to sunrise; they are also to be used in daylight hours when visibility is restricted. Five of the required

lights are of primary interest to most boaters. The other two
are different types of flashing lights with specialized use—one
on hovercraft, the other on certain barges—and are not covered in this book. The five lights of primary interest include:

   Masthead Light: Also called a "steaming light," this light is
raised above deck on some kind of a mast, usually on or close
to the centerline of the boat. Although it is generally called a
"masthead light" and found at the top of the mast on motorboats, it usually is mounted only partway up the mast of a sailboat—the forward mast, if the sailboat has more than one. By
definition, a "masthead light" always is white. It lights an area
from the bow around each side to a point 22.5 degrees abaft
(astern of) the beam, as shown in Figure 51.

   Side Lights: Red on the port side, green on the starboard

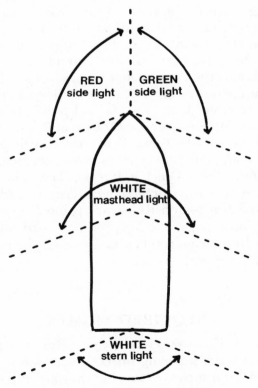

FIG. 51.   Boat navigation lights.

side. Together, these lights cover the same arc of visibility covered by the masthead light—from dead ahead around to 22.5 degrees abaft (astern of) the beam, as shown in Figure 51. Both the red and green lights are visible at the same time only from dead ahead. (You can remember which color is on which side by remembering that "red" has fewer letters than "green" and "port" has fewer letters than "starboard." The shorter words go together—red / port. You can also think in terms of wine—port is red.)

Stern Light: This light also must be white. It is located at the stern of the boat and covers an arc from dead astern forward on both sides to a point 22.5 degrees abaft the beam, as shown in Figure 51. The stern light and the masthead (steaming) light together, and / or the stern light and the red and green side-lights together, make a complete circle.

All-'Round Light: This light can be seen from any direction, as shown in Figure 52(a). Depending upon its purpose, it may be either white, red, or green. It is usually mounted on the boat's mast.

Towing Light: This is a yellow light with the same range of view as the stern light, covering an arc from dead astern forward on both sides to a point 22.5 degrees abaft the beam, as shown in Figure 52(b).

Lights for Motorboats

The rules vary according to length. For purposes of understanding, it is important to start with larger boats.

Less Than 164 Feet (50 Meters) Long: Any boat operating under power at night or in reduced visibility should show a white masthead "steaming light" in the forward half of the boat, a white stern light, and red and green side lights. If the boat has a second mast aft of and taller than the first, it may also show an additional white masthead light on the second mast. The white lights should be visible in good conditions for two to five miles, depending upon function and boat length; the side lights should be visible from one to two miles, depending upon boat length. This rule applies to sailboats running under power, *even if they are motorsailing,* as well as to motorboats.

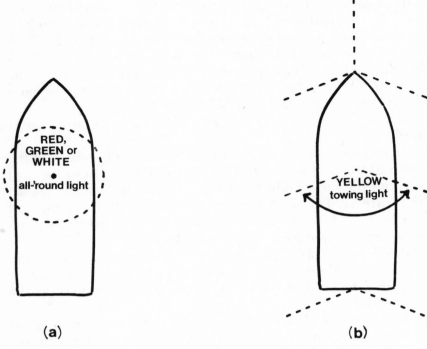

Fɪɢ. 52.   Boat navigation lights (cont.).

Less Than 39.4 Feet (20 Meters) Long: Any boat operating
under power at night or in reduced visibility (this rule, too,
applies to sailboats whose engines are being used, even if they
are motorsailing) should show an all-'round white light and red
and green side lights. As an alternative to the all-'round white
light, the boat may show the same system of two white lights
prescribed for larger motorboats—a masthead (steaming) light
and a stern light. The white lights on boats this size should be
visible in good conditions for at least two miles; the red and
green side lights should be visible for at least one mile.

Less Than 23 Feet (7 Meters) Long: A motorboat less than 23
feet long must show the same lights required for larger motorboats. *This includes dinghies powered by outboard motors.*

Lights for Sailboats

As noted earlier, a sailboat is a sailboat only if it is moving under sail alone.

Any Size: A sailboat underway should show only red and green side lights and a white stern light. *Note: A common error of sailors is to show a white masthead light—the "steaming light"—while under sail.* That can be dangerous. The skipper of another sailboat seeing that steaming light will assume the sailboat is under power and may not grant the "right of way" the sailboat skipper expects—for example, starboard tack over port tack.

In addition to the red and green side lights and white stern light, a sailboat underway may show two all-'round lights at the top of the mast, one atop the other. The upper light must be red, the lower green. It should be emphasized that the masthead red and green lights are *in addition to* the usual side lights and stern light.

Less Than 65.6 Feet (20 Meters) Long: A sailboat underway may show a single red, green, and white "tricolor" light at the top of its mast in place of the red and green side lights and white stern light required on larger sailboats. The tricolor light may not, however, be used in conjunction with the all-'round red and green masthead lights described above.

From a practical perspective, I recommend against using the masthead tricolor light when other pleasure boats are close at hand; the reason is that most boaters are not accustomed to looking 40 or 50 feet in the air to spot another pleasure boat's running lights, and they may not see you. Susan and I discovered that problem firsthand when a motorboater pulled up alongside us, irate that we were sailing through a crowded harbor after dark without any lights; he hadn't seen our masthead tricolor.

Less Than 23 Feet (7 Meters) Long: While it is preferable for smaller sailboats to show the same lights as their larger sisters, it may not be practical. In that instance, the rules allow you to carry a bright, white flashlight or lighted lantern that can be shown in plenty of time to prevent a collision. The light is most easily seen if you shine it on the sail.

Lights for Rowboats

In general, rowboats—including dinghies—are required to show the same lights as small sailboats are. However, if the side lights and stern light are impractical, a boat under oars should have a bright, white flashlight or lighted lantern that can be shown in plenty of time to prevent a collision. Note that while the Navigation Rules do not specifically address the use of canoes, kayaks, paddle boats, etc., our presumption is that these boats would be subject to the same rules as rowboats. In any case, the interests of safety suggest that anyone out in a canoe, kayak, or paddle boat at night where there is any possibility of other boat traffic—including other canoes, kayaks, or paddle boats—should carry a bright flashlight that can be shown in plenty of time if necessary to prevent a collision. He or she should also be wearing a PFD.

READING THE LIGHTS ON OTHER PLEASURE BOATS

When you think about these lighting requirements for a few minutes, you will reach understandings like the following:
• If you see a boat out on the water at night with only a single white light, you may be looking at the stern of either a motorboat or a sailboat. You could also be looking at a small sailboat or rowboat from almost any angle, an anchor light, or at a motorboat or sailboat far enough away that you can't yet see its red / green running lights. There's a crucial point here: You cannot assume that you are seeing all of the lights a boat should be showing. One of the lights may be burned out, improperly shielded by something on the boat, or still below the horizon. The practical implication is that you need to consider all of the possible interpretations of the lights you see and continue checking them until you are safely clear.
• If you see a boat showing only a red side light and a single white light, you could be looking at a motorboat anywhere from the size of a dinghy to some 164 feet long—assuming that some sailor isn't showing his steaming light improperly. It also means

that the other boat is headed in your general direction. If a collision appears possible as the other boat gets closer, the fact that the boat is showing you a red light means that it has the right of way, and you'll have to change course to get out of its way. As the boat gets closer, you'll be able to judge its size more clearly.

• If you see a boat showing only a green side light and a single white light, you could once again be looking at a motorboat anywhere from the size of a dinghy to some 164 feet long. That boat, too, is headed in your general direction; in this case, however, if a collision appears possible as the boat gets closer, you will have the right of way in most circumstances and should maintain your course and speed. The skipper of the other boat should, in turn, change course to get out of your way. *However: You should always assume the other person does not know the "rules of the road" and be ready to change course, if necessary, to avoid a collision, even though you have the right of way. Also, remember that you may not actually have the right of way if you are crossing a channel and the other boat is restricted to the channel by the depth of water.*

• If you see a boat with both its red and green side lights visible, but no white light, you're looking at a sailboat or, possibly, a rowboat headed straight toward you. As the boat draws closer, you should watch carefully to be sure its skipper has seen your boat. You should also be prepared to change course as necessary to avoid a collision if the other boat does not alter course to go around you.

• If you see a boat with both red and green side lights and a white light visible, you're looking at a motorboat headed straight toward you. In this case, too, you should watch the other boat carefully to be sure its skipper has seen your boat. You should also be prepared to change course as necessary to avoid a collision.

READING THE LIGHTS ON COMMERCIAL VESSELS

It isn't enough, however, to recognize the lights on other pleasure boats. Anyone who uses his or her boat in waters where there might be commercial boat traffic must also be able to read the lights of the most common commercial vessels. Moreover, as mentioned earlier, there should be a good light reference handy so that if a set of lights that aren't familiar is encountered, someone can look them up to figure out what those lights are telling you. It could save your life.

HERO SAVES FOUR OFF NEW JERSEY AFTER WRECK—Novice boater Elmer Thomas, 43, of Pipersville, Pennsylvania, doesn't see himself as a hero.

Thomas rescued four boaters off Ocean City, New Jersey, after their 29-foot sportfishing boat capsized and drowned two others.

The 29-foot *Reel Action* rammed a tugboat's 200-yard towline and became entangled, said officer Michael Hickman of the State Police Marine Bureau in Wildwood, New Jersey. The fishing boat was then run over by the barge that the tug was pulling, he said.

An autopsy showed that Gary Endrick, 32, of Warminster, Pennsylvania, and Eden Gasin, 24, of Willow Grove, Pennsylvania, drowned, Hickman said.

The two victims were sleeping in a cabin below deck and were trapped underneath when the barge climbed atop the *Reel Action*, Hickman said.

The survivors were rescued by Thomas after spending almost seven hours in the water.

The *Good Times* rescued the four survivors around 7:50 A.M. and took them back to the Coast Guard's Great Egg station in Ocean City.[3]

From a practical viewpoint, the commercial motor vessels most of us will commonly encounter are large ships, tugs, and fishing boats. We may also share the water with ferryboats, sightseeing boats, and other commercial vessels that fall short of what most of us would consider ships. Any of these commercial boats that are less than 164 feet (50 meters) long are only required to show the same masthead light, red and green side lights, and stern light required of other motorboats of the same size. They may also show a second masthead light if the boat has more than one mast.

3. *Soundings,* November 1988.

More Than 164 Feet (50 Meters) Long: In general, large ships are required to show two white masthead lights, the second aft of and taller than the first; red and green side lights; and a stern light. An exception to this requirement is for large ships on the Great Lakes, which may use an all-'round white light atop the after mast in place of the second masthead light and stern light. The masthead lights (and the all-'round white light on the Great Lakes vessel) should be visible for at least six miles in good conditions. The side lights and stern light should have a visibility range of at least three miles.

One purpose of the two masthead lights is to help others seeing the ship have a clearer understanding of the ship's relative course when the ship is too far away for the side lights to be distinguished. The importance of this becomes apparent when you realize that a ship traveling at 18 knots travels six miles in 20 minutes. This means that while you might look astern now and see nothing, 21 minutes later you can look astern just in time to see the bow of a ship before it overruns your boat. The obvious point is that if you are boating during the day or night in an area where there is large-ship traffic, you need to keep a good and frequent lookout.

Tugboats Pulling Barges: When a tugboat is pulling one or more barges, it must show two masthead lights, one directly above the other in a vertical line, if the length of the tow (the distance from the tug to the stern of the last barge) is less than 200 meters. If the length of the tow is more than 200 meters, the tug must show three masthead lights, each one directly above the other in a vertical line. In addition, the tug must show its normal red and green side lights and a yellow towing light aligned vertically directly above its stern light. In all cases, the vertically aligned lights must be far enough apart that you can easily see that there are two or three lights, one above the other.

Since tugs are also required to show the same navigation lights as those required on other motorboats of their size, some tugs may show lights on two masts. In that case, the vertically aligned masthead lights may be displayed on either mast. Whichever, the other mast must still show its normal masthead light.

Barges being pulled should show red and green side lights mounted on the corners of the bow, and a stern light. Experience suggests the lights on barges are not always easy to see. That's one reason it is so important to know what the tugboat's lights are telling you.

Note: Because there may be more than one barge in a tow, it is important to be extremely careful when passing behind a tug pulling a tow—particularly at night or in poor visibility during daylight hours. People have been known to let one barge pass, only to discover too late that there is a second or maybe even a third barge in the tow, with tragic results.

Tugboats Pushing Barges in Front: There are two possible circumstances here. In the first circumstance, the bow of the tug fits up into the stern of the barge so that they effectively form a single unit. In this case, the tug and barge are treated as a single vessel. As a result, the lights on this "composite" vessel will look just like those of any other motorboat of the same overall length.

In the second circumstance, the tug is simply pushing the barge. In this case, the tug must show two masthead lights, one directly above the other in a vertical line, its normal red and green side lights, and two yellow towing lights in place of the stern light. The barge should show red and green side lights mounted at the corners of the bow and a special yellow flashing light on the bow visible over the same arc as that covered by the tug's masthead lights.

Tugs Towing Barges Alongside: A tugboat towing a barge alongside should show the same lights that are shown when pushing a barge in front—two masthead lights vertically aligned, red and green side lights, and two yellow towing lights vertically aligned in place of the stern light.

A barge being towed alongside should show only red and green side lights mounted at the corners of the bow, and a stern light.

Commercial Fishing Boats: These rules apply to boats fishing with nets, long lines, trawls, and other gear that restricts their maneuverability. They do not apply to boats fishing with trolling lines or other apparatus that does not restrict their maneuverability; in other words, these rules do not apply to sportfishing boats.

In general, a boat engaged in fishing should display on its

mast either an all-'round green light vertically aligned above an all-'round white light if it is trawling, or an all-'round red light vertically aligned above an all-'round white light if engaged in fishing other than trawling. In either case, the boat may have gear stretched far out from the sides or stern. If the boat is moving through the water, it should show red and green side lights and a stern light in addition to the all-'round lights. If the boat is more than 164 feet long, it should also show a masthead light on a mast aft of the all-'round green (or red) and white vertically aligned lights. Key point: If you see either a green light or a red light directly above a white light, you are looking at a fishing boat and should either pass safely in front of it or steer well clear of it.

Other Commercial Vessels: Various other specialized navigation lights may be encountered from time to time. In general, these consist of two or more all-'round red or green lights, or a combination of all-'round red and white lights. Any of these combinations of lights is telling you that the vessel is limited in some way in its ability to maneuver and that you should stay well clear of it. In fact, depending upon the combination, you may be looking at anything from a working dredge to a mine-sweeper to a boat involved in a diving operation or even to a boat that has run aground. In any case, either of the two references suggested earlier should enable you to quickly figure out what the lights mean.

ANCHOR LIGHTS

There is often confusion as to when one should show an anchor light and when it's not required. Starting at the top: Anytime you are anchoring for the night, whether required by the letter of the law or not, your own self-interest requires that you show a nice, bright anchor light.

TWO TEENS INJURED IN ACCIDENT—Two Anne Arundel County, Maryland, teenagers were injured when the Boston Whaler they were in crashed into [an anchored] sailboat.

Rebecca Neel, 14, of Millersville, and William S. Rickelman, 16, of Severna Park, were treated in Anne Arundel General Hospital.

According to published reports, the two were driving the 17-foot Whaler at a high rate of speed in the Magothy River on the evening of August 26. They apparently saw a powerboat in Sillery Bay and, after turning to avoid it, crashed into the port side of an anchored 28-foot Cape Dory sailboat.

Neel and Rickelman were both thrown on impact from the small powerboat into the water. Apparently neither saw the anchored sailboat in their path. The two were rescued by the sailboat owner and taken to Fairwinds Marina before being transferred to the hospital.

The two people in the sailboat, Glenn Kendall and his wife, were not injured. The boat, however, suffered about $5,000 in damage. The Whaler reportedly had damage totaling between $2,000 and $3,000.[4]

In general, boats less than 164 feet long are required to display a single all-'round white light "where it can best be seen." Many motorboats that are less than 39.4 feet (12 meters) long have an all-'round white light on the top of their masts as a navigation light in lieu of the masthead light and stern light required on larger boats. If this light meets the two-mile visibility requirement, it should serve effectively as an anchor light.

Many sailboats also have an all-'round white light at the top of the mast to serve as an anchor light. In my view, mast-top lights on sailboats do not make good anchor lights. Because they are 40 or 50 feet in the air, mast-top lights may not be seen by people running their boats at night, who are generally looking for lights close to the water, not high in the air. For that reason, I recommend using a separate white anchor light that can be hung from a halyard 8 or 10 feet above the cabintop. This light can operate from its own fresh batteries or be connected to the boat's main batteries.

Now, the exceptions to the rule: A boat less than 65.6 feet (20 meters) is not required to show an anchor light if it is anchored in a special anchorage designated by the U.S. Secretary of Transportation. Such anchorages are clearly marked on navigation charts. In addition, boats less than 23 feet (7 meters)

4. *Soundings*, December 1986.

long are not required to show an anchor light if they are anchored in areas where other boats do not normally navigate—in other words, in coves or creeks away from normal boat traffic.

However, while I acknowledge, as noted earlier, that the Navigation Rules make these exceptions, I believe that common safety sense makes no exceptions, and that you should use a good anchor light, whether or not it is required by the Rules.

Testing What You've Learned
(Answers can be found in Appendix C)

1. When are you supposed to use your boat's navigation lights?

2. If you are out on the water at night and see a single white light ahead, what does that light tell you?

3. If you are out on the water at night and see a yellow light directly above a white light, what do those lights tell you?

4. If you are out on the water at night and see a red light, a green light, and, between them, two white lights one above the other, what do those lights tell you?

5. If you are out on the water at night and see a green light and two white lights, one directly above the other, what do those lights tell you?

6. If you are out on the water at night and see a single green light, what does that light tell you?

7. If you are out on the water at night and see a red light directly over a green light, what do those lights tell you?

8. If you are out on the water at night and see a red light directly over a white light, what do those lights tell you?

9. If you are out on the water at night and see a red light directly over a white light and, closer to the water, another red light, what do those lights tell you?

10. TRUE or FALSE: Because of the obvious impracticality, the Navigation Rules do not require any lights to be used at night on small sailboats, rowboats, or dinghies.

17

Sound Signals

Before the days of ship-to-ship radio, large ships needed some way to communicate their intentions to other ships as they approached each other in narrow channels. Their size alone made it impossible for them to turn or stop quickly, making it doubly important to avoid misunderstanding. Moreover, in fog and other conditions when visibility was so reduced that lookouts couldn't seen other boats, even with the help of their navigation lights, some means was needed for boats to tell each other that they were out there. Sound signals had their origins in both of these needs, and are still widely used.

Today, there are a dozen or so specific sound signals to help you get where you're going safely and efficiently. For example, you can use your boat's horn to tell the skipper of another boat what side you plan to pass him on, to warn him that a dangerous situation is developing, and to let other boats know your whereabouts if you get caught out in fog. As described in Chapter 12, you can use your horn to let other boaters know that you're leaving your slip. You can also use it to ask the operator of a drawbridge to raise the bridge for you. In short, sound signals can be really useful.

Most of these sound signals are prescribed by the Navigation Rules. The signals made using the boat's horn are composed of short, long, or a combination of short and long blasts on the horn, with a "short" blast defined as lasting about one second, and a long or "prolonged" blast lasting about four to six seconds. Most bell signals consist of a rapid ringing for about five seconds.

Interestingly, the boats that most of us have—less than 39.4 feet (12 meters) long—are not required to have a horn or bell that meets any particular specifications related to size or loudness. The only requirement is that boats of this size carry some means for making "an efficient sound signal." I carried a good, loud mouth whistle on my sailboat when I was a teenager. Our boat today carries both a horn we hold up to our mouths to blow and a louder Freon canister horn. Many motorboats are equipped with good, strong electric horns that meet the requirements for larger boats.

WARNING AND PASSING SIGNALS

Although the Steering and Sailing Rules define when one boat has the right of way over another, there are times when it would be nice to know that the skipper of the other boat does indeed recognize your right of way. Similarly, sometimes there may be good reason why you want to pass a boat differently than as prescribed by the Steering and Sailing Rules. The "warning" and "passing" signals established by the Navigation Rules enable you and other skippers to discuss these kinds of issues using your boats' horns. They include a specific series of horn signals for boats that are approaching each other, either when meeting head-on, crossing each other's paths, when one boat is overtaking another, or when visibility is blocked and the potential for collision exists. Two of these signals are for providing warning of potential danger; the other three are for negotiating the plans for one boat to pass the other.

Although most pleasure boaters seldom use these signals except when passing, this does not mean that all of the sound signals can't be helpful to those of us who have small boats. To the contrary, there are times in a crowded harbor when sound signals could be well used. Moreover, we can easily find ourselves being signaled by a ship whose skipper or pilot wants to be sure we know how he intends to pass us. Susan and I well remember an occasion in the Chesapeake and Delaware Canal when a cruise ship (a small ocean liner) signaled us, with two short blasts, his intent to leave us on his starboard side when passing us, as required by the fundamental Steering and Sailing Rules noted in Chapter 15. We acknowledged his signals as required by the Navigation Rules by giving two short blasts on our mouth horn—much to the amusement of passengers standing along the ship's rail.

Warning Signals

There are two warning signals. The most important one is the danger signal—five or more short blasts on the horn. This danger signal should be used at any time you do not understand the intentions of another boat and you believe there is imminent danger of collision. It should also be used in response to a passing signal if you believe it is unsafe for the other boat to pass you as planned.

The second warning signal consists of one long blast. It is the signal mentioned earlier that you should use when leaving a slip. Key point: If you are operating your boat near a dock and hear a four- to six-second blast on a boat's horn, start looking around to be sure your way is clear. The skipper of the boat coming out of the dock or slip may not have seen you.

Passing Signals

Passing signals apply only to boats operating under power. They are used in situations in which two motor-driven boats (including sailboats that are "motorsailing") are in sight of each other and are meeting head-on, crossing each other's path, or overtaking one another.

Meeting Head-On or Crossing: These signals can be confusing until you understand the variety of circumstances they must apply to. If the two boats are meeting more or less head-on, it's simple; they are going to pass side by side. If they're crossing, it's more complex, because the signal you make tells the skipper of the other boat whether you plan to pass in front of or behind him. So, you need a definition for these signals that will fit both circumstances—passing side by side, and passing in front of or behind. That's why these signals are defined in a way to tell the other skipper which side of your boat you intend to leave him on. For example:

• **One short blast**—"I intend to leave you on my port side" (Figure 53).

• **Two short blasts**—"I intend to leave you on my starboard side" (Figure 54).

Whenever you give a passing signal to another skipper, he should respond with one of two answers. If he agrees to the proposed passing, he should echo your signal. In other words, if you signal him with one short blast, he should answer with one short blast if he agrees to your proposed passing. If you signal him with two short blasts and he agrees to your proposed passing, he should answer with two short blasts. As noted above, however, if he disagrees with your proposal, he should answer with the danger signal—five or more short blasts.

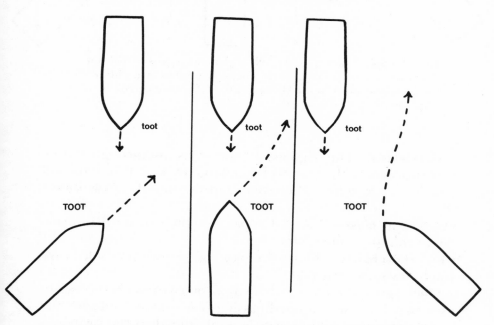

FIG. 53. Sound signals: When planning to pass so that you leave the other boat on your port side, you should signal with one long blast on your horn. If the skipper of the other boat agrees, he should respond with the same signal.

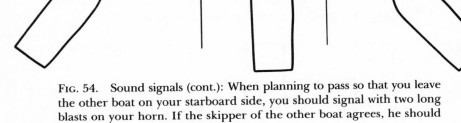

FIG. 54.   Sound signals (cont.): When planning to pass so that you leave the other boat on your starboard side, you should signal with two long blasts on your horn. If the skipper of the other boat agrees, he should respond with the same signal.

Overtaking: The signals in this circumstance are more straightforward. If you are overtaking another boat, you will pass it on one side or the other, and the sound signals reflect that.

• **One short blast**—"I intend to pass you on your starboard side (leave you to my port side)."

• **Two short blasts**—"I intend to pass you on your port side (leave you to my starboard side)."

Once again, there are only two possible correct responses to each signal. If the proposed passing is acceptable and safe, the correct response is to repeat the same signal. If the proposed passing is unsafe, the correct response is to sound the warning signal of five or more short blasts.

Additional Sound Signals

Two additional sound signals should be mentioned here:

• When approaching a blind curve in a channel, you should sound one long blast. A boat coming from the other direction should answer with the same signal—one long blast—to tell you that it is there. If there is no response, it's presumed there's no traffic coming the other way, though you should still proceed cautiously.

• Although this is not described in the Navigation Rules, the generally accepted sound signal to request a bridge opening is one long blast followed by one short blast. The bridge operator should respond with the same signal if he is able to open the bridge at that time. If the bridge operator cannot open the bridge at that time, he should answer with the danger signal of five or more short blasts. In that circumstance, the boat's skipper should indicate his understanding by answering with the same danger signal. You can also arrange a bridge opening by radio; most bridge tenders monitor VHF Channel 13.

SOUND SIGNALS IN FOG (RESTRICTED VISIBILITY)

The greatest danger from collision when you are caught in a fog, or when visibility is reduced in heavy rain or snow, comes about because you can't see the other boats and they can't see you. Radar helps—if you have it and know how to use it well. But even radar may be of little value in heavy rain or snow because the precipitation itself creates interference on the radar screen that can mask the radar images of other small boats.

As noted at the outset, sound signals evolved in part to overcome problems of restricted visibility. While they won't tell another boat where you are, properly used sound signals will at least let other boats know that you are nearby and what you're doing—moving ahead under power, drifting with your engine running, moving but restricted in your ability to maneuver, or lying at anchor to wait it out. Equally important, the same signals from other boats tell you the same information about them—

what they're doing, and whether they're restricted in their ability to maneuver. Changes in the sound of those signals can also help you figure out whether any of the other boats are getting closer to you or farther away. The situations and signals you're most likely to encounter include:

• A boat that is under power and moving through the water—**one long blast on the horn at least every two minutes.**

• A boat that is under power, but stopped and drifting—**two long blasts on the horn at least every two minutes.**

• A boat that's moving, but is limited in its ability to maneuver—**one long blast followed by two short blasts (long, short, short) at least every two minutes.** This might include sailboats under sail, tugs pushing or towing barges, fishing boats, etc.

• A boat or barge being towed, if it is manned—**one long blast followed by three short blasts (long, short, short, short) at least every two minutes and, if practical, immediately after the signal given by the towing vessel.**

• A boat longer than 39.4 feet (12 meters) at anchor—**a bell ringing rapidly for about five seconds at one-minute intervals.** In addition to ringing the bell, you are permitted to give a short blast on your horn, followed by one long blast and one more short blast (short, long, short). Also, ships longer than 100 meters are required to ring two bells, one at the bow for five seconds immediately followed by another bell at the stern for five seconds, both at one-minute intervals.

• A boat less that 39.4 feet long at anchor (and this includes most of us)—**either a bell ringing rapidly for five seconds at one-minute intervals, or some other efficient sound signal, at least every two minutes.** An example of an efficient sound signal in this circumstance might be banging on the bottom of a pan with a spoon. However, it is a small concession to carry a hand-held bell for this eventuality.

As when considering navigation lights, you not only need to know what to do on your boat, you also need to be able to interpret the signals you hear from other boats. So, for example, if you're anchored in a fog ringing your bell every minute and you hear one long blast on another boat's horn, you know there's a boat under power moving through the water somewhere in your neighborhood. In that case, you'll want to listen to the sound of its horn each time it blasts to judge whether the boat is heading toward you.

If, on the other hand, you hear two long blasts, you'll know that the other boat is not moving through the water, but drifting with its engine running. Depending upon where you are and the kind of boat traffic normally found in that area, the sound of one long blast followed by two short ones may tell you that somewhere nearby there's a sailboat under sail, a fishing boat, a tug with a barge, or perhaps one pleasure boat towing another. If that long-short-short signal is followed by one long blast and three short ones, you'll know clearly that there's something being towed nearby. Finally, any time you're in a fog and hear a bell being rung rapidly for five seconds, or a pan being banged for several seconds, every one or two minutes, you know that you are near someone lying at anchor. That is the only circumstance in which you'll hear that kind of sound signal.

Testing What You've Learned
(Answers can be found in Appendix C)

1. What sound-making devices are boats less than 39.4 feet long required to carry? Are there other sound-making devices that are not required, but are worthwhile having aboard?

2. What does it mean if you hear five or more short blasts on a horn?

3. If you're near a dock and hear one long blast from a boat's horn, what does the signal mean, and what should you do about it?

4. If you're meeting another boat head-on and the other skipper signals you with two short blasts of his horn, what is he telling you, and how should you respond?

5. If you're overtaking another boat and want to leave it to port (pass it on its starboard side), what is the correct sound signal? If the other skipper replies with five short blasts, what is he telling you?

6. What is the generally accepted sound signal for requesting a bridge opening? How is the bridge operator supposed to respond?

7. If you're moving under power in the fog, what sound signal should you use?

8. If you're anchored in the fog on a boat less than 39.4 feet long, what sound signal should you use?

18

Distress Signals

If you need help, but can't tell anyone, you've got a problem. By the same token, if you can tell someone, but the other person doesn't understand what you're trying to communicate, you've still got a problem. Both Coast Guard regulations and the Navigation Rules attempt to prevent these situations from arising. The Coast Guard regulations prescribe minimum emergency signaling devices to be carried on your boat if you operate in U.S. coastal waters; the Navigation Rules describe a broader series of signals, most of which are recognized as distress signals the world over.

REQUIRED VISUAL DISTRESS SIGNALS

The regulations requiring visual distress signals approved for day and / or night use apply specifically to boats on the Great Lakes, the various coastal bays and sounds, the mouths of our largest rivers as far upstream as the river is more than two miles wide, and the ocean or Gulf Coast waters out to the three-mile limit. An exception to the requirement is made in daylight hours for recreational motorboats less than 16 feet long, canoes and kayaks, and open sailboats less than 26 feet long, if they do not have a motor.

After sunset, however, all boats are supposed to carry visual distress signals approved for night use. Moreover, even if your boat is one of those exempted from carrying day signals, I suggest you ignore the exemption and carry a daytime signal anyway. I'd also suggest carrying approved distress signals if you're boating on inland lakes or rivers. You may still need help someday, even in those waters.

Signals Approved for Both Day and Night Use

There is only one category of signaling devices approved for both day and night use—flares. They may be either hand-held flares, meteor flares, or parachute flares. A minimum of three is required. All flares meeting Coast Guard specifications as emergency signaling devices are labeled with an expiration date. In general, flares should be replaced every three years.

Standard highway flares are not approved as marine visual distress signals and should not be carried on your boat. Not only are highway flares unlikely to ignite in wet weather, they also are not bright enough to be seen over the distances often required on water.

If you have hand-held flares and must use them, be sure to hold them over the downwind side of the boat so that the wind can't blow the burning material back toward you or the boat. Also, when lighting a flare make certain there are no gasoline containers anywhere nearby. Meteor or parachute flares should be fired from the stern of the boat across the wind so they cannot be blown back down onto the boat. In general, flares should be used only when there is another boat in sight; if you can't see a boat, those aboard it probably will not see your flare.

Signals Approved for Daytime Use

In addition to flares, visual distress signals approved for daytime use include orange smoke devices and a distress flag. Orange smoke devices may be held in your hand or ignited, placed on the stern of your boat, or put out to float on the water. They are useful when the wind is light; if the wind is more than 8 or 10 knots, the smoke will be blown away too fast for it to be an effective signal. In any case, you should use the smoke device only when you can see another boat.

The approved signal flag consists of a black ball and a black square, both on an orange background. The flag can be tied to an oar or strung up a mast. If there's no wind, the flag will be more effective at attracting attention if you wave it from an oar or a boathook than if you let it hang limp from a mast.

Signals Approved for Nighttime Use

Other than flares, the only approved nighttime visual distress signals are a quick-flashing white strobe light and an electric distress-signal lantern. The battery-powered distress-signal lantern is used to flash S.O.S. in Morse code (three short flashes, three long flashes, and three short flashes) four to six times a minute. Some of these lights are programmed to flash the signal for you when they're turned on. Normal flashlights should not be carried in place of an approved distress signal lantern for at least two reasons: Their light probably isn't bright enough to be seen at the distances required; and, flashlights get used so often that their batteries are seldom fresh.

DISTRESS SIGNALS

The Navigation Rules describe seventeen specific distress signals, all but one of which are agreed upon internationally. The exception is the quick-flashing (fifty to seventy times per minute) white strobe light mentioned above, which is recognized officially in U.S. waters as a distress signal, but not in international waters.

There are two reasons for becoming acquainted with these signals. One is that you may need to use one or more of them yourself some day. The other is that you may see one of these signals and must be able to recognize it for what it is—a call for help. In addition to the quick-flashing white strobe, the distress signals are:
• Red star shells (rockets or shells), fired one at a time at short intervals.
• A foghorn sounding continuously, or a continuous noise made with any fog signaling device.
• Flames on a vessel, as from a burning tar barrel, etc.; or, obviously, from the vessel itself being on fire.

- A gun fired at one-minute intervals.
- A distress flag, consisting of a black ball and a black square on an orange background.
- S.O.S., the international Morse code distress signal, sent by radio, with a light, or with a horn. The signal consists of three shorts, three longs, and three shorts, in that order.
- The "Mayday" signal sent by radio (on VHF radio, this is given over Channel 16).
- A parachute red flare, or a hand-held red flare.
- A dye marker in the water.
- The signal flags "November" and "Charlie," the International Code Signal of distress.
- A square black flag flying above or below anything resembling a black ball.
- A person holding his / her arms straight out sideways from the body and moving them up and down slowly, as if they were wings flapping in slow motion.
- Orange smoke.
- A radiotelegraph alarm signal.
- A radiotelephone alarm signal.
- An emergency-position-indicating radio beacon (EPIRB).

Obviously, some of these signals will be used only by larger boats or ships. All but the last three, however, could be seen or heard by any pleasure boater. In any case, use of these signals except in an emergency situation is prohibited.

The "Mayday" Signal

The "Mayday" signal should be used only when life or the vessel is threatened and immediate assistance is required. On VHF radio, the signal is given over Channel 16 and repeated three times: "Mayday, Mayday, Mayday." Following the "Mayday" signal, you should give your boat's name, your location, and, in as few words as possible, the nature of the emergency, the number of people aboard, and a description of your boat, followed by the word "Over." You should then wait a good, solid twenty to thirty seconds for a response to your call. If there is none, repeat the procedure.

If you are using your VHF radio and hear a "Mayday" call,

you should interrupt your conversation immediately and listen to the "Mayday" call. If no other boat comes in to answer the call for help within about twenty seconds, you should respond by calling the name of the boat in distress three times, give your boat name, and say that the "Mayday" message has been received. If you did not hear all of the "Mayday" message, ask to have it repeated and write down the key facts—boat name, location, problem, people, and description of boat.

Once you have responded to a "Mayday" call, you must stick with it until someone else takes if off your hands. You should also alter your course to go to the other boat's aid, if it's possible to do so without endangering your own boat and crew.

An important point is that you may or may not be the best boat to respond to the emergency. For example, if you have a sailboat with a top speed of 7 knots and the emergency is 20 miles away, it would be better for a faster motorboat to respond if there is such a boat in the area. In that situation, after you've changed course to head for the distressed boat, you should ask over the radio whether there are any other boats monitoring the "Mayday" call. If other boats respond in the affirmative, you should determine among you whether one of them is able to render assistance faster or more effectively than you are. If so, the other boat (or boats) should also go to the distressed boat's assistance. However, you should continue toward the distressed boat yourself until you know that the emergency is ended, just in case the other boats encounter problems and cannot provide the assistance needed.

It is not possible in a couple of pages to cover anywhere near all contingencies. In any emergency situation, however, the most important thing is for you to keep calm at all times. Your calm manner not only will instill confidence in those around you, it will also let you make better decisions as events unfold.

Finally, please remember that your first responsibility is to the safety of your crew. While you should make every effort to come to the aid of another boat and its crew if they are in distress, under no circumstances should you expose your crew to unreasonable danger—not even in an effort to rescue someone else. Not only might the result be a double tragedy, but also your effort to lend assistance might discourage other boaters from assisting in the mistaken belief that their help isn't needed, when, in fact, they may be better suited or better equipped than you to give the aid needed.

Testing What You've Learned
(Answers can be found in Appendix C)

1. What kind of visual distress signal is suited for use day or night?

2. TRUE or FALSE: Distress flares that are shot up into the air should be used to attract the attention of boats that are too far away for you to see from the deck of your boat.

3. If you are anchored in a quiet cove away from roads and cars and you hear a noise that sounds as if someone's boat horn is stuck and won't stop making noise, should you complain about the noise or check it out to see what the problem is?

4. Name three flag configurations that mean a boat is in distress.

5. When you are crossing a wide river, your boat hits a submerged log, putting a hole in the bottom and damaging the propeller so that your engine is useless. You quickly see that your boat is sinking and turn on your VHF radio. What should you say into the microphone?

6. If you have nothing but a flashlight at night, how can you send a distress signal?

7. You have been out fishing all morning and now are ready to head back to the boat ramp. When you try to start your engine, however, it doesn't want to start. Moreover, your battery is quickly drained as you keep trying to start the engine, so that now you also have a dead battery. You don't have any visual distress signals because the regulations don't require them on your boat. How can you signal other boats that you have a problem?

8. If you are monitoring VHF Channel 16 and hear a "Mayday" call, what should you do?

19

Anticipating, Avoiding, and Handling Problems

Assuming that you take safety seriously, your time on the water will generally be trouble free. Your boat will perform well. You'll perform well as skipper or crew. And most of the time, the weather will provide the perfect backdrop for your day afloat. From time to time, however, you may run into problems. The weather forecast may turn out to be wrong, for example, with a strong wind coming up unexpectedly. Or, everybody and his brother may be out in their boats so that the waters will be unusually crowded. Or, despite your best efforts to maintain your boat, you may have engine trouble. These things can happen to any of us.

As you think about these kinds of situations, you'll find there are two broad categories of problems you're likely to run into: situations that can be avoided with a bit of knowledge and forethought, and those that will happen despite your precautions. Both kinds of problems are discussed in this chapter, with suggestions offered for avoiding them if you can and for dealing with them when you must.

The overall strategy for avoiding or handling problems boils down to three elements: (1) identifying potential problems ahead of time; (2) developing the knowledge and / or skills needed to avoid them, if possible; and (3) acquiring the knowledge, skills, and equipment for dealing with them. If you can also bring to the situation both an ability to think things through and a spirit of self-reliance, you'll be well prepared to handle whatever arises—including circumstances you haven't anticipated.

The following are a number of areas which either present the potential for problems to develop or are, indeed, problems that many people will encounter at some point in their boating activities, despite their best precautions. All are areas in which forethought and preparation with knowledge, skills, and equipment can make the difference between inconvenience and possible tragedy.

TAKING ON FUEL

The potential for an accident involving your boat's fuel is greatest when you're at the gas dock filling up your tanks. The danger is minimal with diesel fuel. However, it is relatively great when taking on gasoline, and so this series of precautions is strongly recommended:

1. If you are filling a portable gas tank, take it out of the boat and fill it on the dock. In this way, you will not get any gasoline in the boat if you overflow the tank.

2. When getting ready to fill internal tanks, close all windows, ports, and hatches. The idea is to prevent gasoline fumes from getting down into the cabin. Remember, gasoline fumes are heavier than air and will run downhill.

3. Turn off all electrical circuits. That includes refrigerators, air conditioning, fans, radios, etc. It also, of course, means turning off the engine(s).

4. Hold the nozzle of the gasoline hose firmly against the side of the fill pipe as you pump the gasoline. The gasoline running through the hose can build up a static charge. Grounding the nozzle against the fill pipe prevents sparking from static electricity.

5. After filling the tanks, returning the hose to the dock, and closing the fill pipes, open all hatches, windows, and ports to let the interior of the boat air out.

6. Wait four to five minutes to allow for thorough ventilation of the boat.

7. Raise the engine hatch and smell the air down in the bilge. If you do not smell gasoline, turn on your bilge sniffer (if you have one) and check its reading to confirm what your nose has told you.

8. If you have one, turn on the bilge blower to ventilate the bilges. Let it run for about five minutes.

9. After checking the bilge for gasoline fumes again and finding none, you are ready to start the engine(s). *Under no circumstances, however, should you attempt to start an engine if you can smell gasoline in the bilge or your bilge sniffer indicates the presence of explosive fumes.* In that circumstance, you should follow the procedure outlined under the subheading "Starting Your Engine" in Chapter 8.

It is very important to follow this entire procedure each time you take on gasoline. The hundredth time you've gone through this procedure and not smelled any gasoline fumes in your bilges, you may wonder whether it's really necessary. After the hundred-and-first time, when you do smell those fumes, you'll never again question why the procedure is so rigid. As illustrated by the news reports in Chapter 8, the explosive consequences of starting your engine when there are gasoline fumes in the bilge can be tragic.

HEAVY TRAFFIC

During the years I was learning to sail, I was also crewing for my dad on his 30-foot sportfishing boat, as we went fishing offshore most weekends during the summer and early fall. When returning from the day's run, we'd often pass through small fleets of rented rowboats with outboard engines either anchored or adrift for fishing. Sometimes, we'd also come upon a sailboat race. I clearly remember that, in both situations, my dad would slow down from our cruising speed of about 15 knots to our normal trolling speed to go past the other boats, making little or no wake. Sometimes, he'd stop completely to let the racers cross in front of us, rather than try to motor through the fleet.

Once we—or they—were safely past, he'd bring the boat back up on plane, sometimes only to slow down again for another group of boats a half-mile farther along. I knew why he kept slowing down like that, because he told me why he did it; but I didn't really understand the meaning behind the words.

Today, I can see my dad's actions from the viewpoint of the other guy—the guy in the kind of boat that sometimes is rolled rather violently by the wake of a motorboat cruising by—and my understanding is more complete as a result. Among other things, I've come to understand that whether there is "heavy traffic" on the water depends upon your perspective. Certainly a person in a 15-foot johnboat or a 20-foot sailboat has a different perspective on the traffic than the skipper riding high on the flying bridge of a 40-foot sportfishing boat.

There are five situations described here under the heading "heavy traffic." Obviously, there could be more. These five, however, are situations that are present almost every day on many of our waterways. They involve fishing boats, sailboat races, commercial shipping, boats' wakes in narrow channels, and sailboats in narrow channels.

Fishing Boats

Small fishing boats, whether anchored or drifting, present the potential for real danger unless both the people in the fishing boats and the skippers of other boats cruising through the fishing grounds show some courtesy to each other. Fishermen, for example, should stay out of any channel. If it's necessary to anchor along the channel's edge, so be it. But be aware that your position may be precarious if the channel is used by large ships, which simply can't be slowed to a "no wake" speed for every small boat they encounter. Among other reasons, most ships need to be going 6 knots or more to maintain steerage.

If you're in your boat, on the other hand, and come across one or more small fishing boats, you should be sure that your wake won't create a problem for the people aboard. Generally, the farther away you are from the other boat when you go past, the less effect your wake will have. So, one courtesy you can offer is to give smaller boats a wide berth. In any case, it doesn't take long to figure out whether you should be slowing down when you pass other boats. If your wake will roll them severely, or if any of the other boats looks at all overloaded or low in the water, you should slow to a "no wake" speed.

Commercial fishing boats come in many sizes, shapes, and descriptions. They range from the low workboats of crabbers working trot lines, to lobster boats hauling lobster traps, to large trawlers or shrimp boats laying out giant nets. Whatever their activity, it's difficult if not impossible for us as pleasure boaters to anticipate what a commercial fishing boat will do next. The reason is simple: We don't know the boat's work patterns. As a result, we may decide that we can maintain course and speed to pass safely close behind one of these boats, only to discover suddenly that we're facing a collision because the other boat changed course or stopped dead in the water while our attention was elsewhere. As a result, it is almost always wise to give these boats a wide berth—a very wide berth.

Sailboat Races

Any time that the race course for a sailing fleet crosses a well-traveled channel or fairway, the potential exists for frustration—frustration on the part of non-racers whose way is obstructed by the racers, and frustration on the part of the racers whose competitive juices make them resentful of any outside interference with their boats' performance in the race. What's required on both sides is patience and understanding.

From a safety perspective, the best action for a non-racer when he encounters a sailboat race is to stop his boat and watch the competition as the main body of the fleet crosses the channel. Then he can wend his way slowly through the stragglers, using care to avoid interfering with their progress. Trying to thread your way through a bunched group of racing boats is tantamount to asking for an accident, even if technically you have the right of way because you're restricted to the channel by your draft.

On the other hand, racers should be neither cavalier nor stupid. The world does not owe them an unobstructed race course. Every racing skipper has a clear obligation to be ready to change course quickly when requesting a so-called "racer's right of way" over other boat traffic, just in case one of the other skippers fails to grant that privilege. Moreover, no racing skipper should ever assert any right of way over commercial boat traffic. First, he doesn't have the right of way. Second, the skippers of many commercial vessels couldn't grant that privilege to sailboat racers even if they wanted to because of limitations in their vessels' maneuverability. And third, it's just plain dangerous to cross in front of commercial boat traffic unless there's a large margin for error.

Commercial Shipping

There is only one safe way for pleasure boaters to deal with large commercial ships—freighters, tankers, ore ships, container ships, motorized barges, tugs and barges, etc.—and that is to stay well away from them. First, the captain of a ship standing on his bridge may not be able to see your boat in front of his if you're closer than about one-fourth of a mile (Figure 55). The skipper of a tug pushing a barge may have the same kind of blind spot, or difficulty seeing small boats in front of him. Second, chances are good that commercial vessels like these are moving much faster than you think—typically, 12 to 14 knots if it's a large ship, covering a mile every four or five minutes. In

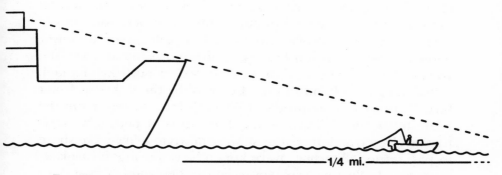

FIG. 55. A ship's blind spot: The skippers of many commercial ships have a blind spot in front of their bows that may extend one-fourth of a mile or more ahead of the ship. As a result, they may not be able to see your boat as you cross too close in front of them.

the open waters of the ocean or the Great Lakes, ships often go even faster. Third, chances are good that the vessel is considerably closer than you think, because its large size makes judging the distance difficult. And fourth, most commercial vessels can't stop or turn sharply—at least, not in time to avoid you if your motor stalls or the wind dies as you're passing in front of them. For all of these reasons, do not cross a channel in front of a ship or a tug unless there is a very large margin of safety. How much sea room you'll want depends, of course, upon your particular boat, but you should always consciously build that margin of safety into your plans.

Boats' Wakes in Narrow Channels

If you have a small runabout or a deep-vee runabout, you may take great delight in jumping other boats' wakes. It can be a dangerous game. The potential for underestimating the size of a given wake and getting into trouble is too great. Instead, you should slow your planing boat down to take wakes at a more moderate speed. When you're overtaking another boat whose wake is large, you should probably cross its waves at a 90-degree angle. It is sometimes difficult to steer a straight course when crossing the wake at a smaller angle, because the waves are pushing your stern sideways. When passing head-on, on the other hand, you should take another boat's wake at an angle of about 30 degrees so that your hull doesn't come off the first wave in a way that makes it pound into the second one.

If you have a displacement boat—a sailboat or a slower motorboat—you obviously have a different situation. In fact, you'll often feel like a victim as your boat is buffeted, rocked, rolled, and yawed almost out of control by the wakes of faster boats. This is a situation that calls both for courtesy from the faster boats and skilled boat handling on your part. The courtesy involved is simply that of slowing down to a low-wake speed to pass, especially when overtaking a boat moving at displacement speed. We are always appreciative when another boat slows to pass us.

Since it's not always reasonable to expect the other skipper to slow down for you if you have a slower and / or smaller boat, your boat-handling skills will involve knowing how to take other boats' wakes. For example, you can keep to the outside of the channel, giving other boats the maximum available space in which to pass you. The farther you are from them, the flatter their wakes will be when they reach your boat. Another example: If you're headed into a wake, you should attack it at an angle of about 30 degrees away from straight on, essentially the same as the planing boat would take it. If you attack it straight on, a large wake can stop your boat dead in the water so that it bucks violently, burying your bow as it comes down off the first or second wave.

Still another example: If you're being overtaken so that the wake comes at you from astern, there are three ways to take those waves. The worst way is to take them on the quarter so that they catch your stern at an angle. If there's room, a better alternative is to turn your boat so that the wake comes square on your stern and gives your boat a push. The best way to take that wake, however, is to turn so that you're headed toward the boat that has just passed you and take its waves almost on your beam (Figure 56). If this is done correctly, you won't feel a thing;

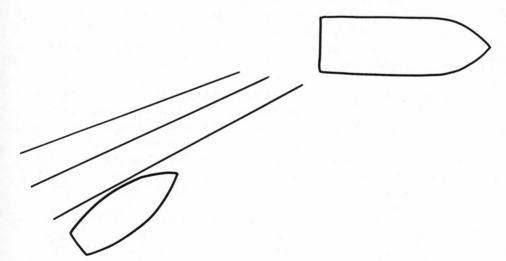

FIG. 56. Taking wakes: When you are passed by a boat making a large wake, you can often minimize its effect on your boat by taking the waves slightly forward of directly abeam, as illustrated.

your boat will just bob straight up and down over the waves as they pass beneath your hull. It takes a little practice, but we've found that if our bow is headed slightly toward the wave, we can take even very large wakes with little or no rolling. I'd suggest practicing first on smaller waves, however. I'll also offer this note of caution: Occasionally, you'll be passed by a series of two or more boats running one right behind the other. *You need to be sure that, in changing your course to take any of those wakes, you won't be creating a dangerous situation by turning unexpectedly in front of another boat.*

When you encounter a large ship in a narrow channel, you should give it as much room as you can so that its wake has a chance to flatten out somewhat before it gets to you. As for taking that wake, follow the same procedures that you would follow for taking any other large waves—with one possible exception. If you have a large enough boat that you don't normally slow down for other pleasure boats' wakes, you should consider slowing down somewhat for the wake of a large ship if you're meeting it head-on.

There is, in addition, another hazard from large ships' wakes that all pleasure boaters should be aware of. That hazard occurs when the shipping channel runs adjacent to relatively shallow water. As the ship's wake leaves the deep water of the channel and enters the shallow area, very large and dangerous waves can be created:

CAUTION FROM THE COAST GUARD—The Coast Guard has issued a strongly worded caution to the skippers of small craft regarding the dangers of operating in shallow waters adjacent to deep channels used by large ships. The normal wake of ships in the channel is no hazard to boats in the deep waters of the channel; however, where these waves reach the shallow waters on either side of the channel, they grow progressively in height and can become dangerous.

Just outside the ship channels of the approaches to Baltimore Harbor [Maryland], wave heights of 10 to 12 feet have been reported. Several injuries and one death have recently occurred. The Coast Guard urges all boaters to use extreme caution in operating or anchoring in shallow waters adjacent to the ship channels.[1]

1. *Motor Boating & Sailing*, Hearst Magazines, New York, December 1986.

Sailboats in Narrow Channels

While sailboats no longer have the right of way over all motor-driven boats in a channel, it's helpful for powerboat operators to understand what sailboats are doing when they zigzag back and forth across a channel. With that understanding, the seemingly erratic behavior of the sailboat skipper becomes reasonably predictable and you can plan to pass him easily and safely.

All of that zigzagging takes place because sailboats can't sail directly into the wind. The closest that most sailboats can point into the wind is at an angle of about 45 degrees. So, if a sailor wants to go up a channel when the wind is coming more or less down that same channel, the only way he can do it is by "tacking" back and fourth—sailing 45 degrees off the wind toward one side of the channel, and then turning to sail 45 degrees off the wind toward the other side of the channel. Depending upon exactly how the wind is blowing relative to the channel, one "tack" may be longer than another, but the pattern will be the same (Figure 57). If you are confronted with this situation, all you need to do is watch the sailboat for a few minutes, and the pattern will become apparent. Then you can plan to pass in a way that is comfortable for both of you. The key point of courtesy is to allow enough room in passing that the sailboat can come about to head back across the channel when it nears the channel's edge.

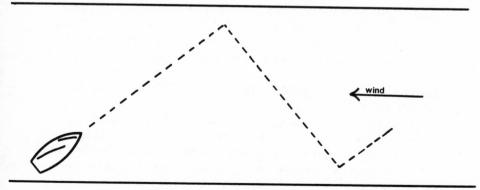

FIG. 57. Tacking up a channel: A sailboat going up a channel against the wind must sail a zigzag course, back and forth across the channel.

STOPPING TO FISH

There are few activities more relaxing than sitting in a boat with a rod in your hand waiting for a fish to take your bait. Sometimes it doesn't even matter whether the fish are biting; the fishing itself is more important than catching any fish. But, whether you're anchored to fish or drifting lazily with the current, there are critical safety considerations to keep in mind. As I've noted several times earlier, nothing will ruin your enjoyment faster than an accident.

When anchoring to fish, how and where you anchor is always a primary consideration—not only for whether you'll catch any fish, but also for reasons of safety. The following three suggestions can help you anchor safely for fishing.

First, as mentioned before, you should not anchor in a channel. If you must anchor at the channel's edge, you should be conscious of the boat traffic and be prepared for heavy rolling. Everyone in your boat should wear a PFD. It is also critically important that your boat not be overloaded; you do not want water pouring over the side if the boat rolls heavily in a large wake.

Second, never tie your boat to a channel marker or to any other navigation buoy. Not only is it against the law, it can make the marker hard for other boaters to see. Also, getting your boat untied from the marker when you're ready to move can be difficult and, therefore, dangerous if a strong current develops.

Third, never anchor your boat from the stern. A strong current or tide pushing against the flat transom of your boat can apply strong pressure on the anchor line, pulling your stern dangerously low in the water. Then, all it takes is a wave. . . .

DETROIT POLICEMAN DROWNS AFTER ASSISTING IN RESCUE—A Detroit police officer drowned in the Detroit River after helping rescue four people whose boat had capsized.

Richard Fortin, 45, had been on the police force for 23 years. . . . He was assigned to a fire department boat on the weekend of June 19 to aid boats that were in the city to watch the Detroit Grand Prix automobile race.

According to officer John Leavens, Fortin helped pull four people to safety after their boat capsized while they were viewing the race. The boat reportedly had been anchored from the stern, and water started coming over the transom.[2]

Even if your boat isn't swamped, the strong pressure on your anchor line will dig your anchor in and may make breaking it loose very difficult.

If you're drifting to fish rather than anchoring, you must keep close tabs on where you are and on all boat traffic around you. It's too easy to become absorbed in your fishing and fail to notice that you've drifted into the middle of a channel, particularly if you're fishing in a large river or bay where channel markers may be one or more miles apart—difficult to see from a small boat in the best of conditions, let alone on a hazy summer day. Moreover, from your position you may not see a freighter until it is only three or four miles away—and it could be on top of you in less than fifteen minutes.

What each drifting fishing boat needs is a "designated" pilot, much as a carload of party-goers needs a designated driver. From a practical perspective, that designated pilot should be you, the skipper. You can't really delegate your responsibility for the boat and the safety of your passengers. Your job as designated pilot is to pay attention to your location, your rate of drift, and other boat traffic so that you can restart your engine and move back to safe waters before you drift into a hazardous situation.

Finally, whether you're anchored or drifting to fish, it's imperative that you keep tabs on the weather. You should carry a weather radio, but it will be useless unless you listen to it periodically. You also need to stay aware of local conditions and head for home if wind and waves begin to build. An important part of preventing problems is knowing when to call it a day.

RUNNING AGROUND

This is one of the more common problems leading to calls for help from the Coast Guard. The potential for damage in run-

2. *Soundings*, September 1987.

ning aground is generally greater for motorboats than it is for sailboats. One reason is that motorboats are usually traveling at higher speeds; as a result, the impacts are greater and so is the damage. Another reason is that most modern motorboats don't have sturdy external keels to take the impact of running aground. As a result, the exposed propeller(s), rudder(s), or drive unit(s) of a motorboat can be seriously damaged by running onto mud or sand even at relatively slow speeds, whereas a sailboat's keel may not even be scratched. Running into rocks or a reef at almost any speed, of course, can seriously damage any boat.

The risk of running aground can be minimized with good piloting, which involves keeping track of where you are by using a navigation chart, and by being alert to both the underwater hazards and the depth of the water as shown on the chart. (The use of charts is discussed in more detail in the next chapter.)

Paying attention to the water around you and to the way your boat is riding can also help keep you out of trouble. For example, if there's enough wind to make waves, you'll tend to see whitecaps sooner in shallow water than in deep water. So, if you're cruising along and see an area of whitecaps ahead, you should recognize the possibility of a shoal (shallow area) and either slow down to approach the area with caution or steer around it. By the same token, if you suddenly find that you've entered an area of whitecaps, you should slow down immediately and check the water's depth by using your depthsounder or lead line, or by looking on the chart. If indeed you've wandered into a shallow area, we'd suggest making a U-turn and, at slow speed, retracing your course back to deep water. For the record, with the exception of high-speed runabouts, most motorboats require about the same depth of water at cruising speed that they need at slow speeds. While the forward two-thirds of the boat is riding on top of the water at planing speeds, the stern section is usually immersed right down to the waterline.

If the water is calm and there aren't any whitecaps, you'll have to rely on other signs to warn you of shallow water. In a planing motorboat, for example, you may notice the waves in your wake becoming steeper in shallow water. If the water begins to get dangerously shallow, your bow will rise, your stern will drop lower, and your stern wave will start coming right up to the back of your boat. Under those circumstances, you should slow down promptly, shift into neutral, and stop to assess the situation. If there's enough water under the boat for you to continue motoring at slow speed, I'd suggest making a U-turn and retracing your path back to deep water, unless you can see a shorter and equally safe way out.

If your boat actually runs aground, the immediate circumstances determine your action. If you've just run aground softly, try sending all or part of your crew up to the bow. In this way, you can often lift the stern enough to put the engine in reverse and back off slowly. Usually, that will do the trick. Once back in deeper water, you should check for damage—water leaking into the bilge, or damage to your propellers. If there's any unusual vibration when you put the engine into gear, you've probably damaged a propeller and should shut that engine down, if you have a twin-screw boat. If you only have one engine, the decision whether to head into port at a slow speed depends upon the seriousness of the vibration. Most of the time, the best course of action is to anchor and signal for help. If you have a VHF radio, you can place a routine call to the Coast Guard or to a local marina and ask for someone to come tow your boat in. Be prepared, however, to pay for the towing service.

If you've run hard aground—with some impact—you should first check to be sure you haven't developed a leak; in other words, check the bilges to be sure you're not taking on water. If the boat is leaking, you should have everyone put on life jackets, and call the Coast Guard on your VHF to advise them of the situation. This is a circumstance that requires a cool head and ingenuity. Often, you can find the source of a leak and stop it in some creative manner. Or, the leak will be slow enough that your bilge pump can keep up with it, as long as you don't run down your battery. In any case, your objective should be to keep your crew calm; to find a way to keep your boat afloat (even though it is aground); and to communicate with the Coast Guard or another boat accurately about your situation so that they can provide any help needed.

Most of the time, of course, your boat won't be taking on water; it will just be stuck in the shallow water. Even if you've hit hard, you may be able to back off by putting people in the bow to lift the stern. If you can't back your way off and there's a wind or current that will push you farther aground, you'll need to get an anchor out promptly. If it's still daylight, you can either take the anchor out in your dinghy or put someone overboard (with shoes and life jacket on) to carry it out to deeper water. You might even float the anchor on a boat cushion, if the water's too deep for someone to carry the anchor out. In most circumstances, you should not try to walk the anchor away from the boat after dark; it's not safe, because you can't see the person in the water well enough and he might step into a hole.

With the anchor set, you can check for damage to your propeller, rudder, or drive unit. If you have an outboard or I/O, you should raise the drive unit for a damage check and then leave it up until the boat is afloat. If you've bent a propeller, you won't be able to use that engine unless you can change the propeller. If you've bent your rudder, you may or may not be able to steer with it. Finally, if you're in tidal waters and don't already know the tide schedule, you should check whether the tide is going out or coming in. All of these factors will determine how much outside help you'll need. In any case, your options will include: (1) waiting for the tide to float you off; (2) "kedging" yourself off by placing your anchor in deep water and pulling the boat toward the anchor; (3) flagging down another boat to pull you off; and (4) getting on the radio to ask for help.

BLIND TURNS

Around marinas and bridges, along the shores of lakes, and in some smaller rivers or deep-water creeks, there are blind turns or corners that demand caution. They're "blind" because you can't see around the corner of the dock, or around the bend of the creek. If someone is coming too fast from the other direction, it's an accident waiting to happen. As the following newspaper articles illustrate, the dangers are real.

TWO ARE KILLED IN BOAT COLLISION—A two-boat accident off Long Island Sound killed two and injured three people. All of the victims were aboard a runabout that crossed the path of a larger cruiser, according to marine police.

The August 13 collision occurred when Matthew McGrath, 25, of North Bellmore, New York, turned his 20-foot outboard boat into the path of a 30-foot Sea Ray that emerged from underneath a parkway bridge over Long Creek at Freeport, New York, police said.

McGrath's sister, Linda McGrath, 20, also of North Bellmore, was thrown overboard, hit by the propeller of the other boat, and killed.

Thomas Cummins, 37, a visitor from Ireland aboard McGrath's boat, died from internal injuries.

"You can't say anybody was in the wrong," said Nassau marine police officer Victor Hansen.

The bridge is "four lanes wide, and you can't see anyone coming through the bridge until he's in the channel—and then it's too late," said Hansen.

Hansen said the deaths of McGrath and Cummins are the second and third recreational boating fatalities in Nassau County during 1988. The other fatality occurred about two months ago when a speedboat crashed into the same bridge, killing a passenger, Hansen said.[3]

The second accident also resulted in two deaths:

BOATER PLEADS INNOCENT IN FATAL BROADKILL CRASH—The driver of a 22-foot boat that collided with a smaller vessel June 16, killing two people, pleaded innocent Thursday in Magistrate Court 2 to three charges of operating his boat negligently.

Delaware Marine Police charged Joseph C. Simpson III, 45, of Edgewood, Maryland, with failing to keep to the right side of a waterway, operating a vessel at an excessive speed when vision was obstructed, and failing to follow the manufacturer's recommendations on the maximum power of the boat's motors.

Simpson and his wife, Paula D., were traveling toward Milton on the Broadkill River north of Roosevelt Inlet about 1:30 P.M. after a fishing trip in Delaware Bay.

At the same time, Oscar F. Henry, 51, and Victoria Boyer-Henry, 38, of Hummelstown, Pennsylvania, were heading south on the Broadkill toward Roosevelt Inlet.

3. *Soundings*, October 1988.

According to marine police, the two boats collided at a bend in the river. The Henrys were thrown from the boat when the two vessels collided. The Simpsons were thrown to the deck of their boat.

Oscar Henry was killed when his 16-foot boat ran over him, said marine police officer Charles P. Fox. His body was pulled from the river by other boaters immediately after the accident.

Victoria Henry's body was recovered about two hours later. Foxwell said she apparently had drowned.

Although there is no speed limit on the Broadkill River, Foxwell said Simpson was charged with operating the boat at an excessive speed because the accident occurred at a spot where vision would have been obscured. Foxwell estimated that the Simpson boat was traveling at 25 to 35 miles per hour.

Marine police also allege that the Simpson boat was traveling along the left side of the river when it should have been on the right.

According to Foxwell, the manufacturer's specifications indicate the Simpson boat, an S-22 North American, should have been equipped with engines totaling no more than 270 horsepower. The boat, according to Simpson, was equipped with two 150-horsepower engines.[4]

Five key points emerge from these and other similar news reports:
• This kind of accident can happen anywhere that your vision is obstructed. A dangerous situation can be as obvious as a sharp turn in a narrow river, or as subtle as an anchorage where two boats (e.g., a dinghy and a runabout) may be on a collision course coming from opposite sides of an anchored boat and not see each other until the last minute.
• Always assume that there's a boat coming from the other direction whenever you approach a blind turn or corner, and keep to the right.
• Unless you're already moving slowly, reduce your boat speed significantly whenever you approach a blind turn or corner.
• Always keep far enough away from the shore, dock, bridge abutment, or other obstruction so that you have room to turn in either direction if someone coming the other way emerges unexpectedly from behind a blind corner.

4. *News-Journal*, Wilmington, Delaware, August 16, 1985.

• For your safety, use the appropriate sound signal—one long blast on your boat's horn—whenever you approach a blind turn or corner to warn other boaters that you're there. Even if the other guy doesn't know enough to reply with the same signal, at least he'll know you're there.

WORSENING WEATHER

The words "worsening weather" have a variety of meanings. With calm seas, cold water, and high humidity, "worsening weather" can mean a change from unlimited visibility to heavy fog. On a hot, muggy July afternoon, it may mean the development of severe thunderstorms. At any time, it may mean the movement of heavy rain and / or wind through your area.

Whatever the change in weather, seldom should you be caught completely by surprise. Not only are major changes in weather forecast with reasonable reliability by the weather service, but you can anticipate them before they develop just by paying attention to what's going on around you. For example, thunderstorms, with their twin dangers of high wind and lightning, are a real possibility on any hot, humid afternoon around inland and coastal waters. Under these circumstances, a prudent boater will head for home when he sees large, puffy, white cumulus clouds beginning to come together and build high up into the atmosphere. If the sky is hazy and you can't see cloud structures, you can listen to an AM radio; distant lightning will cause static. You can also listen for distant thunder. Why be so concerned? Thunderstorms frequently have hurricane-force winds gusting out in front of the advancing storm cloud—winds that can wreak havoc on unwary boaters. Even when you know they're coming, the violence of thunderstorms can be overwhelming.

FOUR DROWN IN TEXAS LAKE STORM—Four people drowned and more than 400 others were helped to shore during powerful spring storms over Galveston Bay and Lake Livingston in Texas.

The four people drowned after being trapped under a capsized 20-foot Stingray powerboat on Lake Livingston, about 80 miles north of Houston.

On May 17, heavy thunderstorms and wind blasted through southeastern Texas, stranding boaters. The storms had been predicted, but not the force with which they hit. On Lake Livingston, sustained winds of 90 miles per hour were recorded about 2:00 P.M. at the Trinity River Authority Dam office, said Sergeant J. C. Robbins of the Polk County Sheriff's office.

About 4:30 P.M., heavy thunderstorms and winds of at least 60 miles per hour were recorded on Galveston Bay, said Chief Michael Martin of the Coast Guard office in Galveston.

"I don't think people realized how intense it was going to be," Martin said. "They were predicting scattered thunderstorms that usually carry 30- to 35-mile-per-hour winds."

Martin said a total of 28 rescue boats responded to 132 vessels in distress [on Galveston Bay]. Sixty-five people were recovered directly from the water and another 359 people were given assistance.

"Boats had capsized or sunk in most cases," Martin said.[5]

What should you do if you're out in your boat and a thunderstorm is going to catch you? Of the following suggestions, the first applies in all situations; the remainder may or may not apply to you, depending upon the kind of boat you have and the circumstances of the moment:

• Determine your location and pinpoint it on the chart so that you know whether you have to worry about shallow water or underwater obstructions. If such hazards do exist, you'll need to determine what course you can steer safely during the storm. When the storm strikes, heavy rain may reduce visibility to zero for several minutes, and then it will be too late to figure out where you are.

• If you have any radio or Loran antennas, or fishing outriggers, lower them. They can attract lightning. Disconnect the antenna leads from your radio and Loran.

• If you're in a small, open motorboat, distribute the weight evenly and have everyone keep low in the boat. If your boat has a cabin, the crew should go down into the cabin unless they're needed on deck. No one should touch any metal on the boat until all danger of lightning is past to avoid the possibility of electrocution in the event of a lightning strike.

5. *Soundings*, August 1986.

• If you are where you can anchor safely, it may be a good idea to do so, using your largest anchor and letting out a length of anchor line equal to ten to twelve times the distance from your foredeck to the water's bottom. If the anchor begins to drag, you can use your engine to take some of the strain off the anchor.

• If you're in a motorboat and can't anchor, you should point your bow toward the thunderstorm cloud as it approaches so that you can take the strongest winds head-on. The initial strong blast of wind roars out in front of the storm cloud and is then followed by the rain. The strongest winds generally last only a few minutes, after which you can resume your course.

• If you're in a sailboat and can't anchor, you should get down to your smallest sails and heave to.* If you've got lots of sea room, you may want to take all sail down, turn away from the storm, and run under bare poles before the wind when it hits. We normally put two reefs in the mainsail, take down the jib, and leave our small staysail up; then we heave to before the storm hits. If you have one, what about your auxiliary engine? Many sailboats' engines are not powerful enough to control the boat in thunderstorm-strength winds. For that reason, you will probably have better control over the boat if you can go down to storm sails. On boats not having storm sails, I'd suggest taking all sails down, lashing them securely, and heading off downwind under bare poles—if you've got the sailing room. Otherwise, you'll need to do the best you can under power to keep your bow into the wind so that you are not blown into danger.

While fog is less dramatic than thunderstorms, it also poses a real hazard. Boaters in the Pacific Northwest and New England know that fog is a distinct possibility whenever winds between about 5 and 15 miles per hour are blowing in from warm off-

---

* "Heaving to" is a procedure in which you neutralize the effects of the wind to a great extent by setting your sails and rudder so that the boat is trying to turn in two directions at the same time. As a result, it goes almost nowhere. "Heaving to" is accomplished by (1) bringing the sails in tight, (2) turning the rudder to come about without releasing the jib sheet, and (3) after coming about (with the jib now backwinded), turning the rudder to head back into the wind. At this point, the boat will come almost to a stop, with the backed jib pushing the bow one way and the mainsail and rudder trying to make it go in the other direction. Even when the waves are quite rough, the boat will feel as if a "calm" has taken over.

shore waters. Such conditions are ready-made for fog as the warm, moist air meets the cold coastal waters. Though less common, fog is also encountered in many other parts of the country, particularly in the fall and early spring. You can usually find out whether conditions are ripe for fog by making a short telephone call to the local weather bureau. Suggestions for dealing with fog are discussed in the next section.

One of the sneakier changes in the weather on any given day may be the "sudden" appearance of strong winds and waves getting too big for comfort. Most of the time, of course, the wind and waves don't really come up suddenly; rather, they've been building for some hours, but the buildup went unnoticed. The trick is to recognize what's happening early, before the wind and waves have the opportunity to get serious. The technique is simple: Every hour (or more often if you think something's building), stop what you're doing, focus your attention on the wind and waves, and write down the time, an estimate of the wind strength, and the size of the waves. In this way, you can compare what you observe now with what you observed in the two or three hours before. When it becomes apparent that the wind is beginning to increase, it's time to head for home— before conditions have a chance to deteriorate.

GETTING CAUGHT OUT AFTER DARK OR IN FOG

It's one thing to go out for an evening's cruise planning to be out after dark . . . or to set out from the dock with fog already overhanging the area. It's quite another to find yourself out after sunset when you had planned to be back ashore well before supper, or to be enveloped by fog when you were expecting clear skies and bright sunshine. In the first instance, you've probably prepared ahead of time for being out after dark or in the fog and should have no trouble. In the second instance, however, you may be unprepared and could easily find yourself in difficulty.

Finding yourself out on the water after dark or fogbound unexpectedly happens more often than you like to think. It's very easy, for example, to stay out longer than you've planned. Perhaps the fish didn't start biting until just before you were going to head home—and then they wouldn't stop coming. Or maybe the wind and waves forced you to run much more slowly than expected so that you couldn't get in before dark. Possibly you had engine trouble. Or maybe you just dozed off for a couple of hours. Whatever the reason, the point is this: Even though you may not ever plan to be out in your boat after dark, you may find yourself in that situation anyway. And you should be prepared for it. The same applies to fog: Unless you go boating in an area where fog is unknown, you should be prepared to handle it if the situation arises.

What can you do to be prepared?

• Make sure your boat is equipped with all navigation lights required for operating at night. Also, every time you get ready to take your boat out, check to be sure those lights are working.

• Carry spare bulbs for each navigation light and the tools required to change the bulbs. Also, make sure that you know how to change the bulbs by practicing on each light at least once at the dock. The deck of a tossing boat after dark is neither the time nor the place to learn how to change a light bulb.

• Take time to study navigation lights, and carry a quick reference of some kind on your boat so that you can interpret other boats' lights.

• Carry a red-filtered flashlight that you can use for reading your navigation chart at night without ruining your night vision.

• Take the time to learn about the lights used as navigation aids in your area, by studying the nautical chart. Also, get in the habit of noting the course between buoys according to your boat's compass. In that way, you'll know where to look to find a buoy at night (or in fog).

And finally, get out on the water at least once after dark to see what night piloting is all about. (Chapter 21 covers night piloting in detail.) If you're concerned about taking your boat out at night, you might try going out at dusk a few times, when it's almost but not quite dark. In that way, you can get a taste of nighttime piloting while there's still some light to help you out. As you gain confidence, you can stay out later and later, gradually developing a good feel for what's involved in nighttime boating. Who knows? You might even discover that you like being out there after dark!

Fog is a little different. Boating in fog is difficult to practice, and I don't think we've ever met anyone who likes it. Even so, you can be prepared for fog. One part of that preparation involves your boat's equipment; the other part involves your boating skills.

Equipping Your Boat for Fog

Basic equipment begins with the horn and bell needed to make required sound signals if you're out in fog. If your boat has an electric horn, or you normally use a gas-powered horn, you should also carry one that you can put up to your mouth to blow. The boat's batteries can fail, and your horn canister can run out of its compressed gas. Hopefully your lungs won't run out of air!

Along with the ability to make sound, you should carry a reference card listing various sound signals used in fog so that you know what ones to make with your horn or bell as well as how to interpret the signals of other boats. All the quick-reference navigation light cards that we've seen also list sound signals.

In addition to the horn and bell, your boat should be equipped with a radar reflector, if you have a place to hang it. Fiberglass boats make poor radar targets, so anything you can do to make it easier for boats equipped with radar to see you, is well worthwhile. Of course, horns, bells, and radar reflectors won't help you find your way. For that you'll need a good compass, a chart of the area, a watch, and some means of telling how fast your boat is going. Without them or some electronic equivalent (Loran, Sat-Nav, GPS, or, close inshore, radar), it's simply not possible to tell where you're going with any degree of accuracy in fog. Even with the proper tools, good skills are needed to get where you want to go.

Boating Skills in Fog

Three habits are invaluable for piloting in fog. The first is always keeping track of where you are on your chart—and writing it down. The second is adjusting your speed so that you can stop in less than half the distance that you can see. In other words, if visibility is 50 feet, you should be going slow enough to stop in less than 25 feet. The third, as mentioned earlier, is taking routine compass bearings from one buoy to another when you're following a channel—and noting them on the chart. You never know when you'll need them.

For example, Susan and I didn't know that we were going to have fog the next morning the first time we went into Province-town Harbor at the tip of Cape Cod. But we routinely jotted down the compass headings as we went from one buoy to the other. The next morning, we were able to go carefully from the harbor by retracing our steps, despite a fog that reduced visibility to about 100 feet. By the time we were a mile north of the Cape, we were in bright sunlight. While we were enshrouded in fog, however, the compass courses jotted down the day before told us what direction to head in; measurements from the chart told us how far it was from one buoy to the next; and the speed curve we've developed for our boat let us determine our boat speed. With that information, we simply divided the distance by our speed to determine how long it should take us to go from one buoy to the next, used the watch as a timer, and trusted the compass to point us in the right direction. Had there been a significant current running, we probably would have waited for the sun to burn off the fog rather than risk being set off course by the current. Since there was no current to speak of, we made the run at slow speed, going from buoy to buoy, with no trouble. If necessary, you can do the same, if you've equipped your boat and yourself properly.

MAN OVERBOARD

One of the potentially most dangerous situations in boating is having someone fall overboard. If that happens, you may not know what condition the victim is in until you can get back to him. He (or she) may have been injured in the fall. He may have fallen because of a fainting spell, a heart attack, or a cramp. He may have been knocked overboard by a swinging boom, or

282 Meeting the Real World

he may have lost his balance and fallen when the boat was rolled violently by a large wave.

When this emergency happens, there are specific procedures that should be followed, and everyone on the boat should know what he's supposed to do—and that means the skipper, all members of the crew, and the passengers. You achieve this state of readiness by briefing people before you leave the dock and *by practicing* man-overboard drills with your crew. Briefing your passengers ensures that they will know what they can do to help, and how to stay out of the way. You can practice with your crew by throwing a boat cushion overboard unexpectedly (a bright yellow, red, or orange cushion, so that you can see it). Going through a man-overboard exercise to retrieve the cushion will ensure that your crew knows what to do if you're ever confronted with the real situation.

Although conventional wisdom argues that most people fall overboard in bad conditions, an analysis of Coast Guard accident reports by BOAT / US shows otherwise:

Open motorboats accounted for 62% of the incidents and 56% of the fatalities; in distant second place came rowboats (14.1% and 9.4% of the fatalities). Sailing auxiliaries—the kind usually illustrated in the books—accounted for only 3.7% of the incidents and 4.1% of the fatalities. The remainder were scattered among cabin motorboats (6.2%); open, unpowered sailboats; canoes and kayaks; inflatables, etc.

The other factors:

Time of day: 64.3% between 2:30 and 9:30 P.M., with the peak in the late afternoon.

Location: Only 2.6% in the ocean, 3.1% on the Great Lakes, 13.5% on bays, 20.8% on rivers—and a whopping 57.3% on inland lakes.

Water conditions: 49.8% occurred in calm conditions and another 23.6% in conditions described as "choppy."

Wind: None, 16.8%; light, 44.3%; moderate, 18.3%; strong, 7.4%; stormy, 1.8%; and unknown / unrecorded, 11.4%.

Visibility: Described as "good" in 76.3% and "dark" in only one-half percent (0.5%) of the cases.

Weather: Clear, 69.5%; cloudy, 13.2%; fog, 1.2%; rain, 3.7%; other / unknown, 12.4%.

Causes of the incident: Operator carelessness seemed to be the cause in 20% to 30% of the cases, depending on the type of craft.

Moving around the boat during turns, high speed, leaning over the side, and other predictable behavior also accounted for the majority of reasons.

Operation of the craft when the incident occurred: 39.3% occurred while the vessel was just plain cruising along; another 18.1% occurred while the vessel was drift fishing, and 11.1% occurred when the vessel was drifting (without a reason given for the drifting).[6]

The picture that emerges from these statistics is pretty clear. Man-overboard situations can happen anytime and anywhere—usually when you least expect it because the weather is good, the water is calm, and everyone is having fun. They tend to occur in the afternoon, when people are more likely to be tired or less careful, perhaps because they've had a chance to drink a few beers. Hopefully, when a man-overboard situation arises, the victim will be wearing a life jacket, but probably not. Seventy percent of the incidents analyzed by BOAT / US involved a fatality; it seems almost certain that those who drowned were not wearing PFDs.

In any case, your preparation for handling this can make the difference between life and death for the victim. The procedures for a man-overboard situation are straightforward—not always easy, but straightforward.

1. *All people* who see the person fall overboard should yell as loudly as they can, "Man overboard!"

2. *Anyone who can* should throw a flotation device to the person in the water. It can be a flotation cushion, a horseshoe buoy, a life ring, or a life vest. Whatever is thrown to the victim, however, *should not be attached to the boat*. Please note, however, that you can't throw it if you don't have it handy in the cockpit. It's not enough to own a throwable flotation device; it also must be kept out where it is readily available in case it is ever needed.

3. *All people* (except the skipper) who can see the person in the water should point toward the person in the water. Once the skipper has the person in sight, one other crew member should be designated to help keep the victim in sight while the others make ready to rescue him—e.g., get out the boarding ladder, prepare the throwable PFD, etc.

6. *Boat / US Reports,* Fall 1986.

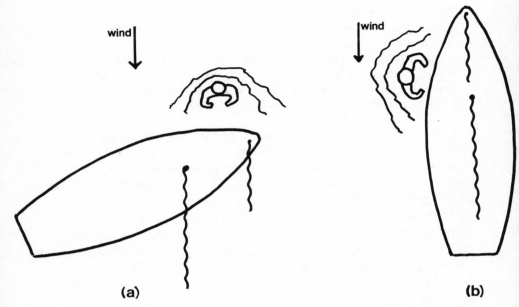

Fɪɢ. 58. Sailing up to a person in the water—two approaches: (a) Sail toward the person, letting out your sails to coast to a stop; (b) head into the wind, and coast to a stop alongside the person in the water.

4. In a motorboat or a sailboat under power, the skipper (or whoever is at the controls) should turn the boat back toward the person in the water and slow the boat down to a safe approach speed. In a sailboat under sail, the boat should be jibed or tacked around to head back toward the victim. In approaching the victim, use the same technique you would use for coming to a stop at a mooring buoy (discussed in Chapter 25). Either head up into the wind to coast to a stop alongside the victim, as in Figure 58(b); or let out the sails so that they lose the wind and the boat coasts to a stop (a). The advantage to approach (a) is that you can pull the sails in to move the boat forward a bit if you are going to come up short. In any case, once the boat is approaching the victim, the procedures you follow to bring him (her) alongside and get him (her) aboard depend upon your boat, your equipment, and the condition of the person in the water. Several alternatives are discussed in the pages that follow.

Healthy Victim

There are two basic approaches to rescuing a conscious, un-injured victim: coming alongside, and what we'll call the "water-ski pickup." The decision to use one approach or the other in a given situation depends upon the conditions of the moment, the characteristics of your boat, and how the boat is behaving.

Coming Alongside: Basically, this approach involves bringing your boat up next to the victim to get him aboard. It sounds simple enough, but sea conditions can make it very difficult. The major question is whether you should come up so that the victim is upwind or downwind of the boat.

The argument for keeping the victim to the leeward (or downwind) side is that the wind will tend to blow your boat toward him, not away from him. Additionally, the calming "shadow" that the boat creates in the wind and waves may make it easier to get the victim aboard. Some people, however, believe the danger of having the boat blown down on top of the victim argues for keeping him on the windward (or upwind) side of boat, particularly for the victim who is able to help himself.

In either case, as soon as you are within range, you should throw the victim a flotation device (if he doesn't have one) attached to a rope that has a loop in the end large enough to be slipped over his shoulders, to hold him around his chest and under his armpits. If the victim is kept to windward, it is doubly important to get a loop under the victim's arms promptly so that he is "attached to the boat." In that way, the boat cannot be blown away, out of reach. Once the person has the loop over his shoulders, the boat should be stopped and the person pulled to the boat. If you're in a sailboat, you should "heave to." Don't try to take down the sails; they will only get in the way. (Getting the victim aboard is discussed after the water-ski pickup.)

The Water-Ski Pickup: As the name implies, this method of recovering a man overboard is much like the technique for hooking up with a fallen water-skier in the water. The ski boat, pulling the ski tow rope behind, makes a circle around the person in the water so that the tow rope comes right up to his hands. In the man-overboard situation, the rescue boat—power

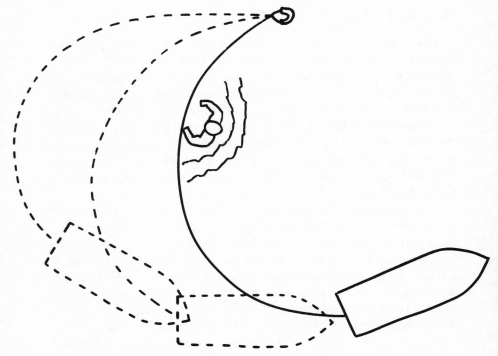

FIG. 59.   Man overboard—a water-ski pick-up: You can get a PFD to a person in the water by trailing it on a long line and making a relatively tight circle around the person in the water—the same way that ski-boat operators get the tow rope and handle to their skiers in the water.

or sail—does the same thing, but pulling a flotation device instead of a water-ski tow rope (Figure 59).

"Life Sling" is the brand name of an excellent system specifically designed for this use. The system includes a long line made of polypropylene (so that it floats) and a sling-shaped flotation device that can be used if necessary to hoist the victim out of the water. In use, you throw the flotation "sling" into the water and pull it behind the boat at the end of its tether. The boat is then steered slowly in a tight circle around the victim and at a safe distance. As the circle is completed, the line will be pulled right up to the victim. When he has hold of the line, you stop turning and coast forward until the flotation device reaches him.

The person in the water then puts the flotation sling around his chest so that you can pull him up to the boat—keeping both the victim and the line clear of your propeller(s). In a sailboat, you would heave to at this point.

Getting the Healthy Victim Aboard: The final step is getting the person aboard. I can tell you, from personal experience, that this can be difficult. I have tried to get out of the water onto our boat without benefit of a ladder, and I couldn't do it, even with the help of a strong male. This is the major reason we purchased a boarding ladder to replace the two-rung rope ladder I'd rigged for the children.

If the victim can use a ladder, by all means get one over the side. A sportfishing boat with a transom door for landing large fish can "land" the victim through that door *as long as all engines are turned off*. If you don't have a ladder or a transom door, you can tie a loop in a mooring line, hang it over the side just below the waterline, and tie the other end of the line securely to a cleat. The victim can then put one foot in that loop and, standing in it, with you pulling on the line under his arms, or pulling on his arms, he can, with help, climb aboard. If you're in an overboard motorboat, you may have a special problem in bringing someone aboard. While it is much easier to bring someone over the side, you need to be careful that you don't swamp the boat as you do it.

Injured Victim

If the victim is unable to help himself, one of your crew may have to go into the water to help him. I say "may have to" because it might not be necessary. If, for example, you have a low boat and can reach the person by leaning over the side, probably no one needs to go into the water; you simply grab the victim and muscle him into the boat. In some smaller boats, you may have to use special care that you don't tip your boat over trying to get the victim aboard.

Swim Platform Pickup: If you have a swim platform, you may be able to reach the victim from there. In all situations, however, the people trying to pull the victim aboard should be wearing life jackets, just in case they fall overboard while trying

to get the victim out of the water. The person on the swim platform is in a more precarious position, so he (she) should also
have a safety harness or a line that is attached securely to the
boat. Of course, with anyone so near the propeller(s), your
engine(s) should be turned off.

From a Sailboat: A larger sailboat sometimes provides an
advantage when you are trying to lift an injured victim from
the water. For example, we have a block and tackle rigged from
about the mid-point of our boom. We normally use this to keep
our sail off the spreaders and to prevent the boom from swinging unexpectedly in an accidental jibe. In an emergency, we can
attach the bottom part of that block and tackle to a sling and
use its four-to-one mechanical advantage to lift someone out of
the water. By running the line from the tackle to one of our
cockpit winches, Susan can readily lift me out of the water.

Alternatively, in a smaller sailboat you can lower the sail into
the water, maneuver the victim up into the sail, and then begin
to pull the sail up onto the boat, using it as a large, canvas sling
to lift the victim.

The key point is that you have to look at your boat—motorboat or sailboat—and make the effort to figure out how you
would get someone back on board if he were injured or unconscious—or, if you are male, how your wife or female friend
would get you out of the water if you were unconscious. It may
take some ingenuity to figure out your system, and it will definitely take practice to make sure that you and your crew know
how to make it work. But if you ever find yourself in a man-
overboard situation, the effort and time invested in your
man-overboard drill will be among the most valuable hours you
have ever spent. The middle of an emergency is no place to
start trying to figure all of this out.

Going Into the Water: Only when there is no alternative should
someone go into the water to help the victim. Moreover, anyone who goes into the water must wear a PFD and be tied to
the boat either with a safety harness or a line tied securely around
his chest. You don't need to create a second victim while trying
to help the first.

Once in the water, the "rescuer" should first get a loop around
the victim's chest, snugly up under the armpits. If possible, the

line should go up the person's back, so that when he is lifted, his back will be against the side of the boat. This helps protect his face and neck when you are pulling him up into the boat. (A conscious victim who can help himself is better served by having the line from the loop go up past his face, so that he is facing the boat and can help get himself up and over the side.)

Next, the "rescuer" should help get the victim aboard by guiding and lifting from below as the crew on deck pulls the person up. This is much more effective if the "rescuer" has something to hold onto with one hand (even if that is only his own safety line) while he helps the victim with the other hand.

Finally, as soon as the victim is safely on deck, the crew should recover the "rescuer." If there are enough people to begin first-aid treatment for the victim while bringing the "rescuer" back on board, by all means begin the first aid at the same time. However, if there are not enough people to do both, first get the "rescuer" back on board and then start administering first aid. Once you begin something like artificial respiration or cardiopulmonary resuscitation, you can't stop to recover the "rescuer" until either the victim regains consciousness, emergency medical people arrive on the scene to take over, or you conclude that the victim has died. In the meantime, the "rescuer" could have become a victim himself if left in the water.

The only exception to the recommendation that you get the "rescuer" out of the water before ministering to the victim would be in the case of heavy bleeding from an injury. In that situation, you should get a pressure pad on the wound immediately to stem the bleeding, recover the rescuer, and go back to the first aid. The minute that you delay recovering the "rescuer" in that circumstance shouldn't hurt him, but it could be the difference between life and death for the victim. For additional information about first-aid skills, call your local Red Cross.

ROUGH INLETS

Boaters along coastal waters who want to get out into the ocean often must go through relatively narrow inlets. Most of the time, these inlets pose few problems if the ocean itself is not particularly rough. Under the wrong combination of wind, tide, and sea conditions, however, running an inlet can present a severe test of your boating skills.

In foul weather, the problems of inlets are caused by the storm-driven ocean waves breaking across the entrance. In fair weather, the problems result mainly from breaking waves created by the wrong combination of wind and tides. Tragedy occurs either when the skipper doesn't recognize the danger, lacks the skills needed to pilot his boat in those conditions, or is taking his boat into waters it wasn't designed or constructed to handle.

One of the deceptive characteristics of inlets is that it is usually easier to go out an inlet into the ocean than it is to return. Many times, a small-boat skipper will go out in the morning when neither the tide nor the wind is a factor, spend several hours fishing or sailing, and then head for home. Ten miles offshore, the wind and waves are moderate, the sky is clear, and everything is in good order. Meanwhile, back at the inlet, a strong sea breeze has come up, the tide has turned and begun to run out strongly, and the clash between the wind and the tide has resulted in large breakers across the channel leading through the inlet. Depending upon the nature of that particular inlet, the strength of the wind and current involved, and the capabilities of your boat, those waves can be very dangerous.

NEW JERSEY CHARTER BOAT RESCUES EIGHT—Eight people, including four children, were rescued by the crew of a commercial fishing boat after their small pleasure boat sank in rough waters off Barnegat Inlet, New Jersey, May 10.

Allan Cunningham's custom-made boat lies submerged in 25 feet of water, but he's grateful his family is safe.

The Howell Township, New Jersey, man, his wife, four of his five young children, and another couple had set out on what they expected to be a pleasant fishing trip, when their boat was swamped by a 15-foot wave. All eight were saved by the crew of the *Carolyn Ann II,* a party boat, which was close enough to see the Cunningham boat sink and arrived on the scene about 10 minutes later.

Cunningham said he wasn't aware that a small craft advisory had been issued for the waters off Manasquan to Cape Henlopen. He first noticed the water was getting rough when he passed the rocks at the mouth of the inlet. He said the wave that swamped the boat "appeared out of nowhere."

Barnegat Inlet, with its bottled-up currents and shifting shoals, is considered the third most hazardous inlet on the East Coast, according to the Coast Guard.[7]

There are four keys to running inlets safely. The first is good judgment. The second is timing. The third is knowing how to handle your boat in a following sea. The fourth is taking common-sense precautions if you have no choice but to go through a rough inlet.

Inlets and Good Judgment

The most fundamental element of good judgment involved in navigating inlets is deciding whether your boat is suited to running the inlet if conditions deteriorate. Virtually any boat can navigate an inlet safely when the water is flat, but that doesn't make it safe to take "virtually any" boat out through that inlet for a day of fishing. In a rare (for me) display of good judgment as a teenager, I turned my sailboat around at the bay-side entrance to Barnegat Inlet despite my very strong desire to go sailing in the ocean. Even as a fourteen-year-old, I was able to figure out that I might not be able to bring my 16-foot sailboat back through the inlet if the tide turned against me.

If your boat is suited for the inlet only in good conditions, I strongly recommend against your taking the boat into the ocean unless you stay close enough to the inlet that you can be sure of getting back while conditions are favorable. If you really want to spend more time in the ocean or range farther afield, I'd suggest curbing your desires until you have a boat better suited for the use you want from it. If you have any question about the suitability of your boat for running local inlets, visit your local marine police or Coast Guard facility and talk with them. They're the people who get called in emergencies.

In addition, if there are breaking waves across an inlet when

7. *Soundings,* August 1986.

you want to go out into the ocean, consider changing your plans unless your boat is large, the waves are small, and you have a lot of experience in handling your boat under rough-water conditions. The face of a wave as it crests is very steep and moving forward with a great deal of force. Depending upon the size of a given wave, the size and weight of your boat, and the way that you happen to hit it, a cresting wave can easily overpower your boat.

Inlets and Timing

Often, the time you choose to run an inlet is as important as any other factor. Two hours can make the difference between encountering very large breaking waves across the inlet and relatively calm water. Why? It's the effect of the tide, or of the wind and tide. Any inlet subject to a strong tidal current is best used at slack tide. Also, if the wind is blowing toward the land, most inlets are considerably rougher with an ebbing (outgoing) tide than when the tide is flooding (coming in). These factors make it worthwhile knowing the times of slack tides and of the strongest ebb and flood tides so that you can plan to enter the inlet when the conditions are most likely to be favorable.

Small-Boat Handling in Following Seas

The danger in coming through an inlet when waves are breaking behind you occurs when your boat gets caught in a breaking wave. If your boat will go fast enough, the best approach in entering the inlet is to ride the back of a wave through the inlet. You simply pick your wave and adjust your boat speed so that you ride its back right on through (Figure 60). When the wave does break, the crest is safely in front of you, and you're safely in front of the next wave in the line.

If you're in a sailboat or a displacement motorboat, you probably don't have sufficient boat speed to avoid getting caught by at least one breaking wave. The danger, of course, is that the breaking wave will take control of your boat and make it broach, rolling dangerously. The danger is caused by two factors: First, the breaking wave changes the flow of water past your rudder

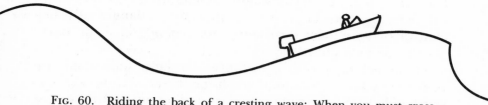

F<small>IG</small>. 60. Riding the back of a cresting wave: When you must cross through an area of breaking waves, you should try to adjust your speed so that you can ride the back of one wave right on through the area. In that way, the wave will break in front of you, not in back of or directly beneath your boat.

because the water is moving faster than your boat. As a result, even though your boat is "racing" forward, the rudder may "think" it's standing still or even moving backward and have just the opposite effect from what you expect. Second, your rudder and propeller are not as effective in the frothy white water of the breaking wave as they are in solid blue water. As a result, your boat is not its normally responsive self.

All of this means that slow-speed boats require excellent boat handling when entering an inlet through breaking waves. Your objective is to time the waves so that you avoid getting caught by a wave just as it begins to break. That may be a surfboarder's dream; in this situation, it is a boat skipper's nightmare.

To do this, you should come into the inlet at a moderate speed, watching the waves to get a sense of their rhythm and pattern. You'll find that the waves come in a series, with one or two large waves followed by several that are smaller. Your objective is to ride the back of the second large wave as far as you can, so that if one of those waves is going to catch up with you when it breaks, it will be one of the smaller waves, not the bigger one. When a wave does break behind you and the foaming front thunders toward you, you want that wave to catch you square on the stern with your rudder straight amidships and your engine running full to give you the strongest possible prop wash past your rudder. If, however, a wave catches you so that it is cresting right behind your boat, reduce speed immediately. Hopefully, you'll slow down enough that the wave will pass under your boat before it breaks, and you can speed up again right

behind it. In any case, you want to avoid racing headlong down
the front of a cresting wave because of the danger of losing
control of your boat, broaching and being rolled, or pitchpoling end over end.

So the technique is this: As the second large wave comes up
under your boat, you should push the throttle all the way forward and, as long as you don't start getting out on the crest of
your wave, keep your engine running flat out until you are
through the breakers. The long keels of displacement motorboats and heavy-displacement sailboats help provide needed
directional stability in this situation. Sailboats also gain stability
if they are able to come through the inlet with a moderate amount
of sail flying. Too much sail, however, may increase the risk of
broaching by making the boat heel over, thereby reducing the
effectiveness of the rudder and keel. It is important to keep
your sailboat straight up.

Common-Sense Precautions in Rough Inlets

If you ever find yourself in a situation in which you're taking
your boat through a rough inlet, there are several precautions
you should take. First, you should have everyone put a life vest
on. You don't have to make a big deal about it; this should be
handled as a routine safety precaution. Second, you should stand
off and watch a few other boats go through the inlet to get a
sense of what it's like. It is very difficult to judge the size and
power of breaking waves by looking at their backs. Watching
how they affect other boats gives you another yardstick. And
third, use a buddy system. Call on the VHF radio or flag down
another boat and ask them to follow you through. In that way,
if you do get into trouble, at least there's someone watching
who can come to your aid. Finally, you may consider whether
conditions in the inlet will be better later in the afternoon either
because the tidal current will ease or the onshore breeze will
weaken late in the day. You may be able to get advice along this
line by using your radio to consult with the marine police or the
Coast Guard.

LOSING AN ENGINE

One of the nice things about having a boat with two engines is the ability to get home if you lose an engine. For most of us, however, it's one engine or nothing. So, what can we do about the possibility of that engine failing? There are two basic alternatives: (1) Become a mechanic; or (2) pay close attention to the care and feeding of your engine. The first alternative isn't practical for most of us. The second, on the other hand, is not only practical, but also effective. As a result, it's the route most of us have to choose.

Most boat-engine failures involve one of five critical engine systems, and they wouldn't happen if the skippers had taken the suggestions that follow. The critical systems are the engine's lubrication, fuel, air-intake, cooling, and (to one extent or another) electrical systems. Your focus should be on making certain that each of these five systems is well cared for and fully fed. This is what's known as "preventive maintenance."

Lubrication System

There are two basic engine types—two-cycle and four-cycle—and they have very different lubrication systems. Two-cycle engines are lubricated by mixing oil with the gasoline that fuels them. Four-cycle engines are lubricated by continually circulating oil from a central reservoir through key engine parts. These systems impose very different requirements on you as the skipper.

Two-Cycle Engines: Most outboard engines are of the two-cycle variety. With many of them, you are supposed to put oil into the fuel every time you take on gasoline. The important point of care with these engines is adding the correct amount of oil to the gasoline. If you guess and add too little, the engine will wear excessively; it may also overheat and, in the extreme, it could seize up. If you guess and add too much oil, it can foul your spark plugs, making the engine run roughly at low speeds and difficult to start. Such fouling can even make your engine stall, particularly at low speeds.

Some two-cycle engines today are equipped with an oil-injection system that mixes the oil and gas for you right in the engine. If you have one of these engines, your primary responsibility is keeping the oil reservoir filled. It's not enough to be sure there's oil in the reservoir before you start the engine to go out for the day. You should make sure the reservoir is filled—adding oil as necessary. You should also have a good idea how many gallons of gasoline are supposed to be served by a filled reservoir, and keep track of your oil consumption. In this way, you have the opportunity to detect any change in your oil consumption before a problem can develop.

Outboard engines also need lubrication around moving parts associated with their transmissions, shafts, and propellers. You should not only follow the servicing recommendations of your owner's manual closely, but also carry spare lubricant on the boat.

Four-Cycle Engines: Some outboards and virtually all I/Os and inboards—gasoline or diesel—are four-cycle engines. These all have essentially the same kind of lubrication requirements that your car has, with one important difference: You change your car engine's oil and filter after so many "miles"; you change your boat engine's oil and filter after so many "hours" of operation, or at least at the end of each boating season. So, you need to consult your owner's manual to learn the recommended time intervals for changing your boat's oil and filter, keep written track of your engine hours, and change the oil and filter at the recommended intervals. You also need to check the oil level before you start each day's boating, and add oil as necessary to keep the oil level full. And you need to do all of this religiously.

Four-cycle engines also have transmissions and drive trains that need lubrication. If the transmission has an oil reservoir of its own, it, too, should be checked regularly, though it shouldn't be necessary to check it every day. The owner's manual will tell you how often this oil should be changed.

Fuel System

You have three jobs when it comes to your boat's fuel system: keeping the fuel tank filled; keeping the fuel clean; and maintaining the integrity of the fuel tank and lines.

Keeping your tank full is the best way known to man to avoid running out of fuel. The technique is simple: First, fill your fuel tank(s) before you start your day's outing; second, keep track of your fuel consumption; and third, start back to a fuel dock while you have more than enough fuel to get you back—with a large safety margin. A strong head wind, a current that's against you, or an error in your calculation could leave you stranded if you try to cut too close on the amount of fuel.

Keeping your fuel clean means having good fuel filters, changing the filter elements regularly, and buying fuel from marinas or gasoline stations that you know have good filter systems in their own pumps. If you have a diesel engine, you should have at least one water separator/filter system in addition to the filters that are mounted on the engine itself. The water separator/filter should have a clear bowl so that you can check for water in the system by looking at that filter bowl. At the first sign of water, you should consult with your marina about getting the water out of your tanks. For the record, you should also store your boat over the winter with its internal fuel tanks filled so that water does not condense from the air in your tanks during the winter months.

Making sure that your fuel tank and fuel lines are in good condition should be part of your pre-start checklist, as mentioned in Chapter 8. In this way, you can detect the potential for fuel leaks before they actually develop.

Air-Intake System

All engines need to breathe. The air they inhale is mixed with the gasoline or diesel fuel so that the fuel will burn. Diesel engines particularly require large amounts of air. Your job is to be sure that the air-intake passages to your engine room are not blocked, and to change or clean the engine's air filters as recommended in your owner's manual.

Cooling System

Nearly all boat engines are cooled by water that is pumped through small channels in the engine block. On some engines, this water is pumped from outside the boat and spit back out again after use. Other engines use a two-step system in which water from outside the boat is used to cool water that is recirculated over and over again through the engine. These recirculating systems are usually called "fresh-water cooling."

Outboard Engines: The cooling systems of outboards generally are vulnerable in two areas—one being the water pump, the second involving possible blockage of the cooling-water system itself. The water pump should be serviced each year—more frequently if your boat gets a lot of use—as recommended in your owner's manual. Most marine water pumps have a rubber impeller that ages with use and can break. Also, any sand, silt, or other stuff that is in the water going through your water pump tends to make the impeller wear excessively. We wiped out a pump on our 40-horsepower outboard almost entirely one season, after running unwittingly through a section of river where there was deep silt on the bottom. We'd been through a half-mile of the silt before we realized what was happening. A few days later, we discovered that our engine was running hot; steam instead of water was coming out with the exhaust. The engine went to a mechanic to repair the water pump.

Blockages in the small water channels in the engine can result from corrosion as well as from dirt. For this reason, it's a good idea to flush the outboard's cooling system with fresh water if you've been operating either in salt water or in water with mud or silt.

I/Os and Inboard Engines: In addition to their water pumps and water channels, inboard engines have two or three other areas of vulnerability. One is the water-intake screen, which is located on the boat's bottom and can be blocked either by marine growth or by a sucked-up piece of paper or plastic. The rubber hose that carries the water from the engine water-intake through-hull fitting to the engine itself is a second area of weakness. Another short section of hose carries the hot water from the engine to the exhaust system. The condition of these cooling-system hoses and their hose clamps should be checked regularly. A leak could not only cause overheating problems with your engine or its exhaust system, it could also sink your boat.

The third area of weakness is the secondary water strainer

some boats have on the inside of the hull between the water intake and the water pump. This strainer also needs to be checked periodically to be sure it doesn't become clogged.

The system on boats with two-stage cooling systems is similar to your car's cooling system. The water that actually cools your engine is circulated through a radiator that, on a boat, is called a heat exchanger. However, instead of using air to cool the water in the radiator as your car does, the boat uses water from the river, lake, or ocean. This so-called "raw water" is drawn into the boat at the water-intake through-hull fitting and is pumped through the heat exchanger, into the exhaust system, and out of the boat. The "raw water" side of the system has the same vulnerabilities at the intake screen, the hoses, and the secondary strainer that are in any other inboard cooling system. In addition, the second stage of the cooling system also has weak spots. It has its own water pump, which can fail, much as your car's water pump can fail. Also, the level of coolant in the second stage needs to be checked regularly, just as you check the coolant in your car's radiator. A problem on either side of the two-stage cooling system can stop your engine.

Electrical System

One area in which diesel engines have a decided advantage over gasoline engines—in addition to the greater safety of diesel fuel compared to gasoline—is in the simplicity of their electrical systems. The primary electrical requirement of a diesel engine is for its starter motor to get the engine started. As a result, the diesel engine's basic electrical system consists only of a battery, a starter motor, and an alternator to keep the battery charged. If you can crank your diesel by hand, no electricity is required.

The most obvious maintenance requirement for the electrical system of diesel engines is to keep the battery fluid up to its recommended level, the battery fully charged, and the battery terminals free of corrosion by cleaning and coating them with grease or Vaseline. Along with this battery maintenance, you'll also need to check the alternator belt regularly to be sure it is properly tightened and not cracked. We also carry a spare alternator belt—and know how to replace it, should that be necessary. One note: You should *never* turn off the ignition before stopping your diesel engine. It's a good way to burn out the alternator—quickly. I know that from personal experience; and I did it in a moment of absentmindedness, even though I knew better.

In addition to the basic battery / starter motor / alternator system of the diesel, gasoline engines also have an electrical or electronic ignition system to provide the spark needed to ignite the gasoline and air mixture in the engine. These ignition systems are at best relatively complex, and at worst extraordinarily so. With an inboard engine, about all you can do for the ignition system is to be sure that your engine receives the recommended tune-ups and maintenance from a professional mechanic. With an outboard, you can also carry spare spark plugs. Then, if your engine fails because the spark plugs have been fouled from too much oil in your gasoline, changing the spark plugs will generally get the engine running long enough for you to run back to shore. For the most part, however, the ignition systems of modern outboard engines are, like their inboard counterparts, too complex to do much troubleshooting if they fail.

What to Do if the Engine Quits

If your engine quits, what should you do? First, if you can, put an anchor down so that you'll stay where you are. Second, get on the radio and notify the Coast Guard or your marina that the engine has quit and what your situation is. If you need assistance because of threatening weather, it's getting dark, or because you're in a dangerous situation, ask for it. If you have no immediate need for assistance, advise them that you're going to try to determine why the engine has stopped, to see whether you can solve the problem or will need help.

And then do that—try to find out why the engine stopped by checking out the five basic systems. Do you have fuel? Is the oil level OK? Did your alternator belt break and the battery run down as a result? If so, and you have two batteries, perhaps you can get started by switching to the second battery after replacing the alternator belt, using the belt from your spare-parts kit. Alternatively, you can fabricate a temporary belt with a piece of rope. Did the engine overheat? If so, you may be able to restart it after an hour or so, but you'll need to figure out why it overheated, or the problem will probably just reoccur. There may be something blocking the water intake. If none of these reveals the problem, check the air intake. It's an unlikely culprit, but. . . .

If you have an engine mechanic's knowledge and skills, there are other troubleshooting steps you can take; you'll know what they are. Otherwise, if you can't restart the engine after checking out all of these systems, it's time to get back on the radio and ask for a tow.

BEING TOWED

The two principal dangers in being towed are: (1) excessive speed, and (2) failure of either the tow rope or the cleat it's tied to. Towing speed is something you need to work out with whoever is going to tow your boat, before the towing procedure is started. Depending upon the size of your boat and the sea conditions, a safe towing speed may be less than one and probably no more than about five knots. If the person volunteering to tow your boat isn't willing to limit his speed to what you believe is safe for your boat, don't give him your tow line; look for another rescuer. The risks involved in being towed faster are simply too great. Not only may excessive towing speeds place dangerous strains on your boat and its fittings, but you don't have the same control over your boat when it's being towed that you would have under your own power.

Note that I have referred to giving the other boat "your tow line." Having your own line is the best way to be sure that the tow line is right for the job. For example, it's just as important that the tow line not be too heavy (strong) for pulling your boat as it is that it be strong enough. An appropriately sized nylon line will stretch enough to soften the impact of wave shocks on your bow cleats. Line that is too heavy will not stretch; instead, it will transmit those shocks directly to your cleats, possibly overloading them. In general, a line of a size suitable for your boat's anchor line is also suitable as a tow line. For that reason, you should be sure to have an anchor line that is long enough to be used as a tow rope if need arises.

Preventing failure of your deck cleats requires an additional step. I strongly suggest that you go through whatever contortions are necessary to look under your deck to find out whether there are sturdy, metal plates backing up all of your deck cleats. If the answer is "Yes," the next question is whether your cleats are actually bolted to those backing plates or fastened with self-tapping screws. Replace any self-tapping screws with bolts, lock washers, and nuts. If the cleats do not have metal backing plates, have backing plates installed and your cleats bolted to them.

In any case, you should never attempt to tow another boat (or allow your boat to be towed) with a rope attached to any cleats not bolted to metal backing plates. Otherwise, the strains involved in towing are likely to tear the cleats right out of the deck, with potentially deadly effect. The same stretchiness that allows nylon line to absorb shock loads when your boat is being towed will make it snap back like a whip if a cleat breaks loose under the strain, turning the rope end and cleat into a potentially deadly missile. In the same way, you should check with the skipper of a potential towing boat to be sure his cleats also are bolted through to sturdy backing plates; you don't want one of his cleats flying back at you if the tow rope snatches it from his stern. If he doesn't know the answer to the question, he should look, to find out.

Rigging for Towing

If you have only one bow cleat, you should simply make the middle of your anchor line fast with a couple of turns around that cleat and pass or throw the other end of the line to the towing boat. When the line has been made secure to the towing boat's stern cleats, you can adjust the length of the line from your foredeck. If you have two cleats on your bow, you can snub the line around one of them until you're ready to adjust the length of the line. Before the towing begins, however, you'll need to get a loop around both cleats so that the pulling force will be applied evenly to each.

FIG. 61.   Towing a boat: When towing a boat (or a dinghy), you should adjust the tow line so that the other boat rides at least two waves behind you. Also, the length of the tow line should be fine-tuned so that both boats are going up the waves or down the waves at the same time.

In the same way, it's generally better if the skipper of the towing boat can put a large eye in the tow line and loop it over his port and starboard stern cleats so that the load is centered in the stern. Towing from a single cleat on one corner or the other of the stern can make steering more difficult for him. In addition, it's (obviously) important for the skipper of the towing boat to keep the tow line away from his propellers.

Once the skipper of the other boat has made the tow line secure to his stern cleats, he should move away slowly, allowing you to adjust the length of the line from your bow. In general, you'll need a longer tow line in open water and a shorter tow line where space is more constricted. You should have a minimum of three boat lengths of tow line so that there is enough distance between your two boats to allow you time to steer off to the side if the towing boat stops or slows unexpectedly. If there are significant waves running and you'll be moving with the waves behind you, the tow line should be adjusted so that you are at least two waves behind the towing boat. In addition, the length of line should be adjusted so that both you and the towing boat are at the same relative position on the waves (Figure 61). The object is for you both to be climbing or going down waves at the same time. This will help prevent the waves from alternately pushing your two boats closer together and snapping you back to the end of the tow line. Finally, with the tow length adjusted, you are ready to begin the slow trip back to port.

Towing Yourself

If you have a dinghy with an outboard motor, you can often tow your own boat back to port—assuming the water's not too

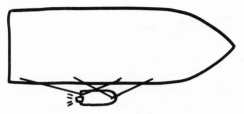

FIG. 62.   Your dinghy as a tugboat: By lashing your dinghy alongside as illustrated, even a very small dinghy can serve as a tug for a rather large boat if the wind and waves are calm.

rough. Rather than putting the dinghy at the end of a tow rope out in front of the larger boat, however, you should put the dinghy along your boat's side much in the same way that a tugboat goes alongside to move a larger ship (Figure 62). After you've put out a couple of fenders to protect your boat's topsides, your dinghy changes roles and becomes a tug. When the dinghy is tied securely with bow and stern lines as well as with forward and aft spring lines, you can start the dinghy's engine, bring it up to the appropriate cruising speed, and steer the two boats with the larger boat's rudder. As for the person in the dinghy . . . for all practical purposes, he's "down in the engine-room." His job is to keep the motor running, to speed it up or slow it down, and to shift into forward, neutral, or reverse as the skipper orders from the larger boat's helm. With an arrangement like this, a 2- or 3-horsepower dinghy outboard can be used to move a 30- to 35-foot boat quite easily in quiet water.

WATER-SKIING

Water-skiing has an image of being fun—and it can be. With two skis, it's not too difficult even for a first-timer to get up and running. Going with one ski offers the more athletically inclined substantially greater challenge. But for all of its image of fun and sunshine, water-skiing is also a sometimes deadly sport.

WATER-SKIER   KILLED   IN   BOATING   ACCIDENT—A Saturday-afternoon boating mishap claimed the life of a Pennsylvania 16-year-old, according to Maryland Natural Resources Police.

Police said the fatality occurred at about 2:00 P.M. on Swan Creek as the unidentified victim was water-skiing while two friends were operating a 19-foot speedboat. The youth, of Lancaster, was apparently struck by the boat as it circled back to the spot where he had fallen into the water.

The official cause of death was listed as drowning, but police said the victim had major cuts to his lower torso, apparently from the boat's propellers.[8]

Sometimes, too, accidents result in double tragedy as boat skippers are held criminally liable for the accident:

BOATER CONVICTED OF NEGLIGENCE IN WATER-SKI FATALITY—A Pasadena, Maryland, man has been acquitted of boat manslaughter charges, but in December faced sentencing on a lesser charge in the accidental water-skiing death of a local teenager.

In a well-publicized trial, Joseph F. DiPiazza was convicted of negligent operation of a motorboat, said Rob Cecil, public affairs officer with the Maryland state attorney's office in Anne Arundel County. At the same time, DiPiazza was acquitted of the boat manslaughter charge and reckless operation of a motorboat.

He faces a maximum penalty of 30 days in jail and a $200 fine.

Stephen Aaron Luck, 18, died May 27, 1985, after being struck in the head by the propeller of the boat DiPiazza was driving. At the time of the accident, Luck was water-skiing in the crowded Severn River around an area known as "ski island." Skiing with him was his friend, Russell Millard. At the helm of the boat was Connie Boyer and as spotter was her sister Cindy.

DiPiazza was also driving a boat pulling a water-skier. He, too, had a spotter on board. According to testimony by the Boyers and other witnesses, DiPiazza's boat was traveling at a high rate of speed about 75 feet behind Luck. They said DiPiazza's boat then began gaining on the front boat, when Luck lost his balance and fell.

DiPiazza, testifying on his own behalf, said he was traveling at a normal rate of speed when suddenly he saw a person in the water, but it was too late to avoid hitting him.[9]

8. *News-Journal,* Wilmington, Delaware, September 23, 1985.
9. *Soundings,* February 1987.

Pulling a water-skier with your boat requires very specific skills that need to be learned with hands-on instruction. You should not try to pick up these skills by reading a book or sitting in a classroom. Rather, you should find an experienced person who can go out with you in your boat and talk you through the procedures involved until you and your crew have them firmly in your heads. Only then should you try to pull any skiers.

There are, however, some key elements of water-ski safety that can be reviewed here and should never be ignored. All are equally important:

• You should have at least one and, preferably, two observers in the boat with you whenever you're pulling a skier. One person's responsibility is to watch the skier at all times. The other observer's job is to help you watch for hazards ahead of the boat. This second observer is particularly important when your attention is on the skier—for example, when you're attempting to get him (or her) up onto the skis or to pick him up after he's fallen. In these circumstances, your second observer should keep an eye out for other boats that may or may not be paying proper attention to you.

• The skier *always* should wear an approved personal flotation device.

• You should adjust your boat speed and turns to the skill of the skier. Skiing is meant to be fun, not thrilling. So, do not try to see how fast your skier can go—even if he (or she) wants you to do so. That's inviting an accident.

• You must pay close attention to the fatigue level of your skiers. It's always tempting to get in one last run, but people frequently don't realize how tired they are. Moreover, you may also be more tired than you realize. Because of the fatigue, both you and your skiers are more susceptible to making mistakes in judgment; also, the skiers are more vulnerable to being injured. So, quit while you're ahead.

• Do not pull skiers in crowded waters. You may be able to maneuver through the crowd, but someone else trying to keep track of all the traffic may fail to see your skier in time to avoid an accident. So, find a place where the traffic is light. And, for goodness' sake, stay out of ship channels!

• Always turn off your engine (with it in gear) when your boat is next to a skier in the water. The risk of a propeller hitting your skier is just too great. So, keep the engine off until the skier is either safely aboard or safely away from the boat.

But again, get someone with experience in pulling skiers to teach you the ropes. And you, in turn, be certain that anyone else (your teenage child, for example) who uses your boat to pull skiers gets good, solid instruction as well as practical, supervised experience before you turn over the keys to the boat.

COMING TO THE AID OF OTHERS

It is sometimes frightening to see how often people rescued from severely disabled boats report that other boaters just cruised on by, apparently oblivious to their distress. Too often, it seems, people mistake a distress signal for a friendly wave. Or, they apparently just don't see the signal in the first place.

For a lot of reasons, safe boating demands that the skipper of every boat and his crew keep a good watch in all directions. And that doesn't mean simply keeping an eye on the water nearby. It means maintaining a sharp lookout all the way to the horizon—in all directions—and paying attention to what you see. The major purpose in this, of course, is to look for other boat traffic, or for landmarks, navigation aids, crab or lobster pots, signs of changing weather, floating debris, etc. Another critical purpose in maintaining this watch, however, is to look for anything unusual or out of the ordinary, particularly as you look at other boats.

BOATERS RESCUE FOUR FROM BURNING BOAT—Two New Jersey men are credited with rescuing four boaters off the state's Ocean County shoreline just minutes before their pleasure craft was consumed by flames August 8, but the rescuers said what they did was just their "duty as boaters."

Ron Chesinski of Little Egg Harbor Township, New Jersey, and Tom VanBlarcum of Franklin Lakes, New Jersey, were aboard VanBlarcum's boat, *Unique,* a 38-foot Bayliner. They were heading from Bricktown to Chesinski's home when they spotted smoke coming from the exhaust of *Daddy's Dream,* a 44-foot cabin cruiser stalled about 1½ miles offshore from Surf City, New Jersey.

They pulled alongside *Daddy's Dream,* which was carrying owner /
operator Arthur Goldstein of Watchung, New Jersey, his wife, and
two others. "It was only common courtesy to stop," VanBlarcum
said.

VanBlarcum told his son, Thomas Jr., 8, to hand him a life jacket,
and the youngster helped his father untie *Unique*'s dinghy to get it
in the water. With Chesinski at *Unique*'s helm, VanBlarcum rowed
over to *Daddy's Dream* and went aboard.

While VanBlarcum was onboard *Daddy's Dream,* there was a second flare-up. "I called the Coast Guard, and they told us to immediately get everyone off the boat," said Chesinski.

VanBlarcum said that when he boarded the boat, he had immediately questioned whether the boaters were using diesel. "They
were using diesel, so there was less chance of an explosion," he said.
"The boat was filled with smoke, and we had closed all the hatches.
But they had no more fire extinguishers. I knew it was time to get
them off."

Shortly after *Daddy's Dream* was evacuated, flames raged through
the craft, which was in water about 25 feet deep. Authorities said
they are still investigating the cause of the fire.[10]

Sometimes, of course, "the unusual" is more subtle.

SHARP LOOKOUT RESCUES FIVE—The sharp eyes and first-
aid training of two BOAT / US members on the Chesapeake Bay
last fall saved the lives of five people after a boating accident.

Member Gene Pontrelli of Wilmington, Delaware, was sailing out
of the Chester River with his wife on a blustery day of 25-knot winds
and a 3- to 5-foot chop when they spotted what looked like debris
in the water about a half-mile away. When Mrs. Pontrelli saw that
the debris appeared to be "moving," they dropped their sails and
motored to the scene.

What they found were five elderly people in the cold water, clinging to a swamped, 15-foot runabout. They had been surviving in
the water for an hour and a half, and no one was wearing a life
jacket.

The Pontrellis were able to pull everyone onboard their sailboat
and quickly saw signs of hypothermia in two of the men. They got
them out of their wet clothes and wrapped themselves with the victims in blankets to warm them up.

10. *Soundings,* October 1987.

A radio call to the Coast Guard was relayed to a nearby marina, where a speedboat and a paramedic were dispatched. All of the victims, who were vacationers out for a day of crabbing in an overloaded boat, were taken to a local hospital.

Both of the Pontrellis have received first-aid and CPR training where they work.[11]

These two news reports have three elements in common: (1) the rescuers were paying attention to what was going on around them—in the second case, looking closely at "debris" a half-mile away; (2) the rescuers were willing to get involved; and (3) the rescuers were prepared to handle the situations they encountered.

The first of those three elements is a matter of developing good habits—the captain and crew keeping a good watch. The second reflects a tradition as old as boating itself—coming to the aid of another boater in distress, or, in VanBlarcum's words, doing their "duty as boaters." And the third demonstrates knowledge, boating skills, and judgment.

The knowledge component—how to recognize signs of hypothermia and then treat it, for example, or to think to differentiate between the dangers of diesel fuel and gasoline—comes either from years of experience or from taking courses offered by the Red Cross, the Coast Guard Auxiliary, the United States Power Squadrons, or, as in the Pontrellis' case, by both the Power Squadrons and their employers. The boating-skills component—VanBlarcum putting on a life jacket before getting into his dinghy to row over to the boat in distress, for example—comes from consciously applying the knowledge gained from boating-safety courses, and from books such as this, to the day-to-day operation of your boat. The judgment component is more difficult. It boils down, however, to acquiring sound knowledge of your own, your crew's, and your boat's capabilities so that you not only provide the maximum assistance possible under the circumstances of the moment, but so that you also have the sense to get help from others when the distress at hand is more than you alone can handle. In both cases reported here, the rescuers called for advice from the Coast Guard.

11. *Boat / US Reports,* January 1989.

COMMON SENSE

One of the most important ingredients of boating safety is plain, old common sense. For example, common sense should suggest that anyone taking out a small sailboat on wintry water be wearing a life jacket and, possibly even a wet suit—especially if the boat is easily tipped over. Without that life jacket, the cold water can quickly overcome even a strong swimmer.

> RHODE ISLAND SAILOR MISSING IN CAPSIZE—A 28-year-old Rhode Island man was missing after the Sunfish he was sailing on the Warren River capsized. Two friends along on the sail April 5 stayed with the boat for a few minutes before swimming to shore and calling police.
>
> A search by local authorities and the Coast Guard failed to turn up any sign of the missing man, Lionel A. Botello of Warren.
>
> The two friends were identified as Frank A. Lewis, 14, and William W. Brackett, 25, the owner of the boat. None of the men had life preservers, according to Chief Emilio Squiloente of the Warren Police Department.
>
> The capsize occurred around 10:30 A.M., less than 100 feet from shore. Squiloente said the three men were sailing in water less than 15 feet deep.[12]

Common sense also suggests that every boat (with the possible exception of canoes and kayaks) always have an anchor available for use quickly. That means the anchor is stowed where it can be reached immediately, that the anchor line is attached to the anchor, and the line is stowed neatly so that you don't have to worry about it becoming snarled if you need to anchor in a hurry. Engines can quit, and Murphy's Law suggests that they will always quit at an awkward time and place. In the same way, winds can die, leaving sailboats at the mercy of the current unless they have an engine to take over where the wind left off.

Less obvious, perhaps, but still an element of common sense, is being sure that someone knows where you are, when you expect to return, and how to identify your boat should that become necessary in a search-and-rescue operation. This is called

12. *Soundings,* June 1986.

"filing a float plan" and is much like airplane pilots filing a flight plan. It's a detail that can save your life.

COPTER SAVES FISHERMEN—Two fishermen were rescued by the crew of a Coast Guard helicopter Friday morning after their boat capsized in the Delaware Bay.

Coast Guard officials said [the two men] were gillnetting in the bay off Broadkill Beach early Friday morning. When they did not return by 11:00 A.M., family members notified the Coast Guard.

A helicopter from the Coast Guard base in Cape May, New Jersey, sighted the two clinging to the overturned hull of their 16-foot outboard boat about noon and picked them out of the water.[13]

There are times also when using common sense means saying "No." For example, it may mean saying "No" to someone who wants to join you because letting that extra person aboard would overload the boat. The basic problem with overloading is that your boat not only floats too low in the water, but becomes "loggy"—meaning, the boat is heavy in the water and won't float up over the waves the way it should. As a result, waves the boat would normally handle easily can come right over the stern or side, filling the boat with water.

Common sense may mean saying "No" to a planned trip because the weather forecast is bad, or cutting an outing short because the weather shows signs of deteriorating. It takes courage to disappoint your guests, but the potential problems from getting caught out in conditions too rough for your boat are much more serious than any disappointment you'll cause. For the record, a common-sense rule of thumb for keeping out of conditions too rough for your boat is this: Don't take your boat out in waters that would be unsafe if the weather deteriorated. Of course, even this rule of thumb requires common sense in its application, or you couldn't put some boats into any body of water. The important factor is how long it'll take you to get back to a safe harbor. The weather seldom deteriorates so quickly that there isn't time to get to safety as long as you're alert to the weather, you haven't ranged too far afield, and you have the self-confidence to cut the day short.

13. *News-Journal*, Wilmington, Delaware, May 4, 1986.

The last area of common sense I'll mention is one discussed in the first chapter—alcoholic beverages. Alcohol—and drugs—do not mix with boating. The mixture of booze or drugs with hours spent out in the sun and the fatigue created by a constantly moving boat creates an accident waiting to happen. Common sense tells us that drinking and boating don't mix. So here, too, it's a matter of knowing when to say "No."

Testing What You've Learned
(Answers can be found in Appendix C)

1. When filling your gas tank, what precaution should you take to prevent sparks resulting from the build-up of static electricity?

2. TRUE or FALSE: It's best to fill the portable tanks for your outboard right in the boat so that you don't risk an accident getting them in and out of the boat.

3. After filling your boat's internal tanks with gasoline, what three steps should you always follow before trying to start the engine(s)?

4. What kinds of boats should pleasure-boat operators always grant the right of way to and stay well away from?

5. When you stop to fish, are you better off anchored from the bow or from the stern? Why?

6. If you run aground with a good, hard impact, what's the first thing you should do after getting your engine throttled down and into neutral?

7. List four precautions you should take when approaching a blind turn.

8. TRUE or FALSE: It doesn't do any good to keep track of the weather when you're out on your boat, because conditions change so fast they usually can't be predicted with any accuracy.

9. TRUE or FALSE: If you don't plan to ever be out on your boat at night, there isn't any need for you to learn about navigation lights or check your boat's running lights.

10. List the three things that should be done immediately if someone falls overboard.

11. What is the main danger to be considered in bringing your boat through an inlet from the ocean when there are waves breaking across the inlet?

12. TRUE or FALSE: Often, conditions in inlets are at their worst in mid-afternoon, and a dangerous entrance can be avoided simply by waiting until evening.

13. List five quick checks you can make to find the source of your trouble if your engine stops unexpectedly.

14. If your boat must be towed, you should be sure that all cleats being used for towing _____, that the tow line is made of _____, and that the tow line is about the same size as _____.

15. When pulling a water-skier, how many observers should you have on your boat?

16. Why are overloaded boats hazardous?

VI

Finding Your Way

Finding your way from one place to another while driving your car isn't really very difficult. You drive along an extensive network of roads guided by a system of signs that not only point the way, but also control your speed, warn you of hazards, and alert you to the availability of food and fuel. Finding your way from one place to another while operating your boat is also not very difficult. It is, however, quite different.

Instead of roads, there are channels, but you may or may not need to use them, depending upon your boat's draft. In place of signs carrying words or symbols, our waterways are marked by a system of buoys and beacons. The buoys are floating navigation aids. The beacons are fixed in position—usually on pilings or towers. After dark, rather than using your lights to change night into "day" by illuminating the road ahead of you, as you would in a car, you try to avoid shining bright lights on and around the water for fear of ruining your night vision. Indeed, for the most part, the lights on your boat are designed only to help other people see you, not the reverse.

Hazards on the water are sometimes marked by buoys. More often than not, however, the only place they're marked is on your navigation chart. It's up to you to find them and then figure out whether they pose any danger to your boat. As a result, while you may occasionally look at a road map while driving your car, you should be looking at your charts continually when out in your boat, both to check for hazards and to keep track of your position and progress.

This section introduces basic piloting, including discussion of the system of buoys and beacons used to mark our waterways and the use of navigation charts. Your boat's compass, adjusting your course to compensate for the effects of the wind and current, estimating your time of arrival, and piloting at night are also covered.

20

Basic Piloting— Daytime

People new to boating often find the idea of having a chart out by the steering wheel or tiller and keeping track of their position on the chart an incredible burden. It gets in the way of their "fun." It's an understandable reaction. Assuming they're in local waters and stay within sight of land, they can rely on familiar landmarks to get where they're going. But then there's the exception that makes all of that chart work worthwhile.

For us, such an exception occurred when we were attending a sailing school in the British Virgin Islands—a great place for sailing, in part because of the reliable winds and in part because everything is so close together that it's virtually impossible to get lost. Basic piloting skills are useful in the Virgin Islands, however, and the course we were taking emphasized piloting as well as sailing. And, thank goodness. After completing the course, Susan and I went out on our own for a few days and were sailing merrily along one afternoon, when a tropical rainstorm swept down on us. The rain was so intense for about fifteen minutes that we couldn't see much past the bow of our boat, and the wind was so strong that, despite our reefed sails, we were racing ahead.

Had that happened to us two weeks earlier, before we'd learned about keeping our position plotted on the chart, we'd have had a potential problem. There were islands ahead and to starboard as well as to port. We had to steer a course that would put us safely between islands—easy enough to do in clear weather, but with visibility reduced to a few yards. . . . We were able to weather the squall safely and with some confidence, however, because we knew where we were and how to use the chart to determine a compass course that would take us safely between the islands, even though we couldn't see them.

But you don't have to go to the Virgin Islands to have the same thing happen to you. Since then, we've had similar experiences in various waters along the East Coast where we've done most of our boating. Each time, the same basic piloting skills have proven very handy.

Today, of course, in this age of electronics, even small boats often have Loran units to assist with piloting. Larger boats, particularly those used in coastal and offshore waters, may even have satellite navigation (Sat-Nav) units. With these electronic marvels, you can often determine your position within a matter of feet. But you still need a chart to see where you are. You also need to know how to use that chart to get where you're going. For example, your Loran unit may tell you that the course back to your starting point is 090 degrees, but it won't tell you that there's a shallow area you'll have to steer around along the way to avoid running aground. That's the kind of information you get from your chart.

Moreover, age of electronics or not, everyone who ventures out from shore in a boat should know how to get where he's going and back using only his chart, his compass, and his knowledge of boat speed. Why? Because electronic systems can fail, as illustrated in one of my favorite excerpts from a major boating magazine. The article featured what was described as the world's largest sportfishing boat:

> Aside from the strength and seaworthiness of the 90-footer, both captain and owner emphasize their boat's strategic redundancy: "On our first trip to Venezuela we left with two Lorans and two Sat-Navs. By the time we got there, both Lorans and one Sat-Nav were out," recounts [Captain Dick] Greiner. The answer? Four Lorans and four Sat-Navs.[1]

1. *Motor Boating & Sailing,* July 1987, pp. 96–98.

Backing up your electronics with traditional piloting and navigation techniques is much less expensive than doubling or quadrupling the number of electronic navigation systems on your boat. We also find it more fun.

EQUIPMENT REQUIRED FOR BASIC PILOTING

Basic piloting requires only a minimum of equipment. Most important is a chart of the waters you'll be using. And you'll need a compass and some method for telling how fast the boat is moving. A few plotting tools are also important—pencils, dividers, and a course plotter.

Navigation Charts

Local charts of coastal waters, navigable rivers, and the Great Lakes are available at most marinas. They may be the large-format charts published by the National Oceanic and Atmospheric Administration (NOAA) or books of charts published either by private companies or many state governments. Boaters on inland lakes and rivers are not so fortunate. There are few navigation charts or maps for inland waters. Those that are available are produced for the most part either by local businesses operating on the lake or river or by the state agency responsible for managing the area. In any case, it is your responsibility to replace your charts with updated versions or to update your charts yourself. Changes in navigation aids and other information relating to changes on charts are published in the Notice to Mariners and are available from the U.S. Coast Guard.

Compasses

If possible, your boat's compass should either be permanently mounted on the boat or held in a permanently mounted bracket. The compass should also be where you can see it easily from the steering wheel or tiller. The reason for having the compass mounted in a fixed location is twofold: First, for accurate reading, the compass must be positioned so that its front and back pins (called the "lubber lines") are aligned with the centerline or keel of the boat; the only way to ensure that alignment is to place the compass in a permanent mounting. Second, the various magnetic forces in or on your boat may create a small amount of error in your compass readings. By keeping the compass in one place, you'll have a reasonably good chance of ensuring that the error—called "deviation"—will be constant.

The location of your compass will also affect the amount of deviation. By locating the compass at least 3 feet from the engine(s), metal tanks, toolboxes, batteries, generators, and any other large metal or electrical items—including your instrument panel—and by twisting pairs of wires that run within that 3-foot perimeter, you can to minimize compass deviation.

Unless you find from experience that your compass deviation is large enough to cause piloting errors, you can probably ignore it. One way to check for deviation is to measure the compass course between two buoys and then turn the boat around to read the compass course while you're headed in the opposite direction. The difference between the two compass readings should be 180 degrees. Any variance from the 180-degree difference is caused by deviation. Since deviation often differs from one course to another, you'll need to check your compass on a number of different courses, obviously using different pairs of buoys. But as long as the difference between opposite headings is only one or two degrees, I wouldn't worry about it. Few people can steer a small boat so accurately that a compass error of one or two degrees has any practical effect. If your deviation is more than two degrees, however, you should find someone who can help you "swing" your compass to develop a deviation table and show you how to use that table.

Determining Boat Speed

Many boats have knotmeters (speedometers). One alternative—obviously not particularly accurate—is to estimate your speed. A second alternative that is much more accurate is to develop a speed curve which tells you how fast your boat is

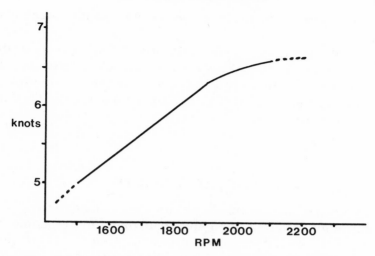

FIG. 63. Using a speed curve: A speed curve allows you to estimate your boat's speed through the water with reasonable accuracy by adjusting your engine RPM. According to this speed curve for our boat, for example, setting the engine speed at 1,825 RPM gives us a boat speed of about 6 knots.

moving at different engine RPM settings (Figure 63). The speed curve is developed by running your boat back and forth over a known distance at different engine RPMs. The key is to run the course—usually a measured half-mile marked by buoys—in both directions at the same RPM, adding the two times together to calculate boat speed for one mile. Running the course in both directions helps to neutralize any current or wind effects, thereby providing a more accurate measure of speed. Such a speed curve can be very useful even as a check on your knotmeter. Whatever method you use, you will need to determine your boat speed for many piloting activities.

Plotting Tools

These are the tools you need to draw your course and plot your progress on the chart. As a minimum, you need a straightedge and pencil so that you can draw a straight line on the chart. You should always write on the chart in pencil so that your lines and notes can be erased when you no longer need them.

You'll also need to measure distance on the chart. A draftsman's compass or a set of dividers works well; a ruler can also be used. An instrument called a "course plotter" is helpful for determining the "true" heading of the course that you've plotted on the chart.*

READING CHARTS

At first glance, navigation charts can appear formidable. They are certainly different than the road maps most people are accustomed to using. As you continue looking at a chart, however, things begin to make some sense (Figure 64).

The first distinction you'll probably notice is between the yellow or green areas, which represent land, and the blue or white areas, which represent the water. In the land sections, you'll notice that some roads are shown, as are towns and cities—but without much detail. In fact, the kind of land detail most likely to be shown on charts includes structures that can be seen from the water and used as landmarks by boaters to help them figure out where they are. Examples are water towers and tanks or radio antennae, which are represented on the chart by small circles with a dot in the middle, labeled "tower," "tank," or "antenna." You may also see docks depicted projecting from the land into the water.

As your eye moves to the blue and white areas, you're likely to notice a lot of numbers scattered around the water. In the charts most of us use, those numbers tell how deep the water is (at low tide) as measured in feet. When you study those numbers a bit, you'll recognize that the blue areas represent shallow water and the white areas, deep water. The fine line between

---

* The Earth has two north poles. One is the geographic North Pole; the other—the one that the compass on your boat points toward—is the magnetic north pole. The "true" headings measured on the chart relate to the geographic North Pole. Magnetic headings and compass courses relate to the magnetic north pole. Converting "true" headings to "magnetic" headings is discussed later in this chapter.

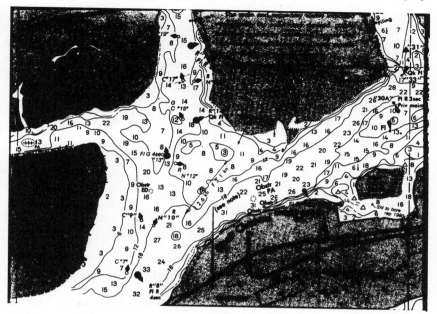

FIG. 64. Navigation chart: This section of chart contains illustrations of many of the chart symbols described. Note that there are three bottom contour lines, variously labeled as 6, 12, or 18 feet deep.

the blue and white areas is a bottom contour line that represents a specific depth of water. That depth—frequently 6 feet—is indicated by a small number which breaks the line, as shown in Figure 64. In that case, the water would be less than 6 feet deep in the blue areas and more than 6 feet deep in the white areas. Insofar as the depth along that transition line may differ from one chart to another, it's a good idea to check that depth on each chart.

As you keep looking at the water areas, you'll begin to notice various symbols. Some of those symbols are shown in Table 20-1. Among them are symbols for underwater hazards and for the major buoys and beacons used to mark the channels that serve as the "roads" along our waterways. A complete listing of all symbols used on charts produced by the National Oceanic and Atmospheric Administration is contained in NOAA Chart No. 1.

TABLE 20-1. Navigation Chart Symbols

NOTE: *If no color is specified, lights are white. If no color is specified for a buoy, color is determined by the number. Odd-numbered buoys are green (or black); even-numbered buoys are red.*

◇ C"1"	Green (or black) can buoy #1
◇ N"2"	Red nun buoy #2
◗ Fl R 4sec "30"	Red light buoy #30, flashing red every 4 seconds
◗ Fl 5sec "31"	Green (or black) light buoy #31, flashing white every 5 seconds
◗ Fl G 4sec "7"	Green (or black) light buoy #7, flashing green every 4 seconds
◗ "5" Fl 3sec	Green (or black) light buoy #5, flashing white every 3 seconds
◈ RW	Red and white buoy with vertical stripes
◈ RG	Red and green buoy with horizontal color bands, red on top
◈ GR	Green and red buoy with horizontal color bands, green on top
◇ "1" BELL	Green (or black) bell buoy #1
◗ Fl R 4sec 12ft 3M	Flashing red light every 4 seconds, mounted on a piling or tower 12 feet above the water; range is 3 nautical miles
*	A rock awash
+	A rock below the water's surface
(+ +)	An area of submerged rocks
(⋈)	An artificial fishing reef
₀°₀ stumps	Tree stumps; may also be labeled "pilings"
(4) obstr	An obstruction 4 feet below the surface at mean low water
BR or ⌣⌣⌣	Breaking waves

U.S. NAVIGATION BUOYS AND BEACONS

In the waters along our coastal rivers, bays, and sounds, channels are marked by a series of buoys and beacons that run from the ocean inland or, in the case of the Intracoastal Waterway, from New England down the Atlantic Coast to Florida, around Florida, and along the Gulf Coast to Mexico. Many of these buoys have radar reflectors built into them. Some, but not all, have lights on them to help with nighttime piloting. Some also have bells, gongs, or whistles, presumably to help us find them in fog. Unfortunately, most of these noise devices rely on the buoys' movement in the waves to produce noise. Since the water is usually relatively calm in fog, they make the least noise when it would be most useful.

All buoys used as aids to navigation also have distinctive colors. Most channel markers are solid red or solid green. Some channel markers may have red and green horizontal stripes; others may have red and white vertical stripes.* Each has a distinct role in marking the channel.

In addition to channel markers, there are buoys for special purposes. For example, buoys used to mark underwater obstructions are white with a horizontal orange color band. Solid yellow buoys are used for such special purposes as marking a fishing area or as weather buoys.

Reading the Channel Markers

The channels in rivers and bays, as well as those leading in from the ocean, are marked principally with solid red and solid green buoys. These buoys are used to mark the edges of channels and are of several types, each distinctive in its appearance (Figure 65).

When coming in from the ocean or going up-river, red channel markers are kept to your starboard side and green ones are

---

* The United States is in the midst of making a transition in the coloring of its buoys from the old color system to that described here, for a uniform international system. As a result, there may still be some buoys that are black and some with black and white vertical stripes. Solid black buoys are being changed to solid green. Black and white stripes are being changed to red and white vertical stripes. The conversion is to be completed by the end of 1993.

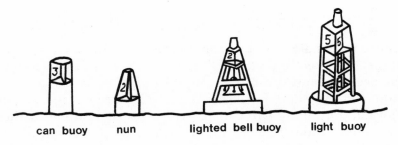

can buoy   nun   lighted bell buoy   light buoy

FIG. 65. Floating navigation aids: These buoys are used to mark the edges of channels. The can buoy would be either green or black. The nun would be red. The lighted bell buoy and the light buoy may be green, black, or red, depending upon which side of the channel they are marking.

kept to your port side. This is the origin of the old saying, "Red right returning." The "Red right returning" adage applies in the Intracoastal Waterway (also called the ICW) when you're headed from north to south along the East Coast or west toward Brownsville, Texas, along the Gulf Coast. While it's sometimes difficult to tell whether you are headed upstream, or in from the ocean by looking at the water around your boat, this is where a chart comes in handy. As long as you know what direction you're traveling, you can tell by looking at the chart which side of your boat to leave the red or green buoys on.

Red-and-green or red-and-white striped buoys provide additional information about the channels (Figure 66). For example, a buoy with red and white vertical stripes is used to mark the center of a channel. The junction of two channels or, more frequently, an obstruction in the channel, is marked by a buoy

mid–channel   junction or obstruction

FIG. 66. Floating navigation aids (cont.): The mid-channel markers (left) are red and white. Junction or obstruction markers (right) are red and green, with the color of the top band indicating the preferred side for passing the buoy.

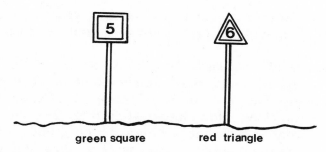

green square red triangle

FIG. 67. Fixed navigation aids—daymarks: The green square has the same meaning as a green can buoy. The red triangle has the same meaning as a red nun buoy.

with red and green horizontal stripes. If the buoy is marking a junction, the color of the stripe on top tells whether the main channel branches off to the left (red) or right (green) as you're coming up the channel. To follow the main channel, you would leave the buoy to starboard or port as indicated by the top color band. To follow the secondary channel, you would do the opposite. If the buoy is marking an obstruction, the top stripe indicates the preferred side to leave the buoy as you go past the obstruction. Assuming you're headed up-channel, you would leave the buoy to starboard if the top band is red or to port if the top band is green. If you are headed down-channel, of course, the directions would be reversed in both situations.

In addition to, or in place of, the solid red and green buoys, channels may be marked with so-called "daymarks"—red triangles or green squares mounted on pilings (usually wooden posts) sticking up from the water (Figure 67). Daymarks are often positioned in relatively shallow water and should be given a wide berth if your boat draws more than a couple of feet. Their name stems from the fact that they are unlighted markers, for the most part useful only during daylight hours.

The Intracoastal Waterway: Buoys and beacons used to mark the ICW follow the same coloring system described for other coastal waterways. In addition, however, they have a distinctive yellow mark to identify them as part of the ICW system. Buoys and beacons in channels that are exclusively a part of the ICW are marked with a yellow horizontal stripe. In places where the

ICW coincides with a regular channel, small yellow triangles or squares are painted on the buoys or beacons in lieu of the horizontal yellow stripe.

Channel Marker Numbers: To help us keep track of our position, most channel markers are numbered. Red buoys and red beacons always have even numbers—two, four, six, etc. Green markers always have odd numbers—one, three, five, etc. These numbers progress from the sea toward a port, but two deviations are important to note. First, the buoys may skip one or more numbers. So, for example, the numbering sequence of red channel markers may be "2," "4," "10," "12," "16," etc. As long as you match the number of the buoy that you are passing with the correct buoy shown on the chart, however, that idiosyncrasy shouldn't cause any difficulty. Second, there may not be buoys marking both sides of a channel. The markers may be all red, mostly red with an occasional green, and so on. But again, as long as you're following the chart, you'll know what buoys to be looking for.

Whenever a new channel branches off from the primary channel, the buoys for the new channel will be numbered starting with "1" or "2," depending on whether the first buoy is green or red. Numbering in the main channel will continue as before. Although mid-channel markers and buoys marking a junction or obstruction are not numbered, they may be identified with a letter—again, to help us find them on the chart.

Identifying Buoys on the Chart

Every buoy and daymark that you see on the water is represented by a specific symbol on the chart, usually a diamond over a dot-sized circle, as illustrated in Table 20-1. If the diamond represents a green, red, or green and red buoy, usually it is printed in the color of the buoy. If it represents a red-and-white vertically striped buoy, it usually is printed with a vertical line dividing the diamond in half.

In addition to the symbol itself, the marker is described by a combination of letters and, if applicable, numbers. For example, a red buoy with the number "2" is described on the chart as R"2." A green buoy normally is described only by its number, e.g., "3." A red and green buoy is described as RG or GR, with the first letter indicating the color of the top stripe. A mid-channel buoy is described as RW or, sometimes, RWVS (red and white vertical stripes).

As shown in Table 20-1, buoys with bells, whistles, or gongs have "Bell," "Whistle," or "Gong" printed alongside the symbol. Buoys with lights are shown with a purple dot (red on some charts) about the size of a small pencil eraser. In addition, a combination of letters and numbers describes the color of the light and how it flashes. Lighted navigation aids are covered in more detail in Chapter 21.

The descriptions of buoys on the charts let you identify each buoy as you pass it. If you're having trouble matching what you see on the water to what's shown on the chart, you should stop your boat to figure out the reason. When I've found myself in that situation, it's been for one of two reasons: Either the buoys or beacons have been renumbered and my charts have not been updated, or I've just changed from one chart to another and failed to notice that the new chart has a larger or smaller scale than the one I had been using. Charts covering large areas are printed on a different scale than are harbor charts. As a result, you may have to make a mental adjustment when changing from one chart to another, particularly in terms of relating the distances shown on the chart to what you see around you.

Piloting Outside of Channels

So far, of course, we've focused on following channels. Much of your boating won't be in channels, however. Rather, you'll be cruising across rivers, lakes, or bays without worrying about where the channels are—except as you have to watch for other traffic. It's just as important, though, to keep track of your position when you're outside a channel as it is when you're in one. That's the only way you can be sure to steer clear of underwater hazards; it's also the only way you can be sure to steer a safe course in the kind of situation described at the beginning of this chapter, when visibility is severely restricted by heavy rain, fog, or darkness.

Piloting across open water requires taking three considerations into account: the direction you're heading in (your course), how fast you're moving (your boat speed), and the effect of wind or current. By drawing a line on your chart before getting underway that takes all of these factors into consideration, and updating that line at regular intervals as you proceed on your course, you'll keep an accurate track of where you think you are. The system is called "dead reckoning." And it works amazingly well.

Plotting Your Course Line: If there's no wind or current to take into consideration, maintaining your DR (dead reckoning) position is quite simple. First, draw a line from where you are to where you want to go and use your course plotter to measure the "true" compass course represented by that line. Next, you'll

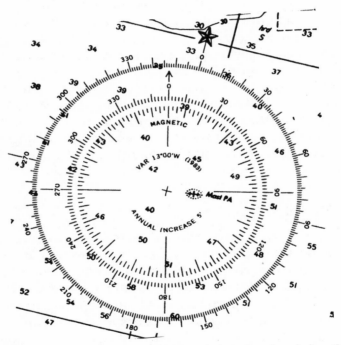

FIG. 68. Compass rose showing local variation: Local variation (Var 13°00′W) is given in the center of the compass rose. Also provided are the year for which that variation applies (1983) and the annual change in "minutes of arc" (Annual increase 5′). This information enables you to bring the variation up to date. For example, in 1990, the local variation in this example would be 13°35′W.

EXAMPLE 20-1.   Converting True Course to Magnetic Course

True course (taken from chart)	= 047°
Variation (taken from compass rose)*	= 13°W
Magnetic course	= 060°

* NOTE: When converting from "true" course to "magnetic" course, add (west) variation; subtract (east) variation.

have to correct the "true" course for variation in the Earth's magnetic field in the area shown on the chart. The local "variation" is noted inside the compass rose on the chart (Figure 68) and is added to or subtracted from the "true" course heading, as explained in Example 20-1. Assuming you do not need to correct for compass deviation, the corrected "magnetic" heading is the course that you would steer, and you should label the course line with that heading, writing it just above the line you've drawn on the chart. While some authorities recommend using the "true" heading to label the course line, we have found it generally less confusing to use the "magnetic" course and label it as such (Figure 69).

If there is a wind or current to take into consideration, you'll need to estimate its effect so that it doesn't push you off into a hazardous area. For example, if the current is moving south at 2 knots, and your course is in a westerly direction, you'll need to compensate for the current by steering a few degrees to the north of your intended course, as illustrated earlier in Chapter 13, Figure 42. In that way, the current will be pushing you a bit to the south while you steer a bit to the north, and the compromise between the current and your steering will be right down the line that you wanted to travel.

FIG. 69.   Labeling your course: In labeling your course line, the "magnetic" heading is penciled above the line.

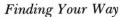

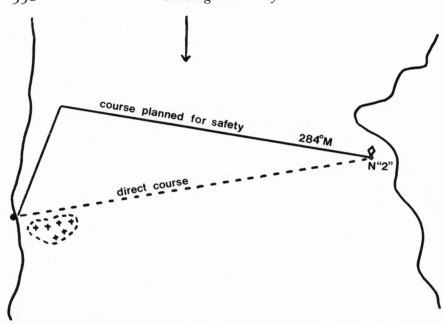

FIG. 70. Introducing a known "error": By plotting your course well to one side of the direct heading so that you have a known "error" in your steering, you ensure not only that you will be clear of any hazards shown on the chart, but also that you'll know which way to turn when you reach the other shore.

If you're unsure of the effect of the wind or current, consult your chart to see whether it makes any difference from a safety perspective whether you err to one side or the other of your desired course line. Then choose which side to err on and adjust your course several degrees in that direction. By doing this, you are creating you own "known" error so that, if you miss your destination, you'll miss it in a specific direction. In that way, you'll not only steer well clear of any underwater hazards, but you'll also know which way to turn to get where you want to go when you reach the other shore, even though you may not know exactly where you are (Figure 70).

Locating Hazards and Landmarks: Once you've drawn (in pencil) your intended course line on the chart, you should look along that line—and for some distance on both sides of the line—

to see whether there are any hazards that you'll need to avoid. If so, you should mark them clearly and decide tentatively what you're going to do to be sure you give them plenty of room. As noted earlier, some of the symbols used in charts to mark underwater hazards are illustrated in Table 20-1.

In addition to looking for hazards on the chart, you'll want to look for landmarks or buoys along your course that you can use to check your position. If, for example, there is a buoy near your course line, you can figure out ahead of time when you should be able to see it by measuring how far along your course it is and applying the same distance/speed/time formula described below for updating your position. Similarly, if there are landmarks you could use to confirm your position, you'll want to know approximately when you should begin looking for them.

Estimating Your Time of Arrival: It's always worth taking a few minutes to estimate how long you plan to be out on your boat—or, if you're going from one place to another, how long you think the trip will take. In that way, you can let other people know when to expect you. You can also use those calculations to make sure you have enough fuel to reach your destination.

The simplest way to calculate an "ETA" (estimated time of arrival) is to measure on the chart how far you'll be going and then divide that distance by your estimated boat speed. The answer will be the number of hours the trip will take if there are no delays. You'll also have to make allowances for delays, however—for areas that may have speed limits, for time you'll have to spend waiting for a bridge to go up, for the time that you plan to spend fishing, or for the time needed to refuel if the day's run will tax your fuel capacity. But, once you've factored in all of those delays, you should have a pretty good estimate of the total time that you'll be gone.

If your course has several distinct parts, or "legs," it's also a good idea to estimate how much time will be needed for each leg. These calculations will let you compare your actual progress to the estimates made before you started. If you find that the trip is taking significantly longer than expected, you may need to make an extra stop to get more fuel or use your VHF

EXAMPLE 20-2.   Calculating Distance Traveled

Speed = 20 knots
Time = 15 minutes (¼ hour)
Distance = Speed × Time (in hours)
= 20 knots × ¼ hour
= 20/4
Distance = 5 nautical miles

---

radio to call ahead and let people know that you're running a bit late, so they won't worry unnecessarily.

Plotting Your Position: Once you get started, you can measure your progress by plotting how many miles you've traveled every fifteen minutes, half hour, or hour using the formula "Distance equals Speed times Time" ($D = S \times T$). So, for example, if you've been traveling at 20 knots for fifteen minutes, the distance traveled is equal to one-quarter hour times 20, or 5 nautical miles (Example 20-2). (For your information, a nautical mile equals about 6,080 feet, or about 1.15 statute miles.)

Next, using the scale provided on the chart, measure five nautical miles along your course line from your starting point, and put a dot with a half-circle around it at the five-mile point (Figure 71). That dot with the half-circle marks your estimated position. You should then write the time next to the position, using the twenty-four-hour clock. You should also write your boat speed under the course line just below where you noted the course earlier. The purpose of recording your course, time, and speed on the chart is twofold: It enables you to reconstruct your progress later in the day if that should become necessary for any reason; it also lets you figure out the actual effects of the wind and current as you mark your progress against buoys and various landmarks. Often, you can then use that information to estimate the wind and current effects more accurately as you continue on your way.

How often you update your position depends in part upon how fast you're going. With our boat moving at only 5 or 6 knots, we update our position once an hour as long as we keep moving the same direction at the same speed. With a boat moving at 20 or 30 knots, you should probably update your position

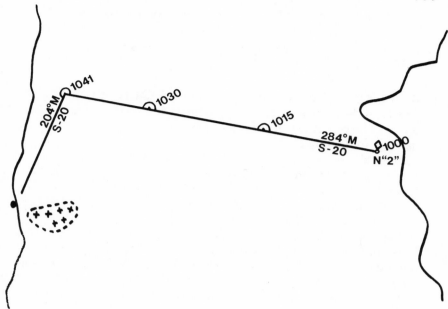

Fig. 71.   Plotting your progress on the chart: Progress along your course line should be updated regularly as shown. Your position and the time also should be plotted whenever your course or speed are changed.

every five or ten minutes. At 30 knots, you'll go two-and-a-half miles in five minutes.

Updating Your Position: In updating your position, you go through the same procedure described above to calculate how far you've traveled in this new time period. When you've calculated the new distance traveled, you plot that by measuring from your last estimated position, as shown in Figure 71.

If you change your cruising speed or your course, you'll need to note the time, figure out your position at the time you made the change, and mark that position on the chart. All of your new measurements will be made from that new position. If you've changed course, you'll also need to draw a new course line from that position, labeling it with the course above the line and the boat speed below, again as illustrated in Figure 71. All this while, of course, you need to be looking at the chart ahead of your

position for any hazards—including just plain shallow water—
that you need to take into consideration. Failure to do this, even
under what are apparently the simplest of situations, can be
troublesome:

> BOAT HITS ROCKS, RUNS ONTO BEACH AT BETTER-
> TON—A 44-foot fiberglass trawler hit submerged rubble off Bet-
> terton [Maryland] beach June 1, causing an unestimated amount of
> damage to the boat.
>
> *Katie Mer,* a 44-foot pleasure boat owned by Barry Weckesser of
> Lutherville, Maryland, struck rubble remnants of the old Ericsson
> Pier in Betterton at 12:45 P.M. According to Guy Berry, an officer
> at the Still Pond Coast Guard Station, there were five passengers
> aboard. All were unharmed.
>
> Apparently the captain was unaware of the concrete, stones, and
> brick that are out of sight below the surface at high tide. After strik-
> ing the debris several hundred yards offshore, the captain then ran
> the boat aground to prevent the boat from sinking.
>
> A boatbuilder at the Georgetown Yacht Basin said the hull had a
> 3-foot puncture.[2]

The "rubble" struck by the trawler is labeled as an "obstruction" on NOAA charts of the area. The hole in the trawler's
bow was less than 18 inches below the waterline, suggesting that
almost any motorboat passing over the rubble would have been
damaged, even if damage was only to the lower unit of the outboard engine.

STATE NAVIGATION BUOYS

There are thousands of rivers and lakes in nearly every state
that do not come under the jurisdiction of the U.S. Coast Guard
buoyage system. These waters also may have buoys and beacons
to help ensure boater safety; the state buoys, which are different than those regulated by the Coast Guard, have been stan-
dardized under the "Uniform State Waterway Marking System"
(Figure 72).

2. *The Mariner,* Cecil County, Maryland, June 1988.

Uniform State Waterway Marking System

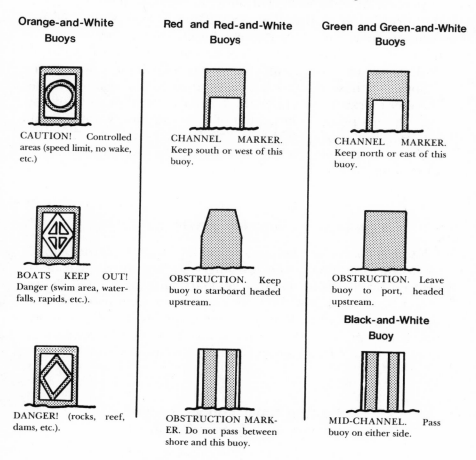

Orange-and-White Buoys

CAUTION! Controlled areas (speed limit, no wake, etc.)

BOATS KEEP OUT! Danger (swim area, waterfalls, rapids, etc.).

DANGER! (rocks, reef, dams, etc.).

Red and Red-and-White Buoys

CHANNEL MARKER. Keep south or west of this buoy.

OBSTRUCTION. Keep buoy to starboard headed upstream.

OBSTRUCTION MARKER. Do not pass between shore and this buoy.

Green and Green-and-White Buoys

CHANNEL MARKER. Keep north or east of this buoy.

OBSTRUCTION. Leave buoy to port, headed upstream.

Black-and-White Buoy

MID-CHANNEL. Pass buoy on either side.

FIG. 72. State navigation aids: While most waterways are regulated by the U.S. Coast Guard, many states maintain local waterways and enforce local restrictions on speed, etc. The buoys illustrated here are those used by states.

Unfortunately, as noted earlier, there are few charts available for these state-controlled waters. What are available are more akin to simple maps showing the locations of various boat ramps or commercial facilities, depending upon who is providing the map.

Still, the buoys in these state-controlled waters serve the same important function as that of buoys in the coastal waters under the jurisdiction of the U.S. Coast Guard. They help you get from one place to another safely. Often, they guide you into a harbor or to a boat ramp. They also are used to warn you of underwater hazards, a waterfall or dam ahead, or a swim area.

Some of these buoys are also used in coastal waters whose channel markers are under the federal system. State buoys in these waters provide some kind of local cautionary notice—for example, notice of speed limits, "No Wake" zones, "No Anchoring" zones, "Water-ski Only" areas, etc. The warning is actually written on the buoy.

LEARNING MORE ABOUT PILOTING

Piloting skills are best learned through practice with the help of an instructor to guide your learning. The boating safety courses offered by the Coast Guard Auxiliary and the United States Power Squadrons provide classroom instruction in piloting skills, including work with charts. Various hands-on boating courses offered by private sailing schools and boat-charter companies often provide instruction in basic piloting as well.

Testing What You've Learned
(Answers can be found in Appendix C)

1. TRUE OR FALSE: As long as your compass is mounted permanently on your boat, you do not need to be concerned about compass deviation.

2. Why is the ability to determine your boat's speed an important part of basic piloting?

3. TRUE OR FALSE: The only important details for boaters on navigation charts are found in the blue and white areas of the chart.

4. TRUE OR FALSE: Blue areas on a navigation chart represent shallow water.

5. You are headed upstream and see a green daymark ahead. On which side of your boat should you keep it? Is it safe to pass close to it?

6. You see a buoy with red and green horizontal stripes. What two things might it be marking? How can you know for sure which of the two it means?

7. On your chart you see a small circle with a red diamond over it and the label R"12". What does this symbol represent?

8. Why is it useful to plot your intended course ahead of time on your chart?

9. You left the harbor buoy an hour and forty-five minutes ago and have been traveling at 16 knots. How far have you come since taking your departure?

10. You are keeping track of your course on a chart. If you change boat speed, why is it necessary to note the time and plot your position as of the time you made that change?

21

Basic Piloting— Nighttime

As twilight fades into darkness, the visible expanse of water around your boat shrinks rapidly. By the time dark is fully upon you, your realm consists mostly of blackness broken only by dim reflections of your own boat lights and a scattering of mainly white, red, and green lights around the now-invisible horizon. At this point, you are encountering one of the largest single differences between boating and driving an automobile: When it is dark on the water, it's dark. You can't see where you are; you can't see where you're going; and you can't see where you've been. All you can see are the lights—shore lights, boat lights, and navigation lights.

The temptation is to turn on a spotlight and use it just as you use the headlights on your car to light up the road. For several reasons, however, headlights won't work out on the water.

First, you're not on a highway where other people will come from predictable directions—e.g., along the same road or from another clearly marked road. On the water, boats can come literally from any direction. The closest comparison to driving that I can think of is going down a road at night in an area where deer are common. Every year, thousands of drivers hit deer at night because "they jump out at you from nowhere." Unfortunately, the same kind of accident happens on the water because someone doesn't see the other boat.

Second, no one else is operating his boat using a spotlight for headlights. All you can rely on to see the other boat is its red, green, or white running lights. As you'll discover, those are not overwhelmingly bright lights, and many times you have to be looking for them to see them before they are very close.

Third, when your spotlight is on and you're looking at that nicely lighted water in front of your boat, your night vision (your ability to see in the dark) is ruined. If you look off to the side where the spotlight is not shining on the water, for example, you may not see another boat's running lights or the flashing red or green light of a distant buoy. In other words, your spotlight may be keeping you from seeing the "deer" running along the side of the "road"—until just before you hit it.

Fourth, your spotlight doesn't reveal underwater hazards; you still must read your chart and maintain careful track of your position on the chart at all times to avoid those hazards. Moreover, if you're relying on a spotlight to illuminate the way while you cruise over the water at your normal running speed, you'll likely have a false sense of security. Boat spotlights aren't much help in seeing floating debris or lobster-pot markers when you're running fast at night; such floating hazards are hidden by the natural camouflage of shadows and reflections created by any light shining on constantly moving waves.

And finally, your spotlight temporarily blinds other boaters if it shines on them and may result in their making a foolish move—just as shining your bright headlights in the eyes of an oncoming driver on the highway could result in an accident.

The point is this: We're all handicapped when it comes to being out in our boats at night, because we can't see very well in the dark. As a result, unless you're well away from shore on a large body of water with no underwater hazards within miles of your course, nighttime is slow-down time on your boat. Your ability to judge distances is impaired. Your ability to see is severely reduced. And you will often need extra time to figure out what various lights are telling you. Otherwise, you're an accident waiting to happen:

NEWLYWED KILLED IN BOAT ACCIDENT—A pair of Florida newlyweds crashed into an abandoned concrete pier Easter Sunday night near Miami, killing the wife instantly and seriously injuring her husband.

Sherry Newton Valdes, 20, of Miramar, died in the accident. Jose Valdes, 24, the boat's driver, was hospitalized with chest and face injuries.

The couple, married just a month, was returning from an outing on the Oleta River in North Miami when their boat hit a 60-foot-long concrete pier about 8:30 P.M., said Captain Mike Lamphear of the Florida Marine Patrol.

Lamphear said paperwork found in the glove box indicated the Valdeses had bought the 20-foot, jet-drive ski boat just the day before. "The odds are pretty good that was the first time they had it in the water," Lamphear said.

"[Valdes] was going at a high speed," Lamphear said. "We have no estimate yet, but fast enough that he didn't even get close to getting around the pier. He simply didn't see it.

"It was one of those tragedies that was preventable. It didn't have to happen. You go too fast, you don't have a good lookout, you overdrive your vision at night. . . ."[1]

Danger can exist even in a well-marked channel if you're traveling too fast and not paying close attention to all of the lights around you. The accident reported here occurred at the edge of the main shipping channel in the Delaware River a few miles south of Philadelphia:

SEARCH CALLED OFF FOR MAN MISSING IN CRASH OF BOAT—The search was indefinitely suspended Sunday for a man missing after a motorboat carrying him and three other Pennsylvania men crashed into a buoy off Little Tinicum Island in the Delaware River, the U.S. Coast Guard said.

A tugboat picked up three of the boaters from beside the damaged 16-foot craft shortly before 11:00 P.M. Saturday, but could not find a man who had been on the bow when the crash occurred about 10:00 P.M., the Coast Guard said.

The buoy off the southeastern tip of the island has green flashing lights and is 8 feet in diameter and 26 feet tall, authorities said.[2]

The keys to safe boating at night are slow speed, maintaining good night vision, keeping an extra-alert watch *including the use*

1. *Soundings*, July 1987.
2. *News-Journal*, Wilmington, Delaware, June 22, 1987.

of your ears, correctly interpreting the lights that you see, maintaining a good dead-reckoning position on your chart, and, whenever possible, following a marked channel.

BOAT SPEED AT NIGHT

Understandably, it can be frustrating to run a high-powered speedboat at 5 or 10 miles per hour, but many times that's exactly what's needed when running your boat at night. In fact, we usually run at about one-half our normal 6-knot cruising speed under power when entering a harbor or traveling even a familiar small river at night when there are unlighted buoys along the way. The reason is simple: Because of the darkness, we can't see well enough to go faster and feel safe at the same time. If we know we should be approaching an unlighted channel marker and can't yet see it, we'll slow even further until we have the marker in sight.

In determining a safe speed at night, you need to answer the following questions: "How far ahead of the boat can I see? How long will it take me to figure out what it is that I'm looking at in the dark? How far will the boat travel at the speed I'm going while I figure out what's happening? And, will I have enough time at this speed to avoid an accident if I come upon something unexpectedly?" If you answer these questions honestly, you'll probably reach the conclusion that it's seldom safe to run at more than 10 or 15 knots and often not safe to run even that fast.

Why is this emphasized so much? Because running at a reasonable speed lies at the core of safe nighttime boating. To understand the importance of slowing down at night, think about all the warnings you receive through your eyes in daylight that you can't get at night. You can see a boat that's anchored along the side of the channel in the daytime when you're still a half-mile away. At night, you may not see the same boat until it's only 50 or 100 feet away. You can also see unlighted buoys during the day when they're a half-mile or so away. At night, you may not see an unlighted buoy until it's 40 or 50 feet away. If that buoy is dead in front of you when you see it, you'll hit it if you're moving at more than a very few miles an hour.

In daylight, you can look at a boat a half-mile away and know right away whether it is coming toward you. Moreover, it doesn't take more than a couple of minutes to have an idea of how fast the two boats are approaching each other. You can also tell at a glance whether it's a motorboat or sailboat, a tug pulling a barge, a large freighter, or whatever. As a result, you know right away how much room you need to give it. At night, depending upon how good you are at reading other boats' running lights, it may take you several minutes to figure out what kind of boat it is and what you should do about it.

All of this means that you have a different decision-making environment at night than in daytime. In some situations, it takes longer to figure out what you're seeing. In others, you may not be able to see a danger until you're almost on top of it. In any of these circumstances, the key to safety is boat speed— going slowly enough to give you the time needed to interpret what you see and to steer away from it if necessary.

NIGHT VISION

As darkness falls, your eyes become adjusted to the lower level of light. By daylight standards, you can't see much. But it's sometimes surprising how much you can see with just the small amount of light provided by the moon and stars or by the loom of your own boat's running lights. Even on dark, cloudy nights, for example, I can still "see" my way forward on our white deck to take down our white sails. Moreover, with the help of a good pair of binoculars we can often see boats in an anchorage or docks sticking out from shore much faster than with the unaided eye.

This "night vision," of course, isn't usually an all-or-nothing phenomenon. Your ability to see in the dark is the work of specialized sensors in your eyes that are sensitive to faint light, but not to red light. The way that your eyes work has some practical implications for nighttime boating. Any bright, white light—for example, the flashlight used to look at your charts, the cabin lights in your boat, the flashlight used as a running light in the rowing dinghy, or a spotlight—can temporarily overwhelm your eyes' sensitivity to faint light and, therefore, greatly reduce your night vision. You can test this yourself by going outside at night away from any street, window, or porch lights, taking a flashlight with you. After about ten minutes away from any lights, you should be able to see to some extent, possibly even quite well. At this point, turn the flashlight on, shine it in your face (at your chin) for a few seconds, turn the flashlight off again, and look around you. The odds are very good that you won't be able to see anything at all for the first minute or so. Then—gradually—your night vision will return until, after eight or ten minutes, you can see as well as before.

The same thing happens on your boat. This does not mean, however, that you must get by on your boat without using any lights to help you see. As mentioned above, the same sensors that are overwhelmed by bright, white lights don't see red. As a result, you can use red lights to help you do many chores. On our boat, for example, the cabin lights can be switched to either red or white. When at anchor or at a dock, we use the white interior lights. When underway at night, we use the red lights. In this way, we can move in and out of the cabin without affecting our night vision. In the same way, we use a flashlight with a red filter to read our chart out in the cockpit—again, without affecting our night vision. That's also why the light on any marine compass is red.

Sometimes, of course, you must use a bright, white light on your boat. You may need the additional light to read the numbers on a buoy, for example, or as a running light in your rowing dinghy or small sailboat. Even in these situations, however, you should think about your night vision. For example, you may have one of your crew use the light to read the number on the buoy while you keep your face turned away. In any case, the goal is to minimize the use of all white lights on your boat.

The Coast Guard has reported another interesting cause of night-vision problems. The culprit in this situation is either the glare or the direct light from the all-'round white stern lights on many motorboats. In effect, these stern lights blind the person steering the boat anytime he turns to check the area behind the boat. The problem occurs either because the light is not high enough to be out of the skipper's field of vision or because it's not shielded to keep the glare away from the boat. The solution to the problem is to mount the light on a taller staff and to build a base under the light that prevents glare from shining down on the boat.

Fortunately, if you're suddenly faced with a bright, white light and your night vision is destroyed, it takes only a matter of minutes for it to recover. Of course, the less intense the light and the shorter the time that it's on, the less impact it will have on your night vision and the faster your eyes will recover.

INTERPRETING LIGHTS

For the most part, interpreting lights on the water at night is a reasonably straightforward job. Under some circumstances, however, it can be confusing—particularly if you don't know where you are, or don't have a chart to help you identify specific lights. One cause of difficulty is the interference from shore lights. Almost any experienced boater can tell stories of mistaking automobile brake lights or turn signals, flashing red traffic lights, or various flashing lights on advertising signs for the lights on channel buoys leading into a harbor. If the shore lights don't cause confusion, they're so bright that they make it difficult to pick out the buoy lights amidst all the glare. One reason for this difficulty is that most of us try to pick up navigation marker lights using just our eyes. Good binoculars often make the job much easier by giving you a sharper view of the lights.

Of course, shore lights aren't the only complicating factor. You also need to be alert for and interpret the running lights on other boats at the same time that you're looking for the lights on channel markers. Insofar as running lights for boats were reviewed thoroughly in Chapter 16, however, we will limit our discussion here to lights used on buoys and other aids to navigation.

Navigation-Buoy Lights

In general, the solid red and solid green markers used to identify the edges of the channel carry either red or green lights.

I say "in general" because the United States is still in the process of changing its channel markers to a uniform international system, as footnoted in the previous chapter. Until that changeover is completed (by the end of 1993), individual red or green channel markers may still be equipped with white lights. Regardless of color, however, most lights on these channel markers flash "on" for about one long second at some regular interval—for example, every four seconds, or every five seconds. The color of the light and the interval at which it flashes are clearly marked on your chart—for example, "Fl G 5sec" for a green light that flashes every five seconds.

Occasionally, you'll see a solid red or solid green channel marker with a "quick-flashing" light. By definition, "quick-flashing" means the light will flash at least sixty times per minute—that is, at least once per second. Quick-flashing lights are used to mark the edges of the channel when extra caution is needed. For example, the channel may make a sharp turn at that point, or there may be some obstruction at the edge of the channel that you must be sure to avoid. Quick-flashing lights may be red, green, or (until 1993) white.

A problem people sometimes run into when trying to identify the light on a specific channel marker involves timing the interval of the flashing light. The interval listed on your chart is the number of seconds from the beginning of one flash to the beginning of the next flash, and that's how you need to time it—from the beginning of one flash to the beginning of another. People also have a tendency to think they can count the seconds in their heads by counting "one thousand one, one thousand two," etc. Frankly, that's a good way to get into trouble. If you're looking for a red light that flashes every four seconds ("Fl R 4sec"), for example, you could easily pace your counting so that you mistake a five-second interval for the four seconds.

That kind of mistake can have you taking an unintended shortcut across a bend in the channel, and could be dangerous. The best way to prevent such mistakes is to use a stopwatch, starting the stopwatch when the light comes on the first time and stopping it when the light comes on the second time. You should then double- and triple-check yourself by timing the same light through several more cycles, using the stopwatch.

The two other major channel markers—buoys used to mark

junctions or obstructions, and mid-channel markers—also carry specific identifying lights. The red-and-green horizontally striped buoys used to mark either the junction of two channels or an obstruction carry what are called "interrupted quick-flashing" lights—marked "I Qk Fl" on your chart. Under the system being phased out, these lights have been white; under the new system, the light is the same color as the top color stripe on the buoy, either red or green. In any case, the light will flash six times in five seconds, be dark for five seconds, and then repeat the cycle. The full cycle takes ten seconds and, of course, is repeated six times every minute. If you are going upstream, an interrupted quick-flashing red light should be left to starboard as you follow the main channel; an interrupted quick-flashing green light should be left to port. Going downstream, of course, the lights would be left on the opposite sides.

Mid-channel markers—red-and-white vertically striped buoys—carry a so-called "Morse A" light. This light is always white and is labeled "Mo A" on the chart. It repeats the letter "A" in Morse code by showing one short flash followed by one long flash and then a pause. The cycle is repeated every eight seconds.

Land-Based or "Fixed" Navigation Lights

There are many lighthouses, light towers, and other land-based lighted aids to navigation that are fixed in position. These "fixed" aids to navigation are in contrast to lighted buoys, which float on the surface of the water and are anchored in position. Although detailed discussion of these lights is beyond the scope of this book, you should be aware of them and know how to recognize them on your chart. Moreover, if your boating will be in an area where land-based or fixed lights are an important part of the local aids to navigation, you should become well acquainted with them. The characteristics of land-based lights are often different than those of lights found on buoys.

One group of these "fixed" navigation aids that have the same light characteristics as those found on channel buoys, however, are the lighted markers used in parts of the Intracoastal Waterway. On the chart, they and all other "fixed" lights—lighthouses, light towers, etc.—are indicated though by a small dot and a purple (or red) flare that resembles a fat exclamation point. The dot marks the light's position precisely. The positions of lighted buoys, on the other hand, are shown on the chart by a large, purple (or red) dot about the size of a small pencil eraser, indicating the approximate position. Thus, just by looking at the shape of the purple (or red) mark in the blue or white water area of the chart, you can determine whether the light belongs to a buoy or is located on some fixed structure planted in the water's bottom. Similarly, you can locate land-based navigation lights simply by looking for large, purple (or red) exclamation points in the land area near the water's edge.

Red Sectors: Sometimes fixed navigation lights show either red or white, depending upon your angle of approach. In effect, the light is designed to warn boaters of a hazardous area. As long as the light appears white, you are on a safe course; if the light becomes red, you are headed toward some kind of hazard.

The first time Susan and I encountered one of these lights was in Delaware Bay. I did not recognize the light for its type and was confused because it kept changing from white to red to white as we tacked back and forth down the channel. Finally, I looked closely at the chart and found what I had missed earlier—the boundary of a red (danger) sector for that light, indicating a shoal area that could have been dangerous to us had we kept ignoring the red-sector warning (Figure 73).

That experience taught us an important lesson: It's not enough to look on the chart for the abbreviations that describe the characteristics of the next light you'll be looking for. You must also look at the bigger picture. That is, you must also look at chart details both in the area of the light and in the area between here (your present position) and there (the next light).

MAINTAINING YOUR DEAD-RECKONING POSITION

Because of fatigue and the difficulty of working in dim lighting conditions, it's easy to put off plotting your course and updating your position when out on your boat at night. If maintain-

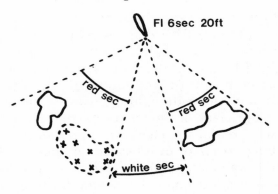

FIG. 73.   Red-sector navigation lights: Some lights have red and white
sectors, but you may not know that unless you look at the chart. The
red sector indicates danger. The white sector is safe for navigation. If
the light seems to change from red to white and back, you are strad-
dling the line between the two zones and need to get safely into the
white.

ing your charted DR position is important in daylight hours,
however, it's doubly important at night.

Why? Consider the following: In daylight, you have a wide
range of visual cues to help you keep track of where you are—
the shoreline, buoys, bridges, prominent landmarks, etc. At night,
you lose most of those reference points. As a result, it's not only
more difficult to judge how far you've come, it's also more difficult to know where you are. The only good means you have
to overcome that added difficulty is in using your piloting skills:
plotting your course carefully on the chart, steering by your
compass, monitoring your boat speed, and updating your dead-
reckoning position frequently—even when you're following a
well-marked channel. Rain and fog can sneak up on you easily
at night (it's much harder to see them coming!) and make seeing
those lighted channel markers more difficult. Moreover, lights
marking major shipping channels are sometimes so far apart
that you can't see the next light in front of you until just before
the light behind you disappears. In such situations, plotting the
course between lights and steering by your compass may be the
only way you have to stay in the channel.

FOLLOWING MARKED CHANNELS

The suggestion that you follow a marked channel at night just makes good common sense. You can be set off course even in daylight by the effects of the wind or current. At least in daylight, however, you have the benefit of being able to see the water and landmarks around you to get clues that you're being set off course. If you're set off course at night, you may not know it until you run aground. Moreover, even in local waters that you travel frequently, the difficulty in judging distances at night can get you in trouble; you'll frequently find that you're not exactly where you think you are relative to the shoreline. By following the channel—even if it's longer—you're less likely to have problems like these because you have a checkpoint at every channel marker to be sure you're on track.

In familiar waters, you can make following the channel at night relatively easy by plotting course lines and measuring the distance between buoys well ahead of time. It's a good rainy-day activity. Then, when you do take your boat out, you can take bearings with your compass on each buoy as you go out the channel and do the same thing on your way back. Of course, you'll need to note the bearings on the chart with the letter "C" after each compass reading to remind yourself that it is a bearing measured with your compass, not a magnetic heading taken from the chart. In that way, you're all set to follow that channel at night, even if some of the buoys aren't lighted.

By following your compass course and figuring out how long it should take you to go from one buoy to the next at your reduced speed, you'll know when you should be coming up on each buoy. If a buoy's not lighted, you can drop to an even slower speed for the last minute or two until you spot it, and then set your course for the next buoy and resume your nighttime cruising speed. As mentioned earlier, a good pair of binoculars can make spotting an unlighted buoy much easier, particularly on a clear night when stars and, possibly, the moon are lighting the sky.

In less-familiar waters, you'll need to plot out the magnetic course and measure the distance to each buoy at least one light ahead of where you are. You need to know the course so that you know where to steer. You need to know the distance so that you can figure out how long it should take you to get to the next buoy. As you pass each buoy, you can use your binoculars (aided, if necessary, by the light from a flashlight) to read the number of the buoy to confirm that, indeed, you are where you think you are.

A word of caution: It is sometimes tempting in a well-lighted channel—particularly late at night—to get a bit lax about the piloting work. When that happens, you're likely to stop plotting your course line, determining your compass heading, and keeping track of your speed, time, and distance. You're also likely to stop looking as closely at the chart for possible obstructions—obstructions that may not be marked by a lighted buoy. The only advice I can offer if you begin to feel that way is, don't. Do not get lax about your piloting, especially at night.

FOUR RESCUED AS SAILBOAT SINKS IN RIVER—Rescue crews early today rescued four people from a 35-foot sailboat that sank just north of Bay View Beach in the Delaware River six miles south of Delaware City.

The 35-foot sloop . . . struck a submerged jetty about 1:30 A.M.

"We didn't know at first what we ran into," said Sherman Rigby, the owner and skipper. "We started the engine and tried to back off. The engine only lasted a few seconds because water got up to the air intake."

The four Massachusetts residents were on a sailing vacation. None of the crew was injured.

"Thank goodness the radio worked," said Rigby. Rigby said they were unfamiliar with the river, but all were experienced sailors.[3]

The channel of the Delaware River is well lighted. The submerged jetty struck by the sailboat is clearly shown on charts of the river. While one cannot determine from the news account why the accident occurred, the report vividly demonstrates the importance of careful attention to your piloting, even when following a well-lighted channel.

3. *News-Journal,* Wilmington, Delaware, June 12, 1986.

Testing What You've Learned
(Answers can be found in Appendix C)

1. Why is it necessary to travel at a reduced speed on the water at night?

2. What do you think would be a maximum safe speed at night in your boat?

3. What are four things you can do to protect your night vision when out on your boat after dark?

4. TRUE or FALSE: You can time a flashing light with good-enough accuracy by counting "one thousand one, one thousand two," and so on.

5. If you see the abbreviation "Qk Fl R" on your chart, what does it stand for? What kind of channel marker carries that light, and what does it mean to you?

6. What kind of channel marker has a "Morse A" light on it? What does that light look like?

7. If a light is represented on a chart by a large purple or red dot, is it a lighted buoy or a fixed light?

8. What does the red sector of a fixed light indicate?

9. TRUE or FALSE: If you are traveling in a well-lighted channel, it's not as necessary to keep track of your position and course line on the chart as it would be if the channel were not so well lighted.

VII

Returning to Port

I'm always a little bit anxious when coming up to a strange dock or into almost any anchorage. The reason is simple: For me, at least, docking is more difficult than undocking. The same is true for getting into a slip, anchoring, picking up a mooring, or coming in to a beach or boat ramp. There's more potential for something to go wrong. For example, when you're getting ready to leave a dock, you can cancel the trip if you don't like the weather. When coming in to a dock, however, you have to take whatever the weatherman hands you. Moreover, if you're away from home waters, you never know fully what you'll find, even when the weather is nice. So, even though I know that most of the time everything will go just as planned, I also know that something can go wrong.

I know there's potential for trouble because of a series of maxims that, according to one encyclopedia, originated in 1949 with an aircraft engineer named Murphy. You've heard of Murphy's Laws. For example, "If anything can go wrong, it will." Or, "It always takes longer than you think it will."

While the encyclopedia didn't indicate whether Murphy was a sailor, he might have been, because his "Laws" certainly have their nautical counterparts. For example:
• *"The water is always shallower than you think."* (That's why boats run aground.)
• *"The shore is always farther away than it looks."* (That's why people

drown while trying to swim ashore after their boat swamps or tips over, when they should stay with the boat.)

- *"If it is meteorologically possible for the weather to change for the worse, it will."* (That's why people get caught out in their boats in bad weather.)

And, finally:

- *"When you are coming in to a dock, the odds of something going wrong are directly proportional to the number of spectators."* (Translated: The larger your audience, the greater the likelihood of a foul-up.)

A safe boater remembers these laws. They are fixed, immutable. All of us are subject to them. And, we escape their effects only by a combination of luck and planning. Or perhaps it's planning and luck, because so often it seems to a great extent that we make our own "luck" by the planning and attention to detail we put into our lives.

Murphy notwithstanding, the key to bringing your boat to a dock, into a slip, to a mooring or boat ramp, or to anchor—safely and without frazzled nerves—is planning and preparation. Returning to port involves: (1) taking your boat slowly past your destination to figure out where and how you're going to make your landing; (2) sizing up ahead of time the effect wind and / or current will have on your boat as you come in and while you're tying up or anchoring, etc.; (3) reviewing your plans with your crew so that each person knows what he or she is to do; (4) getting your fenders out and ready ahead of time; (5) getting all of your lines or your anchor out and ready ahead of time; and (6) reviewing the procedures a final time with the crew. Then, with everyone and everything in position, you take your boat in. That's what this section is all about—returning to port.

22

Docking Under Power

Bringing your boat up to a dock safely and well is basically a matter of balancing the effects of the wind and current on your boat so that it comes to a stop just as you reach the desired place at the dock. If your boat has a motor and you're coming in under power, how well you use your engine and rudder determines how gracefully you'll come up to the dock. The process isn't really complicated. It's mostly just a matter of knowing in your head what to do, and then—as I've said before—driving that knowledge into the seat of your pants by practicing the maneuvers over and over again. In that way, you acquire the skills needed to carry out what your brain tells you to do.

One key to docking your boat under power is to drive it right up to the dock—albeit slowly. If, for example, you try to coast in with an outboard or I/O, you can't steer. So, with those two boat types, at least, you have no choice but to keep them in gear right up to the time you bring the boat to a stop. With a single-engine inboard system, while it's true that you can steer the boat as it coasts through the water, you can steer it better if your propeller is pushing water against the rudder. With a twin-engine inboard, on the other hand, you have maximum control over your boat at slow speeds when you steer it using your engines, not your rudders. So, plan on driving your boat up to the dock, no matter what kind of boat you have.

If your boat is a single-engine inboard, a second key to bringing it up to a dock is using the paddle-wheel effect of your propeller to good advantage. As a result—all other things being equal—you'll want to keep the dock to port in your single-engine inboard if you have a right-hand propeller, or to starboard if you have a left-hand propeller. In this way, when you bring your right-hand-propeller boat up to a dock and shift into reverse to "put on the brakes," the paddle-wheel will tuck your stern right up to the dock. This also puts you in the best position to use your paddle-wheel most effectively when you get ready to leave the dock, as covered in Chapter 11.

Often, of course, all other things are not equal, and you may not have a real choice as to whether you tie up with the dock to port or to starboard. In those situations you'll need to work with the wind or current to get your boat safely to the dock and, where it's appropriate, use your prop wash to offset the paddle-wheel effect.

While you're maneuvering your boat alongside the dock, your crew should be getting ready to put your dock lines ashore. If someone is on the dock to help, you should tell that person specifically where on the dock to make the first line fast, and be ready to tighten the line from the boat. If no one is ashore to help out, your crew should make one end of the line fast to a deck cleat, step (never jump) ashore when the boat is close enough to get ashore safely, and get the first line tied to the dock cleat or piling promptly. When the first dock line is secure, the person on the dock can take the second line and make it fast. Again, the lines should be adjusted from the boat. Finally, depending upon the tide, how strong the current is, and how long the boat will be tied there, you may want to put out one or more spring lines. In any case, fenders should be put out promptly to keep the boat from bumping against the dock.

An added note: The people handling the dock lines generally should not have to pull the boat into position. The skipper's job is to use the engine(s) to get and keep the boat in position until the dock lines are made fast. The engines should not be shut off until the boat is securely tied to the dock.

Situation No. 1
CURRENT / WIND FROM THE BOW

If you have a choice, I'd suggest coming up to a dock headed into the current or wind. The reason is simple: As noted several

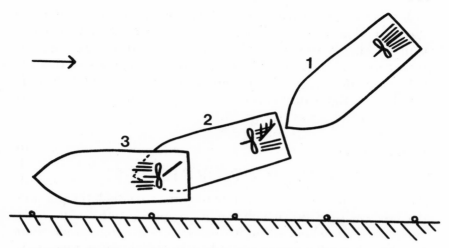

Fig. 74. Docking against the current / wind (under power): If the dock is to port, you can go into reverse as you come alongside the dock, not only stopping the boat but also kicking your stern over to the dock because of the paddle-wheel effect. Leaving the rudder turned away will enable the current to hold the stern in.

times earlier, it's generally easier to control your boat under these circumstances when you are headed into the wind or current. In this situation, you'll want to get your bow line ashore first. In any case, the procedure for docking when headed into the current / wind is as follows:

1. Approach the dock at a slow speed (engine in gear) at an angle of about 30 degrees (Figure 74).

2. When your bow is close by the dock, turn the boat sharply to come up alongside the dock. Turning sharply rather than gradually will help slow the boat; it'll also help lay the boat right up alongside the dock.

3. Stop the boat, and get a bow line ashore. Depending upon how much room you have at the dock, your boat speed, and the force of the current / wind, you can either shift into neutral and coast to a stop before getting the line ashore, or give it some reverse. If your boat has only one engine, however, be sure to plan for the paddle-wheel effect of the propeller in reverse. As noted earlier, the paddle-wheel will either pull the stern toward the dock (helpful) or kick it away (not helpful), depending upon which side the dock is on.

4. Once the boat has stopped, hold it in position by putting the gear in and out of forward as necessary until the bow line is made fast. With the bow line in place, shift into neutral and turn your rudder or drive unit away from the dock so that the current pushing against the rudder or drive unit will help hold the stern in tight until you get a stern line ashore.

Situation No. 2
CURRENT / WIND FROM THE STERN

Although it is usually preferable to come to a dock headed into the current or wind, whichever is stronger, there may be circumstances in which there are good reasons for approaching the dock with the current / wind from astern. If you have lots of room at the dock, that's not a problem because you can just ease alongside and shift into reverse to stop the boat while you get your dock lines ashore. If, however, you need to put your boat into a relatively small space at the dock with a significant current / wind from astern, you have more of a challenge.

In this situation, you'll need to make your approach as nearly parallel to the dock as possible, coming right up alongside the other boats. Susan and I have learned—through a couple of near misses while trying to bring our boat into small dock spaces under these conditions—that the greater your angle to the dock, the more likely you are to overshoot your space. The reason is simple: Since you need your engine in forward to steer, you can't use reverse as a brake to keep the boat from being swept by the current or blown by the wind toward the boat in the next space ahead of you (Figure 75).

So, what do you do? The procedure for coming up to the dock with the current / wind from astern is as follows:

Outboards and I / Os: The strategy is to steer the boat into the space backward—much like parallel parking in a car.

1. Pull up alongside your space a boat width away from the dock, bringing the boat to a stop by giving a short burst of power in reverse. Stay in reverse with just enough power to hold your position against the current / wind.

2. When you have a good position alongside the space you're

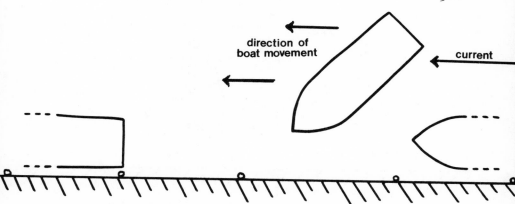

direction of
boat movement

current

Fig. 75. Docking with the current/wind from astern: Coming up to a dock bow-first in this situation can be a prescription for trouble because the current/wind will sweep your boat sideways, making a landing difficult at best, possibly even dangerous. Figures 76–78 illustrate alternatives.

trying to get into, ease the throttle just enough to let the boat drift forward until you have about half a boat length of dock space behind you.

3. Still in reverse, simply increase the throttle and steer the boat backward into the dock, approaching at an angle of about 30 to 35 degrees and turning alongside the dock as you get up to it.

4. Hold position with the engine(s) in reverse until you get a stern line ashore. When the stern line is fast to a cleat or piling several feet behind your boat, put a bow line ashore, turn off your engines, and secure the boat, putting out fenders and spring lines as needed.

Single-Engine Inboards: If the current/wind isn't too strong, you can probably back your boat into the space ("parallel park") much in the same way described for outboards and I/Os. The principal difference is that you'll have to turn your boat for backing before you shift into reverse. The procedure is as follows:

1. Pull up alongside your dock space a boat width away from the dock (Figure 76). Bring the boat to a stop by giving a short burst of power in reverse, then keeping the engine in reverse to hold your position against the current/wind.

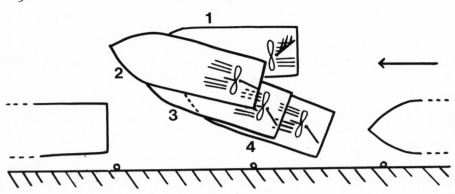

Fig. 76. "Parallel parking," current/wind from astern (single-engine inboard): (1) Kick the stern over using the prop wash. (2) Straighten the rudder and shift into reverse, giving a good surge of power. (3) Continue in reverse, turning the rudder toward the dock. (4) Continue backing toward the dock.

Turn your rudder away from the dock, shift into forward, and give a quick burst of power to kick your stern toward the dock at about a 20-degree angle. The boat should drift forward about half a boat length as you do this.

2. Straighten the rudder and shift into reverse, giving a strong burst of power to begin backing.

3. Turn the rudder toward the dock, and back the boat in, easing the throttle somewhat to let the boat drift forward if necessary to give yourself room to pull your stern up to the dock.

4. Continue backing until the stern is close by the dock.

5. Ease up on the throttle to hold position, and get a stern line ashore and made fast promptly to a dock cleat or piling several feet behind your boat.

6. Ease up completely on the throttle and shift into neutral to let the stern line take the load. The current/wind will swing the bow around to the dock.

Sometimes, of course, the current/wind is too strong for you to back your boat into a small dock space. In that situation, the job of getting your boat in is more difficult. The strategy in this situation is to bring the boat in stern-first but sideways. If the paddle-wheel effect in reverse will help pull your stern toward the dock (e.g., the dock is to port if you have a right-hand propeller), you can get in using your engine and rudder. If the paddle-wheel will pull your stern away from the dock, you'll need to put a line ashore to pull your stern in.

With a helpful paddle-wheel effect, the procedure is as follows:

1. Pull up alongside your dock space about a boat width away from the dock. Bring the boat to a stop by giving a short burst of power in reverse.

2. Easing and increasing the throttle, use the paddle-wheel effect to pull the stern toward the dock while holding your position against the current / wind. If the current is flowing, turn your rudder so that the current pushing against it will help move your stern toward the dock (Figure 77).

3. As soon as the stern comes to the dock, get a stern line ashore. Make it fast several feet in back of your boat, and pull it in tight.

4. Ease the throttle to let the stern line take the load and get a bow line ashore. Turn off your engines and secure the boat—again, putting out fenders and spring lines as needed.

If the paddle-wheel effect will keep your stern off the dock, the procedure is quite different:

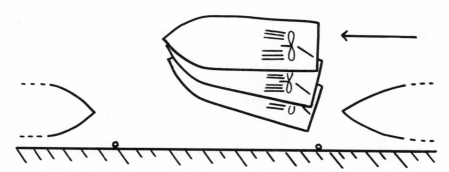

Fig. 77. Sliding your stern sideways to the dock, current from astern (single-engine inboard): If the dock is to port and you have a right-hand propeller, the combined forces of the paddle-wheel effect and the current pushing on your rudder (turned toward the dock as illustrated) will move your boat's stern in to the dock as illustrated here while you use just enough power in reverse to hold your position alongside the dock space.

1. If there is no one on the dock to take your line, either swing around and put a crew member ashore elsewhere along the dock (e.g., at the gas dock) or ease up along a boat that is already tied up and let your crew go across that boat to the dock, being sure to ask permission if anyone is aboard that boat.

2. Pull up alongside your space a boat width away from the dock.

3. Bring the boat to a stop by giving a burst of power in reverse. Stay in reverse to hold your position against the current / wind. Your rudder should be turned so that the current pushing against it will help offset the paddle-wheel effect.

4. Throw your stern line to the person on the dock. Make the end of the line fast to a stern cleat on the side of the boat nearest to the dock.

5. Instruct the person on the dock to pull your stern slowly over to the dock, while you ease or increase the throttle as needed to keep the boat positioned in the dock space. By pulling the stern over slowly, the boat will stay at a relatively small angle to the dock, making it easy to hold your position against the current / wind.

6. When the stern is within two or three feet of the dock, the person ashore should make the line fast to a dock cleat or piling several feet behind the boat.

7. When the stern line is made fast, ease the throttle to let the current / wind swing the boat in to the dock so that you can get a bow line ashore. Stay in reverse, however, until you are sure that the boat will not move too far forward as it swings in to the dock. Be prepared to shorten your stern line if necessary.

8. When the bow line is made fast, you can shut off your engine and adjust your lines as necessary.

Note: This is one of those maneuvers that is worth practicing, preferably when there is lots of space and little traffic. With one of your crew ashore, you can bring your boat up alongside the dock a boat width away as if there were other boats tied alongside and then go through the procedure.

Twin-Engine Inboards: The ability to steer a twin-engine boat in reverse by using the engines instead of the rudders usually will let you back your twin-screw boat into a small space, even with the current / wind from astern—also, much like parallel

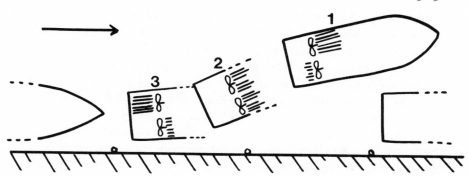

FIG. 78. "Parallel parking," current from astern (twin-engine inboard): (1) The outboard engine is in moderately strong reverse and the inboard engine is in forward at low speed to turn the boat and begin backing in. (2) Both engines are in reverse as you move backward into the space. (3) The outboard engine now is in moderately strong forward to stop backward progress and twist the bow in toward the dock.

parking your car. The rudders are kept straight throughout the procedure so that you have both hands free to work the clutches and throttles. The procedure is as follows:

1. Pull up alongside your space a boat width away from the dock. Bring the boat to a stop by putting both engines in reverse and giving a short burst of power. Ease the throttles slightly to let the boat drift forward until there is about half a boat length of dock space behind you.

Increase the power on the outboard engine (the engine away from the dock) to stop the boat from moving farther forward, and, putting the inboard engine into low forward, start pivoting the bow away from the dock (Figure 78).

2. As the boat comes to about a 20-degree angle to the dock, ease off on the outboard engine somewhat, then shift the inboard engine back into reverse and increase power until both engines are running at the same RPM and the boat starts backing toward the dock.

Caution: If your angle to the dock gets too large, the current / wind will start pushing your boat down the dock toward the boat in front of your space. If you see that starting to happen, give a strong burst of power (in reverse) with the engine closest to the dock. That should overpower the current / wind and help pull your stern more in line with the current so that you can keep backing into the space. If, however, you think you have already been pushed too far down the dock, don't hesitate to shift both engines into forward and give a sharp burst of power to pull out and go around for a second attempt.

3. As the stern approaches the dock, shift the outboard engine into forward to pivot the bow in toward the dock.

4. When the boat is parallel to the dock, adjust the power on both engines so that you are holding your position while you get a stern line made fast to a piling or dock cleat several feet behind your boat.

5. With the stern line made fast, ease the power all the way and shift into neutral so that the stern line takes the load. The current / wind will hold the boat to the dock while you put out a bow line. When the bow line is made fast, you can turn the rudders so that the current will help hold the boat off the dock while you rig your fenders.

This maneuver sounds more complicated than it is in practice. However, it, too, is one you should practice on familiar turf under gentle conditions before you find yourself in unfamiliar waters and severe conditions.

Situation No. 3
WIND BLOWING OFF THE DOCK

In most circumstances, a wind blowing off the dock will have little impact on the process of getting your boat into the assigned space. Since normally you'll head up to the dock bow-first, you can come in at a slightly sharper angle so that the wind's effect is minimized until your bow line is made fast. There is, however, one exception—getting a single-engine inboard boat into a small space when the current is astern.

Basically, this is what happens: As you try to "walk" the stern in toward the dock (or pull it in with the stern line), the wind tries to blow your bow out. The practical effect is that you may have trouble keeping your stern into the current. In this situation, if you can put two people ashore to handle lines, I would recommend it. In that way, one person can help pull in your stern while the other keeps your bow under control. Otherwise, the procedures are the same as those outlined above for getting a single-engine boat in to the dock with the current astern. If you cannot get two people onto the dock to help, you'll just have to work quickly. Again, however, I would try to avoid this situation by finding an alternative—turning around so that the boat is headed into the current, for example. *Caution: If the wind blows your bow out so that the current begins to sweep you down the dock before you can get your stern line made fast, do not try to hold the boat against the current. Cast off the line, pull away and come around for a second attempt.*

Situation No. 4

WIND BLOWING TOWARD SHORE

The first problem of an onshore wind when you're docking is that it wants to blow you into the boats that are already tied up at the dock as you pull alongside. Faced with this situation, you need to make allowance for the wind, leaving extra space between you and the other boats as you make your approach.

If the current is from the bow and the wind not too strong, you can follow the procedure outlined earlier for Situation No. 1. A strong current from astern, however, introduces the second problem of an onshore wind: controlling your bow. In this circumstance, many skippers—particularly those who have sailboats or large motorboats—prefer to bring their boats alongside the dock space and let the wind help them move in to the dock sideways. Once in position, they will use the paddle-wheel effect and / or the current pushing against the rudder(s) to help move the stern toward the dock while the wind blows the bow in.

For all of these situations, it takes time to learn how to bring your boat in like a pro. But all that's required is practice. By getting out in different conditions to practice docking, you'll develop a seat-of-the-pants sense of how to maneuver your boat in these various conditions so that you can come up to any dock safely and cleanly. You'll learn to take the wind into consideration automatically as you make your approach, and to use the current as an ally as you come alongside, or to neutralize it if it's against you.

Testing What You've Learned
(Answers can be found in Appendix C)

1. TRUE or FALSE: To be sure you can stop in time when you are coming up to a dock, it's usually best to coast in.

2. TRUE or FALSE: When docking a single-engine inboard with a right-hand propeller, it's best to come up so that the dock is on your port side—if you have a choice.

3. TRUE or FALSE: If you can come up to a dock so that you're in the best position to use your paddle-wheel to advantage in docking, you'll also be able to use your paddle-wheel to advantage in leaving the dock.

4. TRUE or FALSE: It is generally better to approach a dock with the current or wind behind you.

5. TRUE or FALSE: If the current is from the bow and you are alongside a dock with the bow line made fast and your engine in neutral, you can keep the stern close to the dock by turning the rudder toward the dock.

6. TRUE or FALSE: When the people ashore have your dock lines, you should shift into neutral and let them pull the boat into position.

7. TRUE or FALSE: In general, the best approach when you're docking with the current / wind from behind is to make your approach as nearly parallel to the dock as possible and then go in stern-first.

8. TRUE or FALSE: If you are tied alongside a dock with the current from astern and your engine turned off, you can keep your stern away from the dock by turning your rudder away from the dock.

23

Docking Under Sail

Many of us with auxiliary-powered sailboats don't think much about bringing our boats up to a dock under sail. We just assume that the engine will work when we need it. And most of the time, it does. But, as mentioned earlier, I remember clearly the nice Sunday in June some years ago when I took Susan out for her second sail. I had just met her three weeks before and was somewhat distracted. As a result. I didn't follow my own advice about checking out the boat, and we ran out of gasoline as we started the long run up the river to return to the marina late in the afternoon. Yes, I was embarrassed—especially since I'd done almost the same thing in my car a few days earlier when taking her to a movie. Fortunately, we had been able to coast into a gasoline station. In the boat, however, we had a long sail against the wind up seven miles of river, through a drawbridge, and, finally, up to the gas dock. The point of the story is this: It's worth learning how to sail your boat up to a dock; you never know when you might need that "know-how."

Bringing a small daysailer up to a dock under sail usually isn't very difficult. Even if you get into a little trouble, the boat is small enough and light enough that you can push it away from the dock without much difficulty. Sailing a larger boat up to a dock isn't much different—the same basic sailing techniques are used—but the forces involved are much greater with a bigger boat, and so you can have a larger problem if you get into trouble. Pushing the boat away isn't quite so simple.

Does that mean you shouldn't try to sail a larger boat up to a dock? No. It simply means that you should get out there and practice docking under sail when the wind is light and the dock is clear so that the consequences of any mistakes you make during the learning process are minor. Moreover, you should experiment by coming in with only the jib, with only the mainsail, and with both sails up. We usually prefer to come in under the mainsail alone if the wind is blowing more or less parallel to the dock, but under jib alone if the wind is toward or away from the dock.

The difference is explained this way: When the wind is approximately parallel to the dock, you don't have to let out sail to spill the wind; the wind is spilled automatically as you turn your boat to come alongside the dock. With only the mainsail up, there isn't any sail handling involved. If the jib were up, it would be necessary to cast off the jib sheet. With the wind blowing in any other direction, however, it's necessary to let your sail out to spill the wind as you bring your boat alongside, no matter what sail is up. On our boat, we can do that more easily with the jib than with the mainsail. We can also pull the jib in easily to add some drive if needed. But some boats don't steer well under jib alone, so you'll need to experiment with your boat to learn what's best for you.

If the wind is light, there's usually little difficulty in sailing up to a dock, no matter what the direction of the wind. If at all possible, however, you should head into the current as you come to the dock. In this way, the current helps stop your boat. If you must go with the current, you'll have to rely on your dock lines to stop the boat.

If the wind is strong, you may be better off to sail up close by the dock, get lines ashore, and pull the boat in the last few feet. It may even be necessary to anchor the boat, take lines ashore, and then let the boat be pulled to the dock as you let out on the anchor line. But that's an unusual situation made less difficult as you become more expert at handling your boat and at bringing it alongside under sail.

Situation No. 1
WIND PARALLEL TO THE DOCK

In general, this is the easiest circumstance. You sail the boat closehauled (the sails pulled in tight) (Figure 79) toward the

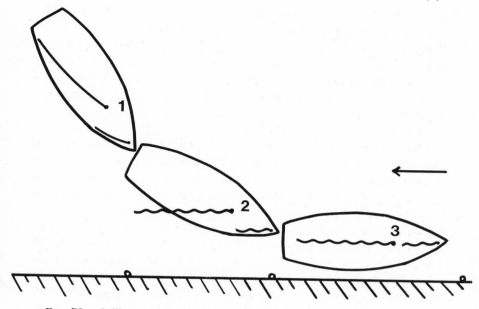

FIG. 79. Sailing up to a dock—wind parallel to the dock: You will (1) come in closehauled, (2) ease the sails to slow the boat, and (3) round into the wind to coast alongside. The key factor is getting an aft spring line ashore promptly to stop the boat (you don't have any brakes), followed by a bow line to hold the bow in.

dock, easing the sail(s) until they are luffing to slow boat speed, and then head into the wind as you turn the boat so that it coasts to a stop alongside the dock. Usually, someone can step ashore with an aft spring line as the boat is coasting to a stop and make it fast. The second line ashore should be a bow line. If you're short-handed and headed into the current, you can give yourself time to get the sail(s) down before putting out a stern line by turning the rudder away from the dock so that the current will hold the stern in.

If the current is from astern and strong enough to keep pushing your boat down the dock very fast after you've headed the boat into the wind, I'd suggest anchoring off and waiting for the current to ease. The reason is that without an engine, you don't have any "brakes"; you have only your first dock line to stop the boat. This is OK if the boat is moving slowly, but risky if it's moving very fast and there are boats in front of you.

If you have any questions about the strength of the current, you can make a trial pass by bringing the boat into the wind a short distance off the dock and waiting to see what the current does. If your boat won't slow down to a crawl after you come into the wind, don't try to sail up to the dock unless you have lots of room—several boat lengths of dock space—in which to get that first line ashore and snubbed around a piling or sturdy dock cleat to bring your boat to a stop.

When you've weighed all the factors and forces and believe that you can sail your boat in to the dock safely, proceed as described above—with one exception. When the current is from astern, your first line ashore should be a spring line leading from a chock amidships to a piling or strong dock cleat near the stern. This spring line can be used to stop the boat; it'll also tend to keep the bow from swinging away from the dock until you can get a bow line made fast and your sail(s) down. If you're short-handed, you can turn your rudder toward the dock so that the current will hold the stern in while you get the bow line rigged and the sail(s) down. Then you can put out your stern line. If you're not short-handed, the stern line should be put out while your crew rolls up or takes down the sail(s).

Situation No. 2
WIND BLOWING OFF THE DOCK

Your strategy in this situation depends on just how the wind is blowing. If it is straight off the dock (about 90 degrees), you'll have to approach the dock at a sharper angle than if it is coming off the dock at a smaller angle—for example, from 30 to 60 degrees. In both instances, however, you can lay the boat right alongside the dock by letting out the sails to stop the boat rather than by heading into the wind.

Wind Nearly Straight Off the Dock: One key to success in this situation is getting a bow line ashore and made fast, followed promptly by your stern line. A second key is to make your approach with the smallest amount of sail necessary—preferably the smallest jib needed to move your boat in those winds.

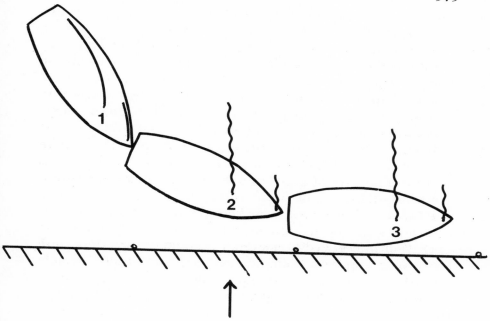

FIG. 80. Sailing up to a dock—wind straight off the dock: (1) Your approach is closehauled. (2) As you turn to come alongside, you should let out the sails to spill the wind and coast up to the dock (3).

The mainsail may be more difficult to use in this situation because it is sometimes more work to get it far enough out to spill all of the wind from the sail quickly. In any case, the procedure is as follows:

1. Note the direction of the current, and make your approach closehauled (at an angle of about 45 degrees to the dock) on a tack that heads you into the current (Figure 80).

2. As you approach the dock, let your sail(s) out so that it begins to luff, slowing the boat. If you slow too much, you can always pull the sail(s) in for a moment to add some drive; but the idea is to slow the boat enough that it coasts up to the dock.

3. When you are close by the dock, let your sail(s) out all the way and steer the boat so that it comes up alongside the dock as it turns, moving very slowly.

4. Once the boat is close enough for you to do so safely, put

the bow line ashore and have it made fast to a dock cleat or piling in front of the boat.

5. As soon as the bow line is made fast, turn the rudder away from the dock so that the current will help hold the stern in, and get a stern line ashore promptly.

6. Roll up or take down your sail(s) promptly. If you have sufficient crew, they should start taking the sail(s) down as soon as the bow line is ashore because the wind, depending upon its strength, may be whipping the sail(s) vigorously. The smaller any sail is and the faster you get it down, the less likelihood there is of it being damaged or a sheet (line) hitting someone as it is whipped around by the fluttering sail.

Wind at a Smaller Angle to the Dock: As the wind moves around so that it is no longer coming straight or nearly straight off the dock, your tactics need to change. Usually, in this situation, you'll make your approach sailing closehauled and headed straight toward the dock. As before, you should not have any more sail up than is necessary to keep your boat moving and responsive to the rudder:

1. Note the direction of the current so that you can plan for its effect on your boat as you dock. Start your approach, sailing closehauled toward the dock (Figure 81) and luffing your sail(s) as needed to slow your boat speed.

2. As you approach the dock, head the boat into the wind, so that it coasts toward the dock with the sail(s) luffing.

3. When the bow is close by the dock, turn your rudder so that the boat lies alongside the dock. How hard you turn the rudder depends upon your boat speed. If the boat is moving slowly, ease the rudder over; if the boat is still moving fairly fast, put the rudder hard over so that it acts as a brake while it turns the boat. In either case, allow the sails to continue luffing.

4. As soon as the boat is alongside the dock, get a bow line ashore and made fast to a dock cleat or piling ahead of the bow.

5. As quickly as the bow line is made fast, turn the rudder so that the current will help hold the stern to the dock, and get a stern line ashore.

6. Roll up or take down the sail(s) promptly.

Note: If you are coming in with a strong current from astern as you head into the wind, the first line ashore should be an aft

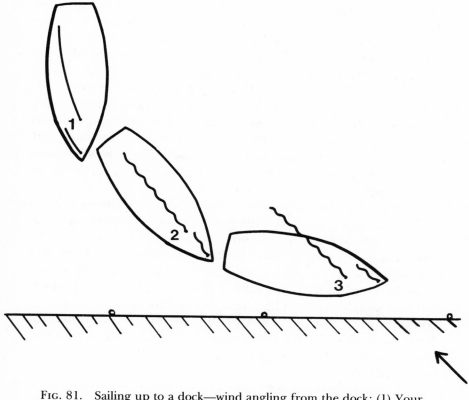

FIG. 81. Sailing up to a dock—wind angling from the dock: (1) Your approach will be nearly straight on as you come in closehauled. (2) As you begin your turn, you'll come up into the wind, then let your sails out (3) so they continue to luff as your turn brings the boat alongside.

spring line leading from a chock amidships. The second line ashore should be a bow line. You can turn the rudder toward the dock to keep the stern close.

Situation No. 3

WIND BLOWING TOWARD THE DOCK

Sailing up to a dock when the wind is blowing from the water onto the dock is generally a more difficult maneuver than other situations. The major problem is that you are forced to let your sails out over the dock in order to spill the wind from them, creating a real risk of snagging a sail or line on the dock and tearing or breaking something.

In the extreme—strong wind blowing down on the dock at an angle of 90 degrees—you may decide to anchor off and go in by dinghy. Even in more moderate conditions, the best decision may be to anchor near the dock and let the boat drop back to the dock by paying out your anchor line (rode). *Under no circumstances should you attempt this maneuver until you have practiced anchoring under sail many times and are confident of your anchoring capabilities.* Why? The answer is easy enough to understand: If your anchor drags, your boat could be blown down onto the dock and other boats. The more practiced you are in anchoring, the more likely you are to do it well and the less likely you are to drag anchor.

Wind Nearly Straight Onto the Dock: Assuming the wind isn't so strong that you should simply anchor out and wait for more favorable conditions, you will probably have to dock by anchoring. You should make at least one dry run to see how your boat handles and to test the effect of the current. You should also check the depth of the water where you will anchor so that you know how far off the dock to place your anchor. The procedure is as follows:

1. Get your anchor ready to be let down.

2. Take down and secure all unnecessary sails. Here again, you should come in with only as much sail as is needed to have good control over your boat.

3. Make your approach on a broad reach, coming in at an angle to the dock of about 30 degrees.

4. As you approach the spot where you want to put your anchor, turn sharply up into the wind and hold your bow there. The sharp, almost U-turn should bring the boat to a stop quickly.

5. When the boat is stopped (completely), let the anchor down, paying out the anchor line as the wind begins to blow the boat back.

6. As the boat is blown back toward the dock, begin snubbing the line gently to dig in the anchor and slow the drift.

7. When the anchor is dug in—and before the boat has drifted all the way back to the dock—the anchor line should be made

fast so that you have time at anchor to take down and secure your sail(s) before attempting to let the boat the last few yards to the dock.

Once the sail(s) have been secured, the dock lines made ready, and your fenders put out, you can let the boat back to dock by paying out the anchor line slowly. As the boat gets to the dock, some of your crew should step ashore and hold the stern off while the bow comes around so that the boat lies up against the dock. When the bow and stern lines are made fast, you'll need to adjust the fenders. Also, you'll either need to let out more on your anchor line so that it will lie flat on the bottom, or go out in another boat to retrieve the anchor so that your anchor line isn't a hazard to other boats.

Note that the critical question in this whole maneuver is how far from the dock to drop your anchor. The answer depends upon the wind's strength, your boat's size, and the water's depth. You'll need to be farther away in a stronger wind so that you can let out enough anchor line to keep from dragging when you try to stop the boat's drift toward the dock. A good rule of thumb is to drop anchor a distance away from the dock equal to the boat's length plus ten to twelve times the depth of the water (ten times the depth for smaller boats, twelve times for larger boats). In other words, if your boat is 20 feet long and the water is 10 feet deep, drop your anchor from 120 to 140 feet off the dock (Figure 82)—farther away in heavy winds.*

Wind at Smaller Angles to the Dock: If the wind is strong, you may choose to anchor upwind from the dock and let your boat drop back to the dock as just described. If conditions are more moderate, however, you may want to sail up to the dock using the smallest amount of sail necessary to control your boat, luffing your sails to stop the boat.

However, because you'll be letting the sails out toward the dock, you must be careful that there isn't anything on that dock—like a piling—to snag your sails and their sheets, or you could end up with a torn sail and / or a damaged boat. In that situa-

---

* Note that we are talking here about "distance off" the dock, not about how much anchor line to let out. Following the rule of thumb suggested here should ensure an adequate length of anchor line for secure anchoring.

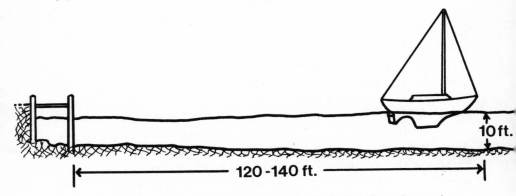

Fig. 82.   Anchoring off to drop back to the dock: You'll need to anchor with an extra margin of safety to be sure your anchor does not drag. Ten to twelve times the depth of the water plus the length of your boat will usually provide an adequate distance off the dock to lower your anchor.

tion, the wiser choice might be to let the boat back to the dock on your anchor line, even in a gentle breeze. In any case, assuming the dock configuration and wind strength will allow you to sail up to the dock, the procedure is as follows:

1. Approach the dock with the wind abeam (Figure 83).

2. As you near the dock, turn closer to the wind and / or let out your sail(s) as necessary to slow down.

3. When the boat is close by the dock, luff the sail(s) further and steer to lay the boat right along the dock as it coasts to a stop. If the current is not a strong factor, you can even be a foot or two off the dock when you come to a stop, because the wind will blow the boat in.

4. As soon as a bow line can be put ashore and made fast, the stern line should be run.

5. Sail(s) should be rolled up or taken down promptly—but also carefully—so that you don't snag any parts of the dock.

And then you can relax for a few minutes before getting up to make sure that everything is secure and shipshape.

An added note: There is another way to take the wind out of your sail(s) that hasn't been mentioned—that is, by dropping (or rolling up) your sail(s) at the last minute. We generally prefer not to take that last sail down until we have the first dock

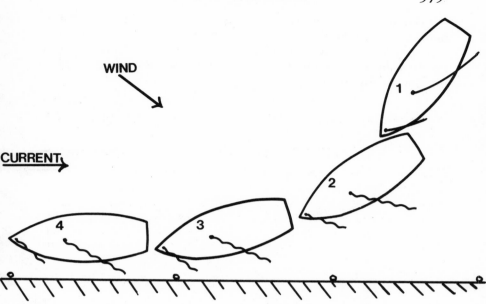

FIG. 83. Sailing up to a dock—wind angling onto the dock: In this situation, you are forced to luff your sails out over the dock. The danger is that your sheets or even the sails themselves will snag on part of the dock structure. Ideally, you would come in carrying the minimum sail required.

line ashore, because once that sail is rolled up or on deck, the boat is powerless. On the other hand, as long as the sail is up and ready, we can abort the docking and head off again.

Testing What You've Learned
(Answers can be found in Appendix C)

1. Why is it advantageous to head into the current when sailing up to a dock?

2. Why do you think it is important to get a bow line on promptly after stopping the boat with the aft spring line?

3. Why is it important to sail up to a dock under the smallest amount of sail necessary to control your boat?

4. If you are sailing short-handed, how can you hold your stern in toward the dock so that you can take your sail down before putting out a stern line?

5. What is the major risk in sailing up to a dock when the wind is blowing toward the dock—even if it is only a moderate breeze?

6. If you are going to anchor and then let your boat drift back to the dock on your anchor line, how far away from the dock should you put down your anchor?

24

Getting into a Slip

Getting your boat into a slip under power is usually pretty straightforward. Trying to sail into a slip can complicate your life unnecessarily unless you're a pretty good sailor and, frankly, I'd recommend against it if you have a choice. You're better off to sail up to the dock or, simply, to anchor out until someone can help you into your slip with a motorboat. You might even be able to use your dinghy with its outboard (if you have one) to tow your boat into the slip, if the wind and current are light.

Assuming, then, that you'll be coming into your slip under power, there are usually only five factors you need to consider: (1) maneuvering space; (2) current; (3) wind; (4) whether you're going into your slip bow-first or stern-first (bow-first is almost always easier); and (5) whether there are dock lines for you to pick up or you have to rig your own.

MANEUVERING SPACE

Some marinas have banks of slips aligned opposite each other, little more than 60 to 80 feet apart. If you have an outboard, I/O, or twin-screw inboard, such close quarters present little problem because of the control you have over your boat when maneuvering in tight spaces. If you have a single inboard engine and a 30- to 40-foot boat, you may have more difficulty. The keys, however, are (1) remembering the techniques learned for turning your boat in a short space by using the paddle-wheel effect of the propeller in reverse and the effect of water thrusting against the rudder in forward, and (2) making allowances for the current and wind.

CURRENT

As noted before, the current will usually run parallel to your slip; it's part of the design in a well-planned marina. In that case, the only question is whether the current is with you or against you. The simplest situation is when the current is against you, because it acts as a brake to help you stop the boat. When it's with you, the current pushes your boat on into the slip and you have to brake against it using your engine. In either case, you also need to make sure that your first line ashore is one that will hold the boat where you want it against the current (Figure 84).

If the current is sideways to the slip, you'll need to take that into account in your approach. Otherwise, you'll either miss the slip or wind up trying to come in at a difficult angle. Compensating for the current is not difficult after you've had some practice estimating its effect on your boat. You can begin by stopping your boat about 25 yards in front of the slip (if you have the space), but headed straight in. Within a minute or so,

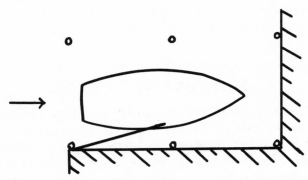

FIG. 84.   Heading into a slip—wind/current from astern: The problem is stopping your boat. For that reason, the first line ashore should be an aft spring line (preferably from amidships). The aft spring will not only stop the boat, but also hold it in position while you make the other lines fast.

you'll be able to see how much the current will move your boat to the side. From that point, you need only position your boat to go into your slip, making an allowance for the current to move your boat sideways as you make your approach. In any case, it is better to overestimate than to underestimate the effect of the current; you can always stop the boat just outside the slip and let the current push you sideways until the boat is lined up properly.

WIND

If the wind is blowing parallel to the slip, it presents essentially the same situation as that provided by a current from the same direction. However, a wind from one side or the other may present a more difficult situation, depending upon the wind's strength; whether it is blowing toward your boat from an angle forward, straight abeam (broadside), or from an angle aft; whether you have one engine or two; and whether you are entering the slip bow- or stern-first.

The major difference between the effects of wind and current when they are coming from the side is that the current tends to move the whole boat downstream, whereas the wind tends to push the bow around while moving the whole boat downwind. Moreover, the farther forward the wind is coming from, the more it tends to blow the bow around.

Heading in Bow-First

When heading into a slip bow-first under these conditions, it's important to keep enough forward motion to control the bow. With twin engines, you can also put the engine closest to the wind in neutral so that the "downwind" engine is pushing the boat. In this way, the engine is tending to push the bow into the wind. If the wind is strong enough, it may also be necessary to put the upwind engine in reverse for short periods to help hold the bow in line.

If you are going into the slip bow-first in a single-engine boat— outboard, I / O, or inboard—with a strong wind from one side

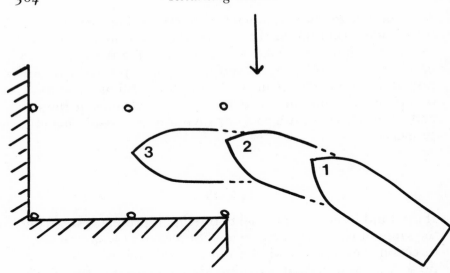

FIG. 85. Heading into a slip—current / wind perpendicular to the slip: In this situation, you should come in (1) at an angle toward the wind / current, (2) turning at the last minute (3) to enter your slip. This will keep the wind / current from pushing you off course.

or the other, you may have to steer a course that is angled somewhat into the wind to keep the bow from being blown off to the side (Figure 85). Once the bow begins to enter the slip, you can bring the stern around to line the boat up with the slip by putting the rudder over and kicking the stern to the side with the prop wash against the rudder. You may also need to make your approach a little faster than normal; the added speed will give you better control of your bow and reduce the time the wind has to work on you. Of course, you'll need to use a good burst in reverse to slow your boat just before actually entering the slip.

Going in Stern-First

When going into the slip stern-first with a twin-engine boat, you'll need to use the "twisting" ability of your engines to control your bow. By keeping the upwind engine in reverse and moving the downwind engine between neutral and forward, it is possible to keep "twisting" or pulling your bow back against the wind as you move backward. The key is to keep your boat parallel to the slip—not letting the wind blow the bow around— so that the wind effectively pushes the whole boat to the side. In fact, it's often a good idea to position your boat so that it's a little upwind from the slip when you first begin reversing, just as you would if the current were from the side. In this way, the wind aligns the boat with the slip as you back up. If you mis-judge and overshoot the slip the first time around, simply go out and make a second pass. There's little sense in trying to salvage a bad approach. If the wind is simply too strong to keep your bow in line, then you should use the technique suggested below for backing a single-engine boat into a slip.

If you have a single-engine boat and want to enter your slip stern-first, your challenge is greater. First, if the wind is essen-tially from abeam and strong, forget it; go in bow-first. If, how-ever, the wind is from an angle of less than about 45 degrees off the bow or stern and not overly strong, you can make it stern-first if you want to. But it takes lots of practice, and even then you may make more than one attempt on any given day before getting into the slip.

The technique is to align your boat with the wind, keep it aligned as you back toward your slip, and then straighten the boat out as you actually enter the slip (Figure 86). If the wind is from what would otherwise be your stern quarter (if you were to back straight into the slip), the idea is to position your boat so that you can back directly into the wind to get to your slip. This means that you start out downwind from the slip with your stern pointed straight into the wind and straight at the slip next to yours on the upwind side. Then:

1. Shift into reverse, and back directly into the wind until your stern is almost to the neighboring slip.

2. At that time, turn your rudder, shift into forward gear, and give a burst of power so that the propeller thrust against the rudder will kick your stern around until it is pointed at your slip.

3. Without turning the rudder, shift back into reverse and

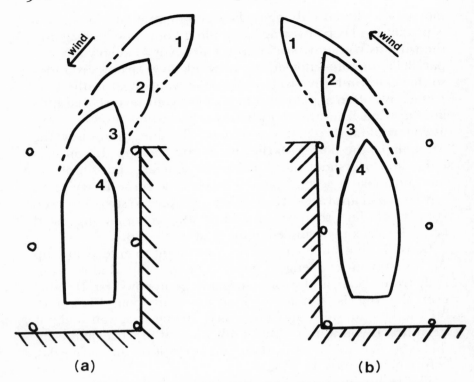

(a) **(b)**

Fig. 86. Backing into a slip—wind at an angle: In both situations (a) and (b), the trick is to (1) align your boat with the wind and back toward your slip at an angle. (2) As the stern begins to enter the slip, you can use your prop wash and rudder as necessary to bring the stern around so that (3) and (4) you can continue right on into the slip. In situation (a), the wind will help bring the bow around as you turn into the slip. In (b), the paddle-wheel effect in reverse will help you steer through the turn.

give as much power as you need to start moving backward into your slip promptly—before the wind can begin to blow your bow around.

4. If needed, shift into forward again to kick your stern around further, and then get back into reverse to continue backing into the slip.

If the wind is from the forward quarter, you align the boat so that when it is headed into the wind, the slip is astern and

slightly downwind. Then you back down on the slip, being careful to keep your bow pointed straight into the wind—a difficult
chore, but made possible by using the paddle-wheel and propeller thrust on the rudder to move the stern to one side or the
other as necessary to maintain your alignment with the wind.
Once your stern is entering the slip, you can let the wind push
the bow around to align the boat with the slip as you complete
the maneuver.

BOW-FIRST VERSUS STERN-FIRST

Walk along any marina pier, and you'll notice that motorboats
with twin engines usually are in their slips stern-first. In contrast, single-engine motorboats and sailboats usually are found
in their slips bow-first. There is really only one reason for this
difference: Twin engines make it relatively easy to put a boat
into its slip stern-first. As just described, however, maneuvering
a single-engine motorboat or sailboat into a slip stern-first can
be difficult even in relatively benign conditions and virtually
impossible if the wind really pipes up. As a result, most skippers
of single-engine boats simply head in bow-first.

DOCK LINES

If you're coming into your own slip, you'll have dock lines already
tied to the pilings, and it's an easy job to pick them up. All your
crew needs to do is to know which lines to pick up first and to
have the boathook ready to help reach them.

If you're coming into a strange slip, however, there probably
won't be any dock lines in place and you'll need to have your
own lines out of the locker and on deck ready for use. It's usually a good idea to get the easiest lines ashore first. For example,
if the slip has a finger pier that extends out along one side, the
lines on that side should be the first ones out. If the current (or
wind) is from the bow, you should start with the bow line; if it's
from the stern, start with the stern line. If the slip is at all short,

a spring line to stop the boat from going too far into the slip should be the first line ashore.

If there is no one on the dock to help you, your crew can fasten one end of a line to the bow or stern cleat and lead the line out through the chock and back over the rail or lifelines. He (or she) can then run the line to a point where he can safely step from the boat to the dock and just walk the line forward or aft, as appropriate, and make it fast to a piling.

Under some circumstances—as when the wind and current are light—you can fasten lines to pilings on both sides of the slip as you bring the boat in. You just stop the boat halfway into the slip while the crew makes one line fast, then push the boat gently toward the other side of the slip to get a line on the opposite piling. With both lines on the first pilings, you can move the boat further into the slip to get lines on the other pilings. Someone will have to handle the first two lines as you move the boat further into the slip, however, to be sure they don't fall into the water.

If the wind is blowing hard from one side or the other, you will probably want to get your lines on the windward pilings first. In all cases, however, remember that you will have to take the lines off the pilings when you are leaving. So, tie them in a manner that will make them relatively easy to get off.

Testing What You've Learned
(Answers can be found in Appendix C)

1. TRUE or FALSE: It is easier to get into a slip when the current is with you.

2. When entering a slip with the current from the side, why is it better to overestimate the effect of the current than to underestimate it?

3. What effect will a wind coming from the side have on a boat, other than pushing it downwind?

4. TRUE or FALSE: If the wind is from the side and you are going into a slip bow-first in a single-engine boat, you may need to approach the slip at an angle. Explain the reason for your answer.

5. TRUE or FALSE: It is generally easier to put a boat into a slip bow-first than stern-first.

6. TRUE or FALSE: When entering a slip stern-first in a single-engine boat with the wind somewhere off the bow or stern, you should align the boat with the wind when approaching the slip.

7. If the current is from the stern, what dock lines should you make fast first, if possible?

25

Picking Up a Mooring, Anchoring, and Beaching Your Boat

On the surface, picking up a mooring, anchoring, and beaching your boat appear to be much easier than coming up to a dock or getting into a slip—and, frequently, they are. However, each maneuver has its potential complications, and Mr. Murphy is ever-present, always waiting for an opportunity to catch you in a moment of carelessness or haste. From a practical viewpoint, therefore, your safety as well as that of your boat requires that each of these maneuvers be carried out with the same attention to detail used in coming alongside a dock or into a slip.

COMING UP TO A MOORING

Picking up a mooring under power is generally a simple maneuver. The key is to look at the other boats on nearby moorings to see what effect the wind and / or current are having on them. It is also important to look at boats that are similar to yours. For example, a sailboat with a deep keel probably will lie differently than a motorboat with a high superstructure when the current is running in a different direction than the wind. The explanation for this difference is that the current will have the dominant influence on the sailboat because of the deep keel hanging from its bottom, whereas the wind will have the dominant influence on the motorboat because the high superstructure acts like a sail.

Once you have an idea how your boat will lie to the mooring, approach the mooring at a slow speed, headed into the wind or current, whichever is dominant. When the bow comes alongside the mooring, stop the boat with a burst of reverse as the crew reaches over the bow to pick up the mooring with his (or her) hand or a boathook. If you are alone, you can walk forward to pick up the mooring after you've stopped the boat. Do not, however, try to bring your stern up to the mooring, because you may get the mooring fouled in your propeller.

If you are sailing up to your mooring, the method is slightly more complicated because you can't use reverse to stop the boat. This is where you really need to know how far your boat will coast after you let the wind out of your sails.

There are two ways to approach the mooring under sail. In the traditional approach—the one I learned as a twelve-year-old—you sail to a point downwind from the mooring and then turn into the wind letting the sail(s) luff up, so that the boat will coast up to the buoy, coming to a stop just as the mooring buoy comes alongside the bow, as illustrated in Figure 87 (a). The problem with this approach—particularly in a crowded mooring area—is that you don't have good control over the boat if it stops short of the mooring.

An alternative approach involves essentially sailing up to your mooring closehauled, letting out your sail(s) to spill the wind so that the boat coasts the last distance, as in Figure 87 (b). If you are going to stop short, you can pull the mainsail in a bit to add a little power, and then let it out again. If for some reason you miss the mooring, you need only pull your sail(s) in to resume sailing with the boat under full control, and you can easily come around for a second try.

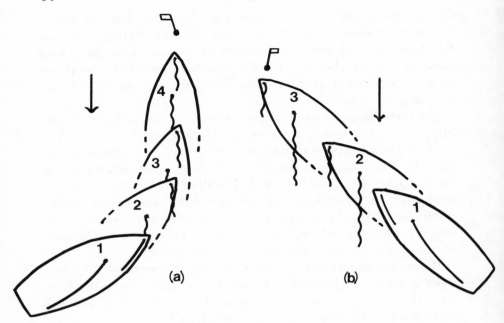

FIG. 87. Sailing up to a mooring buoy—two approaches: In the traditional approach (a), you turn into the wind and coast up to the buoy—if you judge the distance correctly. An alternative approach (b) involves letting out your sails to spill the wind as you coast up to the buoy.

ANCHORING

Whether anchoring under power or under sail, the method is basically the same. You pick a spot, put down your anchor, let out your anchor line (rode), dig in the anchor, and make your anchor line secure.

It sounds so simple. In practice, however, anchoring can be infuriatingly difficult because, even though the basic elements are simple, the maneuver itself seems more akin to art than science. As a result, few elements of boating have been the subject of more articles or book chapters than anchoring. Moreover, in addition to whatever knowledge is needed, anchoring your boat and doing it well require patience, practice, and a conscious awareness of Murphy's most basic law: "If something can go wrong, it will."

The three most common anchoring mistakes are: (1) putting the anchor down while the boat is still moving forward; (2) simply dropping the anchor overboard and letting out some anchor line; and (3) not letting out enough anchor line. The result can include any one or all three of the following: the anchor doesn't get dug into the bottom properly; it's fouled by its own anchor line; and the anchor drags if a stronger wind or current puts additional strain on the system.

The first two mistakes can be eliminated by following good procedures in lowering your anchor and letting out your anchor line as your boat moves back from the anchor. After the boat has been brought to a complete stop, always let your anchor down in a controlled manner. This not only helps you check the water's depth, it also increases the odds that the anchor will lie down on the bottom, ready to be dug in.

By the same token, once the anchor is on the bottom, you should let your anchor line out in a controlled manner. In this way, you can keep it from getting tangled in the anchor, or even in itself. Moreover, every once in a while, you can snub the line briefly to control your boat's drift backward and to start digging in the anchor. You can also have better control over the amount of line you let out.

The third common mistake is also easily eliminated. The correct length of nylon anchor rode in light wind conditions is from five to seven times the distance from the deck of your boat to the bottom (Figure 88). That means that if the water is 10 feet deep and the deck of the boat is 3 feet above the surface of the water, your anchor rode should be from five to seven times the total distance (13 feet), or from 65 to 91 feet long.

The reason for letting out so much line is to allow it to sag into a curve so that the strain on the anchor is sideways, or horizontal, rather than upwards. The horizontal strain will tend to dig the anchor in; the more vertical the pull, the more likely the anchor is to come loose and drag (Figure 89). If the wind strengthens, it may be necessary to let out more line so that the boat doesn't pull the line taut. For example, a scope of ten times the distance from the deck to the bottom is often needed when anchoring overnight in the Chesapeake Bay area to guard against dragging in the event of a nighttime summer storm.

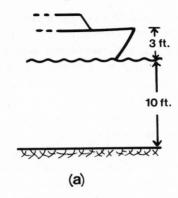

(a)

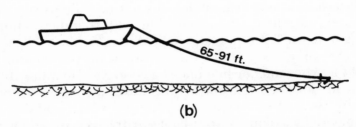

(b)

FIG. 88.   Anchor rode length: The amount of anchor rode (line) required
is determined (a) by adding the distance from your bow chock to the
water and the depth of the water—in this case, 13 feet. The anchor rode
(b) should be from five to seven times that distance—or, in this case,
from 65 to 91 feet long.

Three Keys to Anchoring Under Power

There are three keys to anchoring your motorboat or
auxiliary-powered sailboat securely: (1) picking a good spot to
put down your anchor; (2) the skipper's turning over control to
the person on the bow; and (3) following good anchoring procedures.

Picking Your Spot: No matter how large or small your boat,
you need to pick a good spot to put down your anchor. Hopefully you've chosen an anchorage that is protected from most
winds. If there are other boats around, you'll notice as you enter
the anchorage that people on the boats that are already anchored
will watch you closely. And with good reason: Too often, late-
comers will anchor uncomfortably close to other boats.

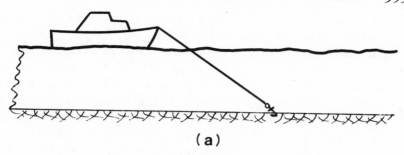

(a)

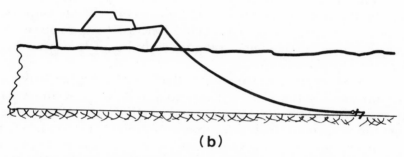

(b)

FIG. 89.   The importance of anchor rode length: If the anchor rode is too short (a) it will not let the anchor dig securely into the bottom. In that situation, the anchor will drag if the wind or current strengthens. The longer anchor rode (b) pulls on the anchor in a way that makes it dig deeper into the bottom as the wind or current strengthens.

If the anchorage is not crowded, you should select a spot a reasonable distance away from other boats so that you don't intrude on your neighbors' privacy. You should also be certain that you are far enough from shore or any other obstacle (a jetty, buoy, or shoal area) that if the wind shifts, you won't swing around and get into trouble. Finally, you need to be sure the water is deep enough that you won't be left sitting on the bottom at low tide.

If the anchorage is crowded, you need to find an area behind another boat that will give you adequate room to swing on both sides. Then pull up behind the boat that will be in front of you (but not too close!), lower your anchor, and fall back on your anchor rode. The idea is to have enough space between you and all of the boats around you so that no matter how all of the boats swing, you will not only stay clear of the other boats, but also of their anchors and anchor lines.

Turning Over Control: The easiest thing any skipper can do to improve his anchoring technique is to let the person on the bow tell him what to do with the boat during the anchoring procedure itself, using the kind of hand signals described in Chapter 9 and illustrated in Figure 20. This means that the skipper and crew need to agree on just where to put down the anchor. Once that spot is chosen and the boat brought around to make an approach, the person on the bow takes charge, telling the skipper how fast to go, where to steer, when to shift into neutral or reverse, and so on. Why? Because the person on the bow usually can see what's going on with the anchor much better than the skipper can.

However, there is an exception: Because the skipper is always responsible for the safety of the boat and crew, he must pay close attention to other boats around him in case a hazard arises that the person on the bow is unaware of. In that case, the skipper should tell the person on the bow that he is taking over and do whatever is necessary to ensure the safety of the boat.

Good Anchoring Procedure: As with many other elements of safe boating, good anchoring procedure involves planning, attention to detail, and practice.

1. Observe other boats, particularly those that are similar to yours, to see how they are lying to the wind and current. You will want to approach your anchoring position so that your course is parallel to those other boats.

2. Pick your spot. You are selecting the place where you will put your anchor so that your boat is free to swing with surrounding boats without hazard of bumping into another boat or fouling another boat's anchor rode.

3. Using either a lead line or a depthsounder, determine the water's depth, add the height of the deck above the water, and then multiply that sum by five, six, or seven, depending upon the circumstances, to determine how much line to let out. The stronger the wind or current, the more you'll want to let out. If the tide is low, let out enough extra line so that you'll have the correct amount of rode at high tide, too.

4. Get your anchor ready to be lowered. This means getting

a length of anchor line up on deck so that it can be let out cleanly. You might also let your anchor down till it is hanging in the water. Sometimes it's easier to tell when the boat stops moving forward by looking at the flow of water around the anchor.

5. Approach the spot from downwind (down-current), coming to a full stop right where you want to put your anchor.

6. When the boat has fully stopped, lower the anchor to the bottom. You can tell when it hits the bottom because the weight comes off the line.

7. Allow the boat to drift backward, perhaps helping it slightly with a small amount of reverse for short intervals. If the boat begins to turn sideways to the wind, just snub the anchor line for a minute to bring the bow around, and then let out more line. Snubbing the line for a minute will help set the anchor.

8. When you've let out the desired length of rode, make it fast, and then dig in the anchor by shifting into reverse and using enough power to pull the rode tight. Ease up as soon as the rode is tight, however. If the anchor is dug in, the anchor line should tighten and then go slack as you take the engine out of reverse and the boat is pulled forward by the anchor line as it relaxes.

9. Note your position relative to fixed landmarks on the shore so that you can check your position later to determine whether you have dragged your anchor. If you are dragging, you can try letting out more line; most likely you'll have to take up your anchor and start over.

10. Check your anchor and position periodically.

There is also one safety note that bears repeating: You generally should not anchor your boat from the stern. Not only is it difficult to pull your boat stern-first up to an anchor against a strong wind or current, but, as noted in Chapter 19, it can be dangerous. A strong current pushing against the flat stern of a motorboat can pull the stern down dangerously low. A strong wind can cause similar problems—particularly for an outboard motorboat—by building up waves that can break over the transom while the pressure on the anchor line holds the stern low. The combination of even a moderate current, a moderate wind, and a stern anchor is often a prescription for trouble.

Anchoring Under Sail

Anchoring under sail is similar in most respects to anchoring under power, but with two important exceptions: The person at the helm cannot turn over control to the crew on the bow because the boat is still under sail coming up to anchor; and there is no engine to help dig in the anchor. These are not problems; you simply do things differently. The steps involved in anchoring under sail are (1) picking a spot, (2) clearing off the foredeck, (3) sailing up to the chosen spot for anchoring, and (4) putting the anchor down securely.

In choosing your spot, you need to consider the wind and possible avenues of escape if you should fail to get the anchor down. Usually it is wise to leave an extra margin of safety between your boat and any other boats that may already be anchored. With the spot selected, you'll need to clear the foredeck. We prefer to get the jib bagged and out of the way. If you have roller-furling gear, the job is obviously easier, but the point is no different: The jib should be out of the way well before you try to anchor.

The techniques for coming up to anchor under sail are essentially the same as for sailing up to a mooring. You should use one of the same two approaches. When the boat comes to a stop, the person on the bow should lower the anchor to the bottom and pay out the line as the boat drifts back. Other crew, or the helmsman, should make sure the mainsheet stays slack so that the mainsail can't fill with wind. As the boat drifts back and the bow begins to fall off, the person on the bow should snub the anchor line gently so that the bow is pulled back into the wind. Each time the line is snubbed, the anchor will tend to dig in.

It's a good idea under these circumstances to let out more rode than you might if you were using an engine to help you anchor. The longer rode will help the anchor dig in if the wind builds. Once the anchor is out as far as you want it, cleat the line and take down the mainsail.

Some sailors like to put their anchor down with the boat still moving forward, with the idea that the boat's momentum will dig in the anchor when they stop letting out on the rode. It works—most of the time. Sometimes, however, the anchor may not dig in and you can suddenly find yourself under sail with an anchor dragging behind you on a hundred feet of anchor line. It's a situation to be avoided if possible.

COMING TO SHORE

Beaching your boat, whether to have a picnic ashore or when coming back to a boat ramp to get back on the trailer, is pretty straightforward. There are two main hazards to watch for in addition to other boats: One is swimmers; the other is the bottom or some other underwater obstruction. The key to managing both hazards safely is to approach the shore slowly—very slowly for the last two or three hundred feet. You may see others come roaring up toward the beach and cutting the power at the last minute to arrive with a splash of big waves, but don't be tempted. Not only is the wave system made by those boaters extraordinarily thoughtless if there are other boats along the beach, but that fast approach is also dangerous. In fact, if the water's a little shallower than you think, it's a good way to damage your boat's bottom or drive unit as you come off a plane and your boat settles down into the water stern-first, dragging your drive unit into the bottom in the process.

When you reach water that is shallow enough for someone to stand in easily, you should turn off your engine and put one of your crew overboard to pull the boat the rest of the way to the shore, even if it's a few hundred feet. It's much safer than trying to drive in and letting your drive unit hit bottom, or sucking silt and sand into your engine's cooling system. *One note of caution: The person in the water should wear shoes of some sort,* to protect his (or her) feet against broken glass, tin cans, rusty nails, coral, jagged rocks, etc. He should also wear a life jacket if he's not a swimmer. He could step into a hole and suddenly be in water over his head.

With the boat beached, the passengers can get off and you can make the boat ready to go on the trailer. Alternatively, if you've stopped for a picnic, I'd suggest anchoring your boat a short distance away from the beach after dropping off your passengers. Boats nuzzled bow-first against the beach look pretty in pictures. In real life, they get left stranded by a falling tide, or floated off by a rising tide, to be pushed sideways against the beach by the wind or waves. Even when you anchor your boat off the beach, you should keep a sharp eye on the water level to be sure a falling tide doesn't leave you stranded. The exception, of course, is on fresh-water lakes and other waters where there are no tides.

Testing What You've Learned
(Answers can be found in Appendix C)

1. Why do different types of boats not lie the same way on their moorings?

2. TRUE or FALSE: Always approach a mooring with the wind or current (whichever is the dominant force on your boat) behind you.

3. Why should you not try to pick up a mooring buoy from the stern?

4. TRUE or FALSE: You should wait until your boat has stopped moving forward before you lower the anchor.

5. TRUE or FALSE: You should generally drop the anchor quickly to be sure it lands exactly where you want it.

6. How can you tell how much anchor rode (line) to let out?

7. TRUE or FALSE: As long as you are going slowly, it's probably safe to drive your powerboat almost to the beach.

26

Closing Up Your Boat

More often than not, boaters headed back to the dock can be likened to horses returning to the barn: We take the bit in our teeth and head back, full-speed ahead. Once we arrive at the dock, we keep right on rushing to get the car loaded and headed for home. With effective planning, that "full-speed ahead" approach can work. As with any other activity, however, "haste makes waste." In the case of your boat, hurrying through the process of getting tied up (or back onto the trailer), and then closing up the boat, increases the likelihood of error that can come back to haunt you a few hours or days later.

Susan and I can vividly remember, for example, visiting our boat one Monday afternoon and noticing that the bilge pump in the 35-foot sailboat next to ours was cycling on and off every minute or two. When the yard crew investigated, they found water leaking into the boat through the head (toilet). The rim of the head bowl was situated an inch or two below the water-line, and if the valve on the head's pump mechanism was left open, water could siphon into the boat. Well, that's exactly what was happening. Had the battery run down before someone noticed the bilge pump cycling on and off, the boat could have sunk in her slip.

In talking to the boat's owners a week or two later, we found out that their young son had used the head just before they returned to the slip, and they had forgotten in the confusion of getting the boat closed up to be sure the boy had closed the valve.

Mishaps like this can happen easily. There are any number

of potential distractions when you're trying to get things together for the trip home in the car and, at the same time, closing up the boat.

For just that reason, the process of closing up your boat should be just as organized as the process of getting ready to take her out. In that way, you can leave the boat, confident that you haven't forgotten to take care of some detail that will haunt you later on—forgetting to shut a head valve, for example, or the valve to the propane tank. In addition, you can use the process of closing up to look for any maintenance needs your boat might have. As you identify those needs, you can either take care of them yourself or arrange for the boatyard to tend to them. In either case, by checking now, you can be certain they are taken care of *before* you next take out your boat, *before* they have opportunity to become problems.

At a minimum, what's required is a well-thought-out, systematic procedure for closing up. A better system employs a checklist so that you don't rely on your memory or on habit to get the job done correctly.

Begin by going through your boat methodically from bow to stern, both above deck and below, to be sure that all items are properly stowed—in other words, that all items are either put away where they belong or, if not, that they are left out in a deliberate manner. For example, you would normally gather all life preservers and put them in their lockers or stowage racks. If, however, some of your life jackets have gotten wet, you should stow them so that they can dry properly, rather than putting them away wet.

When that job is completed, you should have assembled everything that needs to go ashore—trash or garbage, as well as leftover food and various personal items—and ask your crew to take them ashore. Ideally, after that, you are left alone on the boat to run through your checklist without distraction.

Although the specific items on your checklist will depend upon what size and kind of boat you have, your list should take in all of your boat's "systems"—electrical, plumbing, fuel, engine, ventilation, and dock or mooring lines or anchor.

One added note: Unless it is food, water, or fuel, everything that you carry onto your boat should, at one time or another, be carried off your boat. I'm speaking particularly about cans, bottles, paper, plastics, and oil. All of these should be disposed of properly ashore. None should ever be thrown overboard. In fact, Coast Guard regulations now require every boat 26 ft long to display a placard relating to disposal of plastic trash. (See Appendix B, "Pollution Regulations")

ELECTRICAL

At the very least, you should make sure that all systems are turned off. On our boat, we turn off both the circuit breakers and the main battery switch. If you have an electric bilge pump, it should be wired outside of the main switch so that it can operate even when everything else on the boat is turned off. Depending upon where you live, the frequency of thunder and lightning storms, and your personal preference, you may also want to physically unplug electronic gear—radio, depthsounder, Loran, Sat-Nav, etc.—to protect them against lightning damage.

We used to believe that lightning strikes on boats were unusual. Statistically, they probably are unusual. But lightning does strike boats, particularly sailboats or powerboats with high towers or antennas. In the small marina where we kept our boat for several years, for example, boats were struck by lightning while in their slips in successive summers. Our boat was struck while 100 miles off the coast of Maryland en route to Bermuda. In all three instances, all electronic gear on the boats was damaged or destroyed, even though none of it was in use at the time the lightning struck. The only way I know of to protect against such damage is to have your electronic equipment unplugged from both the electrical system and any antennas.

PLUMBING

The plumbing systems you should be most concerned about when closing up are those connected to fittings that go through the hull below or near the waterline. I strongly recommend closing the valves on all through-hull fittings below the water-line. If your boat has underwater exhaust(s), I would also have seacocks fitted to them. It's a foolproof means of being certain that, while you're away, your boat won't sink from a failed hose, exhaust line, or secondary valve. Moreover, if you routinely close those values when getting ready to leave the boat, you're get-ting frequent feedback on their condition. If the valves begin to stiffen, you'll know it before they have frozen in position. And finally, when shutting those valves, it's a simple matter to check the condition of the hose clamps and hoses, both by look-ing them over and by feeling their condition with your fingers.

Finally, it's a good idea to pump the bilge before leaving the boat. If there's an unexpectedly large amount of water in the bilge, that will alert you to the possibility of a leak or of your automatic bilge pump not functioning properly.

FUEL

If you have a gasoline-powered boat with internally mounted tanks, you should have a valve in each fuel line where it comes out of the tank. You should close each of these valves before you leave the boat. At the same time, you should check the con-dition of the fuel lines.

With an outboard engine and removable fuel tanks, the tanks should be depressurized. I also recommend disconnecting the fuel hose at the engine, coiling the hose around the top of the fuel tank, and either taking the tanks from the boat or covering them with a protective fabric to shield the hose and tanks from the elements.

You should also shut off fuel to a stove, if your boat is equipped with one. With a pressure alcohol or kerosene stove, you'll have to open the pressure-release valve at the fuel tank. You should also open the valve that allows fuel to run to the stove to be sure that the entire stove fuel system has been depressurized.

If your stove uses propane or compressed natural gas (CNG), you should close the manual valve at the fuel tank. Do not rely on the solenoid valve. Although it is highly unlikely that the solenoid switch would fail to work properly, it's possible for some contamination to keep the solenoid valve from closing fully, and you wouldn't know it. For that reason, it's worth the small extra effort required to close the hand-operated valve at the top of the tank that serves as a backup to the solenoid.

While there are several differences between CNG and propane, the key difference from the point of view of safety is that CNG is lighter than air and will not collect in the bottom of your boat if a leak develops (CNG can, however, collect in a closed cabin if a leak develops). Propane, on the other hand, is heavier than air and can settle into the bottom of the boat if there's a leak; if that happens, the pool of propane vapor is a time bomb.

ENGINE

In all likelihood, the engine(s) will still be hot from running. As a result, this isn't a good time to check fluid levels. There are, however, two important visual checks to be made if your boat has an inboard or I/O engine system.

The first place to check is the oil drip pan. Every inboard engine is supposed to have an oil drip pan that will prevent oil leaking from the engine from getting into the bilge, where it could be pumped overboard with the bilge water. (As stated clearly on the placard required in your engine compartment by the Coast Guard, there is a $5,000 penalty for pumping oil or oily waste overboard.) You should look at the oil drip pan under your engine(s) for any unusual amount of drippings. You should also wipe the pan clean or replace the oil-absorbent pad periodically to make it easier to monitor the drippings. If there's an increase in the drippings, you should identify and correct the cause.

The second place to check is the stuffing box on your inboard installation or the rubber boot on your I/O system. (The stuffing box is an adjustable gasket-device around the propeller shaft where it goes through the hull. The stuffing box keeps water from leaking into the boat around the shaft, but allows enough water through when the propeller is turning to lubricate and cool the shaft as it rotates in the grasp of the "gasket.") While the stuffing box should allow two or three drops of water per minute while the propeller shaft is turning, it should drip not at all or only very, very slowly when the shaft is not turning.

The rubber boot around the drive unit of the I/O installation should be checked for cracks or tears. If you can inspect the installation from the inside, you should look for any signs of water leaking through. At the first sign of a leak or crack, you should have the system checked by an expert. A leak in the boot can sink your boat.

VENTILATION

While it's nice to have hatches and ports open for comfort in the cabin while you're on the boat, all hatches and ports should be closed securely when you leave unless they are protected from rain. It may seem an innocent mistake to leave a port open so that rain can get in when the only result will be the inconvenience of a wet berth or rain on the galley counter. The problem, however, is that rainwater getting into your boat through an open window or hatch can cause much more than inconvenience. Rain coming into the cabin has an insidious way of leaking into places where it can do serious damage—behind the woodwork into the electrical panel, for example. So, it's important to be certain that all exposed hatches, windows, and ports are closed securely. If additional ventilation is needed when your boat is closed up, you can install ventilators specifically designed to allow air to flow while blocking out rain. In fact, that's a good idea in any case.

DOCK AND MOORING LINES
OR THE ANCHOR

Whether your boat is in a slip, at a dock, on a mooring, or at anchor, the last thing you should do before leaving is to check all of the lines used to make the boat fast to be sure they are adjusted correctly and cleated securely. If you are anchored, you should also make a final check against landmarks to be sure the boat has not dragged anchor. If you are in a slip or tied to a fixed dock, be sure you have made allowance for the rise and fall of the tide. If you are in doubt, ask someone who works at the dock to be sure your dock lines will accommodate the tide changes.

Testing What You've Learned
(See Appendix C)

1. Develop a list of items you should remember to check each time you close up your boat. Test the list the next time you go to your boat, and adjust it as needed. Then, put the list somewhere on the boat where it will be handy for use at the end of every trip.

VIII

Trailering Your Boat

More than 95 percent of the pleasure boats sold in the United States each year can be carried on trailers. And, many of them are. For some people, the only practical way they can have a boat is to keep it on a trailer in the driveway or backyard. In some coastal areas, dockage and marina space is at a premium, and waiting lists for slips or moorings—even for dry storage—require a wait of two or three years or longer. For other people, trailering offers the only way to get their boats to the waters they want to enjoy—to inland lakes and rivers, for example. And for still others, the trailer makes boating more affordable by eliminating costly slip or mooring rental fees. Whatever the reason, the number of boat trailers on the road and at boat ramps across the country is increasing every year.

Along with its convenience and attractions, however, trailer-boating carries a price. That price is the personal responsibility of each trailer-boater to acquire an additional layer of knowledge and skill to ensure safe enjoyment of his or her boat. This section covers safety in towing a trailer, putting the boat into the water, taking it out, and readying both boat and trailer once again for the highway.

27

Over the Road

Getting from your home to the boat ramp and back again safely with the boat and trailer hitched behind your car involves three key elements. The first one is having the right equipment—a trailer that fits your boat, a car or truck that fits the loaded trailer, and the spare parts and equipment needed to handle likely problems. The second is maintaining your equipment properly and checking it out carefully before and during trips. The third element is knowing how to use your equipment—in this case, how to drive the rig safely over streets and highways.

THE RIGHT EQUIPMENT

In choosing your equipment, everything begins with the boat. Or, does it start with the car or truck that you'll use to haul the boat around? A case can be made for either approach.

Starting with the Boat: Until you decide what boat you're going to buy, it's difficult to choose a trailer. And, until you know what size trailer you need, you can't really determine how heavy a load you'll be pulling. Only then do you know how big your car or truck must be to haul your boat down the highway and up and down the boat ramps.

Starting with the Car: Unless you can afford to buy a new (to you) car or truck to suit your boat-trailering needs, the towing capability of your present vehicle will limit how much boat and trailer you can buy. Of course, you may be able to increase your car's towing ability by the kind of trailer hitch you install, by beefing up its suspension system, by adding extra cooling systems for your radiator and automatic transmission, and by beefing up your brakes. But, even so, you'll need to know the limitations of your car or truck as a towing vehicle before you go boat shopping so that you don't inadvertently purchase a boat-and-trailer system too big for you to pull safely. And, there's the key word—*safely*.

So, I ask you: Which comes first? The chicken or the egg? The car or the boat and trailer?

The point of this exercise, of course, is that trailer-boating involves a system consisting of two major components—the towing vehicle and the boat / trailer combination that it tows. Both components must work together. And both must be taken into consideration in choosing your equipment.

The Towing Vehicle

You can probably find something in your car or truck owner's manual that tells you the maximum weight you should tow with your vehicle. In general, you shouldn't try to tow a trailer that weighs more than your car. However, if your car or truck isn't set up for towing its own weight, even that may be too much.

Your chief concerns are stopping ability, strain on the transmission or wear on the clutch, engine overheating, and stability—that is, your car's suspension. All of these concerns can be taken care of by purchasing the right trailer or adding equipment to your car.

Trailer brakes can do a lot to increase stopping ability. It's also possible to increase the capability of your car's cooling system to prevent engine overheating, and to install a small radiator to keep the transmission fluid from overheating and thinning out, which might result in damage to your automatic transmission. Similarly, you can strengthen the suspension system by adding heavy-duty shock absorbers and, possibly, booster springs. You can use a "weight distribution" or "load equalizing" trailer hitch to help prevent overloading the car's rear end.

But if you have a standard transmission and your car or truck doesn't have the power to pull your boat out of the water on a

TABLE 27-1.   Trailer Hitch Ball Sizes

Ball Diameter	Shank of Ball Diameter	Maximum GVW* of Trailer
1⅞″	¾″	1,500 lbs.
2″	¾″	3,000 lbs.
2″	1″	5,000 lbs.
2⁵⁄₁₆″	1″	7,500 lbs.
2⁵⁄₁₆″	1¼″	10,000 lbs.
2⁵⁄₁₆″	1⅜″	13,000 lbs.

* GVW (Gross Vehicle Weight) represents the combined weight of the trailer and its load.

steep boat ramp without excessive wear on your clutch, you have a problem. In fact, if your car is underpowered, you may have a problem, even with an automatic transmission.

All these things must be taken into consideration, and the best advice is to be conservative: Do not try to get the largest possible boat / trailer system that your car supposedly will handle. Or, if the boat you want is simply too big for your car, bite the bullet and trade your car for something that can handle the load you want to haul. The risks involved in cutting corners here are not worth taking.

Assuming that your car or truck is adequate for the towing job, the remaining question involves the trailer hitch. Unless you are pulling a very light load for a short distance (say, just a few miles), you should not use a bumper hitch. The trailer hitch should be permanently attached to your car's frame. The size of ball required for your hitch depends upon the "Gross Vehicle Weight" (GVW) rating of your trailer. Table 26-1 shows the ball size to be used for different trailer weights. In all cases, the ball size must match the coupling.

The Trailer / Boat Combination

Although ideally the boat and trailer should be considered as a unit, most people focus on the boat first and think about the trailer second. It's not a bad way to go, as long as you don't stretch so far financially to get the boat that you end up skimp-

TABLE 27-2. Boat Trailer Classification
by gross weight of trailer and load (GVW)

Class 1—Gross weight of trailer and load (GVW) not to exceed 2,000 lbs.
Class 2—Trailer GVW between 2,001 and 2,500 lbs.
Class 3—Trailer GVW between 3,501 and 5,000 lbs.
Class 4—Trailer GVW more than 5,000 lbs.

ing on the trailer. Both are equally important when it comes to safety.

Normally, the dealer or builder will recommend one or more specific trailers. Alternatively, he may try to sell you the boat and trailer as a package deal. However, the ultimate responsibility for making sure that the trailer matches the boat belongs to you, not the dealer. As a result, it's worth acquainting yourself with the major considerations involved in selecting a trailer so that you can be sure the trailer included in that "low cost, once-in-a-lifetime package deal" really will meet your needs. Those considerations include the following:

• The trailer should be long enough that the stern of the boat is well supported. This is particularly important for outboard motorboats, where the full weight of the motor or motors is on the transom.

• Trailers are classified according to their weight-carrying capacity (Table 26-2). As a rule of thumb, if the combined weight of the trailer itself, the boat, the motor, and all the gear you'll carry in the boat adds up to 85 percent or more of the maximum weight for that class of trailer, you should go to the next higher class of trailer.

However, *trailers are not necessarily built to carry the maximum load allowed in their class. For that reason, you should check the specific GVW of the trailer you are considering.* If the trailer doesn't have a capacity plate on the frame, obtain the information from the papers that come with the trailer. If for some reason the GVW for that trailer is not shown with its papers or on a capacity plate, find another trailer. Finally, if the combined weight of the trailer, boat, motor, fuel, and all the gear you'll carry in the boat exceeds 85 percent of the trailer's GVW, go for a trailer with a higher GVW rating.

• Trailer tires also should be of a size to carry the load you'll be pulling. It would be surprising if they were not—particularly on a new trailer—but it's still worth checking. The capacity plate on the trailer should specify the tire size, and you can simply check to be sure the tires are the correct size. However, if that specification is not available for some reason, divide the GVW of the trailer by the number of tires and check the resulting weight against the load capacity printed on each of the tires. For example, if the GVW is 3,000 pounds and the trailer has two tires, the load on each tire is 3,000 divided by 2, or 1,500 pounds. The maximum load rating of each tire in this example should exceed 1,500 pounds by a significant amount. Going through the math may seem like you're carrying things a bit too far, but if you're buying a used trailer, someone may have tried to save a few bucks along the way by purchasing undersized tires. It's also possible that the wrong tires got put on the trailer by mistake somewhere along the line—not likely, but possible.

• If the gross weight of your trailer when it's fully loaded exceeds 1,500 pounds, the trailer should be equipped with brakes of its own. Many states—but not all—require brakes for loads exceeding 1,500 pounds. We would have them even if our state did not require it to reduce wear on our car's brakes and to give us emergency stopping capability.

• Trailer brakes are one of three kinds: surge brakes, electric brakes, or electrically controlled hydraulic brakes. I recommend against surge brakes for two reasons: There's a built-in delay in activating them that can cause your car and trailer to jackknife if you have to make a sudden stop; and, perhaps even more important, they don't work when you're backing up. As steep as some boat ramps are, we'd like to have our trailer brakes helping when we're backing down the ramp!

The best bet is to have electrically activated brakes that work right in sync with your car (or truck) brakes. If possible, it's also worth the extra cost to have an emergency breakaway system that will trigger the trailer brakes automatically if the trailer comes loose from the car.

• If the trailer does not come equipped with "bearing protectors" (also called "bearing buddies"), you should have them installed. Essentially, these are spring-loaded grease cups that keep your trailer wheel bearings fully greased all of the time, helping protect them from water intrusion.

• If there's any possibility that your trailer will be used around salt water—or even around brackish water—the trailer frame and axles should be made of galvanized steel or aluminum. Otherwise, you'll fight a losing battle against rust.

• The weight on the trailer tongue should be about 5 to 7 percent of the gross vehicle weight. This means that a boat, motor, trailer, and gear combination that weighs 1,000 pounds should be loaded so that the weight on the trailer hitch is at least 50 but no more than 70 pounds. Too little weight on the tongue may make the trailer sway back and forth as you go down the road. Too much weight on the tongue can have the same effect, but for a different reason: the excessive weight on the trailer hitch, combined with the weight of everything else that's loaded into the car, can make it difficult to steer.

Of course, the time to discover that the loaded trailer has too much or too little weight on the tongue is before you buy it, not afterwards. For that reason, before you close the deal, check the tongue weight after your boat (with the outboard or I/O unit mounted) is positioned properly on the trailer bed. Depending upon the placement of the wheels on that particular trailer, you may find that the weight distribution is not what it should be for your boat. In that case, you'll need to look for a different trailer.

You can "weigh" the weight on the hitch by putting the trailer tongue on a set of bathroom scales—assuming the tongue doesn't weigh more than about 250 pounds. You might put a piece of wood across the top of the scales to distribute the weight so that you don't dent or damage the scales when you "weigh" the trailer tongue.

• A trailer with a GVW of more than 1,000 pounds should be equipped with a wheel jack on the tongue that you can use to support the tongue when the trailer is not attached to the towing vehicle. The wheel jack will save much wear and tear on your back.

• The trailer's safety chains should be strong enough to carry well over the GVW rating of the trailer and be bolted securely to the trailer tongue. They should also be long enough to be crossed under the trailer hitch and attached securely to the car, but short enough that they won't drag on the ground.

• Supports for the boat—bunk boards or rollers—should be readily adjustable so that you can fit them to your boat. Bunk boards, which are simply padded boards used to help hold the boat in position, provide the best support, but the friction between them and the boat bottom makes it difficult to load or unload heavier boats. For that reason, trailers for heavier boats usually are equipped with banks of rollers to support the boat. However, rollers must be spaced so that support is spread out over a large area and not concentrated at a few small points, which might distort or stress the hull.

From bow to stern, the key areas to be supported are: (1) just under the bow, (2) along the keel, (3) along the chines, and (4) under the transom. If the boat has an inboard engine and tanks, the areas beneath them also should be well supported.

• The trailer must have tail lights, brake lights, turn signals, and a license-plate light. Ideally, the lights are mounted on a sturdy pole which keeps them out of the water. Alternatively, they're removable so that you can take them off before backing down into the water. Most often, however, the lights are bolted to the trailer frame just behind the wheels so that they're dunked every time you load or unload your boat. For that reason, at the very least, the lights should be sealed so that they cannot fill up with water.

• There must be means for tying the boat down to the trailer. As a minimum, tie-downs should be provided at the bow and stern so that the boat can't bounce in the trailer. With lighter boats, there should be provision for additional tie-downs along the sides of the trailer.

• The winch must have a positive brake on it. In addition, if the winch is electric, it should have a handle so that it can be operated manually if necessary.

• The trailer coupling should be matched to the GVW of the trailer. All couplings produced since 1973 are supposed to be marked with the GVW rating.

Spare Parts and Equipment

You don't need to bring many tools and spare parts when trailering your boat, but if something goes wrong and you don't have the right items—plus the know-how—to remedy the situation, you're out of luck. So, when you buy your trailer, be sure you also get the spare parts and equipment you'll need. Then practice with them at home so that you'll know how to use everything. If you don't, Murphy will surely strike. And, as sure as you're reading these words, the first problem with your trailer will arise on a dark, rainy night on a lonely country road twenty miles from the nearest telephone. So, have the spare parts and equipment with you, and know how to use them.

For the Towing Vehicle: The list is short, centering around two systems—your tires and your electrical system.

• **A full-sized spare tire.** Many cars today are equipped with under-sized "donuts" for spare tires that are intended only to get you to the nearest service station. Those "donuts" are not good for anything if you're pulling a trailer. So, spend the extra money to have a full-sized spare tire for your towing vehicle, and keep it properly inflated.

• **Chocks for your car wheels.** Wheel chocks have only one function—they keep your car (and trailer) from rolling either backward or forward, depending upon how you place them. You'll need two chocks, and I'd suggest buying them because they'll probably work more effectively than any you would make. These chocks are particularly important if you must park on a hill. They also may be useful on a boat ramp. It's embarrassing—not to mention inconvenient, expensive, and potentially dangerous—if the jostling from loading or unloading your boat starts your car and trailer rolling back into the water, even though you thought you had put the brakes on securely.

• **A good jack.** If you have a bumper jack, you should unhook your trailer if you have to jack the car up from the rear bumper. The added weight from the trailer may be more than the bumper jack (and bumper) are designed to handle. A hydraulic or screw-type "scissors" jack that fits under the frame is preferable.

• **A good lug wrench.** You'll probably need to get one of these from an auto-supply house; the one that came with your car is probably inadequate. It should be the cross-type lug wrench with the longest arms you can find. You may need the leverage to loosen the lug nuts. If your lug nuts are a metric size, be sure that your lug wrench also is metric.

• **Penetrating oil.** If the lug nuts are difficult to break loose, sometimes a squirt of penetrating oil and a few minutes of patience to let the oil do its job will make your task much easier.

• **Spare fuses.** You'll need spare fuses for all of the towing vehicle's light circuits as well as for the circuit carrying the electric brakes for your trailer (if your trailer is so equipped). Make sure you know which fuses in the fuse block serve the light and brake circuits so that you won't have to guess which fuse to replace if a problem arises. Any short in the trailer's wiring can blow fuses in the car.

For the Trailer: The list is only slightly longer. In addition to focusing on the wheels and electrical circuits, it also includes tie-downs for the boat.

• **A spare tire.** The spare tire for the trailer should be of the same size and rating as the main tires. Don't try to save a few dollars by getting a cheaper tire for a spare. Also, be sure to keep it properly inflated.

• **A good jack for the trailer.** The best is a hydraulic jack. A distant second-best is a screw-type "scissors" jack.

• **A good lug wrench.** The cross-shaped lug wrench for the car may fit the trailer lugs, too, but be sure that it does. If the lug nuts on your towing vehicle are metric, double-check the size of the trailer's lug nuts. If your trailer was made in the United States, chances are its lugs are sized in inches and you'll need a separate lug wrench for the trailer.

• **Penetrating oil.** The same can of penetrating oil you have for the towing vehicle will work for the trailer.

• **A spare set of wheel bearings.** If you back the trailer into the water when the bearings are hot, you could crack a bearing and find out later on that you have a problem. So, it's worthwhile to carry a spare set of bearings with you—a small effort that can pay big dividends.

• **Grease for your wheel bearings.** If you have "bearing buddies," you should carry a grease gun—loaded—so that you can top off the grease reservoir.

• **Spare bulbs.** You'll need spare bulbs for all of the trailer lights and the tools needed to change them. If not, the only light to burn out will be the one you don't have the spare bulb to fit—according to Murphy's Law.

• **Tools.** You should carry any tools required to adjust the supports for the boat—the rollers and the bunk boards.

• **Spare polyester rope.** Spare rope is always useful to help tie down the boat, just in case you misplace or damage one of your usual tie-downs. *Do not use nylon rope to tie down your boat.* Nylon stretches too easily, and the ties will soon become slack. I recommend polyester rope because it's easier on your hands and because you can tie secure knots more easily with it. Polypropylene rope can be used, but it is stiffer than polyester and more difficult to tie knots with reliably.

MAINTAINING AND CHECKING YOUR TRAILER

The amount of maintenance your trailer requires will depend to some extent on how you use it. For example, if you use your boat in salt water, you should hose your trailer down thoroughly at the end of every trip to help protect it from rust. If you take it down a lot of gravel roads, you'll probably need to touch up the paint on the frame, fenders, and axles frequently. Except for these kinds of special circumstances, however, your boat trailer probably won't require much day-to-day maintenance beyond lubricating the wheel bearings, rollers, winch, and any latching mechanisms—for example, the trailer coupling, the winch latch, and the latch for the tilt lock, if you have a tilt-type trailer. The electrical system needs little ongoing maintenance, just an occasional check to be certain all wires are taped or tied securely in place.

Every few months or so, however, you'll need to do a bit more. If you live where the climate requires that you winterize your boat, spring and fall will give you a nice maintenance schedule. If you're lucky enough to have year-round boating, you'll have to establish your own twice-a-year schedule. In either case, periodic maintenance should include the following. Some of these jobs must be done with the boat off the trailer.

• Remove light bulbs, clean and spray the sockets with a spray lubricant such as WD-40 or CRC, and put in new light bulbs. Clean and spray electrical connections with the WD-40 or CRC. Tie or tape up any wires that have come loose.

• Clean and spray the winch mechanism with the spray lubricant. Lubricate the winch bearings with a waterproof grease.

• Check the winch brake or latch mechanism to be certain it works properly. Although this should be a part of day-to-day maintenance, it's worth a special look every few months as well.

• Check that the winch rope or wire is securely fastened to the hook that goes in the bow eye when you're loading your boat. Also, check the full length of the winch rope or wire to be certain it's in good condition. If the rope is frayed, or the wire has any broken strands, replace it.

• Check that the safety chains are still securely fastened to the trailer and that the chain is in good condition. For example, if part of one chain has dragged on the pavement, a link may be worn thin and the chain should be replaced.

• Check tread wear on the trailer tires. The tires should wear evenly. If not, the wheels may need balancing. It's also possible, though less likely, that the wheels are out of alignment.

• Check the tire pressure and the condition of the valve stems. Valve stems do age and can be broken. Also, make sure all valve stems have caps.

• Remove the wheel bearings, clean them in mineral spirits, and examine them carefully. If you see any evidence of rust or pitting, replace the bearings. In any case, repack the bearings with grease. And if you don't have "bearing buddies," this is a good time to install them.

• Check the trailer brake linings, brake fluid level, and the brake lines.

• If your trailer has bunk boards, check the carpet or felt padding for wear and to be sure it is still securely fastened. If the padding is worn, replace it.

• Check the adjustment of the bunk boards or roller banks as well as the rollers under the keel to be certain all are supporting the boat properly. Adjust as necessary.

• Lubricate all of the rollers with waterproof grease.

• Double-check the trailer frame, axles, and wheels for rust spots.

Use a wire brush to remove any rust before touching up with paint. (If you've been touching up chips and scratches in the paint as part of your routine maintenance, you should have little to do here.)

• If you have a tilt-type trailer, lubricate the tilting hinges and the tilt latching mechanism.

• If you will be storing the boat for several months—for example, over the winter—jack up the trailer and put blocks under the frame to take weight off the wheels. Also, remove heavy items from the boat to help prevent hull distortion during the storage period.

THE PRE-TRIP CHECKLIST

Just as you need to check your boat and its systems thoroughly before heading out onto the water, you need to check your trailer / boat / towing vehicle system before you head out onto the road. In fact, when pulling a boat trailer, you should also stop after about ten minutes to do a second safety check. Here again, a checklist will help you be sure that you don't skip over something important.

Before starting from your driveway, or from the boat ramp for the return trip, your checklist should include:

Lights: You need to be certain that all lights are working. This means putting someone behind your trailer to check the tail lights, turn signals, and brake lights. It's important to check them in that order to be sure that your turn signals and brake lights are working while your car lights and trailer tail lights are turned on.

Trailer Hitch: You should also double-check that your safety chains are properly hooked up and the trailer coupling is securely fastened to the ball hitch.

Tires: You'll need to check the tires on both the trailer and the car. The car tires particularly may need air because of the added weight of the trailer. If they are low, you should head for a service station first thing.

Car Engine Fluids: Always—always—check your car's oil level, transmission fluid (if automatic), and radiator coolant level before setting out to haul your trailer more than a few miles.

The Boat: Finally, you should make sure that the boat is sitting squarely on the trailer, the tie-downs are tight, the winch brake or latch is set, the bow eye is tied to the winch drum with a separate piece of line as a back-up to the winch hook, and that there aren't any loose items in the boat that could be blown out by the swirling wind as you travel down the highway at 55 miles an hour.

Once you've started your trip—after your stop at the service station to put air in the tires, gas up, and add that quart of oil— you'll need to stop after about the first ten minutes of highway driving and every two hours thereafter to check your load. The two major things you'll need to check at these times are the boat tie-downs and the trailer hitch and safety chains—just to be sure all is secure. Because problems can develop.

BOAT FLIPS FROM ROAD, OVER BRIDGE, IN RIVER—A South Carolina man hadn't quite made it to the boat ramp when he "launched" his boat into the Cooper River.

This past spring, Lawrence Mundy of Windsor was towing his 16-foot Westwind, with a 115-hp engine, across the Silas N. Pearman Bridge, when the boat flipped out of its trailer and went over the side of the bridge.

After hitting the superstructure of the Charleston bridge in two places, it fell 180 feet into the river, said Petty Officer Greg Stannard of the Coast Guard's Charleston station.

Mundy's boat sank almost immediately, according to witnesses. It was unsalvageable by the time the Coast Guard got to the area a short time after the accident.

Stannard said it is not completely clear how the accident occurred. The trailer may have gone over a bump or hit the side of the bridge. The trailer came loose from Mundy's car and, after it skidded along the edge of the bridge for a while, the tongue caught on something, flipping the boat out of the trailer and over the side.[1]

Second-guessing on the basis of news reports is risky at best . . . but, if you've ever wondered why trailers have safety chains, or about the value of pulling off the road periodically and

1. *Soundings*, July 1986.

checking over your rig, that news story should answer your questions.

HOW TO PULL YOUR TRAILER

Pulling a boat trailer safely involves a lot more than hitching it to your car and setting off down the highway. As with operating your boat, pulling a trailer safely involves learning and practicing new skills.

One overriding fact of pulling a trailer is that you're driving a lot more weight than most of us are accustomed to pulling around or bringing to a stop. It takes longer to accelerate, so you have to allow more space for pulling out into traffic. It takes longer to slow down or stop, so you have to allow more space between you and the car in front. You also have to anticipate the need to slow down or stop well ahead of time so that you don't get caught trying to stop in a hurry. Unless your trailer also has a good set of brakes, you can jackknife the rig in a matter of seconds if you have to hit your brakes suddenly and hard.

Another overriding fact is that the rig is much bigger than most of us are accustomed to driving. Not only is the car / boat / trailer combination longer, it may also be taller. The extra length means that you have to allow more room to turn corners. The trailer will not follow the car; it cuts the corner short. If there is a curb in the way, the trailer will try to jump over it. If there is a tree, a telephone pole, parked car, or—heaven forbid— a person at the corner and your car gets around that obstacle but your trailer doesn't, the consequences could be very serious. So you have to swing corners wider than you're accustomed to doing.

The extra height could mean that your trailer is somewhat top-heavy—not a problem when you're going down the highway (unless there are strong crosswinds), but potentially very dangerous if you take a corner or an exit ramp too fast. The centrifugal forces involved in the turn can easily roll the trailer over. The difficulty is not hard to avoid: Simply drive a lot more slowly around those turns than you would in your car alone.

The third overriding fact of pulling a trailer is that it's sometimes too easy to forget that the trailer's back there. When you're riding down a highway, particularly if the car or truck is packed so that you can't see the trailer through your rear-view mirror, the whole rig can slip from your consciousness because it's just following quietly along behind you. *If that happens, you're an accident waiting to take place.* How do you stay aware of the trailer? Make sure that when you look in your rear-view mirror, you're looking right at your boat. If it's a small boat and hidden from view by the back of your car, mount a flag on the trailer next to the winch so that the flag is fluttering right in the middle of your rear-view mirror's field of vision. And, most important, pay attention to your driving.

How do you learn to drive your trailer? The same way that you learn anything else—by getting out and practicing, preferably at times when there is little traffic. Start slowly. Stop slowly. Follow at exaggeratedly long distances. Swing corners wide— but not so wide that you go into the lanes for oncoming traffic. And learn to use your mirrors, particularly the mirror on the passenger side of your car. (Backing up a trailer is discussed in the next chapter.)

Testing What You've Learned
(Answers can be found in Appendix C)

1. How do you determine whether your trailer should have its own brakes?

2. What is the advantage of putting "bearing buddies" on your trailer wheels?

3. What might make your trailer sway back and forth as you drive down the road?

4. List five pieces of equipment and / or spare parts needed for the towing vehicle.

5. List nine pieces of equipment and / or spare parts needed for the trailer.

6. List five things you should always check before starting to tow a trailer.

7. What precaution must you take when turning corners while towing a trailer?

28

At the Boat Ramp

Although you may not believe it if you've spent any time watching the activity around a boat ramp, getting your boat off and back onto your trailer is not difficult. When problems arise, usually they're the result of too little advance planning and too much hurry. As a result, someone either forgets to do something important—like putting the drain plug in the boat—or ignores the wind, current, or tide. As in other circumstances, however, these kinds of mistakes can be avoided by using a simple checklist. This chapter includes sample lists of steps involved in putting your boat into the water and in getting it back onto the trailer.

LAUNCHING YOUR BOAT

The most important thing when launching your boat is patience. Do not hurry. First of all, if you've driven more than a mile or so, you should wait at least a half-hour after getting to the launching area to let your trailer's wheel bearings cool down before backing your wheels into the water. As mentioned earlier, hot wheel bearings will simply draw the cold water right in past the grease, and you may get a cracked bearing as a result. So, if you can start off by accepting that you have a half-hour to kill before you try to launch your boat, you'll have plenty of time to work through the checklist—a real, written, step-by-step checklist that you carry right along with your spare parts and tools. (If you have a sailboat, you should not try to save time by rigging your mast now—but more about that later.) Your checklist might include the following:

1. Park your car and trailer, set your brakes, turn off the engine, and put your wheel chocks in place, if the parking area is sloped.

2. Walk down to the water's edge alongside the boat ramp. Note which way the current is running, what the wind is doing (if anything), and check out the condition of the ramp. If these are tidal waters, check the present tide situation and find out how much the tide rises and falls. It may be much more difficult to get the boat out at low tide.

3. If anyone else is launching or loading a boat, watch to see how his trailer and towing vehicle take the ramp. For example, does the ramp extend far enough into the water to launch the boat without the trailer wheels going off the end of the ramp? Is the surface of the ramp slippery with mud or slime so that the car has trouble getting up the ramp?

4. Think through in your mind what you will have to do with your car and trailer. Think about whether you'll need a stern line on your boat to hold the stern against the current or wind as the boat goes into the water.

5. Return to your boat, and take off and stow the tie-downs.

6. Install the drain plug.

7. Tie a line to the bow cleat, and hang the coiled line over the trailer winch.

8. If you've decided you need one, tie a line to the up-current or windward stern cleat, lead it forward, and hang the coiled line over the winch next to the bow line.

9. Be sure your drive unit or outboard motor is raised. If you have a sailboat, leave the mast and boom tied securely to the boat.

10. If you have a tilt-type trailer, release the latch pin for the tilt-latching mechanism.

11. Load any gear from the car into the boat.

12. If your trailer lights are removable, unplug them and take them off the trailer so they won't get wet. If they are not removable, unplug the lights at the trailer hitch; the brake-light bulb will heat up as you are backing down the ramp with your foot on the brake and may crack if cold water gets to it.

13. Assemble your crew, explain to them what you're going to do in launching the boat, and assign each of them their responsibilities. Be sure they understand not only what they're supposed to do, but why. If they know why they're doing the job, it may help them react correctly if something unexpected happens.

14. Review your checklist to this point. Literally, check each item off. If you've done everything so far, check your wheel bearings (put your hand on the hub) and, if they're cool, remove the wheel chocks and drive to the boat ramp.

15. When you've backed the trailer far enough down the ramp to launch the boat (but no farther), set the brake, turn off the engine, and leave the gear-shift lever in low (first) gear if you have a manual transmission and in "park" if an automatic. (Ideally, you can go far enough down that the back of the trailer frame is just in the water.)

16. Place the wheel chocks behind the front wheels of your car.

17. Walk back to the trailer winch, being careful that you do not fall if the boat ramp is slippery.

18. Give the bow and stern lines to your line handlers, who should be standing on the up-current or windward side of the boat.

19. Remove the short piece of line used to tie the bow eye securely to the winch drum as a back-up to the winch hook. Tie the line to the winch bracket so that it will be readily available for loading the boat.

20. Release the winch latch (or winch brake) and ease out enough slack in the winch line to take the hook out of the bow eye. (The winch line should be disconnected so that the winch handle doesn't whirl around like a propeller as the boat is pushed back on the trailer. Use the line you've tied to the bow cleat to control the boat if needed.)

21. Push the boat backward off the trailer and into the water. *Under no circumstances should you get into the boat and start the motor while it is partially on the trailer.*

22. Now that the boat is launched, leave her in the good hands of your line handlers, pull the wheel chocks from under your tires, put them in the car, and then drive the car and trailer to

the parking lot. Secure the car and trailer and go back down to your boat, which by now your crew will have pulled off to the side of the ramp. *Here you can begin checking the boat and safety gear before starting the engine, as outlined in Chapter 8.* If yours is a sailboat, now is the time to put up your mast.

LOADING YOUR BOAT

The logic behind the routine suggested for loading your boat is similar to that behind the launching procedures. First, don't hurry. Second, check out the situation ahead of time, and plan your moves. And third, use your checklist.

1. Bring your boat into the ramp area upwind or up-current from the boat ramp itself. In this way, the wind and / or current will help you move your boat to the ramp when it's time to load.

2. Shut down your engine(s) and raise your drive units for loading.

3. Turn off all electrical systems, and get your gear organized to be taken off the boat.

4. Tie one line to the bow cleat and a second line to the windward or up-current stern cleat. If the wind and current are contrary or there are a lot of waves, you may need two stern lines, one from each side.

5. If yours is a sailboat, take down your mast and tie it and the boom securely on the boat.

6. Get all your crew members ashore, and assign one or more of them to hold your boat in position with the bow and stern lines while you check out the boat ramp and plan the loading process. Whether your line handlers need to be in the water or can work from shore depends upon the specific nature of the launching area. What's important is that they can hold the boat in position for you.

7. Review with your crew all steps of the loading process so that they know what to do and why they are doing each step.

8. Go to the parking lot, start your car, and let the engine warm up for a few minutes. (You don't want the engine to stall at an awkward time because it was cold.)

9. While the engine is warming up, pull out the winch line,

hooking the end to the rear of the trailer. Also, check to be sure the tilt mechanism is unlatched, if you have a tilt-type trailer.

10. Review your checklist to this point to be sure you haven't forgotten something.

11. Drive to the boat ramp and back your trailer down the ramp, going only as far down as necessary to load the boat— generally until the back roller on the trailer is just about to get wet. Set the brake; turn off the engine, leaving the gear in first or park, whichever is appropriate; and put the wheel chocks behind your front wheels.

12. Walk down the ramp carefully so that you do not slip while your line handlers let your boat drift down to the trailer. Retrieve the hook from the rear of the trailer and hook it securely to the bow eye.

13. Go back to the winch, engage the winch latch or brake mechanism, and begin winding in the winch line. As the bow comes up to the first roller, instruct the person with the bow line to pull or slack off as necessary to bring the boat right up onto that roller.

14. As you continue to winch the boat onto the trailer, instruct the person with the stern line to pull in or slack off so that he (or she) keeps the boat lined up properly and the keel runs right up the center rollers.

15. Bring the boat in quickly, but be ready to pause if she starts to come onto the trailer incorrectly. If necessary, slack off a bit, get the boat lined up again, and resume winching. If there are a lot of waves, they can make it hard to keep the boat lined up. What's needed in that situation is good timing (winch quickly when the boat is lined up, stop winching as the wave knocks the alignment out, and resume winching quickly when the line handlers get the boat lined up again). A little patience helps a bit, too.

16. When the boat is fully loaded onto the trailer, check the winch brake or latch mechanism to be certain it's secure. Also, tie the bow line to the winch bracket as added insurance that the boat cannot slip backward off the trailer when you start up the ramp. Coil the excess bow line, and hang it over the winch.

17. Put the stern line securely into the boat.

18. After you're in the car and the engine is started, put your

foot firmly on the brake, and instruct your crew to remove the wheel chocks and step well clear of the car and trailer.

19. With the wheel chocks removed and all people clear of the car and trailer, put the car in gear and drive slowly to the parking lot.

20. After parking securely (using the wheel chocks, if necessary), remove the drain plug from the boat and unload any gear you will carry in the car. Also, remove the stern and bow lines from the boat.

21. Using the short piece of line, tie the bow eye securely to the winch drum as a back-up to the hook.

22. Put the drive unit in proper position for traveling.

23. Put on all of the tie-downs, being sure to pull them tight.

24. Latch the tilt mechanism securely.

25. Reconnect the trailer lights.

26. Review your loading checklist to be sure you haven't forgotten something.

27. Go to your pre-trip checklist to be sure your car, trailer, and boat are ready for the highway.

BOAT RAMP ETIQUETTE

Every institution has its own social rules, and the situation at boat ramps is no different. Knowing those rules can make life easier for you, help keep the peace, and be a source of some frustration. It can make life easier because you'll understand the system and be able to fit right into it. It can help keep the peace because you won't inadvertently make someone angry by messing up the system. It can be a source of frustration because you'll know it when someone else who doesn't know the rules starts fouling up the system.

The First Rule

Learn how to back your trailer before you get to the boat ramp.
Do not use the ramp area as a stage for learning. Instead, find a friend or acquaintance who knows how to back a trailer, and get that person to teach you how to do it. Then practice,

practice, practice—until you have it down pat. Even if you know how to back a trailer, get out and practice with your new boat trailer. The backing characteristics of every towing vehicle / trailer combination depend upon (a) the distance between the trailer wheels and the trailer hitch, and (b) the turning characteristics of the towing vehicle. As a result, every new combination of trailer and towing vehicle is a bit different than another.

So, practice, practice, practice. You might use a shopping center parking lot on a weekend morning before the stores open, or the local high school parking lot when it's not being used. You need to be able to back up in a straight line and to make both sharp and gradual turns while backing up. And you need lots of room for practicing. Then, try backing the trailer into your driveway—again and again, until you have it down pat.

The Second Rule

Get your boat ready for launching before you back it down the boat ramp.

The thoughtfulness behind this rule is that the less time you take at the ramp, the more quickly the boaters behind you can get into the water. This has a practical side, too: it gives you time to let your trailer wheel bearings cool down so they won't suck in the cold water. It also makes it easy for you to be very methodical. You can work down your checklist without the pressure of twenty other boaters waiting in line for you to get your rig out of their way.

The Third Rule

Get your car and trailer off the boat ramp and out of the way of other boaters as soon as your boat is launched.

This seems self-evident, but you'll be frustrated more than once by someone tending to his boat for several minutes before he gets around to moving his car and trailer from the boat ramp. The trick is to delegate to your crew either the job of pulling the trailer from the ramp to the parking area, or the responsibility for using the bow and stern lines to guide your boat off to the side, away from the ramp.

But, an observation: If you forget to use your wheel chocks and, as a result, your trailer and car slip back into the water, you will tie up the boat ramp for quite some time. Moreover, you'll get little sympathy from the many boaters you keep from putting their boats in the water because of your carelessness. So, remember to use those wheel chocks.

The Fourth Rule

Get both your boat and the trailer ready for hauling before you move your car and trailer to the boat ramp.

In this way, you won't tie up the boat ramp unnecessarily while you take care of details that could have been dealt with before you went to get your car and trailer. This preparatory work includes reviewing with your crew what each of them should do to help get the boat onto the trailer.

The Fifth Rule

Move your boat and trailer from the boat ramp to the parking area promptly after getting the boat onto the trailer.

If the ramp is slippery and you have a rear-wheel-drive vehicle, you can often increase traction for your drive wheels by putting two or three people in the back seat, or in the back of the truck over the wheels. If there's much water in the boat, it will also be a good idea to remove the drain plug so that the water begins to drain before you try to pull the boat and trailer up the ramp.

Following these rules and the checklists will get your boat in and out of the water with a minimum of fuss. But you aren't finished yet. Once the boat is out of the water and you've moved it safely to the parking area, you still need to make all of the preparations required for the drive home, as covered in Chapter 26. At the end of a day on the water, everyone in the crew—including you—will be tired and anxious to be headed home. As a result, there is strong temptation to hurry, taking shortcuts. But this is no time for shortcuts. Too often, shortcuts lead to difficulties that take more time in the long run.

SAILBOAT MASTS

Finally, there is one additional area of trailer-boating safety that applies specifically to sailboats. It involves sailboat masts and electrical wires.

NEW JERSEY PAIR ELECTROCUTED—A police detective and his 16-year-old son were electrocuted in Waretown, New Jersey, when the aluminum mast of their catamaran touched overhead electrical lines.

Detective John Francis Maybank, 39, and John Francis, Jr., were killed July 18 when the mast of their 16-foot catamaran touched overhead electrical wires near their new home on Custer Drive. They were walking their sailboat on its trailer down the street in an attempt to launch it on Barnegat Bay.

Workers at the scene said the trailer and the victims were in the middle of the street under the electrical wires. At least one of the victims was holding the trailer hitch when electrical contact was made, according to Police Chief William T. Snedon.[1]

Although the accident in this report did not happen at a boat ramp, many like it have happened at boat ramps or even at yacht clubs or marinas—anywhere that there have been overhead electrical wires and sailboats on trailers.

There is only one way to avoid this kind of accident: *Do not put up your mast until after the sailboat is safely in the water*—and then only after you've checked to be sure there are no electrical wires crossing over the water in the area of the boat ramp. Similarly, take the mast down *before* loading the boat onto the trailer.

The temptation is strong to save time by putting up your mast while you are waiting for ramp space or for your wheel bearings to cool, or to get the boat out of the water quickly and then take down the mast. But, resist it—even if you don't see any wires overhead. If you *never* put up your mast while the boat is on the trailer, and *never* pull the boat out with the mast standing, you cannot make a mistake by not seeing an overhead wire. Also, if you find a boat ramp at which there are any overhead wires in either the ramp area, the parking lot, or across the

1. *Soundings*, October 1986.

road joining the two, report the wires to the state boating safety office. Your report may help prevent tragedy for someone else.

Testing What You've Learned
(Answers can be found in Appendix C)

1. Why is it generally best not to back your trailer into the water as soon as you have arrived at the launching area?

2. If you do nothing else, what is the one thing you should do before you back your trailer and boat down the launch ramp?

3. TRUE or FALSE: Wheel chocks need to be placed behind the front wheels of the towing vehicle only when the boat ramp is slippery.

4. TRUE or FALSE: Your line handlers should be upwind or upcurrent of the boat and be holding their lines before the boat is pushed off the trailer.

5. TRUE or FALSE: When you are taking your boat out of the water, you should crank the winch rapidly and not stop cranking until the boat is all of the way onto the trailer.

6. What is the best time to step the mast when you are launching a sailboat from a trailer? Explain your answer.

IX

Boat Maintenance

Keeping your boat in safe operating condition is as important as anything else for maximizing the enjoyment that you, your family, and friends derive from your outings. For example, it is neither safe nor fun when, out in the middle of a thunderstorm or a rough inlet, your engine runs out of oil and seizes because you haven't bothered to check the oil. It's neither safe nor fun when a hose fails and seawater starts pouring into your boat because the valve on the through-hull fitting is frozen open as a result of your neglect—or when you find yourself out on the water after dark and discover that your running lights don't work. But all of these things and many more happen to boaters virtually every day of the year. Why? Because too many of us don't pay enough attention to our boats' maintenance needs.

From the perspective of safety, boat maintenance could be called "preventive maintenance." What you're trying to do, after all, is *prevent* problems from arising while you're out on your boat, away from the safety of your marina or the boat ramp.

Boat maintenance involves three fundamental activities: (1) continually checking your boat, its systems, and equipment to be sure they're all in good working order; (2) correcting deficiencies promptly when they're discovered; and (3) performing routine service on your boat's systems—for example, changing the oil and checking the condition of your anchor lines.

The first two maintenance activities—continually checking your boat and correcting deficiencies—have been covered in earlier sections. Chapter 8, for example, presented a systematic approach to checking out your boat and equipment so that deficiencies can be corrected before leaving the dock or boat ramp. A similar approach to inspecting your boat and its systems at the end of your boating day is described in Chapter 26.

This section wraps up the subject of maintenance by reviewing the service requirements for the basic systems of your boat—including the engine, the fuel system, the propeller-shaft system (shaftlog and cutless bearing), the steering system, through-hull fittings and shut-off valves, hoses and hose connections, the potable-water system, the electrical system—as well as the hull itself, required and recommended safety equipment, and lines (dock lines, anchor lines, and spare lines). Procedures for both winter storage and spring commissioning are covered for each system. Finally, I'll describe a novel approach to performing your pre-launching checkout.

29

Keeping Your Boat in Safe Operating Condition

Talk about boat maintenance with any group of boat owners, and you'll get reactions ranging from love to hate, and then to disdain. Anything between "love" and "hate" is probably OK, because it suggests that people are probably maintaining their boats adequately. Anything approaching "disdain" is suspect, however, because it suggests that boat maintenance is ignored— until something goes wrong. By the time something does go wrong, depending upon the situation, that boater may well find himself or herself between a rock and a hard place. For example, the Coast Guard files, as well as those of private boat-towing services, are filled with reports of rescues required because boat engines have failed. And apparent leaks in fuel systems have resulted in far too many boat fires. While it is not possible to attribute the cause of the incident described in the following newspaper article to a neglect of maintenance, the incident illustrates the potentially severe consequences of failing to maintain your boat's fuel system in a way that prevents gasoline leaks.

TWO SAVED IN BOAT EXPLOSION—Two persons were pulled unharmed from the Metedeconk River after their boat exploded and sank.

The owner, Ronald Marchak, and a passenger, Janice Lovullo, both of Nutley, New Jersey, jumped overboard when their 23-foot Century cabin cruiser burst into flames September 14 about 100 yards off the Wehrlen Brothers Marina in Brick Township.

They were plucked from the water by the operator of another pleasure boat.

The boat was westbound when the engine stalled, according to Marine Police Officer Janet Gilrain. Marchak opened the engine cover and discovered a fire.[1]

Some of the work involved in boat maintenance, of course, can be delegated. You may want your boatyard to service your engine, for example, if you're unsure about what needs to be done. Or, while you may feel competent to change the oil and filter, you may want a mechanic to do the periodic servicing recommended in the owner's manual. It's much like taking your car to a mechanic for the 15,000-mile checkup.

But, for all the work that you can hire out, the one thing you cannot delegate is the responsibility for recognizing when work is needed, getting that work done, and ensuring that it's done correctly. This means that you have to understand your boat's servicing needs; it also means that you need to review work that's been done with the yard foreman before you pay the bill to be sure the job has been completed correctly.

The service requirements for your boat depend, of course, on specifically what kind of boat you have. Some of those service needs are ongoing; others are seasonal. The suggestions that follow include recommendations for both regular and seasonal maintenance. They cover the basic systems and equipment found on most boats, beginning with the hull and continuing on through to key safety equipment.

THE HULL

If your boat normally is kept in the water during boating season, the only time you have a chance to look at the hull is when it's out of the water, blocked up for storage. If your boat is also

1. *Soundings,* October 1986.

kept in the water during the off season, your only chance may be the couple of days it's out of the water to have the bottom painted. Even if you keep the boat on a trailer, you can't really get a good look at the bottom until the boat is off the trailer for painting; otherwise, the trailer's framework and supports get in the way. Whatever your situation, you need to look at your hull closely each chance you get.

In principle, the best time to go over the hull is right after your boat has been blocked up and made ready for storage. Since the boat will be out of service anyway, there is ample time to do whatever needs to be done if you find any problems. In practice, however, most people seem to wait until it's time to get the boat ready for the new season before pausing to take that good, hard look at the hull. Whenever you do this, there are three key things you'll need to look for in checking your fiberglass hull: blisters, cracking, and deformation.*

Blisters

Gelcoat blisters are almost commonplace in fiberglass boats that spend much time in the water. They begin to appear as small, raised spots the size of a pencil eraser or smaller. You look for them by running your finger tips lightly and your eyes carefully over every inch of your boat below the waterline, looking for innocent little bumps. There may be a lot or a few; and they may be isolated or clustered. In any case, undiscovered or ignored, they can grow to the size of your hand and reach deep into the fiberglass structure of your hull. If your boat does not now have blisters, I suggest that you remove the bottom paint and apply a two-part epoxy water-barrier coating to prevent— or at least delay—their development. If you do find blisters, I suggest that you circle the areas with a marker pen and seek a second opinion from someone who is knowledgeable about gel-

---

* Wooden and metal hulls need similar examination. However, maintenance of wooden and metal hulls is outside the author's area of competence. I would suggest enlisting your local marina operator to advise you on the maintenance of a wooden or metal hull. You could also consult books about wooden boat construction and maintenance as well as *WoodenBoat* magazine, which regularly carries articles about the care and maintenance of wooden boats.

coat blisters. Assuming they really are blisters, get them repaired or repair them yourself—but do it before the boat goes back in the water. If you let them go until "next year," the problem will become much worse, and the repairs will be much more costly.*
Warning: If you do any work on your boat that involves the use of solvents, paints, or resins, carefully follow the manufacturer's recommendations for safe use of the product.

Cracking

Cracking in your hull most likely will come from one or more of three sources: (1) The gelcoat may craze, simply from age and the rigors of use; (2) the gelcoat and, subsequently, the hull laminate itself may crack from flexing over a "hard spot" in the hull; and / or (3) the gelcoat and laminate may be cracked by some external stress—running into a floating log, inadequate support on a trailer, or even being blocked up improperly for storage.

Crazing consists of a spidery web of hair-like surface cracks in the gelcoat. Generalized crazing is easily corrected by removing all paint from the bottom and applying two or three coatings of a two-part epoxy water-barrier coat. Cracks caused by the hull's flexing over some interior component require major repair that should be done only by an expert. You can identify areas where such cracking may occur by looking along the lines of the hull for irregularities in the surface. Any place you see an irregularity that can be matched up with an interior structural member or component (e.g., the galley floor or a bulkhead), you've identified a "hard spot" that should be checked each year for signs of crazing or cracking in the gelcoat. Surface crazing in that area may be a warning that more serious cracking is developing.

Deformation

Deformation is caused by blocking a boat improperly during storage, or from putting it on the trailer incorrectly and letting

---

* For more detailed information about fiberglass repairs, see *Fiber Glass Boats: Construction, Repair and Maintenance* by John Roberts, W. W. Norton, New York, 1984.

it sit that way for a period of time. The result can be serious permanent changes in the shape of the hull, with resulting structural stresses. This kind of damage simply must be repaired. It's important, however, to try to identify the cause of the damage. If, for example, the damage is related to your trailer, you may need to change the trailer supports. Or, you may simply need to make sure the boat is sitting on the trailer properly before storing it. If the boat has been blocked up improperly so that excessive stress was put on some section of the hull, you'll want to be sure the mistake is not repeated. Even if your hull is not damaged, part of your preventive maintenance should include routinely checking the way your boat is supported in storage to be sure the hull will not be deformed or otherwise damaged through inadequate or improper blocking.

ENGINES

Periodic maintenance for your boat engine(s) falls into two categories. The first is the maintenance recommended in your owner's manual, usually on the basis of "engine hours." The second is seasonal maintenance that should be done whether or not it's called for on the basis of engine hours.

With regard to the first category, you should follow the recommendations in your owner's manual scrupulously. While it may take some adjustment to get used to scheduling maintenance on the basis of "engine hours," you can help yourself by keeping a separate engine log in a spiral notebook. It is much like keeping a diary, only you make entries about your engine's operation and maintenance. If your boat is not equipped with an engine-hour meter, you can keep track of how many hours your engine is operated by noting the time you start the engine and shut it off each day and staying up to date with a running total of the engine hours.

You can also use the engine log to keep track of oil consumption, average hourly fuel consumption, and a history of your maintenance activities. Susan and I did not maintain such a log for the first few years we had our present boat, because the engine was used so little that it didn't seem necessary. The first summer that we began to cruise more extensively, our casual approach almost proved expensive when we very nearly ran our engine dry of oil. Since that experience, we have found that our engine log is useful not only for keeping track of maintenance needs, but also for keeping tabs on the overall condition and performance of our engine.

Engine Maintenance Before Storage

Seasonal maintenance is somewhat different than operational maintenance in that the need for it is based on disuse rather than use. In other words, the fact that your boat will be idle for several months means that different maintenance is needed before it goes into storage than what is required before it's put back into commission.

Your owner's manual probably includes directions for winterizing your engine(s). You should follow those procedures closely. At the minimum, you should do the procedures outlined below—and in the order presented.

Cooling System: Whether or not you live in a climate where temperatures drop below freezing, you should flush your engine's cooling system with a 50 / 50 mixture of antifreeze and fresh water before storing your boat for the off season. While the cooling systems of outboard engines probably will drain completely, inboard engines are best left with fresh antifreeze mixture throughout the cooling system to reduce rusting.

To ensure that the fresh antifreeze mixture gets to all parts of the cooling system, you should let your engine run long enough to reach a normal operating temperature. This means recirculating the antifreeze mixture until it becomes hot—no problem at all if your engine has a fresh-water cooling system, a little more complicated but still easily done if your engine is cooled directly by seawater.

If your boat is equipped with fresh-water cooling, you should also flush the raw-water side of the system with the antifreeze mixture, particularly if there is any possibility of below-freezing temperatures. In that way, the raw-water pump will be left filled with the antifreeze mixture.

Exhaust System: Be certain that you flush an antifreeze mixture through the exhaust system so that your muffler is left filled with antifreeze. If you have a seacock on your exhaust through-hull fitting, close the seacock after shutting down the engine for the last time. Otherwise, put a wooden plug securely in the open end of your exhaust pipe to close off the system.

Fuel System: Before storage, the primary objective in preparing your fuel system for months of disuse is to prevent the accumulation of moisture in the fuel tanks and, in gasoline engines, to prevent the formation of "varnish" in the carburetor or injector system.

Portable fuel tanks can be emptied into your automobile's gas tank and stored upside down with the cap off in an area having good ventilation. In this way, any residual gasoline will evaporate and the fumes will run down out of the tank to be dispersed.

You can protect fixed fuel tanks—that is, tanks that are not portable—by filling them immediately before winterizing the engine. This will leave little or no air space in the tanks for condensation of moisture. As during the boating season, you should not fill the tanks to the brim, however. You need to leave room for expansion and contraction of the tank walls with the temperature changes.

When running the antifreeze mixture through the cooling system, you should turn off the fuel supply on gasoline engines and allow them to "run out of gas" so that the carburetor bowl and valves are left empty during the off-season. Diesel engines should be shut down normally, leaving the fuel system filled.

Engine Oil and Filter: After flushing the cooling system, you should change the engine oil and the oil filter. It is easier to pump oil from the crankcase if you change the oil while the engine (and, therefore, the oil) is still warm. If you have an outboard, you should follow the owner's manual's recommendations for lubricating the cylinder heads and pistons.

Engine Belts: Remove the engine belts. This enables you to inspect them carefully. It also relieves pressure on the bearings of the alternator and any other belt-driven accessories. Do not replace the belts until commissioning time; in that way, you can't forget to tighten them.

Air Filters: Remove the air filters, and shoot some spray

lubricant into accessible air-intake throats. Plug the air-intake throats with oversized rags—oversized so that you can't possibly forget to remove them when commissioning the engine(s) before the next boating season. Permanent-type air filters should be cleaned using kerosene or mineral spirits during the off season. *Do not use gasoline to clean air filters.* Disposable air filters should be changed.

Alternator and Starter Motor: Apply a liberal mist of spray lubricant to protect wiring, etc., from moisture during storage.

Ignition System: Spray the exterior with WD-40. Other maintenance should follow the recommendations of the owner's manual.

Engine Maintenance Before Spring Commissioning

In part, spring-commissioning engine maintenance involves completing jobs started when the boat was put into storage. This means removing any rags from air-intake throats and replacing the air filters. Similarly, it means replacing the engine belts—either putting on new belts or, if still in good condition, reinstalling the old ones—and adjusting them as recommended in the owner's manual. In addition, after running the engine for the first time, you'll have to check the oil. Running the engine the first time will fill the new oil filter, leaving the level in the engine a bit low if you did not add extra oil earlier to compensate for that. Before starting up the engine, however, your engine has additional discrete maintenance needs.

Cooling System: You should replace the water-pump impeller(s) in your engine's cooling system at the beginning of each new boating season. The reason for this recommendation is that a breakdown in your engine's cooling system puts the engine out of service. And, the impeller is the weak part in the system.

The water-pump impeller is essentially a small, rubber paddle wheel used to pump cooling fluid through your engine. And the rubber gets tired. Moreover, if the engine lies idle for several months, the rubber blades of the paddle wheel take on a set that may make them less efficient. In any case, your owner's manual will recommend replacing the impeller after a certain number of engine hours. Even if the impeller had to be replaced late during the previous boating season and was used for only a small number of engine hours before the boat was put into storage, it is good practice to replace it as part of your new-season commissioning process.

What difference does it make? As the rubber blades on the paddle wheel fatigue, pieces break off and are pushed into the cooling system, where they can get stuck and block the flow of cooling water. So, changing the impeller is cheap insurance.

Fuel System: Dirt or water in the fuel is the most likely cause of problems with diesel engines. As a result, you should start the new boating season by replacing all fuel filters—even if you don't think you need to change them. It's another bit of inexpensive insurance. However, recognize that you probably will have to bleed air from the fuel system to get your diesel engine started after changing the filters. Dirt in the fuel can also stop a gasoline engine, so it's worth the effort to change or clean the element in the fuel filter of a gasoline engine, too. Finally, once your engine is running, check the filters to be sure there are no fuel leaks.

• If you have portable fuel tanks, three areas will need to be checked. First, inspect the exterior surface for signs of rust. Any rust spots, or scratches in the painted surface where rust might begin, should be sanded clean and painted with a rust-inhibiting paint. If the rust is substantial, take the tank to an expert for advice; it may be a candidate for replacement.

Second, check the inside for dirt. The tank has had months to dry out, and any dirt should be obvious. The difficult part is getting it out.

Third, check the fitting for the fuel hose, to be sure it is secure and clean.

• If you have fixed fuel tanks, you should first check the condition of the hose and hose clamps that connect the fill pipe on the deck and the fill pipe of the fuel tank. The hose should be firm, free from chafe, and the hose clamps secure. If you find that the hose is chafing, or it is soft or mushy when you squeeze it, the hose needs to be replaced. Also, if chafe is evident, you'll need to correct the situation that is causing it.

Second, check out the tank's air vent. The air-vent hose also should be firm, chafe-free, and its hose clamps secure. You'll need to check the outside end of the vent to be sure a mud wasp or other insect has not plugged the system. Here, too, you should make corrections as needed. If in doubt, ask for advice from an expert.

Third, you'll need to check the tank itself and the brackets or straps used to hold it in place. If you find rust or signs of corrosion here, get advice from an expert.

• The final link between your fuel tank and engine consists of the fuel line itself. Every inch of this line—or these lines, if you have more than one tank—should be checked carefully for signs of chafe if they are rubber, or evidence of embrittlement if they are copper. The embrittlement is caused by flexing or vibration and is noticeable because the surface texture of the tubing loses the super-smooth sheen that characterizes healthy copper tubing, and begins to look grainy instead. Similarly, all joints and fittings need to be inspected carefully to be sure they are tight and not leaking. For the record, all lines—fuel lines, air-vent and fill-pipe lines—should come from the top of your tank. If any come from the side, end, or bottom of the tank, you would be wise to replace the tank. Not only is it difficult or impossible to turn off the fuel on tanks with side or bottom fittings, but any leakage is much more difficult to detect.

Gasoline Engine Ignition System: Your gasoline engine's ignition system deserves special attention because of the harsh marine environment. For that reason, your engine should be given a complete tune-up as part of the spring-commissioning process. Specific recommendations as to what a tune-up involves for your particular engine are contained in your owner's manual. At the least, it's a good idea to start the season with new spark plugs. You should also check all ignition wires carefully; if they have gotten stiff or developed cracks in the insulation, they should be replaced.

Sometimes, too, you'll find new problems when you try to start your gasoline engine after the long winter lay-up. If these problems involve replacing any engine parts—for example, the alternator, distributor, starter motor, starter solenoid, or any accessory motor—*do not use automotive parts*. It's tempting to use automotive parts because they are almost always much cheaper than marine parts. But, *it's very dangerous to use automotive parts on your boat's engine.*

The Coast Guard has established "Electrical and Fuel System Standards" which mandate significant differences in these components, compared to those made for cars, to reduce the risk of fire and explosion from gasoline fumes in your boat's engine compartment. For example, automotive alternators, starters, starter solenoid switches, and accessory motors have either exposed contacts, exposed brushes, or vent holes which allow sparks that could trigger an explosion on your boat. The marine versions of these parts are sealed so that no internal sparks can escape. Although carburetors and fuel pumps are obviously not part of the ignition system, similar risk exists with using automotive versions of these on your boat's engine. Carburetors and fuel pumps made for automotive use have vents that can leak gasoline into the engineroom, creating an explosive condition. (Remember the gasoline smell the last time you flooded your car's engine?) So, yes, the marine versions are more expensive, but they are also safer.

ENGINEROOM VENTILATION SYSTEM

All boats with inboard engines in enclosed spaces must have adequate ventilation systems. These systems, which are more often than not neglected, frequently use 3- or 4-inch-diameter thin plastic clothes-dryer exhaust hoses to provide airways from the engine compartment to the deck ventilator by way of stowage lockers. As a matter of practicality, these hoses may be torn or even pulled away from the deck vents from the abuse they receive as items are put in and out of the lockers, or tossed around in rough waters. So, at least once each year—preferably as part of spring commissioning—you should check all of these hoses and vents to be sure that air has an unobstructed pathway between the deck vents and the engine compartment. It's also a good idea to make sure that no creatures have set up housekeeping in one of your ventilators; stranger things have happened.

PROPELLER-SHAFT SYSTEM

If your boat is an I / O, this is the time to take a very close look at the rubber boot that surrounds your drive system where it comes through the transom. Even though you check this boot regularly during the boating season, you should take extra time to inspect it carefully while commissioning the boat for the new season. Now, when you are not hurried and there's plenty of time to make repairs if they're needed, is the best time to find the first signs of aging, or cracking in the rubber.

If your boat is an inboard, you have three things to check—two before the boat goes into the water, the third after it's been launched.

Before Launching

The two items to check while the boat is on land are the cutless bearing and the stuffing box. The cutless bearing is just forward of the propeller, either in the hull where the shaft emerges, or in a strut that helps support the shaft. In either case, the shaft should be snug in the bearing. If you can grab the propeller and wiggle the shaft sideways or up and down in the bearing, it probably should be replaced; consult with an expert.

The stuffing box is the gasket device that keeps water from leaking into the boat alongside the propeller shaft. What you can see when you look at the propeller shaft where it comes into the boat is a large, bronze nut surrounding the shaft. That nut can be tightened down on a threaded bronze tube. The bronze tube, in turn, is secured into a short length of heavy, black hose with two hose clamps. Finally, the hose is clamped securely over the inboard end of a tube (the so-called "shaftlog") permanently fitted into the hull to form the opening for the propeller shaft to go through the boat's bottom.

The actual "stuffing box" is the small area inside the nut where it tightens on the bronze tube. The nut is hollowed out so that two or three wraps of a heavy, greased "rope"—on our boat, about ¼ inch in diameter—can be placed around the propeller shaft inside the nut. As the nut is threaded onto the bronze tube and tightened, the greased rope is compressed around the shaft, creating a gasket in which the shaft can turn, but which generally keeps water from passing. In fact, if it is tightened correctly, no water will get through when the engine has been turned off, and only two or three drops per minute will come through to help lubricate the system when the propeller shaft is turning at cruising speed.

Key point: Periodically, the "stuffing" in the stuffing box needs to be replaced. Usually, that time will come after a season in which you've had to tighten the nut several times to keep too much water from coming through. The time to replace the "stuffing" is while the boat is out of the water. A note of caution: Normally, you need to tighten the stuffing-box nut only a small fraction of a turn to slow the drip to an acceptable level. If you tighten down on it too hard, the shaft will overheat, burning the greased rope in the stuffing box so that the gasket becomes hard and ineffective. Also, a groove can be worn into the shaft. So, tighten stuffing boxes as little as necessary.

After Launching

Many boats—power and sail—with inboard engines are susceptible to having their propeller shafts and engines put out of alignment during off-season storage on land. The problem is simple: When the boat is in the water, the hull is supported all around by the water. When on land, most of the weight rests on the keel; as a result, to some small extent, the rest of the boat settles down around the keel. Over the period of months, a misalignment between the propeller shaft and engine may occur.

For that reason, you should check your shaft alignment—or have it checked—after your inboard boat has been back in the water for a few days, but before you take off for your first day's run. If the alignment is out more than three or four thousandths of an inch, the resulting stresses can damage an oil seal, prematurely wear your cutless bearing, or even lead to a breakdown. Again, I speak from experience. One Sunday afternoon, although our engine continued chugging merrily, we suddenly found ourselves going nowhere. We soon discovered that the coupling between our engine and propeller shaft had failed. After sailing back to our slip at the marina, we found that the bolts connecting the shaft / engine coupling had become loose and then had sheared. Exploring further, we found the shaft alignment out significantly. The following winter, we also had to replace the cutless bearing. We have learned our lesson.

ELECTRICAL SYSTEM

When you're getting your boat ready for storage, there are three key maintenance points for your electrical system that can help prevent problems from developing while the boat is in storage. First, it's a good idea to remove your boat's electronic equipment and take it home for the winter. Most of the time, atmospheric conditions will be better in your home than they will in your boat while it's in storage; as a result, the opportunity for moisture or corrosion damage to your electronics will be reduced. Second, you should protect your electrical panel—and as many of the electrical connections as you can reach—from moisture during lay-up by opening them up, spraying with WD-40 or another similar product, and then closing them up again. This will provide a protective film without interfering with the conductivity of the system. This chore includes taking light bulbs out of sockets, spraying the sockets, and putting the bulbs back. And, third, you should charge your batteries, preferably using a slow charger. Depending upon how heavy they are, you might also take them home where you can keep them warm. In extremely cold winter climates, batteries should be kept indoors, in any case.

Commissioning maintenance for the electrical system is geared toward making sure all systems are ready for the new boating season. While boats differ in the size and complexity of their electrical systems, these five maintenance steps apply to most boats of about 16 feet long or longer:

• Check your battery's charge as well as its water. If the charge has dropped significantly over the storage period, you should have it checked to be sure it is still able to hold a charge adequately. If there's any doubt, get a new battery. In any case, be sure the battery has a full charge when you put it back into your boat. In addition, you should clean the battery posts and battery-cable connectors to ensure a good, clean electrical connection.

• Take the time to go over every inch of wiring in your boat. You are looking for signs of chafe or cracks in the plastic insulation on the wires. You're also looking for any sign of corrosion at connectors. If chafe is found, you may have to replace that section of wire; in any case, you'll need to take action to eliminate the chafing. An electrical short can easily start a fire on almost any boat.

• Check all lights—particularly the running lights and anchor light. I recommend removing the lens and changing all bulbs, spraying WD-40 into the socket before putting in the new bulb, and then turning on the light to make sure it's working before and after putting it back together. If you do this on a cool, low-humidity day, you might use a silicone caulk to seal the light fixture against moisture when you reassemble it. By doing this, we've had excellent success in keeping the interior of our running lights looking in new condition. A note of caution: If you have a sailboat that is stored on land with the mast standing, do not go up the mast to service any lights until the boat is in the water. In any case, do not go up the mast unless you are certain that it, your halyard (including the masthead block), and your winch are strong enough to handle the load. If in doubt, consult with your marina about alternative ways to service the lights on your mast.

• If your boat is normally kept in the water and you have any metal parts below the waterline—e.g., bronze through-hull fittings, propeller shaft and propeller, or I/O drive unit—your boat should be equipped with sacrificial zincs to protect those underwater metal parts from galvanic corrosion. If your boat does not have any zincs, consult with an expert at your marina about the possible need for them. If it does have one or more zincs, you should replace them before each boating season, even if they've been only partially consumed. Note also that there are special considerations for wooden boats because overuse of zincs can cause degradation of the wood.*

---

*See *WoodenBoat* magazine, No. 93, March/April 1990; "Corrosion-Related Problems," by Ed McClave.

• If you have an outboard or I / O, check your owner's manual for the location of the zincs on your drive units. Virtually all I / Os will have one or more zincs to protect the drive unit from galvanic corrosion. Many outboard motors—especially larger motors than can't be taken off the transom easily—also are equipped with one or more zincs. Check the zincs, replacing them if they show evidence of deterioration. Outboard and I / O drive units are particularly vulnerable to galvanic corrosion if your boat spends much time at a marina, because stray electrical currents are common around dock areas.

STEERING SYSTEM

Steering systems are something we frequently take for granted. If your boat has a simple tiller arrangement, there may not be a lot to check. On our boat, which does have a tiller, we check the fitting at the bottom of the rudder to be certain it is secure and free of corrosion, and we check to be sure the rudder turns easily from side to side. Once the boat is in the water, we check the stuffing box where the rudderpost passes through the hull, to be sure there is no leakage. If there were any leakage, we would tighten the stuffing-box nut a fraction of a turn.

If your boat has a mechanical wheel-steering system, you should check to see that it is properly lubricated. If cables are involved, you need to be sure that they're tensioned correctly so they can't jump a pulley. Until you learn exactly what's required to check the wheel steering on your boat, you should get someone who knows what he's doing to check it for you, and watch and ask questions while he's doing it. Hydraulic steering systems also will require a professional checkup.

THROUGH-HULL FITTINGS AND VALVES

If you store your boat in an area subject to freezing temperatures, you'll need to make sure there is no water in the valves to any of your through-hull fittings before you store the boat. That means you should open the valve to let any water drain out and then close the valve again after your boat has been taken out of the water.

In commissioning your boat for the next boating season, maintenance requirements depend upon the kind of through-hulls and valves your boat is equipped with. All bronze through-hull fittings, for example, should be checked for possible corrosion. Tap them lightly with a hammer. Scratch them with a screwdriver blade. Look at their color. If the sound is dull when you tap them, the color funny when you scratch them, or their surface texture and color just look different somehow, then get someone else to check them out. Plastic through-hulls don't suffer from corrosion, but they can become embrittled over time. So they, too, should be checked, particularly on the inside of the hull, for any signs of aging.

All valves on through-hull fittings should open and close easily. Bronze seacocks should be taken apart and lubricated with a waterproof grease—unless they are constructed with a Teflon lining (the Teflon is inherently slippery). Plastic seacocks may also require lubrication, particularly since their plastic handles may break if the valve becomes too stiff. Consult with your marina or the manufacturer about procedures for servicing your boat's plastic seacocks. If your boat is equipped with gate valves, which you open and close by turning a knob similar to that on an outside water spigot, this is a good time to replace them. At the very least, they should be taken apart and carefully checked for deterioration of brass components from galvanic corrosion. Any suggestion of corrosion should lead you to replace the parts involved. The valve also should be lubricated when it is reassembled. But, do yourself a favor, and replace the gate valve with a quality seacock. Like so many other things of this sort, quality parts in good condition provide cheap insurance.

HOSES AND CONNECTIONS

Again, if your boat will be subject to freezing temperatures during storage, you should drain or blow out all hoses connected to any through-hulls as you prepare your boat for off-season storage. And then, of course, you should also make sure each through-hull fitting and shut-off valve are free of water, as outlined above.

Before commissioning, you'll need to crawl around the interior of your boat to check carefully the entire length of any hose connected to a through-hull fitting for signs of chafe, cracking, or loss of strength. At the first sign of deterioration, the hose should be replaced. Also, you should carefully check all hose clamps at both ends of these hoses. There should be two hose clamps at each end, if the fitting permits. And at this time, it's not enough simply to look for evidence of rust. You should use a screwdriver to loosen and retighten the screw on each hose clamp to be certain the screw mechanism is in good condition.

THE POTABLE-WATER SYSTEM

Before storage, you should pump out your water tanks (pump out all of the water) and run some kind of antifreeze for potable water through the system. More than one person—ourselves included—has used cheap vodka for plastic water tanks so that the tanks would not pick up the taste of the antifreeze. If freezing weather is likely, you'll need to be sure you have enough antifreeze in the bottom of your tanks to prevent hard freezing. Our goal is to have only undiluted antifreeze in the tanks. When using commercial potable-water antifreeze, we judge the mixture by the color coming out the faucet. When using vodka, we judged the mixture by the taste—but in very small amounts!

I also suggest that you disconnect the hoses to your potable-water pumps after running antifreeze through the system. This allows liquid in the system to drain or be blown back into the tanks to keep the plastic water lines from picking up the taste of antifreeze during storage. Then work the pumps to blow out all liquid in them.

At commissioning time, you'll need to reconnect the hoses to your potable-water pumps and flush out your water tank until the taste of antifreeze disappears. You should also make certain you have a spare-parts kit for your potable-water pump. Pumps tend to fail when you are well away from the dock and easy access to a marine store.

DOCK AND ANCHOR LINES

Commissioning time provides a good opportunity to check the condition of your dock and anchor lines. If you have a sailboat, it's an equally good time to check the condition of all of your running rigging.

The old manila rope used for lines on boats before the development of nylon and Dacron cordage had only one advantage that I can think of—it was easy to tell when the lines should be replaced. You just twisted the three strands to open them up and looked at the color on the inside. As long as it was a "healthy" golden brown, the rope was probably still in good shape—assuming it hadn't been severely chafed somewhere.

Today, it isn't always quite as easy to tell when a line needs replacing, especially with braided line. But even nylon and Dacron lines do get old—and dirty. Sometimes they also get stiff. As a rule of thumb, you should replace any line that looks old or that has become stiff enough that tying knots with it is difficult. You may want to keep the old line for occasional light duty where its stiffness or age won't be a handicap. But your primary dock and anchor lines should always look and feel in good shape.

Sometimes, of course, most of a line is in good shape, but it may be worn where it has been passed through a chock. The simple solution may be to shorten the line by cutting off the worn portion. You just need to make sure that the line's still long enough to do its job. If it's the anchor line that must be cut, you might consider converting the old anchor line into dock lines and getting a new anchor line. *Do not cut out a section of anchor line and splice the two good pieces together. The splice represents a weak spot in the line.*

SAFETY EQUIPMENT

In preparing your boat for the beginning of a new boating season, you'll need to check all of your safety equipment in the same way that you do before leaving the dock (as described in Chapter 8), using your checklist to be certain that all equipment is on the boat, in proper condition, and ready to use. In addition, however, some things require special attention:

• **Air horn.** If you rely on a gas-powered air horn, you should be sure you have a fresh gas canister. If you don't have a horn you can put up to your mouth to blow, you should get one. If makes a marvelous back-up.

• **Emergency flares.** Flares have a limited lifetime, and all Coast Guard–approved flares have an expiration date printed on them. If that date has already passed, or will pass during the upcoming boating season, replace the flares before the boat goes into the water. *Do not shoot off out-of-date flares without notifying the Coast Guard and local marine police that you plan to do so.* Also, be very careful if you do fire off any flares; they can be dangerous if not used properly. If you need to dispose of out-of-date flares, call the local fire department.

• **First-aid kit.** Some items in your first-aid kit may have expiration dates. Check all items to be sure they are not past their expiration dates and that their packages are in good shape.

• **Emergency stores.** Some boaters carry emergency water and food rations. Expiration dates should be checked, as should the packages. Even if the expiration date is well in the future, the item should be replaced if the package has deteriorated.

• **Flashlights, etc.** All boat kits should include at least one flashlight, preferably two. Also, some boaters use a self-contained anchor light that operates on its own battery. You may also have a weather radio or radio direction finder that is powered by its own batteries. All batteries in such lights or other battery-operated equipment should be replaced with the spare batteries you carried last season, and you should purchase new spare batteries and stow them aboard the boat before it is launched.

WOULD YOU BUY YOUR OWN BOAT?

Too often, checking your boat over before the start of a new boating season becomes a ritual—or a chore. One way to add a little interest, we've found, is to look at your boat as a prospective purchaser. Assume, for example, that you are in the market for a newer boat—and a boat like the one you now own will meet all of your needs. So, while you're not looking for a different boat, you are looking for one like yours that is equipped and maintained in a condition that would make you want to buy it.

Does your boat fill that bill?

How do you go about figuring that out? The method is easy. By now, you have developed a complete checklist for inspecting your boat before starting the engine to go out for a ride or sail. You also have a checklist for items to be examined before launching the boat for a new boating season. You simply sit down, combine those two lists, and plan an orderly and thorough survey of your boat—but from the viewpoint of someone who is considering purchasing it.

If you go through this process honestly, you'll give your boat a good, tough examination. If you find that you would not buy your boat—i.e., that it is not in the kind of condition that would make you want to buy it—you've got to question whether it's in good enough condition for you to be using it. In that situation, the best approach is to list all the deficiencies you've found, prioritize them from a safety perspective, and start at the top of the list to correct them.

Of course, that's an unlikely scenario. If you've been reasonably diligent about maintaining your boat, you'll probably decide that yes, you'd buy your boat. You may also find there are a few items that you'd want corrected before you closed the deal, but that's OK. Once those items have been taken care of, your boat will be safer. You and your crew will be safer. And you'll enjoy your boating more as a result.

Testing What You've Learned
(See Appendix C)

1. Develop two separate maintenance lists for your boat—one for the end of boating season, the other for the beginning of boating

season. These lists can be used to help you keep your boat in good operating order. They probably will be improved as you work through them on your boat, perhaps finding some items that don't really need such attention, more likely finding items that should be added. Remember to consider all of your boat's structural and working systems as well as its equipment.

Appendix A

How To Find a Boating Safety Course

Courses about boating safety are being offered with increasing frequency by a variety of agencies. They vary from two- or three-hour short courses that can do little more than increase your awareness of the importance of safety in boating, to the six-week courses offered by the U.S. Coast Guard Auxiliary and the U.S. Power Squadrons.

The telephone offers the shortest route to find out what courses are available near your community. The Boat Owners Association of the United States—better known as BOAT/US—has a toll-free number which you can call to find out whether there is a Coast Guard Auxiliary, Power Squadron, Red Cross, or state-sponsored boating safety course offered in your area and, if so, whom to contact. That BOAT/US telephone number is 1–800–336–2628, except in Virginia, where it is 1–800–245–2628. There is no cost to you for this reference service.

The second major source of information about boating safety courses in your community is your state's Boating Law Administrator. The following are addresses of the Boating Law Administrators in all major jurisdictions of the United States, listed alphabetically. The telephone numbers for these agencies should be listed wherever the telephone numbers for state offices are found in your local telephone book.

Director, Marine Police Division
Department of Conservation and Natural Resources
64 North Union Street, Room 756
Montgomery, Alabama 36130

Department of Public Safety
P.O. Box 6188 Annex
Anchorage, Alaska 99502

Department of Port Administration
P.O. Box 1539
Pago Pago, American Samoa 96799

State Boating Administrator
Arizona Game and Fish Department
2222 West Greenway Road
Phoenix, Arizona 85023

State Boating Law Administrator
Arkansas Game and Fish Commission
#2 Natural Resources Drive
Little Rock, Arkansas 72205

Director, Department of Boating and Waterways
1629 "S" Street
Sacramento, California 95814

Boating Administrator
Division of Parks and Outdoor Recreation
13787 South Highway 85
Littleton, Colorado 80125

Boating Law Administrator
Marine Patrol Headquarters
333 Perry Road
Old Lyme, Connecticut 06371

Boating Administrator
Department of Natural Resources and Environmental Control
Division of Fish and Wildlife
89 Kings Highway
P.O. Box 1401
Dover, Delaware 19903

Metropolitan Police Department
Harbor Section, SOD
550 Water Street, S.W.
Washington, D.C. 20024

Boating Law Administrator
Division of Law Enforcement
3900 Commonwealth Boulevard
Tallahassee, Florida 32303

Georgia Department of Natural Resources
Law Enforcement Section, Suite 1366
205 Butler Street, S.W.
Atlanta, Georgia 30334

Territory of Guam
Office of the Director
Department of Public Safety
Pedro's Plaza
287 West O'Brien Drive
Agana, Guam 96910

State Boating Manager
Department of Transportation
79 South Nimitz Highway
Honolulu, Hawaii 96813

Planner, Boating Safety
Department of Parks and
  Recreation
2177 Warm Springs Avenue
Statehouse Mail
Boise, Idaho 83720

Deputy Chief, Department of
  Conservation
Division of Law Enforcement
524 South Second Street
Springfield, Illinois 62701–
  1787

State Boating Law Administrator
Department of Natural
  Resources
606 State Office Building
100 North Senate Avenue
Indianapolis, Indiana 46204

Director
Iowa Conservation Commission
Wallace State Office Building
Des Moines, Iowa 50319

Boating Administrator
Kansas Fish & Game Commission
R.R. No. 2, Box 54A
Pratt, Kansas 67124

Director, Kentucky Division
  of Water Safety
Department of Natural
  Resources and Environmental Protection
107 Metro Street
Frankfort, Kentucky 40601

Boating Law Administrator
Department of Wildlife &
  Fisheries
P.O. Box 15570
Baton Rouge, Louisiana
  70895

Director of Licensing
Department of Inland Fishing and Wildlife
284 State Street
Augusta, Maine 04333

Superintendent, Natural
  Resources Police
580 Taylor Avenue
Tawes State Office Building
Annapolis, Maryland 21401

Director, Division of Law
  Enforcement
100 Nashua Street
Boston, Massachusetts 02114

Assistant Chief
Law Enforcement Division
Department of Natural
  Resources
Steven T. Mason Building
Lansing, Michigan 48909

State Boating Law Administrator
Minnesota Department of Natural Resources
500 Lafayette Road
St. Paul, Minnesota 55146

State Boating Law Administrator
Department of Wildlife Conservation
Bureau of Fisheries and Wildlife
P.O. Box 451
Jackson, Mississippi 39205

Commissioner
Missouri State Water Patrol
Department of Public Safety
2222 Weathered Rock Road
Jefferson City, Missouri 65102

Assistant Administrator
Division of Law Enforcement
Department of Fish, Wildlife and Parks
1420 East 6th Avenue
Helena, Montana 59620

State Boating Law Administrator
State Game and Parks Commission
P.O. Box 30370
2200 North 33rd Street
Lincoln, Nebraska 68503

Chief, Division of Enforcement
Department of Wildlife
P.O. Box 10678
Reno, Nevada 89520

Supervisor of Navigation
Division of Safety Services
New Hampshire Department of Safety
James H. Hayes Safety Building
Hazen Drive
Concord, New Hampshire 03305

New Jersey State Police
Marine Law Enforcement Bureau
P.O. Box 7068
River Road
West Trenton, New Jersey 08625

Boating Administrator
Park & Recreation Division
Natural Resources Department
P.O. Box 1147
Santa Fe, New Mexico 87504–1147

Director, Bureau of Marine and Recreational Vehicles
Agency Building #1
Empire State Plaza
Albany, New York 12238

Director of Field Operations
Wildlife Resources Commission
Archdale Building
Raleigh, North Carolina 27611

Boat & Water Safety Coordinator
State Game and Fish Department
100 North Bismarck Expressway
Bismarck, North Dakota 58501

Chief, Division of Watercraft
Ohio Department of Natural Resources
Fountain Square
Columbus, Ohio 43224

Director, Lake Patrol Division
Department of Public Safety
P.O. Box 11415
Oklahoma City, Oklahoma 73136

Director, Oregon State Marine Board
3000 Market Street, N.E. #505
Salem, Oregon 97310

Director, Bureau of Waterways
Fish Commission
3532 Walnut Street
P.O. Box 1673
Harrisburg, Pennsylvania 17105–1673

Executive Director
Puerto Rico Ports Authority
GPO Box 2829
San Juan, Puerto Rico 00936

Assistant Director of Operations
Department of Environmental Management
83 Park Street
Providence, Rhode Island 02903

Chief, Division of Boating
Wildlife & Marine Resources Department
P.O. Box 12559
Charleston, South Carolina 29412

Boating and Hunter Safety Coordinator
Department of Game, Fish and Parks
Anderson Building
Pierre, South Dakota 57501

Boating Law Administrator
Tennessee Wildlife Resources Agency
P.O. Box 40747
Nashville, Tennessee 37204

Supervisor, Water Safety Law Enforcement
Texas Parks and Wildlife Department
4200 Smith School Road
Austin, Texas 78744

Boating and R.V. Supervisor
Division of Parks and Recreation
Department of Natural Resources
1636 West North Temple Street
Salt Lake City, Utah 84116

Director, Marine Division
Department of Public Safety
103 South Main Street
Waterbury, Vermont 05676–0850

Boating Law Administrator
Department of Conservation and Cultural Affairs
P.O. Box 4399
Charlotte Amalie, St. Thomas
Virgin Islands 00801

Boating Law Administrator
Commission of Game and Inland Fisheries
P.O. Box 11104
Richmond, Virginia 23230

Boating Safety Administrator
Washington State Parks & Recreation Commission
7150 Cleanwater Lane (KY-11)
Olympia, Washington 98504

Chief, Law Enforcement Section
Department of Natural Resources
State Office Building
1800 East Washington Street
Charleston, West Virginia 25305

Boating Law Administrator
Department of Natural Resources
P.O. Box 7921
Madison, Wisconsin 53707

Watercraft Supervisor
Game & Fish Department
5400 Bishop Boulevard
Cheyenne, Wyoming 82002

Appendix B

Safety Equipment Required by the U.S. Coast Guard

The following information is excerpted from the U.S. Coast Guard pamphlet *Federal Requirements for Recreational Boats,* the edition current at the time of this writing. However, because regulations change, you should contact your state boating safety office or the nearest U.S. Coast Guard (USCG) office to receive the most up-to-date requirements.*

REGISTRATION AND NUMBERING REQUIREMENTS

All undocumented vessels equipped with propulsion machinery must be registered in the state of principal use. A certificate of number will be issued upon registering the vessel. These numbers must also be displayed on your vessel. Since some states require all vessels to be numbered (i.e., even boats not having motors), check with your local state boating authority for numbering requirements.

---

* Insofar as boating is regulated by both the federal and state governments, you may have to satisfy additional requirements of the state in which your boat is registered. For information, contact your state's boating safety office, as listed in Appendix A.

Display of Number

Registration numbers must be painted or permanently attached to each side of the forward half of the vessel. The Coast Guard and many states issue two validation stickers. They must be affixed within 6 inches of the registration number. No other letters or numbers may be displayed nearby. (The numbers must be plain block characters in a color contrasting with the background and not less than 3 inches in height.)

Certificate of Number

The owner / operator of a vessel must carry a valid certificate of number whenever the vessel is in use. When a vessel is moved to a new state of principal use, the certificate of number is valid for sixty days. The Coast Guard issues the certificate of number in Alaska.

COAST GUARD APPROVED EQUIPMENT

The Coast Guard sets minimum safety standards for vessels and associated equipment. To meet these standards, various equipment must be Coast Guard approved. "Coast Guard Approved Equipment" has been determined to be in compliance with the USCG specifications and regulations relating to performance, construction, and materials.

Personal Flotation Devices (PFDs)

PFDs must be Coast Guard approved, in good and serviceable condition, and of appropriate size for the intended user. Wearable PFDs must be readily accessible, meaning you must be able to put them on in a reasonable amount of time in an emergency (vessel sinking, on fire, etc.). They should *not* be stowed in plastic bags, in locked or closed compartments, or have other gear stowed on top of them. Throwable devices must be immediately available for use. Though not required, a PFD should be worn at all times when the vessel is underway. *A wearable PFD can save your life, but only if you wear it.*

Boats less than 16 feet in length (including canoes and kayaks of any length) must be equipped with one Type I, II, III, IV, or V PFD for each person aboard.

Boats 16 feet and longer must be equipped with one Type I, II, III, or V for each person aboard *plus* one Type IV.

Federal law does not require PFDs on racing shells, rowing sculls, and racing kayaks; states laws vary.

Types of PFDs: A **Type I PFD,** or **Off-Shore Life Jacket,** provides the most buoyancy. It is effective for all waters, especially open, rough, or remote waters where rescue may be delayed. It is designed to turn most unconscious wearers in the water to a face-up position. The Type I comes in two sizes. The adult size provides at least 22 pounds buoyancy; the child size, 11 pounds, minimum.

A **Type II PFD,** or **Near-Shore Buoyant Vest,** is intended for calm, inland water or where there is good chance of quick rescue. This type will turn *some* unconscious wearers to a face-up position in the water. The turning action is not as pronounced, and it will not turn as many persons under the same conditions as a Type I. An adult size device provides at least 15½ pounds buoyancy; a medium child size provides 11 pounds. Infant and small child sizes each provide at least 7 pounds buoyancy.

A **Type III PFD,** or **Flotation Aid,** is good for calm, inland water, or where there is good chance of quick rescue. It is designed so wearers can place themselves in a face-up position in the water. The wearer may have to tilt head-back to avoid turning face-down in the water. The Type III has the same minimum buoyancy as a Type II PFD. It comes in many styles, colors, and sizes and is generally the most comfortable type for continuous wear. Float coats, fishing vests, and vests designed with features suitable for various sports activities are examples of this type PFD.

A **Type IV PFD,** or **Throwable Device,** is intended for calm, inland water with heavy boat traffic, where help is always present. It is designed to be thrown to a person in the water and grasped and held by the user until rescued. It is *not* designed to be worn. Type IV devices include buoyant cushions, ring buoys, and horseshoe buoys.

A **Type V PFD,** or **Special Use Device,** is intended for specific activities and may be carried instead of another PFD only if used according to the approval conditions on the label. Some Type V devices provide significant hypothermia protection. Varieties include deck suits, work vests, boardsailing vests, and Hybrid PFDs.

A **Type V Hybrid Inflatable PFD** is the least bulky of all PFD types. It contains a small amount of inherent buoyancy, and an inflatable chamber. Its performance is equal to a Type I, II, or III PFD (as noted on the PFD label) when inflated. Hybrid PFDs satisfy the PFD requirement only if they are being worn (uninflated).

[Author's note: PFDs and their use are covered in Chapter 8.]

Water-Skiing: A water-skier, while being towed, is considered on board the vessel, and a PFD is required for the purposes of compliance with the PFD carriage requirements. Although not required by federal law, it is advisable and recommended for a skier to wear a PFD designed and intended to withstand the impact of hitting the water at high speed, as when a skier falls. "Impact Class" marking refers to PFD strength, not personal protection. Some state laws require skiers to wear a PFD.

[Author's note: Water-skiing safety is covered in Chapter 19.]

VISUAL DISTRESS SIGNALS

All recreational boats, when used on coastal waters, the Great Lakes, territorial seas, and those waters connected directly to the Great Lakes and the territorial seas, up to a point where a body of water is less than two miles wide, must be equipped with visual distress signals. Vessels owned in the United States operating on the high seas must be equipped with visual distress signals. The following vessels are not required to carry day signals, but must carry night signals when operating from sunset to sunrise:

• Recreational boats *less than* 16 feet in length.
• Boats participating in organized events such as races, regattas, or marine parades.
• Open sailboats less than 26 feet in length not equipped with propulsion machinery.
• Manually propelled boats.

Pyrotechnic Visual Distress Signals must be Coast Guard approved, in serviceable condition, and readily accessible. They are marked with a date showing the service life, which must not be expired. If pyrotechnic devices are selected, a minimum of three are required. That is, three signals for day use and three signals for night. Some pyrotechnic signals meet both day and night use requirements. Pyrotechnic devices should be stored in a cool, dry location.

USCG-approved pyrotechnic visual distress signals and associated devices include:
• Pyrotechnic red flares, hand-held or aerial.
• Pyrotechnic orange smoke, hand-held or floating.
• Launchers for aerial red meteors or parachute flares.

Non-Pyrotechnic Visual Distress Signals must be in serviceable condition, readily accessible, and certified by the manufacturer as complying with USCG requirements. They include:
• Orange distress flag.
• Electric distress light.

Regulations prohibit display of visual distress signals on the water under any circumstances except when assistance is required, to prevent immediate or potential danger to persons on board a vessel.

All distress signals have distinct advantages and disadvantages. No single device is ideal under all conditions or suitable for all purposes. Pyrotechnics are excellent distress signals, universally recognized. However, there is potential for injury and property damage if they are not properly handled. These devices produce a very hot flame. The residue can cause burns and ignite flammable materials. Pistol-launched and hand-held parachute flares and meteors have many characteristics of a firearm and must be handled with caution.

[Author's note: Visual distress signals are discussed in more detail in Chapter 18.]

Fire Extinguishers

Approved fire extinguishers are classified by a letter and number symbol. The letter indicates the type fire the unit is designed to extinguish. (Type B is designed to extinguish flammable liquids such as gasoline, oil, and grease fires.) The number indicates the relative size of the extinguisher (minimum extinguishing agent weight). Approved extinguishers are hand-portable, either B-I or B-II classification.

Fire extinguishers are required if any one or more of the following conditions exist:

• Inboard engines.

• Closed compartments under thwarts and seats where portable fuel tanks may be stored.

• Double bottoms not sealed to the hull or which are not completely filled with flotation materials.

• Closed living spaces.

• Closed stowage compartments in which combustible or flammable materials are stored.

• Permanently installed fuel tanks. Fuel tanks secured so they cannot be moved in case of fire or other emergency are considered permanently installed. There are no gallon capacity limits to determine if a fuel tank is portable. If the weight of the fuel tank is such that persons on board cannot move it, then the Coast Guard considers it permanently installed.

Minimum number of hand-portable fire extinguishers required:

Boats less than 26 feet in length with *no* fixed fire-extinguishing system installed in machinery spaces must have at least one Type B-I approved hand-portable fire extinguisher. When an approved fixed fire-extinguishing system is installed in machinery spaces, no Type B-I extinguisher is required.

Boats 26 feet to less than 40 feet in length must have at least two Type B-I or at least one Type B-II approved hand-portable fire extinguisher. When an approved fixed fire-extinguishing system is installed, the vessel must also carry one Type B-I.

Boats 40 feet to not more than 65 feet in length must have at least three Type B-I or at least one Type B-I plus one Type B-II approved portable fire extinguishers. When an approved fixed fire-extinguishing system is installed, one less Type B-I extinguisher is required.

[Author's note: See Chapter 8 for additional information about fire extinguishers.]

Backfire Flame Control

Gasoline engines installed in a vessel after April 25, 1940, except outboard motors, must be equipped with an acceptable means of backfire flame control. The device must be suitably attached to the air intake with a flame-tight connection and is required to be Coast Guard approved.

REQUIRED NONAPPROVED EQUIPMENT

Natural Ventilation

All vessels with propulsion machinery that use gasoline for fuel, with enclosed engines and / or fuel tank compartments built after April 25, 1940, and before August 1, 1980, are required to have natural ventilation.

Natural ventilation consists of at least two ventilation ducts fitted with cowls or their equivalent for the purpose of efficiently ventilating the bilges of every engine and fuel-tank compartment. At least one exhaust duct extending to the lower portion of the bilge and at least one intake duct extending to a point midway to the bilge or at least below the level of the carburetor intake is required.

Vessels built after July 31, 1978, but prior to August 1, 1980, have no requirement for ventilation of the fuel-tank compartment if there is no electrical source in the compartment and the fuel tank vents to the outside of the vessel.

Powered Ventilation

Vessels built after July 31, 1980, that have gasoline engines with a cranking motor (starter) for electrical generation, mechanical power, or propulsion in a closed compartment are required to have a powered ventilation system. This includes each compartment with such an engine.

No person may operate a vessel built after July 31, 1980, with a gasoline engine in a closed compartment unless it is equipped with an operable ventilation system that meets Coast Guard standards. The operator is required to keep the system in operating condition and ensure that cowls and ducting are not blocked or torn.

Sound Signaling Devices
Less Than 20 Meters (65.6 feet)

Regulations do not specifically require vessels less than 12 meters (39.4 feet) in length to carry a whistle, horn, or bell. However, the navigation rules require sound signals to be made under certain circumstances. [Author's note: See Chapter 17.] Therefore, you must have some means of making an efficient sound signal.

Vessels 12 meters or more in length are required to carry on board a power whistle or power horn and a bell.

Navigation Lights

Recreational vessels are required to display navigation lights between sunset and sunrise and other periods of reduced visibility (fog, rain, haze, etc.). The U.S. Coast Guard *Navigation Rules, International-Inland* encompasses lighting requirements for every description of watercraft.

[Author's note: Navigation lights are discussed in detail in Chapter 16.]

POLLUTION REGULATIONS

The Refuse Act of 1989 prohibits the throwing, discharging, or depositing of any refuse matter of any kind (including trash, garbage, oil, and other liquid pollutants) into the waters of the United States. The Federal Water Pollution Control Act prohibits the discharge of oil or hazardous substances which may be harmful into U.S. navigable waters.

Regulations issued under the Federal Water Pollution Control Act require all vessels with machinery propulsion to have a capacity to retain oily mixtures on board. A fixed or portable means to discharge oily waste to a reception facility is required. A bucket or bailer is suitable as a portable means of discharging oily waste on recreational vessels.

No person may intentionally drain oil or oily waste from any source into the bilge of any vessel.

Vessels 26 feet in length and over must display a placard at least 5 by 8 inches, made of durable material, fixed in a conspicuous place in the machinery spaces, or at the bilge pump control station, stating the following:

"Discharge of Oil Prohibited—The Federal Water Pollution Control Act prohibits the discharge of oil or oily waste into or upon the navigable waters of the United States or waters of the contiguous zone if such discharge causes a film or sheen upon, or discoloration of, the surface of the water, or causes a sludge or emulsion beneath the surface of the water. Violators are subject to a penalty of $5,000."

Similarly, vessels 26 feet in length and over must display a placard relating to disposal of plastic trash. The placard, which must be mounted where it is readily visible, reads in part: "It is illegal for any vessel to dump plastic trash anywhere in the ocean or navigable waters of the United States. Annex V of the MARPOL TREATY is an international law for a cleaner, safer marine environment. Violation of these requirements may result in civil penalty up to $25,000 fine and imprisonment." The placard goes on to note that, in addition to plastic, it is illegal to dump paper, rags, glass, food, garbage, metal, crockery, and dunnage in *any* U.S. waters.

[Author's note: "Discharge of oil prohibited" and "plastic trash" placards are available in marine supply stores and mail order catalogs.]

Marine Sanitation Devices

All recreational boats with installed toilet facilities must have an operable marine sanitation device (MSD) on board. Vessels 65 feet and under in length may use a Type I, II, or III MSD. Boats over 65 feet in length must install a Type II or III MSD.

All installed MSDs must be Coast Guard certified. Coast Guard certified devices are so labeled except for some holding tanks, which are already certified by definition under the regulations.

REPORTING BOATING ACCIDENTS

All boating accidents or accidents resulting from the use of related equipment (which meets the criteria below) must be reported by the operator or owner of the vessel to the proper marine law-enforcement authority for the state in which the accident occurred.

Immediate Notification Required for Fatal Accidents. If a person dies or disappears as a result of a recreational boating accident, the nearest state boating authority must be notified without delay, providing the following information:
• Date, time, and exact location of the accident.
• Name of each person who died or disappeared.
• Number and name of the vessel.
• Names and addresses of the owner and operator.

A Formal Report of Injury Must Be Filed Within Forty-Eight Hours. If, as a result of a boating or related-equipment accident, a person sustains injuries that require more than first aid, a formal report must be filed.

Accidents involving more than $400 damage (or complete loss of the vessel) must be reported within ten days.

If you need further information regarding accident reporting, please call the Boating Safety Hotline, 1–800–268–5647.

ADDITIONAL EQUIPMENT AND ADVICE

As the operator and / or owner, you are responsible for the prudent and safe operation of your vessel, and for the lives and safety of your passengers and others around you. You should become familiar with federal, state, and local rules and regulations regarding safe boat operation and attempt to learn and practice good seamanship, boat handling, navigation, and piloting, etc.

Besides meeting the legal requirements, prudent boaters carry additional safety equipment.

Additional Means of Propulsion

Vessels less than 16 feet in length should carry alternate propulsion, such as a paddle or oars. If an alternate means of mechanical propulsion (e.g., another outboard or trolling motor) is carried, it should use a separate fuel tank and starting source from the main propulsion motor.

Anchoring

All vessels should be equipped with an anchor and line of suitable size and length for the vessel and the waters in which it is being operated. Choose the right anchor for your vessel and the type of bottom you expect to be anchoring in.

[Author's note: Anchors and anchoring are covered in Chapters 8 and 25.]

Bailer

All vessels should carry at least one effective manual device (portable bilge pump, bucket, scoop, etc.) for bailing water, in addition to any installed electric bilge pump.

First-Aid Kit

As the operator of a small boat, you should consider taking a First Aid course and becoming proficient in its application. A first-aid kit and manual, bandages, gauze, adhesive tape, antiseptic, aspirin, etc., is suggested.

Float Plan

Tell a friend or relative where you are going and when you plan to return. Make sure they have a description of your vessel and other information that will make identification easier should the need arise.

Appendix C

Answers: Testing What You've Learned

Chapter 1:

1. You can be held legally responsible for damage or injury caused by your boat if you fail to maintain or operate your boat by generally accepted standards of good seamanship. At a minimum, this would include your boat meeting federally mandated safety standards, being equipped with all required safety equipment (Appendix B) in good working order, being operated in accordance with the "rules of the road" (Chapter 15), and being operated within the requirements of local or state laws.

2. Most states at this writing have no restrictions on who may operate a motorboat.

3. At this writing, only Connecticut has a law to require a boat operator's license. In the area of boating safety education, Maryland, New Jersey, and Vermont have laws requiring people born after certain dates to obtain a "certificate of boating safety education" before operating a state-registered motorboat. The certificate is obtained by successfully completing an approved boating safety course or by passing an approved boating safety examination.

4. The author and his father made the mistake of assuming that a twelve-year-old has the depth of experience and judgment required to apply instructions learned from a book to the variety of situations that are encountered on the water, without first getting some practical experience in his boat under the guidance of an experienced boater. Even adults should have an experienced boater go with them the first two or three times they take their boat out to help them obtain some basic, practical experience.

5. Three sources of boating safety courses are the United States

Power Squadrons, the U.S. Coast Guard Auxiliary, and your state's Office of Boating Safety. For information on how to find a course in your area, see Appendix A.

Chapter 2:

1. Examples of five factors that may create safety hazards around boats but are not normally present around cars include: (a) the danger of falling overboard, (b) the danger of explosion and fire from gasoline leaks on a boat, (c) the fact that boats do not have brakes, (d) the completely different system in boating for finding your way at night (i.e., no headlights), and (e) the potentially large impact on boats from changes in the weather that have relatively little effect on land.

2. The boats most often involved in accidents are motorboats less than 26 feet long.

3. FALSE. Nearly half of pleasure-boating accidents involve motorboats with engines of more than 75 horsepower. Another 15 percent of accidents involve boats with motors of between 26 and 75 horsepower.

4. b. The largest single cause of boating accidents is *operator error*—in other words, human error. That's why there is a growing focus on boating safety education. The more you can learn about your boat, its equipment and systems, and how to handle it in different situations, the less likely you are to become involved in a boating accident.

5. TRUE. An estimated 38 percent of all boating accidents involve people who are legally drunk. In some areas, the impact of alcohol is even greater. In any case, there is no longer any question that drinking even a couple of beers out on the water, when combined with the sun, wind, and motion of the boat, can seriously affect your ability to operate your boat safely. Additionally, the impact of alcohol on your passengers' coordination can seriously increase the risk of their falling overboard if the boat lurches unexpectedly.

6. No matter where you live in the United States of America, there are laws making it illegal to operate a boat under the influence of alcohol. If your locality does not have such laws of its own, federal regulations fill the gap and can be enforced by local authorities. Moreover, under the federal regulations, while a breathalyzer or other measure of blood alcohol can be used as evidence for conviction, it is not required; you can be judged guilty of operating your boat under the influence of alcohol on the basis of your behavior.

Chapter 3:

1. FALSE. It should certainly be possible to go from your boat to another one just like yours and be able to operate it safely. However,

differences in hull shape, size, engine systems, propellers, steering, etc., make it more difficult to move from one boat to another. For example, going from an outboard or I/O (inboard/outboard) motorboat to an inboard system requires learning a whole new set of skills for maneuvering in close quarters. The point is this: Don't just assume that, because you know how to run one or two boats, you can simply jump into a third boat and take it out safely. First spend some time to be sure you know how to handle the new boat in whatever situation you may encounter.

2. *Displacement.* Any boat put into the water will displace an amount of water equal to the boat's weight.

3. The heavier a boat's displacement, the more *volume* it will have below the waterline.

4. c. A boat designed to get up and run on top of the water has a *planing hull.*

5. A boat that can get only partway up onto a plane is said to have either a *semi-planing* or a *semi-displacement* hull.

6. FALSE. A displacement hull is not intended for speed. In fact, its speed is limited by the length of its waterline.

7. FALSE. Although it's relatively easy to get a displacement hull moving up to about 80 percent of its theoretical maximum hull speed, substantial increases in engine or wind power are needed to increase speed over the last 20 percent.

8. Hull speed equals 1.34 times the square root of the waterline length, or, for this boat, $1.34 \times 5 = 6.7$ *knots.*

9. Again, the answer focuses on waterline length, not boat length. Hull speed for this boat is 1.34×6, or *about 8 knots.*

10. The two dangerous situations that can arise when a boat is surfing are *pitchpoling* and *broaching.* A boat is pitchpoled when it begins surfing down a wave so fast that its bow digs into the water and the stern is flipped over the bow by the wave. A boat broaches when it slues sideways as it surfs down the wave and is rolled onto its side, or all the way over. In both instances, the crew can be thrown overboard and the boat sunk.

11. Three factors affecting boat stability include the distribution of weight, the boat's beam, and the hull shape. In general, keeping weight low, increasing the beam, and designing deeper and fuller chine areas tend to increase stability.

12. Standing up in a small boat is unsafe because it reduces the boat's stability by taking weight out of the bottom and putting it up high. Also, standing up in a small boat increases the risk of losing your balance and falling overboard.

Chapter 4:

1. Two advantages of flat-bottomed boats are *stability* and *easy planing*. Two disadvantages are a *quick-rocking motion* and *pounding* when planing over even small waves.

2. The vee bottom helps reduce pounding when planing.

3. The cathedral hull provides increased stability by boosting buoyancy along the sides. As a result, people can sit near the side while fishing without the boat tipping as much as it would with a plain vee bottom.

4. The principal advantage of the deep-vee design is the ability to run through waves at higher speeds. The principal disadvantages are reduced stability at low speed and the need for larger engines to get the boat planing.

5. FALSE. In general, round-bottomed boats do not provide the planing surfaces needed to achieve the speed potential of deep-vee designs.

6. A round-bottomed boat will have a softer motion than a boat with a vee bottom.

7. A light-displacement boat generally has a significantly flatter bottom than a heavy-displacement boat. This applies to both motorboats and sailboats.

8. The internal keel is a structural frame which runs the length of the boat bottom along the centerline. It can be compared to the backbone. It provides a strong, central frame for attaching the boat's ribs.

9. On a motorboat, the external keel helps keep the boat steering in a straight line, helps prevent it from skidding sideways in a turn, and protects the hull, the propeller, and the rudder. A sailboat's external keel helps offset the force of the wind on the sails so that the boat is not simply blown over on its side, and helps the boat sail somewhat into the wind.

10. A skeg on a motorboat can protect the propeller, protect and possibly strengthen the rudder, and help keep the boat moving in a straight line.

11. The skeg on a sailboat serves to strengthen the rudder and, depending upon its design, improve the flow of water over the rudder, increasing the rudder's effectiveness, particularly in downwind sailing.

Chapter 5:

1. Advantages of outboard motors include: Outboard motorboats cost less; outboard motors can be replaced easily; and outboards generally weigh less per horsepower than inboard engines do.

2. Disadvantages of outboard motors include: The sophistication of outboard systems requires specialized knowledge to repair and maintain them; even if you know how to troubleshoot your outboard, it is difficult to work on when the boat is in the water; and the engine weight is all the way aft, making the boat heavy in the stern.

3. When slowing down in an outboard boat, you should bring the boat off the plane gradually so that the stern wave doesn't pile up on the transom. Also, if there are significant wind-blown waves on the water, it's best to bring the bow into the waves as you slow down so that the boat's stern wave isn't enlarged by merging with one of the wind waves to come surging over the transom.

4. Bracket-mounted outboards are gaining in popularity because they eliminate the need for cut-outs in the transom and they enable the propeller to push the boat more efficiently. The result is improved safety from a transom-design perspective as well as improved boat speed and fuel efficiency.

5. FALSE. Conventional outboard motorboats are not suited for bracket mounts. The transom must be reinforced specifically to carry the extra loads caused by hanging the motor a couple of feet behind the transom. The best bet is to be sure that the boatbuilder has designed and constructed the boat specifically for bracket mounting.

6. Advantages of I/Os over outboards include: The engines tend to last longer because they operate at lower speeds; the engines are easier for the boat owner to service and troubleshoot; the I/O boat has a full transom; and larger engines can be used in smaller boats because the engine weight in the I/O system is farther forward.

7. Principal disadvantages of I/Os include: I/Os are more expensive than outboards; they have higher maintenance costs because the drive units are more complex; and it is difficult to change to a larger engine.

8. The rubber boot on the drive units of I/O systems deteriorates with use and age. If not replaced in a timely manner, the boot will begin to leak, and the boat can sink as a result. Boots can need replacing after as little as a single boating season.

9. TRUE. The incentive to use I/Os or outboards on boats larger than 30 feet in length is lost for two reasons: The expense of the I/O system is no longer justified because the boat can't be trailered; and the larger boats often need larger engines than are practical with I/O systems.

10. The major difference, from a safety perspective, between an inboard system and an I/O is in steering the boat at slow speeds. The

inboard must have water going past the rudder to steer the boat. An I/O is more easily maneuvered because the propeller itself is used to steer the boat.

11. A boat with an inboard engine system must be moving relative to the water for its rudder to have any steering effect. As a result, an inboard drifting with the current cannot be easily turned. An I/O being swept along by the current can be steered easily by turning the drive unit and putting it in gear. The propeller will simply push the stern around and point the boat in the direction you want to go.

12. Twin engines offer two advantages of safety. The primary advantage is that you have a spare engine. If one quits running, you can get home on the second engine. Also, for inboards, two engines greatly simplify problems of maneuvering the boat around docks. To the extent that they give the skipper more control over the boat in such tight situations, safety is enhanced.

13. Diesel engines offer a great advantage in safety, because diesel fuel will not explode; it also does not ignite as easily as gasoline. So, the risk of fire and explosion is much lower on a boat with diesel engines. Additionally, diesel-powered boats generally use considerably less fuel to get where they're going, and maintenance is less because diesels do not have the complex electrical systems required on gasoline engines.

14. The two principal advantages gasoline engines offer over diesel engines are lower initial cost and more horsepower per pound. In other words, the engines don't cost as much and they are not as heavy.

15. Diesels have taken over the auxiliary sailboat market because the added safety and reliability of the diesel engine is worth the added cost. The explanation is that sailboats usually need smaller engines, so the extra cost for the diesel power is much less than on motorboats of comparable size.

Chapter 6:

1. A johnboat is a simple, flat-bottomed boat used for basic transportation or fishing in protected areas where the waters are predictably calm. Johnboats are generally meant to be rowed or used with a small outboard motor.

2. The major difference between a runabout and a utility/fishing boat is in the area of stability. A runabout is intended basically for scooting around at good speed. The utility/fishing boat is intended more for fishing, diving, and/or swimming from the boat; as a result, it tends to be beamier and typically have some variation of a cathedral

hull to provide more flotation out along the sides, making the boat less tippy than a runabout when the boat is not moving or is moving very slowly.

3. In general, sportfishing boats are designed to handle ocean waves when running at cruising speed. In addition, they tend to be beamier than other cabin cruisers; to have larger cockpits with lower transoms to make bringing fish aboard easier; and to come equipped with a flying bridge and, possibly, a tuna tower for spotting fish.

4. In an effort to meet consumer demand for comfortable living accommodations, manufacturers have made many small cruisers somewhat tall for their length. As a result, these boats have a relatively high center of gravity (i.e., they have more of their weight up high), making them less stable in rough water. For that reason, many of these smaller cabin cruisers should only be used in protected and semi-protected waters where they can get into a safe harbor quickly if the weather begins to deteriorate.

5. FALSE. I know of no houseboat design that I consider suitable for use more than a few miles from a safe haven in coastal waters or on large lakes or bays where a strong wind can get up substantial waves quickly.

Chapter 7:

1. (A) Cutter matches with (7); (B) Catboat matches with (6); (C) Schooner matches with (4); (D) Sloop matches with (1); (E) Ketch matches with (2); (F) Yawl matches with (5); and (G) Cat Ketch matches with (3).

2. Sloops offer the most efficient rig for sailing close to the wind, with cutters and yawls generally coming in second and third, respectively.

3. Once boats reach the neighborhood of 40 feet in length, their sails begin to get fairly large, unless the rig is broken into smaller pieces. Using a ketch, schooner, or yawl rig breaks up the sail plan so that individual sails are generally smaller and more easily handled than they would be on a sloop or cutter of the same size.

4. The cutter rig results in a smaller mainsail and usually two smaller headsails in place of the single large jib commonly found on sloops. The smaller sails are easier to handle in adverse conditions.

5. Multihulls are generally faster than monohulls for two reasons: They don't rely on weight for stability; and their hulls are designed for planing. Their relatively light weight makes it possible for them to extract enough power from the wind to get out of their "hole in

the water" and up onto a plane, where they can exceed hull speed easily.

6. Multihulls are more stable initially than monohulls. That is, they are not as easily heeled (leaned) over by the force of the wind. However, multihulls lose all stability once they have been blown over onto one side, and they will simply continue going over until they are upside down. Once there, they stay that way—upside down. Monohulls with ballast keels, on the other hand, should come back up onto their "feet" no matter how far over they are rolled. For that reason, monohulls are said to have greater "ultimate stability" than multihulls.

7. Racing boats generally have lighter displacements and, therefore, less hull surface to create friction with the water. In light winds, the reduced friction makes it easier to get the lighter-displacement boat moving. As wind strength increases, the racing boat will get up to its hull speed faster, because it doesn't need as much power to push its smaller underbody through the water. In strong winds, the racing boat often loses its advantage.

8. Cruising boats need to carry a variety of gear and supplies that the racer will happily leave ashore. All of these require internal space; they also add weight. The two add up to heavier displacement.

Chapter 8:

1. Obviously, the list you have made is specific to your boat and can't be fully predicted here. However, at the very least you should have included checking your boat's bilges, its running lights (if you have them), the fuel system (if you have an engine), the steering system, anchor and anchor line, and all Coast Guard-required equipment.

2. Exhaust leaks are insidious. Any leak may fill the boat's cabin with carbon monoxide gas and cause the death of anyone in the cabin. Carbon monoxide has no odor. It simply makes its victim sleepy and gradually causes death while you, the skipper, are up in the cockpit running your boat under the impression that your crew or passenger is down below taking a nap. Leaks in the exhaust of an onboard generator are equally dangerous, particularly if the boat is closed up while everyone sleeps at night.

3. You should check the fabric, the straps, and, if it is kapok in a plastic bag, the flotation of your PFDs. The fabric and straps are checked simply by tugging on them to make sure they don't tear easily. The flotation bags are checked for punctures (leaks) by squeezing them tightly in your hands.

4. FALSE. While the flotation does not need checking, the fabric and straps should be checked regularly.

5. FALSE. Any cushion no longer suitable as a PFD should be disposed of and replaced. It should not even be used in the cabin because of the possibility that it could inadvertently be brought to the cockpit and subsequently used as a throwable PFD in an emergency.

6. You really should sacrifice one of your fire extinguishers to practice with it. To put out a fire, you should direct the spray to the base of the fire and sweep back and forth over the burning material or liquid. You can practice this without actually having a fire simply by spraying the contents of the extinguisher back and forth over a small area of dirt, grass, or driveway. Go back to Chapter 8 to review procedures for checking the readiness of your fire extinguisher.

7. The only legal uses of Channel 16 are to initiate a call and to call for help in an emergency. Whenever a call for help ("Mayday, Mayday, Mayday") is heard, everyone else should stop talking to let the emergency call have priority.

8. FALSE. PFDs are not only intended for use in an emergency, they are also intended to prevent emergencies from occurring. In fact, one of the best-known ways to prevent an emergency is to ensure that young children and weak or non-swimmer larger children and adults wear PFDs in open boats or on deck on larger boats. In heavy weather, it is advisable for all hands to wear their PFDs.

9. In addition to required equipment, small boats should carry a bailer, one or more oars or paddles, and a spare container of fuel. Two other essential items on many smaller boats are an anchor and anchor line—securely attached to the boat—and a swim ladder in case someone falls overboard.

10. *Always,* before you turn on the ignition of any gasoline-powered boat with an I/O or inboard engine, you should get down on your knees, put your nose in the bilge, and smell the air in the bilge to be sure there are no gasoline fumes that could explode. Under no circumstances should you try to start the engine if you smell any gasoline fumes.

11. The first two things to consider when planning your departure are the wind and current (tide). The third thing is the environment—the obstacles you may have to avoid as you get underway.

12. There is no right or wrong answer to this question. While I would hope that few boaters would find a potential problem almost every time they got ready to go out, any of the answers listed is possible depending upon the condition of your boat and your maintenance efforts. The key point is this: Even if you never find a potential

problem while going through your pre-start checklist, all of the checks are worthwhile if only because you and your crew have the comfort of knowing that your boat and its equipment are in good working order. In point of fact, however, going through the checklist will probably uncover something every now and then that needs correcting, making the effort doubly worthwhile.

Chapter 9:

1. If the bottom falls off gradually, you should walk the boat out to deeper water. The problem is that sand, mud, and other debris suspended in very shallow water, or stirred up by your propeller in reverse, will be drawn into the engine cooling-water system and can damage the water pump. The problem exists for outboard, I / O, and inboard installations.

2. FALSE. For the reason explained just above, you are better off not running your engine until there is a couple of feet of water (depth) between your engine water intake and the bottom.

3. The combination of people in the water and a rotating propeller is a serious accident waiting to happen. The only way to be 100 percent safe in the water around a propeller is to have the engine turned off. For that reason, you should not start your engine until all crew members are safely aboard your boat.

4. The best procedure for taking a 25-foot sailboat out from a beach under sail would be to walk it out to deep water, put down an anchor, bring your crew aboard, and then sail away from anchor. If the wind were light, you could safely put up sails while drifting—as long as you had your crew safely aboard first.

5. The bow of a sailboat usually should be headed into the wind when you raise sails.

6. Pulling the anchor in through a bow chock will keep the bow headed into any waves, reducing the risk of waves swamping the boat.

7. Hand signals provide an effective way to ensure good communication between the person on the bow and the person at the controls when working with your anchor. The signals need not be fancy; they need only be easily understood.

8. The best way to move a large boat up to its anchor is to use the engine, with the person on the bow giving the directions.

9. The best way to break your anchor loose from the bottom is to let the boat do it. When the boat is directly over the anchor, snub the anchor line on a cleat and either let the force of the wind or waves do the job, or use your engine or jib to break it loose.

10. The difficulty in leaving anchor under sail is getting the anchor

up so that wind is on the desired side of the boat. Insofar as you cannot be certain which direction you will have to start sailing, you should have planned out ahead of time what you will do in both possible circumstances—starting off on the port tack, or the starboard tack.

11. FALSE. After casting off your mooring line and pendant, you should reverse away from the mooring until you are safely clear of those two pieces of rope so they can't get wrapped around your propeller. Only when you are clear of that hazard should you shift into forward and begin to move ahead.

Chapter 10:

1. FALSE. The paddle-wheel effect is strongest either when the boat is lying still in the water, or when in reverse.

2. When a boat is moving forward, the rudder easily overcomes the paddle-wheel effect because both the prop wash and the boat's movement through the water work directly upon the rudder. In reverse, the prop wash is directed away from the rudder and cannot, therefore, offset the paddle-wheel effect.

3. TRUE. Most single-engine boats do have right-hand propellers.

4. A right-hand propeller kicks the stern to starboard when in forward.

5. A right-hand propeller kicks the stern to port when in reverse.

6. With a right-hand propeller, you would prefer to come up with the dock to port if the wind and current are not important considerations. In this way, the paddle-wheel will kick your stern toward the dock when you put the engine into reverse to stop alongside the dock.

7. In twin-engine inboards, the port engine usually has a left-hand propeller and the starboard engine a right-hand propeller.

8. The stream of water pushed out by the propeller is called the "propeller wash," or "prop wash."

9. FALSE. The prop wash will have essentially no impact on steering when the engine is in reverse. The propeller is pushing the wash forward, away from the rudder.

10. If the current is coming from the bow and your boat is tied up at a dock, you will turn your rudder away from the dock to have the current push your stern toward the dock. To hold your stern off, you would turn your rudder toward the dock.

11. Forward springs are used to keep your boat from drifting back along the dock. Aft springs are used to keep it from drifting forward.

12. When a boat is in a slip, the distance from the stern cleat to the

dock cleat on the same side may be only a few feet. That doesn't give much freedom for the boat to move up and down with the tide unless it is tied to a floating dock. By crossing the lines so that the line from the starboard cleat is made fast ashore on the port side of the boat, and vice versa, the stern lines are made long enough to allow for a larger tide change.

Chapter 11:

1. In an ideal world, you would begin planning for leaving the dock before you ever tied up. In that way, to the extent that docking circumstances permitted, you could come in to the dock so that you would be in the best possible situation when the time came to cast off your lines and head back out onto the waterways.

2. The strength and direction of any wind and current and the presence of other boats are the three key factors in determining what you have to do to leave a dock safely. You'll also have to take the paddle-wheel effect of your propeller into consideration as you actually begin to move out.

3. FALSE. To ensure that all lines are taken off in an orderly manner and put where they can't fall into the water to foul your propeller, the lines should come off in an order determined by the circumstances at the moment. In general, the lines doing the least amount of work come off first; the line doing the most to hold your boat in position comes off last.

4. If the last line off is either a stern line or a forward spring line, that line itself will help you control your stern. In addition, you can use the paddle-wheel effect of your propeller and / or the force of the prop wash or current on your rudder to hold your stern close to or away from the dock.

5. With a right-hand propeller, you'd like to tie up with the dock to port. With a left-hand propeller, you'd like the dock to starboard. In that way, when you shift into forward, the paddle-wheel effect will pull your stern away from the dock. Similarly, going into reverse will snug your stern right up against the dock—a big help when you are coming in to tie up!

6. First, the boat described in this situation has a right-hand propeller (it moves the stern to starboard in forward and to port in reverse). To offset its tendency to pull the stern to port in reverse, you would put the rudder to starboard while backing. When using the prop wash to kick the stern to starboard, however, you'll have to move the rudder to port before shifting into forward.

7. If the current / wind is coming from the bow, you normally would plan to leave the dock headed into it—moving forward—because that will give you the most control over your boat.

8. If there are no boats or other obstacles in front of you, you would probably go out in forward because you've got lots of room in which to maneuver. If, however, there are boats or other obstacles in front of you and the current / wind is coming from the stern, you would normally plan to spring your stern away from the dock and go out in reverse, because that would give you the best control over your boat.

Chapter 12:

1. Before planning your departure from a slip, you should note the strength and direction of the *wind* and the *current*.

2. When the wind and current are from opposite directions, the stronger one will push the boat so that the lines are slack at the other end. For example, if the current is from the bow, the wind is from the stern, and the bow lines are slack, the wind is having more effect than the current.

3. When the wind is from the side, you would shorten the windward dock lines before casting off to give yourself some extra space to leeward in case the wind blows you sideways as you begin to move out.

4. FALSE. When leaving a slip, the order in which you cast off your dock lines can make a big difference. The idea is to cast off the lines doing the least work first, leaving until last those that are doing the most to hold your boat in position.

5. You should always look outside your slip to be sure the way is clear, and then give a four- to six-second blast on your horn just before starting out. If someone answers your horn with a series of five or more quick blasts on his horn, stop your boat and get the dock lines back on. Do not come out of the slip until you find out what's going on. That answer means that someone else thinks there would be danger of collision if you came out of your slip at that time.

6. If your boat is moving at a slow speed in the same direction as the current, you'll have trouble steering—particularly if your boat is steered with a rudder. Two alternative solutions are suggested: When conditions permit, you can speed up a bit so that you are moving through the water fast enough for better steering; or you can steer diagonally across the current so that you get more water flowing past your rudder and / or drive unit.

7. If you're in the slip bow-first, you'll have to come out backwards. Moreover, if you use your engine to reverse out, you'll have to com-

pensate for the paddle-wheel effect. If, however, you just cast off your lines and let the current or wind push you out of the slip, there isn't any paddle-wheel effect to overcome, and your boat just drifts on out. You should have your engine running, however, so that it's ready to go into gear as you clear the slip.

8. With the wind reasonably strong and coming from the side of your slip, the only practical way to keep your bow from being blown off to leeward is to "walk" one of the windward dock lines along the boat as it moves out of the slip, You should also back out of the slip quickly, giving the wind less time to work on you.

Chapter 13:

1. Either the wind, current, or some combination of the two can push your boat sideways, an effect called making "leeway." Unless you compensate for this effect, your boat will gradually be pushed off course. The technique for offsetting leeway involves steering a course so that you are heading somewhat into the wind or current.

2. Boats turn from the stern (rear), pivoting around a point about one-third of the way back from the bow. From a practical point of view, this means that the stern of your boat makes a wider swing around a turn than does the bow, and you need to allow room for it.

3. TRUE. Although the amount of slippage varies from boat to boat, depending upon hull design, any individual boat will slip sideways in a turn more at higher speeds than it will when running at slower speeds.

4. FALSE. Any time there are significant waves, whether from wind or from other boat traffic, you need to make turns carefully so that the waves don't roll the boat dangerously.

5. TRUE. When you want to turn your boat within a space of just one boat length, whether you have a single- or twin-engine boat, you need to bring the boat to a complete stop before starting your turn. Otherwise, the forward momentum will force a wider turn.

6. To turn a single-engine inboard in its own length, you make use of the *prop wash* against the turned rudder in forward and the *paddle-wheel effect* of the propeller in reverse.

7. In this situation, you would turn to starboard so that you can use the paddle-wheel effect in reverse part way through the turn. By shifting into reverse just long enough to give a short-but-good burst of power and then shifting back into forward with another short burst of power, it's possible to shorten the turn without ever stopping the boat. (Note: Because a boat turns from the rear, the stern swings to the side opposite the direction of the turn. Therefore, if you are turning to starboard, the stern swings to port—aided by the paddle-

wheel effect of a right-hand propeller when you give that burst of power in reverse.)

8. Again, turn to port. As above, you are using the prop wash on the rudder to help turn when in forward and the paddle-wheel effect when in reverse.

9. The best way to accelerate your boat in most circumstances is to increase the throttle gradually—quickly, perhaps, but still with a steady motion, not by simply shoving the throttle forward all at once.

10. In general, you should not slow your boat abruptly when you have a following sea, particularly if you have a boat with a cut-out in the transom.

11. FALSE. While it is important to maintain steerage, coming up to a dock slowly gives you more time in which to maneuver if something unexpected takes place—for example, the engine quits.

12. A boat makes its largest wake when it is almost but not quite planing.

13. FALSE. You are responsible for your wake at all times. So, you always need to be aware of its potential for causing problems to other boaters—even if you are out in the middle of a lake or bay.

Chapter 14:

1. Four keys to safe boating in heavy traffic are: (1) being alert at all times; (2) being predictable, so that other boaters are not surprised by something you do; (3) adjusting your speed to that of other traffic; and (4) being courteous to other boaters.

2. The two major factors you need to consider in holding your boat in position are the *speed* and *direction* of the wind and current.

3. To hold your boat in position, you must strike a balance between the force of the wind and / or current on your boat and the forces created by your *propeller* and *rudder*.

4. A boat with an outboard motor is generally easier to steer in reverse than a single-engine inboard because you can turn the drive unit to pull the stern wherever you want it to go.

5. When in reverse, the bow makes a wider swing through a turn than the stern, particularly if the turn is sharp. That means you have to allow extra room for your bow in the turn.

6. You should never back your boat up to a person in the water because of the danger of him / her getting caught in your propeller. Instead, you should come up alongside the swimmer and turn your engine off until he or she is either safely aboard the boat or safely away from the boat where there is no possibility of being injured by the propeller.

7. The paddle-wheel effect of the propeller in reverse in a single-engine inboard attempts to kick your stern to one side—but only so long as the propeller is turning. When you shift into neutral, the paddle-wheel effect is stopped and the boat can coast backward while you use your rudder to keep the boat moving more or less in a straight line.

Chapter 15:

1. Any time a sailboat's engine is being used to help move it through the water—whether or not its sails are up—that boat is considered a motorboat under the Navigation Rules. The reasoning behind this definition is that a sailboat using its engine is no longer limited in its maneuverability by the direction and strength of the wind; instead, it has the same degree of maneuverability as a motorboat.

2. FALSE, and on several counts. First, there are no speed limits on most waterways. More important, however, a safe speed is determined by the amount and kind of boat traffic, the wind and wave conditions, the depth and breadth of the waterway, the maneuverability of your individual boat, and by the visibility. There may also be speed limits, but those limits are in fact limits, not license to go that fast. Depending upon the conditions, a safe speed may be slower than the posted "speed limit."

3. FALSE. While sailboats under sail have the right of way over most motor-driven pleasure boats, sailboats generally must keep out of the way of any motorboat restricted in its ability to maneuver—e.g., boats that are restricted to a channel or that are engaged in fishing as defined by the Navigation Rules.

4. In general, traffic traveling with the current has the right of way at an opening bridge over traffic traveling against the current. The rationale for this practice is that boats moving in the same direction as the current are less maneuverable than boats heading against the current.

5. The so-called "overriding" rule says essentially that the need to avoid a collision overrides specific rules of the road. Therefore, if collision is imminent, the skipper of any boat must take whatever action is necessary to avoid that collision, even if that action violates any of the other Navigation Rules.

6. When two boats under power meet head-on, they should each steer to starboard so that they pass port-side to port-side. The only exception to this rule is when the two skippers have agreed on a different passing pattern ahead of time.

7. When two boats under power are crossing each other's path, the

boat to starboard has the right of way. In other words, if the other boat is approaching from your starboard side, it has the right of way. At night, you would be looking at the other skipper's red ("stop") light; he would be looking at your green ("go") light.

8. If one boat is overtaking another, the boat being overtaken has the right of way. In other words, if you are overtaking another boat, you must keep clear of it until you are safely past.

9. When two boats are sailing on different tacks, the boat on the starboard tack has the right of way. By definition, a boat is said to be on the starboard tack if its mainsail is out on the port side, or would be if it were up.

10. If two boats are on the same tack, the boat to leeward (down-wind from the other boat) has the right of way. In other words, if you are looking past or under your mainsail at another sailboat, it has the right of way.

11. If you're sailing on the port tack and see another sailboat upwind but can't tell what tack it's on, you should assume it's on a starboard tack and grant the other skipper the right of way. This is particularly important at night, when the other boat's red and green running lights may confuse the issue. So, if in doubt and on a port tack, grant the other skipper the right of way, adjusting your course in plenty of time for him to recognize what you are doing.

Chapter 16:

1. Your boat's navigation lights must always be turned on when you are out running between sunset and sunrise. They should also be turned on at any time during daylight hours that visibility is reduced, as in fog, darkness from heavy cloud cover, or in heavy rain or snow.

2. A single white light ahead suggests that you're looking at the stern light of another boat. If you are overtaking it, the other boat has the right of way. However, you also need to consider other possibilities—for example, that the white light may be an anchor light, or the mast-head light of a boat whose other lights are obscured or burned out.

3. When you see a single white light with a single yellow light directly above it, you are looking at the stern of a tugboat pulling a tow. Remember, however, that you can see those lights anywhere along an arc from 67.5 degrees off the port stern to 67.5 degrees off the star-board stern. You may be overtaking the tug from anywhere on that arc and should keep a sharp eye for the tow, keeping well clear.

4. Anytime you see both the red and green running lights of another boat at once, you are looking at its bow. The two white lights one above the other are either the masthead lights on a ship's two masts

lined up one behind the other, or the two masthead towing lights of a tugboat. So, in this situation, you are looking either at a large ship or a tug pulling a tow. In either case, the ship or tug is headed straight for you. If those lights are either directly ahead of or directly astern of your boat, you should change your course to head off at a 90-degree angle either to port or starboard to take your boat out of the other boat's path.

5. If you see a green light and two white lights, one above the other, you're looking at a tugboat either pushing or pulling a tow on a course to cross your path. If the tug is pushing a barge, you should be able to see a green light at the front of the barge (binoculars may make it easier to see the lights). If the tug is pulling a barge, the tow could be up to 200 meters long; here, too, you should be able to see a green light at the front of the barge. Because the tug is restricted in its ability to maneuver, it has the right of way, even though the captain is showing you a green side light.

6. A single green light should mean that you are looking at a sailboat under sail. If it is upwind of you and you are on the port tack, you should give the other boat the right of way. However, you need to consider also the possibility that it's a motorboat or sailboat under power whose masthead light is not working. In that situation, you would have the right of way and be expected to maintain your course and speed.

7. An all-'round red light directly over a green light is a special light combination allowed sailboats under sail. However, this combination is carried at the masthead and must be used in addition to the normal running lights, so you're probably just too far away to see the other running lights. As you get closer, you'll see either a white stern light if the other boat is headed in approximately the same direction you are, or its red and / or green side lights if the boat is headed toward you or on a crossing course.

8. If you see a red light directly over a white light, but no other lights, you are looking at a fishing boat standing still in the water.

9. If you see a red light directly over a white light and, closer to the water, a red side light, you're looking at a fishing boat moving through the water.

10. FALSE. At a minimum, sailboats, rowboats, and rowing dinghies are required to carry a bright flashlight that can be used to alert another boat to their presence. If practical, however, even small sailboats, rowboats, and rowing dinghies should show the same lights required of larger sailboats—that is, red and green side lights and a white stern light. Small outboard motorboats (less than 23 feet, or 7 meters),

including motorized dinghies, must show red and green side lights and either an all-'round white light or white masthead and stern lights.

Chapter 17:

1. The only requirement for sound-signaling devices on boats less than 39.4 feet long is that there be means to make "an efficient sound signal." Acceptable devices can range from a mouth whistle to a Freon horn to an electric air horn. While not required, it is also a good idea to carry a bell for use in fog.

2. Five or more short blasts on a horn are a danger signal. If you hear that signal, you should look around immediately to find the source and make certain you are not in danger of collision.

3. One long blast of a boat's horn near a dock probably means that someone is preparing to leave his slip. You should be sure that you are well clear of any slip from which a boat might be exiting, and stay alert.

4. In a head-on situation, two short blasts mean that the skipper of the other boat is planning to pass you on his starboard side. In other words, is leaving you to starboard. If that is acceptable, you should answer his signal with two short blasts—the same signal he gave you.

5. If you're overtaking another boat and want to pass it on its starboard side, you should signal with one short blast. If the other skipper responds with the danger signal (five short blasts), he's refusing permission for you to pass him in that manner. If it appears safe for you to pass him on his port side, you should signal that intent with two short blasts. He should respond with two short blasts on his own horn if it is safe to pass him in that manner.

6. The generally accepted sound signal to request a bridge opening is a long blast followed by a short blast. The bridge tender should respond with the same signal if he is able to open the bridge. If he can't open the bridge, he should respond with the danger signal of five short blasts.

7. If you're moving under power in fog, you should give one long blast on your horn at least every two minutes.

8. If you're anchored in fog on a boat less than 39.4 feet long, you should be ringing a bell, banging a pot, or making some other such noise for five seconds at one- or two-minute intervals.

Chapter 18:

1. The only visual distress signals suitable for both day and night use are flares. They may be one of three types: hand-held, meteor, or

parachute flares. Under no circumstances should highway flares be used as visual distress signals.

2. FALSE. If you cannot see another boat, you should not use your flares. The closer a boat is to you, the greater the chance of someone aboard it seeing your flares.

3. If you hear a horn sounding continuously, you should definitely investigate. It may well be another boat in distress; a continuously sounding foghorn is an internationally recognized distress signal.

4. Three internationally recognized distress flag signals are: an orange flag with a black square and a black ball; a square black flag flown above a black ball; and the code flags "November" and "Charlie." Though this is not officially recognized, many boaters will also recognize the American flag flying upside down as a signal of distress.

5. If your boat is taking on water dangerously, you should turn the radio to Channel 16 and say the following: "Mayday, Mayday, Mayday." You should then give your boat's name, your location, and, very succinctly, the nature of the emergency, the number of people aboard, and a description of your boat, followed by the word "Over" to signal that your message is completed. If you do not receive a reply in thirty seconds, you should repeat the call.

In the meantime, everyone should be putting on PFDs and preparing either to abandon ship or, if the boat contains flotation that will keep it from sinking, to stay with the boat even after it is filled with water.

6. If it is dark, you can use a flashlight to send the Morse code distress signal, S.O.S.—three short flashes, three long flashes, three short flashes. However, you must be pointing the flashlight toward another boat for your signal to be seen. Even then, of course, there is no guarantee that the signal will be seen by the first boat you flash.

7. Even if you have no visual distress signals on your boat, you have the ability to give an approved distress signal so long as you have two arms. Simply stand up, facing another boat, with someone steadying you if necessary, hold your arms straight out from your sides, and wave them up and down as if you were trying to fly.

8. If you hear a "Mayday" call over the radio, you should immediately note the information being provided. If no one else has responded to the call within twenty seconds, you should respond by calling the name of the boat in distress three times. (If you missed the boat's name, you can respond, "Calling the boat in distress," repeating it three times.) Then, give your boat name and say that the "Mayday" message has been received or partially received. If you did not hear

all of the message, ask to have it repeated and write down the key facts—particularly the location. You should then determine how long it will take you to reach the boat in distress and tell them that information. For further review, go back to Chapter 18.

Chapter 19:
1. When taking on gasoline, the nozzle of the gas hose should be kept firmly against the filler hole in the gas can or the fill pipe on your boat to prevent sparks resulting from built-up static electricity.

2. FALSE. Portable tanks should be filled on the dock so that you cannot run gasoline into the bottom of your boat if you overflow the tank.

3. After filling the tanks, returning the gas hose to the dock, and putting the caps on the fill pipes, you should: (1) open all hatches and cabin windows to air out the boat's interior; (2) raise the engine hatch, put your head in the bilge, and sniff to see if you can smell gasoline; and (3) turn on your bilge blower and let it run for four or five minutes to ventilate the bilges. If there's still no gas smell, it should be safe to start your engine(s). If you can smell gasoline, under no circumstances should you try to start the engine(s).

4. Pleasure boats should always grant the right of way and lots of room to ships, tugs pushing or pulling barges, and working commercial fishing boats.

5. You should not anchor from the stern. If a wind or current begins to make your boat pull hard on the anchor line, your stern will be pulled lower in the water, making it easier for waves to come over the transom and into the boat.

6. Anytime you hit bottom with a hard impact, you should immediately check the bilges for water to see if the impact caused a leak.

7. When approaching a blind turn, you should: (1) always assume someone is coming from the other direction; (2) keep well away from the shore, bridge abutment, or whatever is obstructing your view; (3) slow down, unless you're already moving slowly; and (4) blow one long blast on your horn to alert others that you're coming around the turn. Even if you don't get a response to your sound signal, assume someone's coming from the other direction. He may not know enough to answer your signal.

8. FALSE. While official weather forecasts may miss deteriorating weather in your local area, you can often see the warning signs of bad weather yourself simply by paying attention to the buildup of clouds, the strength of the wind, and the size of the waves.

9. FALSE. One of the most important parts of boating safety is being

prepared for the unexpected. Even though you may not plan on it, such circumstances as engine trouble, bad weather, the need to help another boat, etc., may result in your being out in your boat after dark.

10. If someone falls overboard, anyone seeing the person fall should shout "Man overboard!", throw a flotation device to the victim, and then point toward the victim and continue pointing toward him or her until the boat has turned around and the victim is nearby and in clear sight of the person who is steering the boat.

11. When you are going through an inlet, the primary danger of breaking waves is that they'll take control of your boat, turn it sideways to the waves, and roll it over. In short, breaking waves in an inlet can be very dangerous.

12. TRUE. If an inlet is rough when the ocean itself is not particularly rough, the likely cause of waves breaking across the inlet is a mixture of an out-flowing tide and an afternoon sea breeze. If you simply wait a few hours, the odds are good that the tide will turn and the sea breeze will die, with the result that the inlet will be as calm as it was in the morning when you went out.

13. If your engine quits, you should check your fuel, oil, alternator belt, engine water intake, and the air intake and filter. A problem with any one of these can shut your engine down.

14. If your boat must be towed, you should be sure that all cleats used for towing *are bolted to sturdy backing plates,* that the tow line is made of *nylon,* and that the tow line is about the same size as *your anchor line.*

15. Although state laws may require having only one observer, you really should have two observers on your boat when you're pulling a water-skier—one to watch the skier, the other to watch for boat traffic. With only a single observer, the helmsman's time inevitably is split between watching the skier, watching where he's steering, and looking out for other traffic—not a satisfactory situation, in my view.

16. Overloaded boats are hazardous because they're low in the water and slow to react to waves. As a result, they do not float up over waves the way they should and can be swamped even by small waves. Also, because they're low in the water, overloaded boats can be tipped more easily and swamped by what would otherwise be normal movements of people in the boat.

Chapter 20:

1. FALSE. Compass deviation results from the presence of certain metals and electrical wiring near your compass. This can happen

whether or not the compass is mounted permanently.

2. Part of basic piloting involves determining how far you've traveled along a course, or how long it will take you to get somewhere. Both require knowing your boat's speed.

3. FALSE. The land portion of charts may show prominent structures that can be used as landmarks or which serve as navigation aids.

4. TRUE. The blue portion of a chart represents shallow water; the white represents deeper water.

5. When you are headed upstream (returning to port), green markers are kept to the port side. Insofar as daymarks are sometimes located in relatively shallow water, it's best to give them a bit of room.

6. A buoy with red and green horizontal stripes is used either to mark a junction of two channels or an obstruction in the channel. The best way to figure out what the buoy means is to look at your chart.

7. A small circle-dot with a red diamond represents a simple red buoy. The R"12" tells you that this red buoy has the number "12" painted on it.

8. By plotting your intended course ahead of time, you can look for possible underwater obstructions that you'll need to avoid. You can also identify various buoys and landmarks that you can use to confirm whether you're on your intended track as you go along.

9. If you have been traveling at 16 knots for an hour and forty-five minutes, you have traveled *28 nautical miles*. You arrive at that answer by converting the hours and minutes into hours—1.75 hours—plugging the numbers into the formula "Distance equals Speed times Time" ($D = S \times T$).

10. In order to plot your position, you must be able to measure the distance and direction you've traveled from some beginning point. Whenever you change either your boat's speed or the direction in which you're steering, you need to plot a new beginning point, or you won't know where to begin measuring your progress as you proceed at the new speed or along the new course.

Chapter 21:

1. Unless you are well away from land and in deep water, you need to slow down at night for a variety of reasons: You often can't see floating hazards. It's more difficult to judge distances. You don't have all the visual cues that are available in daytime to tell you where you are. And it's more difficult to keep track of other traffic. All in all, nighttime presents a very different decision-making environment than daytime, and your safety on the water at night demands that you run at much slower speeds.

2. There is no set answer to this question. In general, though, if you travel at more than 10 to 15 knots at night, you're probably going too fast. As the room for error decreases, either because the waters become more congested or narrower, a safe speed may well be only 5 or 6 knots, or even less.

3. To protect your night vision, you can: (1) install red lights in your boat's cabin; (2) use a red-filtered flashlight whenever you need extra light to look at your charts or get around in the boat; (3) use binoculars instead of a spotlight to help you read the numbers on buoys; and (4) let a crew member use the spotlight if one is needed to search out a buoy while you look away from the light so that it can't damage your night vision.

4. FALSE. The potential for trouble is too great to risk an error in "counting" the seconds to time the interval of a navigation light. For that reason, the only acceptable way to time lights is to use some kind of timepiece.

5. The abbreviation "Qk Fl R" on your chart signifies a "quick-flashing red light"—i.e., a red light flashing at least sixty times per minute. That light is found only on a red channel marker and tells you that extra caution is needed at that point in the channel. The channel may turn abruptly. It may become quite narrow at that point. Or there may be a major obstruction right at the channel's edge that you need to be certain to avoid. A look at your chart will quickly show you what you need to know.

6. The light signal "Morse A" is found only on mid-channel markers. This white light is seen as a quick flash followed by a longer flash followed by a few seconds of darkness. The signal recycles every eight seconds.

7. A light shown on the chart by a large purple or red dot is a floating navigation aid—that is, a lighted buoy. The large dot, which is about the size of a small pencil eraser, is meant to indicate that the position of the buoy is not exact.

8. The red sector of a fixed light is best described as a danger zone. If you keep heading toward the red light, you will probably run into some kind of obstruction. In that situation, you should consult your chart immediately to determine which direction you should head in to find safe water.

9. FALSE. It is particularly important at night to maintain your course line and to update your position on the chart frequently, even when following a well-lighted channel. Otherwise, you risk losing track of where you are, failing to see warning of a hazard on the chart, and making a critical mistake in interpreting the channel.

Chapter 22:

1. FALSE. You should generally come up to a dock under power to give yourself maximum control over your boat. Outboards and I / Os have no steering when coasting; inboards have less effective steering when coasting.

2. TRUE. A single-engine inboard with a right-hand propeller will be easier to bring alongside if the dock is to port. The paddle-wheel effect of the right-hand propeller will tuck the stern right up next to the dock when you shift into reverse to bring the boat to a stop.

3. TRUE. Whether you'll be leaving the dock by pushing the bow off and going out forward or springing the stern away and backing out, the paddle-wheel effect will make leaving the dock easier.

4. FALSE. If you have a choice, approach a dock headed into the current / wind, whichever is having the greater effect on your boat.

5. FALSE. With the current from the bow, the rudder should be turned away from the dock to hold your stern in.

6. FALSE. In most circumstances, people on the dock should simply make your lines fast and let you move the boat into position using the engine. If adjustments are needed in the lines, they should be made from the boat.

7. TRUE. If the current / wind is from astern, you should align your boat parallel to the dock space and then go in stern-first. In this way, you maintain positive control over your boat.

8. TRUE. If you are tied alongside a dock with the current from astern, you can help keep your stern off the dock by turning your rudder away from the dock.

Chapter 23:

1. A boat under sail has no "brakes." By coming up to a dock against the current, you're using the current to help stop your boat.

2. When sailing up to a dock, it's important to keep your sails from catching the wind while you're putting your dock lines ashore. This is done most effectively by getting a bow line on promptly.

3. When sailing up to a dock, you should use the smallest amount of sail needed to control your boat so that you have fewer control lines to worry about, less commotion from flapping sails, and less chance of being overpowered by an unexpected gust or shift in the wind.

4. On sailboats as well as on powerboats, you can use the force of the current pushing against your rudder to hold your stern close to the dock until you can get a stern line on. Assuming that you're headed into the current, just turn your rudder away from the dock and tie the tiller or wheel to hold it there.

5. When the wind is blowing toward the dock (the dock is to lee-ward), the major risk occurs because you have to let your sail out over the dock to spill the wind. With the sail and its sheet flapping in the breeze while the boat coasts to a stop, there is a real risk of snagging some part of the dock and damaging the sail. In this situation, coming in under a small staysail or a mostly furled roller-furling jib can be useful.

6. When anchoring to let your boat drift back to the dock, you should put your anchor down a distance upwind from the dock equal to ten to twelve times the depth of the water *plus* the length of your boat. If the wind is strong, add a few more depths of the water to your calculation.

Chapter 24:

1. FALSE. It's easier to get into a slip when the current is against you. When the current is in the same direction you're moving, steering is impaired at low speeds and you must use your engine or dock lines to bring the boat to a stop.

2. It's best to overestimate the sideways push of the current so that you don't overshoot the slip. If you've overestimated, you can always just stop the boat for a minute to let the current push you into align-ment with the slip. If, on the other hand, you've underestimated its effect by much, you'll probably have to go around and make a second try.

3. If the wind is from the side and you are moving at a slow speed, it tends to push your bow around, making it difficult to stay aligned with your slip—particularly if you are backing in.

4. TRUE. If the wind is from the side and you are headed into the slip bow-first in a single-engine boat, you may have difficulty keeping your bow from being blown off to the side if the wind is very strong. One way to offset the wind's effect is to approach the slip from an angle so that you are headed partially into the wind, and then turn into the slip as the bow reaches the first pilings. Remember, a boat turns from the stern.

5. TRUE. It is generally easier to head bow-first into a slip.

6. TRUE. As in answer number 4, one way to offset the wind's effect is to approach the slip at an angle so that your boat is more nearly aligned with the wind.

7. If the current is from astern, the first line ashore should be one you can use to stop the boat, i.e., either a stern line or an aft spring line run from a chock or cleat amidships.

Chapter 25:

1. The way that boats lie at their moorings may be influenced by both their underwater and above-water designs. For example, a shallow-bottomed boat with no keel will tend to line up with the wind, whereas a deeper boat with a long keel and a relatively small deckhouse will tend to line up with the current.

2. FALSE. You should generally approach a mooring so that you are headed into the wind or current; in this way, you will have maximum control over your boat.

3. You should generally not try to pick up moorings from the stern for two reasons: It's a good way to get the mooring line or its pendant caught in your propeller; and there is too much potential for a problem to develop in trying to walk the mooring line forward to make it fast, particularly if the wind or current is strong.

4. TRUE. You should always wait until the boat has stopped moving forward before lowering your anchor to the bottom. Then, as the current or wind pushes the boat backward, you can let out your anchor line.

5. FALSE. The anchor should always be lowered in a controlled manner (a) so that you can stop lowering it at any time and (b) so that you can tell when it reaches the bottom.

6. In normal conditions, you should let out anchor rode (line) equal to five to seven times the distance between your foredeck and the bottom. In strong winds, you should let out even more.

7. There is no single answer to this question. If the bottom falls off sharply from the beach, it may be perfectly safe to drive your powerboat slowly almost to the beach. If the water shoals gradually, however, it's usually best to stop your engine while there is still a foot or so of water below your propeller and walk the boat in the rest of the way.

Chapter 26:

1. There is no "right" checklist. The list that you make should be specific to your boat. However, after developing your list, you might consider paging through Chapter 26 to double-check that you haven't forgotten something.

Chapter 27:

1. If the total weight of your trailer, boat, and all the gear you'll carry in the boat exceeds 1,500 pounds, the trailer should have brakes of its own. You may want brakes on the trailer even if the total weight is less than 1,500 pounds.

2. "Bearing buddies" or "bearing protectors" keep your trailer wheel bearings fully lubricated at all times, protecting against water damage.

3. If you have either too much or too little weight on the trailer hitch, the trailer may start swaying as you drive down the highway. In general, the weight on the trailer hitch should be from 5 to 7 percent of the total weight of the loaded trailer.

4. Equipment or spare parts recommended for the towing vehicle include a full-sized spare tire, a jack, a lug wrench, penetrating oil, and wheel chocks.

5. Equipment or spare parts recommended for the trailer include a spare tire, a trailer jack, a lug wrench to fit the trailer lugs, penetrating oil, spare wheel bearings, grease for wheel bearings, spare bulbs for all trailer lights, tools needed to replace bulbs and adjust boat supports, and spare polyester rope.

6. Before heading out onto the road towing a trailer, you should check to be sure the safety chains are fastened, the trailer lights all work, the coupling is properly fastened on the trailer hitch, the tires on both the car and trailer are properly inflated, the engine oil and radiator fluid are OK, and that the boat is tied securely.

7. When turning corners while towing a trailer, you must always remember that the trailer will cut the corner short . . . and allow for it by taking the corner a little wider than you would normally.

Chapter 28:

1. After running down the highway, the wheel bearings on your trailer are hot. If you back the wheels into the water while the bearings are hot, they will suck in the cold water and may crack.

2. If you do nothing else before backing your trailer down the boat ramp, you should check to be certain that the drain plug is securely in the boat so that it won't sink when you launch it.

3. FALSE. Wheel chocks should always be put behind the front wheels of the towing vehicle when it's stopped on a boat ramp. The purpose of chocks is to keep the car from rolling into the water if the brakes fail or the car jumps out of "Park," with an automatic transmission.

4. TRUE. Before the boat comes off the trailer, your line handlers should stand upwind or up-current from the boat with their lines in place, ready to hold the boat when you push it off the trailer.

5. FALSE. While you'll want to crank the boat onto the trailer rapidly when taking it out of the water, you need to stop cranking and, possibly, back off a bit on the winch if the boat begins to come onto the trailer incorrectly. The most important thing is to get the boat onto the trailer correctly.

6. Generally speaking, you should not step your sailboat's mast until the boat is in the water. Two reasons: You shouldn't get into a habit of stepping the mast while awaiting your turn at the boat ramp, because there may be an overhead electrical wire between you and the boat ramp—a downright dangerous situation. You also shouldn't step your mast while the trailer is on the ramp. Not only will you be working at an odd angle, increasing the likelihood of a slip, but also you'll probably be delaying someone else who wants to use the ramp.

Chapter 29:

1. Developing these maintenance lists is considerably more important than going through an exercise at the end of the last chapter of a book. Too often, in the fall, we are anxious to get the boat out of the water and under wraps; as a result, it's easy to forego maintenance elements that are not absolutely necessary. When spring comes, our energy is focused on getting the boat back into the water, and maintenance once again can be short-changed. The value of maintenance lists is that they enforce a discipline which ensures that maintenance gets done—but only if you use them.

Index